Records

Scottish Volu

1859–1908

BY

MAJOR-GENERAL J. M. GRIERSON,

C.V.O., C.B., C.M.G.

COMMANDING THE FIRST DIVISION OF THE ARMY,
ALDERSHOT COMMAND

The Naval & Military Press Ltd

Reproduced by kind permission of the Central Library,
Royal Military Academy, Sandhurst

Published by

The Naval & Military Press Ltd

Unit 10, Ridgewood Industrial Park,

Uckfield, East Sussex,

TN22 5QE England

Tel: +44 (0) 1825 749494

Fax: +44 (0) 1825 765701

www.naval–military–press.com

© The Naval & Military Press Ltd 2004

In reprinting in facsimile from the original, any imperfections are inevitably reproduced and the quality may fall short of modern type and cartographic standards.

Printed and bound by Antony Rowe Ltd, Eastbourne

Records of the
Scottish Volunteer Force

PREFACE.

THESE " Records " are designed as a contribution to the military annals of Scotland — to "the warlike repute of our history." It is true that the records of the volunteer army cover—with the exception of their services, mostly in small bodies attached to regular units, during the war in South Africa—no ground of warlike exploits, yet they spread over nigh upon half a century of the national life, and that, too, a period in which the regular forces of the Crown have been placed upon an entirely new basis, and converted from a long-service army of the old type into a short-service, largely territorialised force, with distinct local associations, and with an ever and ever increasing connection with the second line or auxiliary forces of the nation. To this connection, to this increase of the power of the forces of the Crown, to this national —as distinguished from purely professional—military spirit, no factor has been more potent than the " volunteer movement," and in no part of His Majesty's dominions has the movement been more enthusiastically taken up — and maintained — than in the northern portion of the United Kingdom. The Scottish volunteers have proved by the large proportion which their numbers have always borne to the male population, by the high degree of efficiency to which they have attained, as attested by the Royal approbation frequently bestowed upon them, and by the generous support which they have afforded in times of stress to their national regular regiments, that the old warlike spirit runs as high as ever in Scotland, and their chronicles cannot therefore fail to be of interest to all patriotic Scots.

The present seems a peculiarly appropriate time when some record of the origin and history of the force should be compiled, as, firstly, its character and organisation have been changed and it has furnished the cadres for the territorial army of the future; and secondly, in a few years' time any attempt to arrive at data as to the earliest formations of the volunteer corps would be in vain. From the list appended to this Preface it will be seen how few are the efforts which have been made to commit to paper the histories of volunteer corps; indeed in the earlier days no records at all were kept in most cases. Nowadays, therefore, the bare facts disclosed by a study of army lists and other official documents can generally be only amplified by the personal recollections of those who took part in the movement in its early days. Those men are now passing away from among us, and with them their knowledge will be buried in the grave; so it becomes a pious military duty to collect as much as possible of what they have to tell and to record it in a permanent form.

In Part I. of these "Records" an attempt is made to give a general sketch of the rise and progress of the volunteer movement with special reference to Scotland. The bulk of this portion is of necessity derived from official documents, returns, army orders, manuals, regulations, and reports of commissions, but special attention has been paid to accounts of the three great reviews of Scottish volunteers held by her late

Majesty Queen Victoria in 1860 and 1881, and by his present Majesty in 1905, as typical of the state of the force at these periods, and general details as to the force have been summarised in the Appendices. Part II. must be read in connection with Part I., as the general account in the latter is common to all the individual records of corps in the former.

Deprived of the details of organisation, training, equipment, and historical gatherings, collected together in Part I. and the Appendices, the individual records of corps reduce themselves to summaries of their special origin, formation, uniform, changes in strength and distribution, the numbers supplied for active service, and the names of their commanding officers. Some records, where published histories or private memoranda were obtainable, are fuller than others, but, in all, every available source of information has been utilised. The Plates showing the uniforms have been drawn by me from authentic sources, mostly original photographs, and the colouring is taken either from official descriptions or, in the case of many of the older types, from statements made by those who have worn the uniform depicted, or, in a few cases, from the actual garments then worn, and in no case has any attempt been made to reproduce a uniform from unauthenticated data. It is hoped, therefore, that the Plates showing the uniforms are as near absolute accuracy as is possible.

I have been assisted in the preparation of these "Records" by very many members of the Scottish volunteer force and others, but by none more effectually than by my valued friend Major - General Sir Alexander J. F. Reid, K.C.B., whose efforts at unearthing old records have been untiring. My grateful thanks are also due to the following, who have furnished information, lent photographs, or otherwise helped in the work :—

Alexander, Captain A. C. B., Seaforth Highlanders, Adjutant 2nd V.B. K.O. Scottish Borderers.
Alston, J. Carfrae, Esq., late Major 1st Lanark V.R.C.
Anstruther, Colonel Sir R. W., Bart., 6th V.B. Black Watch.
Arbuthnot, Major K. W., Seaforth Highlanders, Adjutant 1st V.B. Seaforth Highlanders.
Bailey, Colonel R., late R.A. and 1st Orkney R.G.A.(V.)
Baillie, Colonel J. E. B., M.V.O., V.D., Highland R.G.A.(V.)
Balfour, R. R., Esq., Montrose.
Batchelor, Lieut.-Colonel C., V.D., 3rd V.B. Black Watch.
Birrell, Colonel A., V.D., 5th V.B. Highland Light Infantry.
Black, Sergeant R. E., 6th V.B. Royal Scots, Penicuik.
Brade, R. H., Esq., C.B., Assistant Secretary, War Office.
Breadalbane, Colonel the Marquess of, K.G., A.D.C., 5th V.B. Black Watch.
Brock, Lieut.-Colonel H., V.D., 1st Dumbarton V.R.C.
Browne, Thomas, Esq., late 5th Fife R.V., St Andrews.
Campbell, Colonel C. G. P., 1st Argyll and Bute R.G.A.(V.)
Campbell, Captain D. F., D.S.O., Lancashire Fusiliers, Adjutant 2nd V.B. Argyll and Sutherland Highlanders.
Campbell, Colonel F., late 1st Argyll and Bute R.G.A.(V.)
Campbell, the late John, Esq. of Kilberry, late 93rd Highlanders.
Campbell, Captain (hon. major) J., 1st V.B. Cameron Highlanders.
Cary, A. D. L., Esq., War Office.
Chalmers, Colonel H. D. D., 2nd V.B. Highland Light Infantry.
Chinn, Major J. H., Royal Artillery, Adjutant 1st Banff R.G.A.(V.)
Clark, Colonel Sir J. M., Bart., V.D., 5th V.B. Royal Scots.
Cranston, Colonel Sir R., K.C.V.O., V.D., Commanding 1st Lothian V.I. Brigade.
Crawford, Colonel E. R., V.D., late 1st Lanark R.E.(V.)
Cruden, Colonel G., V.D., late 1st V.B. Gordon Highlanders.
Dalmahoy, Colonel J. A., M.V.O., V.D., 1st Mid-Lothian R.G.A.(V.)
Darling, P. Stormonth, Esq., Kelso, late Border Mounted Rifles.
Donald, Colonel A. H., V.D., late 1st Lanark V.R.C.
Duncan, Colonel D., V.D., late 1st V.B. Gordon Highlanders.

Dunlop, Colonel J. W., C.B., Royal Artillery.

Ewing, Captain (hon. major) James, V.D., late 1st V.B. Gordon Highlanders.

Fraser, Captain (hon. major) H., 1st V.B. Cameron Highlanders.

Gibson, Captain T., 1st V.B. Cameron Highlanders.

Grant, Colonel A. B., M.V.O., V.D., late 1st Lanark R.G.A.(V.)

Hadden, Lieut.-Colonel A., V.D., The Border V.R.C.

Harvey, Thomas, Esq., late Captain 1st Dumbarton V.R.C.

Henderson, Brigadier-General David, D.S.O.

Henderson, Major M. W., 8th V.B. Royal Scots.

Hendry, Colonel P. W., V.D., Brigade-Major Highland Light Infantry V.I. Brigade.

Heron-Maxwell, Sir John, Bart., late 15th Hussars and 1st Dumfries Mounted Rifles.

Hill, Lieut.-Colonel H., V.D., 1st V.B. Black Watch.

Hudleston, F. J., Esq., Librarian, General Staff, War Office.

Johnston, Colonel C. J., V.D., Hon. Colonel 3rd V.B. Seaforth Highlanders.

Johnston, Colonel J. W., M.V.O., V.D., late 1st Fife R.G.A.(V.)

Johnston, John, Esq., Glasgow.

Kay, Captain F. W., 1st Aberdeen R.G.A.(V.)

Lennox, Lieut.-Colonel J., V.D., Galloway V.R.C.

Lockie, Captain and Quartermaster J., 1st V.B. Cameron Highlanders.

MacInnes, Lieut.-Colonel J., V.D., late 5th V.B. Argyll and Sutherland Highlanders.

Mackenzie, Colonel R. C., V.D., Commanding Highland Light Infantry V.I. Brigade.

Main, Colonel R. M., V.D., 7th V.B. Royal Scots.

Mellis, Colonel W. A., V.D., 4th V.B. Gordon Highlanders.

Menzies, Colonel R., V.D., late Q.R.V.B. Royal Scots.

Mitford, Captain W. B. J., Gordon Highlanders, Adjutant 6th V.B. Royal Scots.

Moncreiffe, Colonel Sir R. D., Bart., V.D., 4th V.B. Black Watch.

Morrison, Colonel F. L., V.D., 1st V.B. Highland Light Infantry.

Morrison, Colonel J., V.D., 1st Sutherland V.R.C.

Morton, Major D. S., late 1st V.B. Highland Light Infantry.

Muir, Captain G. W., Argyll and Sutherland Highlanders, Adjutant 5th V.B. Argyll and Sutherland Highlanders.

Munro, Lieut.-Colonel C., V.D., late 5th V.B. Black Watch.

Neish, Major F. H., Gordon Highlanders.

Oliver, W. H., Esq., Hawick, late Border Mounted Rifles.

Osborn, Lieut.-Colonel G., Royal Garrison Artillery.

Outram, Colonel J., V.D., 1st V.B. Highland Light Infantry.

Park, Colonel W. U., M.V.O., V.D., 1st V.B. Argyll and Sutherland Highlanders.

Paterson, Lieut.-Colonel R., V.D., 5th V.B. Argyll and Sutherland
Highlanders.

Paul, Major W. J., 4th V.B. Scottish Rifles.

Peace, Colonel T. S., V.D., 1st Orkney R.G.A.(V.)

Ralston, Colonel T. B., V.D., 2nd V.B. Scottish Rifles.

Reid, Lieut.-Colonel J. L., 2nd V.B. Gordon Highlanders.

Rose, Colonel George, V.D., late 1st V.B. Cameron Highlanders.

Sadler, Captain B., 4th V.B. Black Watch.

Scott, Colonel R., V.D., late 3rd V.B. Gordon Highlanders.

Shaw, Lieut.-Colonel J. E., 2nd V.B. Royal Scots Fusiliers.

Shearer, Lieut.-Colonel A. R., V.D., 6th V.B. Black Watch.

Singleton, Captain H. T. C., D.S.O., Highland Light Infantry,
Adjutant 5th V.B. Gordon Highlanders.

Smith, the late C. H., Esq., late Major 1st Lanark R.V.

Stansfeld, Captain J. R. E., D.S.O., Gordon Highlanders, Adjutant
3rd V.B. Gordon Highlanders.

Stevenson, Colonel J., C.B., A.D.C., late 9th Lanark V.R.C.

Stewart-Mackenzie, Colonel J. A. F. H., of Seaforth, Honorary
Colonel 1st V.B. Seaforth Highlanders.

Storrar, Colonel D., late 1st Fife R.G.A.(V.), Kirkcaldy.

Stuart, Lieut.-Colonel T. R., 1st Ayr and Galloway R.G.A.(V.)

Walker, Lieutenant H. W., Royal Field Artillery.

Warrand, Colonel A. R. B., 1st V.B. Seaforth Highlanders.

Wilson, Colonel J. B., V.D., 3rd Lanark V.R.C.

Youngson, Colonel J. A. W. A., V.D., late 1st Aberdeen R.G.A.(V.)

I shall be very glad if any one will point out to me errors in the work, or afford me any information to supplement the records.

JAMES MONCRIEFF GRIERSON,
Major-General.

Aldershot, *April* 1909.

CONTENTS.

PART I.

GENERAL ACCOUNT OF THE ORIGIN AND HISTORY OF THE FORCE.

Contents.

PART II.

RECORDS OF THE SEVERAL CORPS WHICH HAVE CONSTITUTED THE SCOTTISH VOLUNTEER FORCE, 1859–1908.

Contents.

Contents.

APPENDICES.

LIST OF PLATES OF UNIFORMS.

PLATE I.

1st Fife Mounted Rifles. Private 1860

1st Fife Light Horse. Captain 1890

1st Forfar Light Horse. Captain (Undress) 1890

1st Dumfries Mounted Rifles. Private 1874–1880

Border Mounted Rifles. Corporal 1872–1880   Private 1880–1892

McLagan & Cumming, Edin^r

PLATE II.

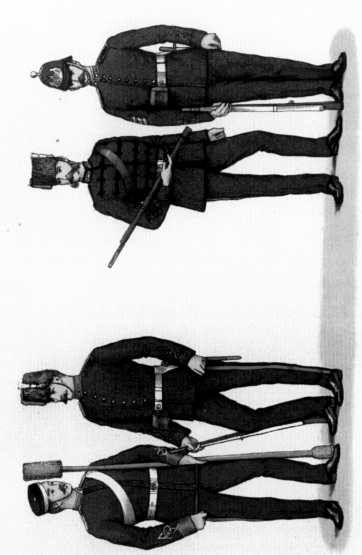

GUNNER (in Forage Cap)   GUNNER
1st EDINBURGH A.V.   1st EDINBURGH R.G.A. (V.)
1866   1907

1st EDINBURGH (CITY) R.G.A. (V.)

GUNNER   SERJEANT
1st MIDLOTHIAN A.V.   1st MIDLOTHIAN R.G.A. (V.)
1860   1905

1st MIDLOTHIAN R.G.A. (V.)

MᶜLagan & Cumming, Edinʳ

PLATE III.

LIEUTENANT (Review Order)   GUNNER   PIPER
1ST ABERDEEN A.V.   2ND BANFF A.V.   1905
    1860   1875

1ST BANFF R.G.A. (V.)

CAPTAIN   LIEUTENANT   GUNNER
1ST FORFAR A.V   3RD FORFAR A.V.   1ST FORFAR A.V.
    1860   1860   1881

1ST FORFAR R.G.A. (V.)

M°Lagan & Cumming Edin^r

PLATE IV.

McLagan & Cumming, Edinᵣ

GUNNER
3RD FIFE A.V.
1860

CAPTAIN
1ST STIRLING A.V.
1860

GUNNER
1907

BATTERY SERJEANT-MAJOR
1880

COMPANY SERJEANT-MAJOR
1907

1ST FIFE R.G.A. (V.)

1ST RENFREW AND DUMBARTON R.G.A. (V.)

PLATE V.

SERJEANT   GUNNER   GUNNER   BOMBARDIER   CAPTAIN   DRIVER
3rd ARGYLL A.V. (in Forage Cap) 2nd AYRSHIRE A.V (in Forage Cap) 1st LANARK A.V 1st LANARK R.G.A. (V.)
1866   1896   1860   1890   1862   1907

1st ARGYLL AND BUTE   1st AYR AND GALLOWAY   1st LANARKSHIRE R.G.A. (V.)
R.G.A. (V.)   R.G.A. (V.)

M⸱Lagan & Cumming, Edin⸱

PLATE VI.

LIEUTENANT   LIEUTENANT   LIEUT. COLONEL   GUNNER   CAPTAIN   GUNNER
(in Patrol Jacket and   1st SUTHERLAND A.V.   (Review Order)   4th ABERDEEN A.V.   3rd ABERDEEN A.V.   HEAVY BATTERIES
Forage Cap)   1860   1907   1860   1868   (in Forage Cap)
1890   1907

1ST BERWICK   1ST CAITHNESS   1ST ABERDEENSHIRE R.G.A. (V.)
R.G.A. (V.)   R.G.A. (V.)

McLagan & Cumming, Edin^r

PLATE VII.

M⁽ᶜ⁾Lagan & Cumming, Edinʳ

CAPTAIN, 1ST ORKNEY A.V.   TRUMPETER   CAPTAIN, 1ST INVERNESS A.V.   LIEUTENANT (Review Order)
1860   1905   1860   1907

1ST ORKNEY R.G.A. (V.)   HIGHLAND R.G.A. (V)

PLATE VIII.

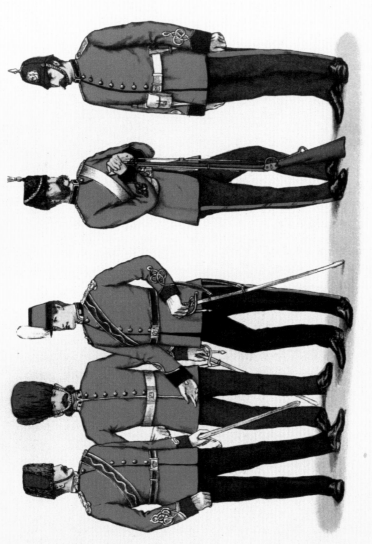

CAPTAIN
1ST LANARK E.V.
1860

CAPTAIN
97th LANARK R.V.
1862

LIEUTENANT
2nd LANARK E.V.
1860

SAPPER
1881

SAPPER
1907

1st LANARKSHIRE R.E. (V.)

McLegan & Cumming Edin^r

PLATE IX.

SAPPER
1st ABERDEEN E.V.
1881

MAJOR 2nd LANARKSHIRE R.E. (V.)
1905

SAPPER

M'Lagan & Cumming Edinr

PLATE X.

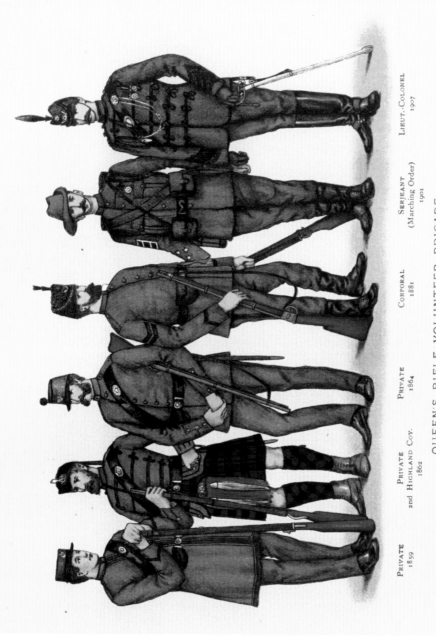

PRIVATE   PRIVATE   PRIVATE   CORPORAL   SERJEANT   LIEUT.-COLONEL
1859   2nd HIGHLAND COY.   1864   1881   (Marching Order)   1907
             1862   1901

QUEEN'S RIFLE VOLUNTEER BRIGADE,
THE ROYAL SCOTS.

PLATE XI.

PRIVATE
3rd (later 2nd) EDINBURGH R.V.
1867-1882

LIEUTENANT
1904-1908

PRIVATE
1900-1908
9TH VOL. BN. (HIGHRS)
ROYAL SCOTS

PRIVATE
1900-1908
8TH (SCOTTISH) VOL. BN.
THE KINGS

4TH VOL. BN. THE ROYAL SCOTS

MᶜLagan & Cumming Edinᵣ

PLATE XII.

PRIVATE
1st Midlothian R.V.
(in Undress Blouse)
1860-1863

CAPTAIN
1st Midlothian R.V.
1863-1878

PRIVATE
1st Midlothian R.V.
(5th V.B.R.S.)
1885-1890

CAPTAIN
5th V.B. Royal Scots
1890-1905

PRIVATE
1905-1907

5TH VOL. BN. THE ROYAL SCOTS

M'Lagan & Cumming Edin

PLATE XIII.

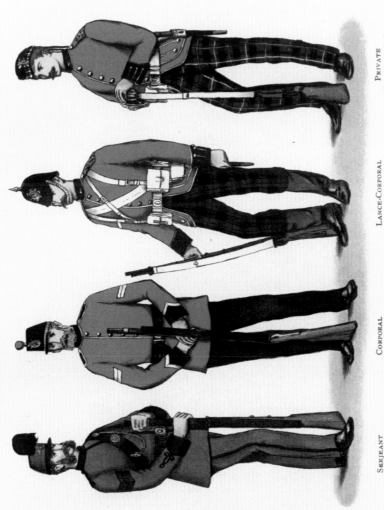

SERJEANT
3rd MIDLOTHIAN R.V.
1860-1864

CORPORAL
1st A.B. MIDLOTHIAN AND
PEEBLES R.V.
1864-1874

LANCE-CORPORAL
(Marching Order)
1888-1900

PRIVATE
(Review Order)
1904-1908

6TH VOL. BN. THE ROYAL SCOTS

M°Lagan & Cumming Edin°

PLATE XIV.

PRIVATE   PRIVATE   CORPORAL   PRIVATE   PRIVATE   CAPTAIN
1st A.B. HADDINGTON R.V.   1895–1904   1904–1908   1st A.B. LINLITHGOW R.V.   1890–1903   1903–1908
1864–1880   1876–1890

7TH VOL. BN. THE ROYAL SCOTS   8TH VOL. BN. THE ROYAL SCOTS

McLagan & Cumming Edin^r

PLATE XV.

SERJEANT   PRIVATE   CORPORAL   PRIVATE   FIELD OFFICER   SERJEANT
2ND AYRSHIRE R.V.   1ST AYRSHIRE R.V.   (Marching Order)   3RD AYRSHIRE R.V.   1ST A.B. AYRSHIRE R.V.   1898-1908
1860   1880-1887   1888-1908   1860   1870

1ST VOL. BN. ROY. SCOTS FUSILIERS   2ND VOL. BN. ROY. SCOTS FUSILIERS

McLagan & Cumming, Edin.

PLATE XVI.

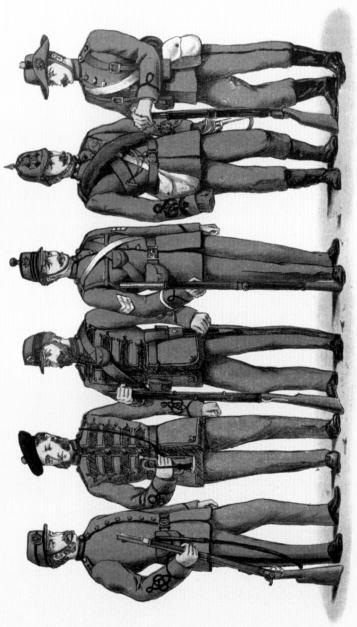

McLagan & Cumming, Edin.

PRIVATE
2nd ROXBURGH R.V.
1860

BUGLER
4th ROXBURGH R.V.
1860

PRIVATE
1st SELKIRK R.V.
1860

SERJEANT
1st A.B. ROXBURGH AND
SELKIRK R.V.
1863-1877

CAPTAIN
1879-1902

PRIVATE
1902-1907

THE BORDER RIFLE VOLUNTEER CORPS

PLATE XVII.

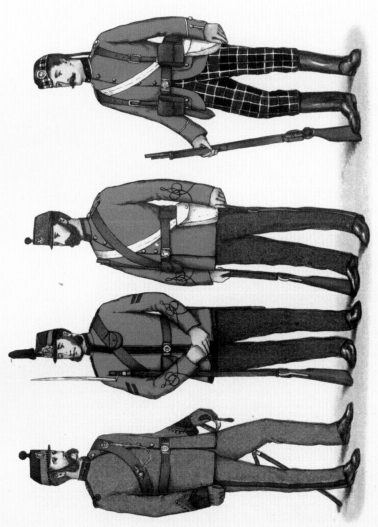

ENSIGN
4th A.B. BERWICK R.V.
1860-1863

CORPORAL
1st A.B. BERWICK R.V.
1864-1874

PRIVATE
1st A.B. BERWICK R.V.
1875-1880

PRIVATE
1900-1908

2ND VOL. BN. K.O. SCOTTISH BORDERERS

PLATE XVIII.

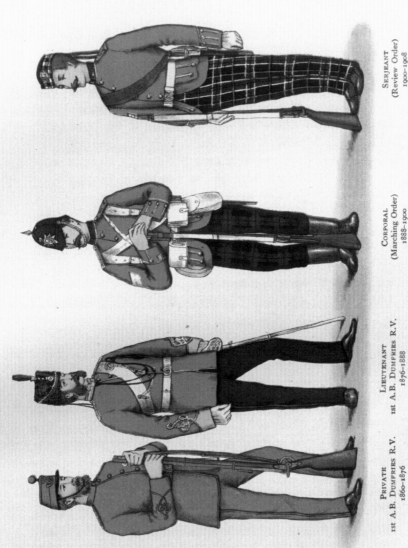

PRIVATE
1st A.B. DUMFRIES R.V.
1860–1876

LIEUTENANT
1st A.B. DUMFRIES R.V.
1876–1888

CORPORAL
(Marching Order)
1888–1900

SERJEANT
(Review Order)
1900–1908

3RD VOL. BN. K.O. SCOTTISH BORDERERS

MᶜLagan & Cumming, Edinᵣ

PLATE XIX.

SERJEANT, 1873–1883

LIEUTENANT, 1883–1905
(in Patrol Jacket)

PRIVATE, 1905–1908

GALLOWAY V.R.C.

McLagan & Cumming, Edin^r

PLATE XX.

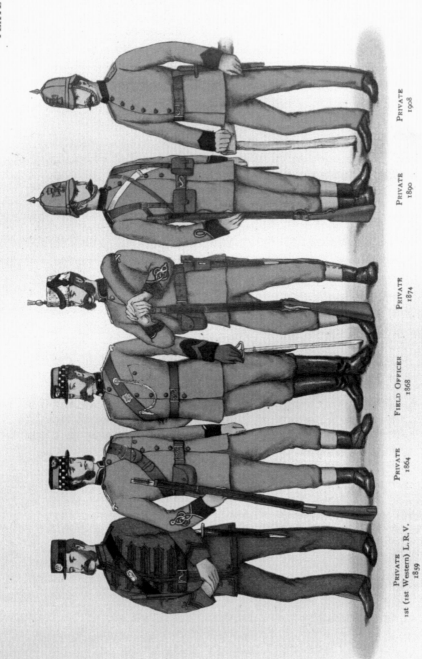

PRIVATE
1st (1st Western) L.R.V.
1859

PRIVATE
1864

FIELD OFFICER
1868

PRIVATE
1874

PRIVATE
1890

PRIVATE
1908

1ST LANARKSHIRE V.R.C.

McLagan & Cumming, Edinr

PLATE XXI.

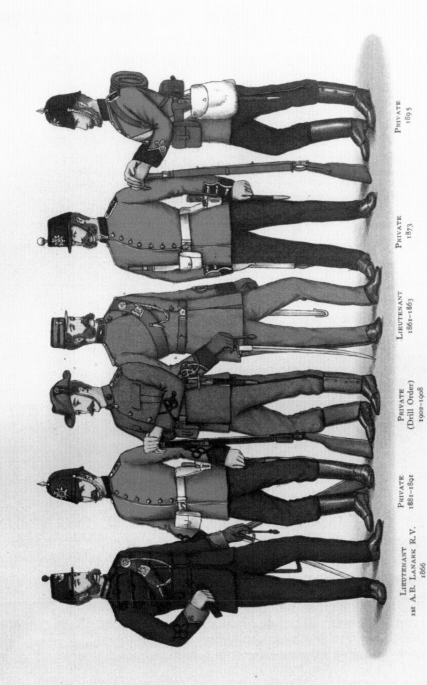

LIEUTENANT   PRIVATE   PRIVATE   LIEUTENANT   PRIVATE   PRIVATE
1st A.B. LANARK R.V.   1881-1891   (Drill Order)   1861-1863   1873   1895
1866   1902-1908

2ND VOL. BN. SCOTTISH RIFLES   3RD LANARKSHIRE V.R.C.

M'Lagan & Cumming, Edinr

PLATE XXII.

Mc Lagan & Cumming, Edin^r

LIEUTENANT
4TH LK. R.V.
1860

CAPTAIN
6TH LK. R.V.
1860

BUGLER
6TH LK. R.V.
1859

PRIVATE
4TH LK. R.V.
1863-1876

CAPTAIN
HIGHLAND COYS.
4TH L.R.V.
1867

PRIVATE
4TH V.B.S.R.
1878-1904

PRIVATE
4TH V.B.S.R.
1904-1908

4TH VOL. BN. SCOTTISH RIFLES

PLATE XXIII.

PRIVATE, 4TH AD. BN. LK. R.V.   PRIVATE, 4TH A.B. (29TH) L.R.V.   PRIVATE, 29TH (7TH) L.R.V. and 5TH V.B.S.R.
1865–1871   1871–1879   1879–1897

5TH VOL. BN. SCOTTISH RIFLES

McLagan & Cumming. Edinʳ

PLATE XXIV.

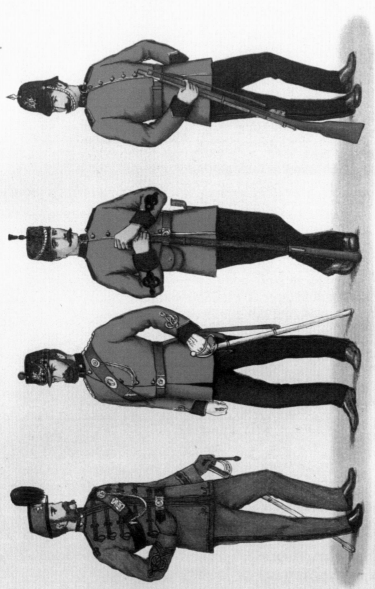

CAPTAIN, 1st FORFAR R.V.   LIEUTENANT, 1st FORFAR R.V.   PRIVATE, 1st FORFAR R.V.   PRIVATE
1860   1862–1877   1877–1880   1904–1908

1st VOL. BN. ROYAL HIGHLANDERS

McLagan & Cumming, Edinʳ

PLATE XXV.

PRIVATE
5th FORFAR R.V.
1860–64

PRIVATE
1872–82
Cap worn
1864–72

SERJEANT
1882–1908

2ND VOL. BN. ROYAL HIGHLANDERS

ENSIGN
10th FORFAR R. V.
1862–1880

PRIVATE
(Review Order)
1887–1908

3RD VOL. BN. ROYAL HIGHLANDERS

McLagan & Cumming Edin^r

PLATE XXVI.

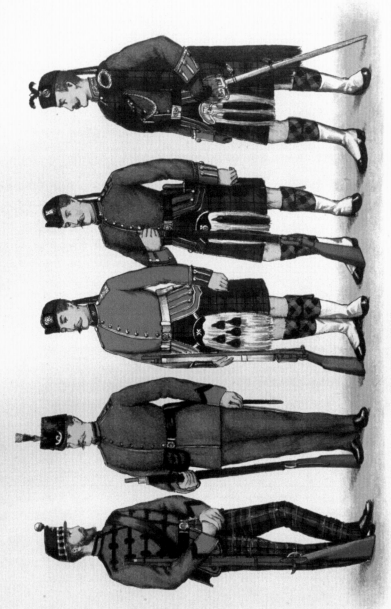

PRIVATE
18th PERTH R.V.
1868-1878

PRIVATE
1st PERTHSHIRE R.V.
1876-1883

PRIVATE
1901-1908

PRIVATE
2nd PERTHSHIRE R.V.
(5th V.B.R.H.)
1883-1908

LIEUTENANT
2nd PERTHSHIRE R.V.
(5th V.B.R.H.)
1883-1908

4TH VOL. BN. ROYAL HIGHLANDERS   5TH VOL. BN. ROYAL HIGHLANDERS

M'Lagan & Cumming Edin?

PLATE XXVII.

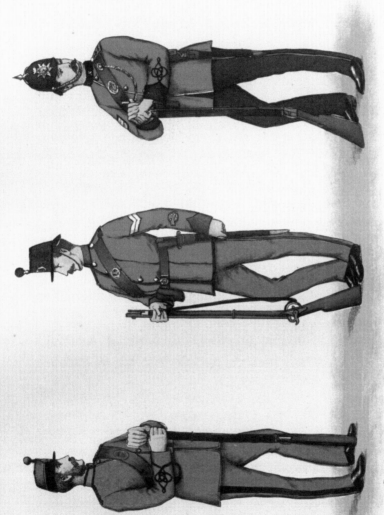

PRIVATE
5th FIFE R.V.
1860-1863

CORPORAL
1st ADM. BN. FIFE R.V.
1863-1875

SERJEANT
1st FIFE R.V. later 6th V.B.R.H.
1880-1908

6TH VOL. BN. ROYAL HIGHLANDERS

Mᶜ Lagan & Cumming, Edinᵣ

PLATE XXVIII.

LIEUTENANT
19th LANARK R.V.
1860–63

PRIVATE
19th LANARK R.V.
1863–70

PRIVATE
19th LANARK R.V.
1870–74

CORPORAL
19th (5th) LANARK R.V.
1874–83

SERJEANT
(Review Order)
1903–08

1ST VOL. BN. HIGHLAND LIGHT INFANTRY

MᶜLagan & Cumming Edinᵗ

PLATE XXIX.

ENSIGN
25th LANARK R.V.
1860

PRIVATE
25th LANARK R.V.
1861-73

CORPORAL
1880-98

FIELD OFFICER
1905

PRIVATE
1906-08

2ND. VOL. BN. HIGHLAND LIGHT INFANTRY

McLagan & Cumming Edinr

PLATE XXX.

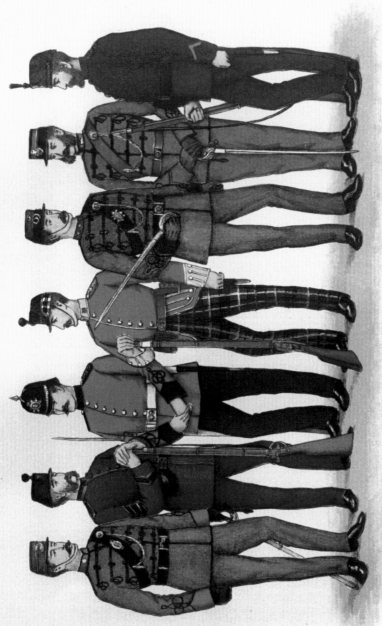

LIEUTENANT   SERJEANT   PRIVATE   PRIVATE   CAPTAIN   LIEUTENANT   PRIVATE
31st LANARK R.V.   2nd ADM. BN.   31st or 8th   1886-1908   5th L.R.V.   64th L.R.V.   5th L.R.V.
1860   or 31st LANARK R.V.   LANARK   1860   1860   1872
1861-74   R.V.
1878-86

3RD VOL. BN. HIGHLAND L.I.   5TH LANARK R.V. (1860-1873)

PLATE XXXI.

PRIVATE   SERJEANT   PRIVATE   COLONEL   PRIVATE   LIEUTENANT
37th LANARK R.V. 3rd A.B. LANARK R.V. 1883–1904 1904–1908 105th (10th) LANARK R.V. 1902–08
1860–62   1862–80   1868–1885

9TH LANARKSHIRE V.R.C.   5TH VOL. BN. HIGHLAND L.I.

MᶜLagan & Cumming, Edinᴿ

PLATE XXXII.

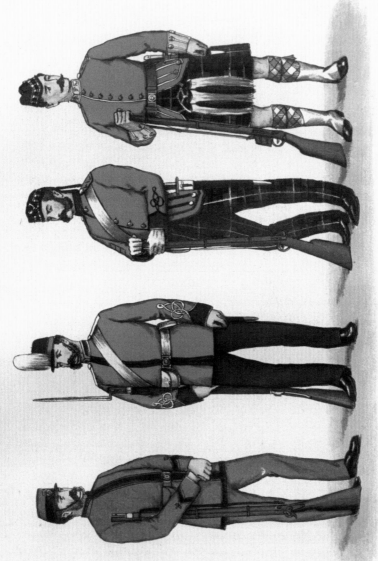

PRIVATE
1st ROSS R.V.
1860-64

PRIVATE
1st ROSS R.V.
1864-76

SERJEANT
1st A.B. ROSS R.V.
1876-88

PRIVATE
1903-1908

1ST VOL. BN. SEAFORTH HIGHLANDERS

McLagan & Cumming, Edinr

PLATE XXXIII.

ENSIGN
4th SUTHD. R.V.
1860

PRIVATE
1st SUTHD. R.V.
1860

PRIVATE
3rd SUTHD. R.V.
1865-67

PRIVATE
2nd CAITHNESS R.V.
1864-70

CAPTAIN
1880-99

PIPER
1883-1908

PRIVATE
1899-1908

1st SUTHERLAND V.R.C.

MᶜLagan & Cumming Edinᵣ

PLATE XXXIV.

LIEUTENANT   PRIVATE   ENSIGN   LIEUTENANT   CAPTAIN   PRIVATE
3RD ELGIN R.V.   1ST A.B. ELGIN, R.V.   6TH ELGIN R.V.   1ST ELGIN R.V.   1886–1898   1905–1908
1861   (except 6th & 7th Corps)   1862–1879   1880–1886
           1862–1879

3RD VOL. BN SEAFORTH HIGHLANDERS

PLATE XXXV.

PRIVATE
1st ABERDEEN R.V.
1860–1862

PRIVATE
No. 11 COY., 1st A.R.V.
1861–1862

SERJEANT
1st A.R.V.
1862–1879

COLOUR-SERJEANT
1880

PRIVATE
1895–1907

1ST VOL. BN. GORDON HIGHLANDERS

McLagan & Cumming, Edinᴿ

PLATE XXXVI.

LIEUTENANT   PRIVATE   CAPTAIN   PRIVATE   PRIVATE

6th ABERDEEN R.V. 2nd A.B. ABERDEEN R.V. 1880–1908 1st A.B. KINCARDINE R.V. 1876–1908

1860–1864   1864–1875   1864–1876

2ND VOL. BN. GORDON HIGHLANDERS   5TH VOL. BN. GORDON HIGHLANDERS

PLATE XXXVII.

M°LAGAN & CUMMING, Edin?

ENSIGN	LIEUTENANT	LIEUTENANT	CAPTAIN	CAPTAIN	CAPTAIN	CORPORAL
5th ABERDEEN R.V. 1860	9th ABERDEEN R.V. 1860	17th ABERDEEN R.V. 1860	20th ABERDEEN R.V. 1860	2nd A.B. ABERDEEN R.V. 1863–1868	3rd A.B. or 3rd ABERDEEN R.V. 1872–1883	1903–1908

3RD VOL. BN. GORDON HIGHLANDERS

PLATE XXXVIII.

PRIVATE
10TH ABERDEEN
R.V.
1860

PRIVATE
11TH ABERDEEN
R.V.
1860

CORPORAL
7TH ABERDEEN
R.V.
1860

PRIVATE
1ST A.B. ABERDEEN R.V.
1864–1869

SERJEANT
1869–1887

PRIVATE
1887–1903

SERJEANT
1903–1908

4TH VOL. BN. GORDON HIGHLANDERS

M. Lagan & Cumming, Edin.

PLATE XXXIX.

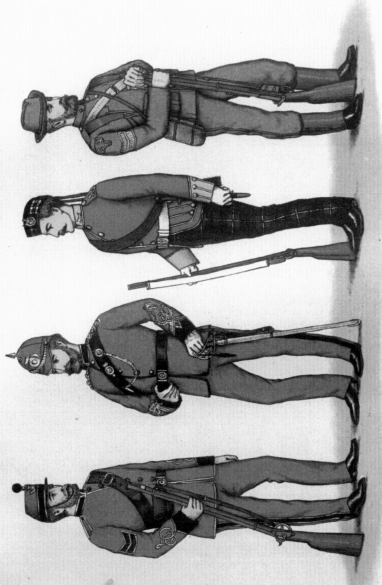

CORPORAL
1ST A.B. BANFF R.V.
1861–1880

CAPTAIN
1887–1891

6TH VOL. BN. GORDON HIGHLANDERS

SERJEANT
1891–1908

CORPORAL
1900–1908

7TH V.B. GORDON
HIGHLANDERS

McLagan & Cumming Edin.

PLATE XL.

LIEUTENANT   SERJEANT   PRIVATE   PRIVATE   CAPTAIN   PRIVATE   PRIVATE
5th INVERNESS R.V.   1st INVERNESS R.V.   6th INVERNESS R.V.   2nd INVERNESS R.V.   1st INVERNESS H.R.V.
1860-63   1860-63   1863-1880   1863-1880   1880-1893   1893-1908

1ST VOL. BN. CAMERON HIGHLANDERS

McLagan & Cumming Edinr

PLATE XLI.

CAPTAIN
10th RENFREW R.V.
1860–1877

CAPTAIN
1st R.R.V.
1881–1889

PRIVATE
1899–1908

1st V.B. ARGYLL AND SUTHERLAND
HIGHLANDERS

LIEUTENANT
2nd A.B.R.R.V.
1862–1875

PRIVATE
2nd R.R.V.
1881–1898

LIEUTENANT
1903–1908

2nd V.B. ARGYLL AND SUTHERLAND
HIGHLANDERS

MᶜLagan & Cumming Edinᵀ

PLATE XLII.

PRIVATE   PRIVATE   PRIVATE   PRIVATE   LANCE-CORPORAL
3RD A.B. RENFREW R.V.   1889-1908   3RD STIRLING R.V.   1ST A.B. STIRLING R.V.   1886-1908
1862-1874   1862-1863   1863-1882

3RD V.B. ARGYLL AND SUTHERLAND   4TH V.B. ARGYLL AND SUTHERLAND
HIGHLANDERS   HIGHLANDERS

PLATE XLIII.

CAPTAIN   PRIVATE   LIEUTENANT   PRIVATE   PRIVATE

2nd ARGYLL R.V.   13th ARGYLL R.V.   8th ARGYLL R.V.   1st A.B. (later 1st) ARGYLL R.V.   1902–1908

1868   1867   1866   1874–1883

5TH V.B. ARGYLL AND SUTHERLAND HIGHLANDERS

PLATE XLIV.

PRIVATE
6th DUMBARTON R.V.
1860

PRIVATE
6th DUMBARTON R.V.
1861–1864

SERJEANT
1st A B,
DUMBARTON R.V.
1864–1874

PRIVATE
1874–1882

LIEUTENANT
1882–1887

COLOUR-SERJEANT
Review Order
1887–1908

1st DUMBARTON V.R.C.

Mᶜ Lagan & Cumming Edinᵣ

PLATE XLV.

PRIVATE
1st CLACKMANNAN R.V.
1860

PRIVATE
1st A.B. CLACKMANNAN R.V.
1867–1874

CAPTAIN
1st A.B. (later 1st)
CLACKMANNAN AND KINROSS
R.V., 1874–1888

FIELD OFFICER
7th V.B. A. and S. HRS.
1888–1903

7TH VOL. BN. ARGYLL AND SUTHERLAND HIGHLANDERS

M'Lagan & Cumming Edin.

PLATE XLVI.

McLagan & Cumming Edinr

PRIVATE
1860

PRIVATE (Kilted Company)
1860

LIEUTENANT
1907

PRIVATE
1907

7TH MIDDLESEX (LONDON SCOTTISH) V.R.C.

PLATE XLVII.

Private

Private

ARMY SERVICE CORPS   ROY. ARMY MEDICAL CORPS

(Volrs.) 1907   (Volrs.) 1907

LIST OF WORKS, &c., CONSULTED.

Monthly Army Lists, 1859 to date.

'Narrative of the Royal Scottish Volunteer Review in Holyrood Park on the 7th August 1860.' By E. R. Vernon. Edinburgh: W. P. Nimmo, 1860.

Files of the 'Scotsman' and 'Glasgow Herald,' 1860 and 1881.

'History of Defensive Organisation.' By John Crawford, Captain, late 19th Lanark R.V. Glasgow: David Robertson & Co., 1878.

'History of the Volunteer Infantry.' By R. P. Berry, late Lieutenant 6th West York R.V. Simpkin, Marshall, Hamilton, Kent & Co., Limited, 1903.

Painting of "The Glasgow Volunteers, 1861-63." By Thomas Robertson, W.S.A., 1863, in the possession of Lieut.-Colonel R. Patterson, V.D., 5th V.B. Argyll and Sutherland Highlanders, 8 Clairmont Gardens, Glasgow.

'History of the Fife Light Horse.' By Colonel Anstruther Thomson. Edinburgh: William Blackwood & Sons, 1892.

'History of the Queen's Edinburgh Rifle Volunteer Brigade.' By William Stephen. Edinburgh: William Blackwood & Sons, 1881.

Bazaar Handbook of the Hawick Volunteers.' 1902.

'History of Galashiels.' By Robert Hall. Galashiels: Alexander Walker & Son, 1898.

'History of the 1st Lanark Rifle Volunteers.' By David Howie. Glasgow: David Robertson & Co., 1887.

'History of the 7th Lanark Rifle Volunteers.' By Captain James Orr, late R.E., and Adjutant of the Battalion. Glasgow: Robert Anderson, 22 Ann Street. 1884.

'History of the 1st Volunteer Battalion Highland Light Infantry' (written for their bazaar). 1891.

'The 1st Lanark Rifles Gazette.'

'The Pibroch' (Glasgow Highlanders' Annual Record).

'Sutherland and the Reay Country.' By the Rev. Adam Gunn, M.A., and John Mackay. Glasgow : 'Celtic Monthly' Office, 1897.

'History of the 3rd Volunteer Battalion, Seaforth Highlanders, 1860-1906.' Elgin : 'Northern Scot' Office, 1906.

'History of the Aberdeen Volunteers.' By Donald Sinclair, Solicitor, Aberdeen. 'Aberdeen Daily Journal' Office, 1907.

'Records of the 3rd (The Buchan) Volunteer Battalion, Gordon Highlanders.' By Captain and Hon. Major James Ferguson. Peterhead : David Scott, 1894.

'Records of the 5th (Deeside Highland) Volunteer Battalion, Gordon Highlanders.' Compiled by Major P. L. Davidson. Printed for private circulation, 1898.

'History of the Volunteers of Clackmannan and Kinross.' By Surgeon-Captain E. E. Dyer, 7th V.B. Argyll & Sutherland Highlanders. Alva : Robert Cunningham, 1907.

'The London Scottish Regimental Gazette.'

'The Royal Review,' special number of 'The Scottish Review.' September 14, 1905.

'Historical Sketch of the 4th (Perthshire) Volunteer Battalion, The Black Watch.' By Captain G. D. Pullar. Edinburgh : Hillside Printing Works, 1907.

'A Military History of Perthshire, 1660-1902.' Edited by the Marchioness of Tullibardine. Perth : R. A. & J. Hay, 1908.

LIST OF SUBSCRIBERS.

Adam, Arthur, V.D., Lieut.-Col. (retired), 5th V.B.R.S.

Aitken, Arthur Campbell, Lieut., 9th V.B.R.S.

Anderson, C. W., Major, 4th Bn. K.O.S.B.

Anderson, D. P., 2nd Lieut., 8th Bn. S.R.

Anderson, Wm., & Sons, Military Outfitters.

Anstruther, Sir Ralph, Bart., Colonel commanding late 6th V.B. Black Watch (R.H.)

Arrol, A. Theodore, Esq.

Arthur, David S., Captain, 8th Bn. S.R.

Atkinson, Herbert E., late Sergeant, London Scottish.

Auld, William, Major, 1st L.R.V.

Barnett, Hugh, V.D., Major and Hon. Lieut.-Col., 1st V.B.R.S.F., now 4th Bn. R.S.F.

Beatson, Sir George Thomas, K.C.B., M.D., Colonel, R.A.M.C. (Territorial).

Bennett, Alex. J. M., Captain and Hon. Major, 8th Bn. A. & S.H.

Bennett, Robt. J., Lieut.-Col. commanding 1st L.A.V.

Bethune, H. A., Major, 7th Bn. Black Watch.

Birrell, A., Colonel, 9th Bn. H.L.I.

Blackwood, William, formerly Lieut. 1st Artisan Coy. Q.R.V.B.

Broadfoot, Wm. R., V.D., Colonel (retired), 1st L.R.E.

Brock, H., Colonel, 9th Bn. A. & S.H.

Burns-Macdonald, Arch., Captain, 9th Argyllshire R.V. (1860).

Cadell, Henry M., V.D., Lieut.-Col. and Hon. Col., lately commanding Forth Division R.E., Submarine Miners.

Campbell, John, Major, 4th Q.O.C.H.

Campbell, M. Pearce, Captain and Hon. Major (retired), 1st L.R.V.

Campbell, Mrs.

Campbeltown Free Library.

Cargill, John T., Esq.

Chalmers, Hugh D. D., Colonel commanding 6th Bn. H.L.I.

Clarke, Seymour, Major, Q.O.C.H.

Cockburn, David, Major, 9th A. & S.H.

Connal, R. H. M., Major, Queen's Own Royal Glasgow.

Corsar, Charles, Captain, 1st Forfar R.G.A.V.

Crawford, Euing R., V.D., Lieut.-Col. and Hon. Col., late commanding 1st L.R.E.V.

Cuthbert, T. W., J.P., Captain, 4th V.B. Seaforth Highlanders.

Dalmahoy, J. A., M.V.O., V.D., 1st Lowland Brigade R.F.A.

Dickson, David, Lieut.-Col., Q.R.V.B.

Donald, A. H., Lieut.-Col., 1st L.R.V.

Donald, C. G., C.B., Brigadier - General, commanding Home Counties Division.

Douglas, Bailie R. A., J.P., late Q.R.V.B.

Douglas, Robert Jeffrey, Major, 5th Bn. S.R.

Duke, David, V.D., Captain and Hon. Major, 2nd (Angus) V.B. The Black Watch (R.H.)

Duncan, W. V., Major, 1st V.B. The Gordon Highlanders.

Dundee Free Library.

Dunlop, J. W., C.B., Colonel, R.A.

Dunlop, Thomas, Captain (retired), 1st L.R.V.

Edinburgh Public Library.

Edington, George H., Captain, R.A.M.C.(T.)

Elliot, Stuart Douglas, V.D., Lieut.-Col. and Hon. Col. (retired), 4th V.B.R.S.

Fergusson, James, Colonel (retired), 9th V.B.R.S.

Findlay, James M., Captain, 8th Cameronians (S.R.)

Fleming, William G., V.D., Colonel, 9th Bn. H.L.I.

Forsyth, R. W., Limited.

Fraser, Hugh Munro, Lieut.-Col., 1st V.B. Seaforth Highlanders.

Frew, William, Surgeon-Colonel (retired), 4th V.B.R.S. Fusiliers.

Garroway, John, V.D., Major, 5th V.B.S.R.

Gentles, Norman, Captain, 6th V.B.S.R.

Gilmour, Sir John, Bart., late Colonel commanding Fife and Forfar I.Y.

Gordon, Alex., F.S.M., Captain, 3rd V.B. A. & S.H.

Graham, Balfour, V.D., F.R.C.S.E., Lieut.-Col., A.M.R., and R.A.M.C.(T.F.)

Graham, D. Runciman, V.D., Colonel, late commanding 3rd V.B.H.L.I.

Grant, A. B., M.V.O., V.D., Colonel, late commanding 1st L.R.G.A.V.

Grierson, John M., V.D., Major, 5th Bn. S.R.

Griffith, Sir R. Waldie, Bart., 1st Roxburgh and Selkirk V.R.C.

Haddon, And., Lieut.-Col.

Halley, George, F.R.C.S.Ed., R.A.M.C.(*y*)

Hamilton, His Grace the Duke of.

Hamilton, William, Esq.

Hannan, H. M., Major, 8th S.R., Brigade-Major Scot. Rifle Br.

Harvey, Thomas, late Captain 1st Dumbartonshire V.R.C. (2 copies.)

Hatrick, William Lindsay, Captain, 5th V.B.H.L.I.

Henderson, M. W., Lieut.-Col., 10th R.S.

Hendry, P. W., Colonel, Brigade-Major H.L.I.

Heys, Z. H., Lieut.-Col., 3rd V.B. A. & S.H.

Hill, G. W., Esq.

Hill, Howard, Lieut.-Col. commanding 4th Bn. R.H.

Hope, Charles, Colonel, late commanding 2nd V.B.K.O.S.B.

Hope, James A., V.D., Lieut.-Col., A.S.C.(T.)

Hopkins, Hugh, Esq. (2 copies.)

Hunter, Andrew A., Esq., late London Scottish.

Jackson, Thomas, Lieut.-Col., 7th L.R.V.

Johnston, Jas. W., M.V.O., V.D., Lieut.-Col. Commandant (Hon. Col.) 1st Fifeshire R.G.A.V.

Kay, W. Martin, Major, 6th S.R.

Kennedy, Walter Philips, V.D., Major, Border Rifles.

Knight, C. A., Hon. Major, 1st V.B.H.L.I.

Laidlaw, D., Lieut.-Col. Commandant and Hon. Col. Scot. Telegraph Coys. R.E. and 2nd Highland Field Coy. R.E.

Lang, James, Lieut.-Col., 1st L.R.E. (for Officers' Library).
Lennox, Colonel.
Leslie, John H., Major, R.A.
Lomax, S. H., Major-General.
Loudon, J. Livingstone, Surgeon-Captain, 2nd V.B.S.R.
Love, J. J., Captain, 4th Bn. R.S.F.
Lowson, James, Major, 1st L.R.V.

M'Dougal, James, Captain, 2nd V.B.K.O.S.B.
Macfie, A. L., V.D., Lieut.-Col. and Hon. Col. commanding "Liverpool Scottish."
Mackenzie, R. C., Colonel commanding H.L.I. Brigade Territorial Force.
Mackenzie, Stewart, of Brahan Castle, Colonel.   (2 copies.)
Mackintosh, St Angus, Royal Horse Guards.
M'Niel, John, V.D., Lieut.-Col. commanding Forth and Clyde R.G.A.
Mann, Robert M., Major, 1st L.R.V.
Marryat, Lieut.-Col., late commanding 1st Bn. Manchester Regiment.
Maxwell, Warden R., Hon. Col., 8th S.R.
Mellis, Wm. A., V.D., Colonel, 6th Bn. Gordon Highlanders.
Melvill-Simons, Mrs H.
Millar, A., Hon. Major, 3rd V.B.H.L.I.
Mitchell Library, Glasgow.
Montefiore, Cecil Sebog, Major, 2nd London Divisional Engineers.   (2 copies.)
Morrison, Fred L., Lieut.-Col., 1st V.B.H.L.I.
Morton, D. S., Lieut.-Col., 1st V.B.H.L.I.

Nicoll, P. S., Major, 5th Bn. Black Watch.

Outram, James, Colonel, 5th H.L.I.

Park, J. Smith, M.V.O., V.D., Lieut.-Col. and Hon. Col., 1st L.R.E.V.
Paul, Thos. Alex., Colonel, later Lieut.-Col. and Hon. Col., 1st L.R.V.
Paul, W. J., Major (retired), 4th V.B.S.R.
Pease, G. Smith, Lieut.-Col. and Hon. Col., 1st Orkney R.G.A.

Rae, Captain, Vancouver.
Reid, A. T., V.D., Lieut.-Col., late 4th V.B. Black Watch (R.H.)
Reid, James A., V.D., Hon. Col., 5th Bn. S.R.
Robertson, H. Gordon, Major, 1st Renfrew and Dumbarton R.G.A.
Robertson, Robert, M.V.O., V.D., Colonel, late commanding 3rd
 V.B. Gordon Highlanders.
Robinson, T. Eaton, Major (retired), 1st L.R.V.
Rodger, J. G., Captain and Hon. Major (retired), 1st L.R.V.
Ross, Arthur Victor, Lieut., 5th Bn. H.L.I.
Rottenburg, Fritz, Esq.
Rottenburg, Paul, Esq., LL.D.
Roxburgh, J. A., V.D., Hon. Col., Lieut.-Col. commanding 5th
 Bn. S.R.

Sanderson, Arthur W., Captain, 7th Bn. R.S.
Sherriff, George, Esq.
Signet Library, Edinburgh.
Simpson, E., Colonel, 4th V.B. A. & S.H.
Smith, Fred. J., Lieut.-Col. and Hon. Col. commanding 8th Bn.
 S.R.
Smith, J. Guthrie, Hon. Major (retired), 3rd V.B.H.L.I.
Smith, W. A., V.D., Lieut.-Col., 1st L.R.V.
Spencer, Miss.
Stamfield, John, Captain, Royal Scots Greys.
Stevenson, Allan, V.D., Captain and Hon. Major, 4th Bn. K.O.S.B.
Stewart, C. Murray, Captain, 6th Bn. Black Watch (R.H.)
Sutherland, Jas. B., V.D., Colonel (retired), Q.R.V.B. (R.S.)

"The Adjutant," 4th Bn. K.O.S.B.
The Prince Consort's Library, Aldershot.
Todd, G. Bell, V.D., Surgeon-Lieut.-Col., 9th H.L.I.
Tulloch, W. Forbes, Captain, 8th V.B.S.R.

University Library, King's College, Aberdeen, per P. J. Anderson, Esq., Librarian.
Urquhart, R., M.V.O., V.D., Colonel, 3rd V.B. Seaforth Highlanders.

Walker, H. W., Lieut., R.F.A.
Walker, James W., Captain, 1st Ayr and Galloway R.G.A.

Walker, Miss Sophia I.
Watt, Edward W., Captain, 4th Gordon Highlanders.
Whigham, George, Lieut.-Col., Q.R.V.B.
Wilson, H. Arnold, Captain, 5th Bn. S.R.
Wilson, John B., V.D., J.P., Colonel, 7th Bn. S.R.
Wright, John P., Esq.
Wylie, James K. M., Lieut., 8th Bn. S.R.

ERRATA.

Page 183, line 18 from top, *for* "now" *read* "latterly."

„ 276, „ 17 „ top, *delete* "(later buff)."

„ „ „ 22 „ top, *for* "white" *read* "blue."

„ 340, „ 4 „ foot, *for* "Gun" *read* "Green."

Records of the

Scottish Volunteer Force.

———•———

I.

GENERAL ACCOUNT OF THE ORIGIN AND HISTORY OF THE FORCE.

THE year 1859 dawned amidst the mutterings of storm-clouds in Europe. Since the birth of the third French Empire, the aim of its rulers had been to distract the attention of the people of France from internal affairs by an active foreign policy, and to keep the army, on whose support the throne depended, employed in gathering that glory of which the French soldier has from all time been so avid. Mainly to these reasons had been due the participation of France in the war which, for nigh upon two years, had raged in the East. Fresh from its victories in the Crimea, the French army fancied itself, possibly with right, the most powerful military instrument in Europe, and its leaders eagerly sought for new fields wherein

The political situation in 1859.

A

they might add to the laurels already gained against
Russia.   To the rulers of France the cause of Italian
unity seemed therefore a proper field for their exploits,
and a sensation of imminent danger of war ran through
Europe when, on the 1st January 1859, at the New
Year's reception at the Tuileries, the Emperor Napoleon
III. said to the Austrian Ambassador that he regretted
that his "relations with the Austrian Government were
not so good as in the past."   Mainly directed, of course,
against Austria as this threat was, it nevertheless
caused alarm in other countries, as showing the mili-
tant temper of the French Government, and nowhere
more so than in Great Britain.   There had not been
wanting previous signs of a growing hostility to this
country in France, especially in the army, and all the
more so since the plot against the Emperor's life, which
had been hatched by Orsini and others in England, and
which had so nearly succeeded in its dastardly purpose.
The Emperor of the French had for some time been
strengthening his navy and pushing on the great
harbour works and fortifications of Cherbourg, and
the tone of the officially inspired French press had
gradually become extremely hostile to Great Britain.
Certain French colonels, in their congratulations to
the Emperor on his escape from assassination, had
permitted themselves to indulge in threats to cross the
Channel and plant the Imperial eagles on the Tower
of London, and these, officially published in the 'Moni-
teur,' though afterwards disclaimed, raised public feeling in Great Britain to fever-heat.

For long there had been an uneasy feeling in the
Military unprepared- ness of Great Britain. country that its defences were in an unsatisfactory state, and the minds of thinking
men had been exercised on the subject ever
since the publication in 1847 of the famous letter from

the Duke of Wellington to Sir John Burgoyne, insist-
ing on the danger of the situation and the necessity of
preparation for war, which had made a great impres-
sion on the country at the time.   In 1852 the militia
had been revived, and it had rendered splendid service
during the Crimean War and Indian Mutiny; but men's
minds now reverted to the period when Great Britain
had been threatened by France at the beginning of the
century, and they remembered that at that time their
fathers had volunteered to supplement the regular
army and the constitutional militia in the defence of
the country.   True to the great traditions of their
race, as their fathers had done before them so would
they do now, and patriotic men felt that the hour had
come to offer their services.   A mass meeting was held
in April 1859 in St Martin's Hall, Longacre, to protest
against the insufficiency of the national defences, offers
to form volunteer corps began to pour in upon the
Government, and the Poet-Laureate, Tennyson, voiced
the national attitude in an ode published in 'The
Times' of May 9, 1859, the first verse of which
ran—

> " There is a sound of thunder afar,
>   Storm in the South that darkens the day !
>   Storm of battle and thunder of war !
>   Well if it do not roll our way.
>   Storm, Storm, Riflemen form !
>   Ready, be ready against the storm !
>   Riflemen, Riflemen, Riflemen form ! "

In Scotland all traces of the Volunteers of 1803 and
the Sharpshooters of 1819, except the memory of them,
Volunteer corps existing in 1859. had passed away, but in England one corps
existed which traced its origin to the time
of the great wars.   This was the " Royal
Victoria Rifles," which, originally known as " The Duke

of Cumberland's Sharpshooters," had been raised in 1803 and had escaped extinction. It for long existed only as a rifle club in London, with a rifle-range at Kilburn, and only in 1853 was it allowed to assemble as volunteers for drill. In 1858 it only numbered 57 men, but in it was serving as captain a Mr Hans Busk, who was strongly impressed with the defenceless state of the Kingdom and devoted his time to advocating the formation of a Volunteer force, and, as an example of what it might be made, laboured to increase the Victoria Rifles. In this he was successful. By the middle of 1859 the corps mustered 800 men, and it existed till 1908 as portion of the 1st Middlesex Rifle Volunteer Corps.

But though undoubtedly of the greater antiquity, the Victoria Rifles were not awarded precedence for their county as the first in the volunteer force, as in 1852 an offer had been made by certain citizens of Exeter to form a volunteer corps, and their services had been accepted by the Government of the day. This corps became in 1859 the 1st Devonshire Rifle Volunteers, and gained for its county the first place in the table of precedence for rifle volunteers by virtue of its having been constituted as a corps a year earlier than the Victoria Rifles.

Liverpool also was early afoot in the formation of a volunteer corps, for in 1855 Mr Nathaniel Bousfield founded in that city the "Liverpool Drill Club," consisting of about a hundred members, who were uniformed and armed; but their services were not accepted as volunteers until 1859, when Mr Bousfield had the honour of receiving the first commission granted to a volunteer on June 11, and his club formed the nucleus of the 1st Lancashire Rifle Volunteers.

But if, prior to 1859, Scotland had no nuclei of

volunteers, it was not long before the surviving representatives of the former existing forces banded themselves together once more, for in February 1860 a meeting of the survivors of the Glasgow Light Horse of 1796, the volunteers of 1803, and the Sharpshooters of 1819 was held in Glasgow, one of the only two survivors of the first-named corps (Mr Robert Reid, eighty-eight years of age) being present. It was resolved that they should form themselves into a veteran rifle corps, to be designated " The Old Guard of Glasgow," armed and clothed at their own expense, and an offer of their services was transmitted to the proper authorities. This was acknowledged by the military secretary to the General Commanding-in-Chief on February 7, 1860, who added that it was " gratifying to his Royal Highness to be thus assured that the military spirit still exists among those who came forward in past years when the country was likely to require their services." The date of the official acceptance of the services of the corps was April 3, 1860, and it was numbered the 78th Lanark. It does not appear that the members ever appeared in uniform or did any drill, but they set an example to the younger generation which was of much value to the cause of volunteering. The corps was subsequently merged in the 3rd Lanark Rifle Volunteers.

The Government of the day was slow to move in the matter of accepting the services of volunteer corps, too slow to please the ardent advocates of the **Attitude of the Government to the Volunteer movement.** movement, who naturally accused the Government of apathy and its military advisers of active opposition to the " amateur soldier," but, viewed dispassionately at this lapse of time, the action of the authorities appears to have been guided by sound sense. It was desirable that, before sanctioning the formation of a new military force, it should be ascertained whether its establishment was likely to be a success, whether the promises of those offering their services were likely to be borne out by their performances, whether the new levies would interfere with the recruiting of other branches of the national forces,—in short, the advisability of encouraging the movement had to be debated from the hard matter-of-fact point of view, patriotic exultation being put on one side. The decision was taken in the affirmative, and, as the official account [1] puts it : " No exaggerated view was held by the War Minister of what volunteers could achieve. It was sufficient to utilise the ardent feeling of the nation to create a defensive force of ordinary citizens of the middle class, and to leave that force to work out its own development by constantly aiming at higher military efficiency, by a gradual tightening of the bonds of discipline, and by a closer drawing of the links which attach it to the regular army. . . . From the first, the judicious policy of giving assistance in proportion to efficiency was adopted by the War Office, and it is probably to this as much as to any other cause that the system has developed lasting qualities." On May 12, 1859, the establishment of the volunteer force in Great Britain was sanctioned.

This sanction was conveyed by a War Office circular of the date just mentioned, signed by General The War Peel, Secretary of State for War, which au-Office Cir-cular of May thorised the formation of volunteer corps 12, 1859. under the provisions of Act 44, George III., cap. 54, dated June 5, 1804. This circular was addressed to the Lords-Lieutenant of counties, and authorised them to submit proposals for the formation

---

[1] The Army Book of the British Empire, p. 381.

of volunteer rifle corps, and of artillery corps in maritime towns where there might be forts and batteries. The principal provisions of the Act of 1804, which were recapitulated in the circular, were that the officers should be commissioned by the Lord-Lieutenant; that the members should take the oath of allegiance; that the force might be called out in case of actual invasion, appearance of an enemy on the coast, or rebellion arising from either of these emergencies; that while under arms the members should be subject to military law, and be paid and billeted like regular soldiers, half-pay or pensions being the right of those disabled in actual service; that members could not quit the corps when on actual service, but at other times could do so on giving fourteen days' notice; that members who had attended eight days in each four months, or a total of twenty-four days' drill in the year, should be returned as effective; that members should be exempt from ballot for the militia; that all property of the corps should be legally vested in the commanding officer; and that subscriptions and fines under the rules of the corps should be recoverable by him before a magistrate. The circular went on to state that Her Majesty's Government would recommend to Her Majesty the acceptance of any proposal for the formation of a corps submitted by the Lord-Lieutenant under the above conditions, provided that the members undertook to provide their own arms and equipment, and to defray all expenses attending the corps, except in the event of its being assembled for actual service. Rules and regulations were to be submitted for each corps. The uniform and equipment might be settled by the members, subject to the approval of the Lord-Lieutenant; but the arms had to be furnished under the superintendence of the War Office, so as to secure uniformity of gauge. The establishments were to be fixed by the Secretary of State upon the Lord - Lieutenant reporting the number of privates recommended and the number of companies into which it was proposed to divide them. The closing sentence reminded the Lord-Lieutenant that he was responsible for the nomination of "proper persons" to be appointed officers.

On May 25, 1859, General Peel issued a second circular explanatory of the views of Government on the

The second War Office Circular of May 25, 1859.

organisation of the force. Premising that it was essential that volunteers should not be left in ignorance of the nature and character of the service to which they were binding themselves, that military discipline was the first essential, and that the conditions of service should be such that, while enforcing the necessary discipline, those classes should be induced to serve in the volunteers who did not enter the regular army or militia, the circular recommended that the system of drill and instruction should not be such as to render the service unnecessarily irksome, or make such demands on the time of members as interfered with their ordinary avocations. Rifle volunteers should therefore not be drilled or organised "as soldiers expected to take their place in line," but each man should be so thoroughly instructed in the use of his weapon as to enable the force to act as a useful auxiliary to the regular army and militia. These objects could best be attained by the organisation of rifle volunteers in companies of an establishment of one captain, one lieutenant, one ensign, and 100 of all ranks as a maximum, or in subdivisions, or even sections of a company, the great object being that the members should have "a knowledge of and thorough dependence upon each other personally." The enclosed nature of the country would give peculiar importance to the services of bodies of riflemen so composed, and with a thorough knowledge of their weapon, who should " hang with the most telling effect upon the flanks and communications of a hostile army." Ranges should be established in each locality where volunteer corps were formed, and the issue, at cost price, from Government stores, was authorised of targets and of an annual allowance of ammunition of, for each trained volunteer, 90 rounds of ball and 60 of blank cartridge and 165 percussion-caps, and for each recruit, of 110 ball and 20 blank cartridges and 163 percussion-caps. The rifles should be uniform in gauge (0·577 in. to 0·580 in.) and size of nipple, and store-rooms for the arms near the ranges should be provided. Uniforms should be as simple as possible, and those of the different companies in each county should be similar.

The Volunteer Artillery Corps should have as their first object the manning of the batteries erected for the protection of coast towns, and should be recruited from local men who might be married, or tied by business to the locality, or less fit for field duties, but who, nevertheless, could find time to learn " how to work a great gun mounted in their immediate neighbourhood." The principles of organisation should be the same as for rifle corps, but the bodies might be even smaller. " For instance, the most effective system would be that which would associate ten or twelve men, all neighbours intimately acquainted with each other, in the charge and working of a particular gun mounted, so to speak, at their door." One man should be appointed " captain of the gun," an artilleryman should act as instructor, and " all that would be required of them would be that they should be able to prove, on a half-yearly inspection, that they had duly profited by the instruction so given, and had qualified themselves for the important trust reposed in them." In seaport towns, associations should be formed to man and work boats with a single gun in the bow, and it was hoped that shipowners, &c., would place their spare boats at the disposal of volunteers for this purpose.

Under the conditions laid down in these two circulars, the volunteer force in Great Britain was initiated and The the "movement" began in earnest, each local-Volunteer ity seeming to vie with the other in the work movement taken up of volunteer organisation. "Defence and not by the country. defiance" was adopted as the motto of the force, and everywhere those in a position to head public efforts or to lead public opinion took up enthusiastically the task of organisation for the defence of hearth and home. The movement was a thoroughly national one, and all ranks and classes took part in it. In the counties the lairds put themselves at the head of their neighbours and tenants, and in the towns the chiefs of the mercantile communities organised their employés. In many cases, gentlemen of position formed themselves into self-supporting corps and purchased their own arms and equipment, and at first, indeed, the move-ment was confined to such as could afford to do so; but as all classes desired to take part in the defence of the country, it soon became evident that men of the artisan class would be unable to give their services free unless arms and equipment were provided for them, and accordingly measures were taken to raise the necessary funds by public subscription, or by the con-tributions of honorary members.

The usual way in which a volunteer corps was formed, was that the local authorities or some leading inhabit-ants called a public meeting to discuss the subject, and then, if it was found that the general feeling was in favour of the formation of a corps, lists were drawn up and signed by those willing to join. When the numbers laid down in the circulars above quoted were attained, an application was submitted to the Lord-Lieutenant for the formation of the corps, and by him was transmitted to the Secretary of State for War, who in due course, and after the necessary conditions had been fulfilled, conveyed to the corps Her Majesty's acceptance of its services. The next step was the appointment of officers and non-commissioned officers, and at first (until later regulations placed the nomination of the officers in the hands of the Lord-Lieutenant, and that of the non-commissioned officers in those of the commanding officer) these were elected by the members of the corps. These appointments were not unfrequently keenly canvassed, and meetings were held at which the candidates were voted for. In other cases, corps were raised by country gentlemen among their tenants, or by factory owners employing large numbers of men, and these usually nominated themselves, their sons, or their managers to commissions, and paid for the privilege by contributing largely to the funds of the corps. A large voice was at first accorded to all members in the management of the finances of the corps and its general arrangements, and the difficulty as to knowing where to draw the line between civil and military affairs was great. Hence often arose a want of discipline, which was intensified in many cases by the military ignorance of those appointed officers and non-commissioned officers, many of whom accepted these appointments from the love of position, dress, or notoriety, and, once appointed, failed to take the necessary steps to qualify themselves for their position. But the general spirit of the volunteers was enthusiastically patriotic, and their discipline improved rapidly, towards which the presence of a goodly number of former officers of the regular army in their ranks as officers or in lower grades [1] contributed not a little.

The enthusiasm displayed by all ranks in the earliest days of the force may well be exemplified by an extract from an article entitled "A Brigadier's Retrospect," written in 1902 by Lord Kingsburgh (Colonel the Right Hon. Sir J. H. A. Macdonald, K.C.B.) for 'A Volunteer Haversack,' published by the Queen's Edinburgh V.B. He wrote :—

The volunteer of to-day can have little idea of the enthusiasm of that time. When a citizen joins the volunteer ranks to-day he enters a developed organisation in which his duties are pre-scribed, all that is necessary is provided, and he fulfils his part if he goes through a limited amount of training. In 1859 every-thing was novel, unorganised, and ill-provided. But what a life was in it! The volunteer of that day had no thought of minimum in his drills. Many went regularly to two and even three drills a-day. I have myself drilled at seven in the morning with the Writers to the Signet, in the forenoon in the Parliament House, and in the afternoon out of doors with the Advocates, and in the Queen's Park in the evening with an artisan company. We plunged eagerly into all the complicated cat's-cradle drill of the Red Book of those days, and despised the simple Green Book that was specially prepared to meet our condition of greenness. We went to the targets in all weathers. . . . No doubt much of our zeal was of the "zeal without knowledge" kind, but it made up for that by being really hot. We did as many drills before any arms were served out to us as a volunteer of to-day does in his whole training. My roll-book when I commanded a company showed many volunteers attending ninety drills in one season, and very few fell below fifty. And how and where did we drill? In Exchange Squares and Meadow Walks, by the light of the rat's-tail gas-burners of those days, when weather permitted; in

---

[1] For example, Major-General William Riddell of Camieston, C.B., late H.E.I.C.S., served as a private in the 3rd Roxburgh R.V. (Melrose) from February 26, 1861, to April 30, 1871, and never aspired to promotion.

small steaming rooms below the Council Chambers when driven in by rain or snow. Night after night, through the long winter and into spring, we laboured. Rich companies had drill instructors in their pay, but we who had artisan companies had to do all our own drilling, getting our musketry certificates by judging distance in two inches of snow in the Meadows, and firing our course when one was glad to warm one's fingers between shots on the heated barrels of our muzzle-loaders, which, after the fouling of a few rounds, kicked us unmercifully. Yet I will venture to say that no man now alive who went through that ordeal but looks back on those days with pleasant recollections. I doubt not that much of our doing was not according to knowledge, and I know now that much we had to do was antiquated and inadequate to modern war conditions, but we did it heartily, with a real interest and enthusiasm which the volunteer of to-day would be quite unable to understand.

As in Edinburgh, so it was throughout the country, and never in the course of Scottish history was the old warlike spirit of the nation more thoroughly aroused than in 1859.

To exemplify the various methods by which corps were originated, and the difficulties which were met with, it is of interest to record the beginnings of the movement in Edinburgh and Glasgow.

In the capital, in March 1859, A. W. Macrae, Esq., W.S. (later a major in the Queen's Edinburgh R.V.), and Mr A. Henry (the inventor of the rifle bearing his name) had consulted together and decided to try to raise a rifle corps. The list for the signature of intending members remained hanging in Mr Henry's shop for some time, but few names were received, and it was not until May of that year that the movement was started effectually in Edinburgh by the Highland Society petitioning the Secretary of State for War for permission to form themselves into a Highland volunteer company. The Society of Advo-

The movement in Edinburgh.

cates made similar application early in the month, and
it was only on May 26, in consequence of the issue of
the War Office circular of May 12, that a meeting of
Lieutenancy was held to consider what steps should be
taken, and it was agreed that a regiment of rifles should
be formed in the city, in which all the corps raised
should be included.   The Highland Society's Company
became the 1st Highland, the Advocates the 1st on the
general list, and the 1st Citizens' Company, the members
of which subscribed their names immediately after the
above meeting to a roll, in which those on Mr Henry's
list were also incorporated, the 2nd.   The members of
all these, and of four more companies composed of professional gentlemen and formed shortly afterwards, paid
all their own expenses and provided their own arms,
equipment, and uniform.   The next company was
formed of bank clerks, for whom the various banks
subscribed to provide arms, equipment, and uniform,
and then followed two companies of artisans, the first
raised in Scotland, of which the men of the first paid a
contribution of 30s. in instalments, the remainder of the
expenses being defrayed by public subscription, those
of the second paying 45s. for their uniforms, other
charges being met out of funds subscribed by employers.
These were the original companies of what latterly was
termed the Queen's Rifle Volunteer Brigade, The Royal
Scots, the premier volunteer infantry corps in Scotland,
and they gained for the capital, by their early offer of
service, the senior place in order of precedence of the
counties in the force.   It was not until August 31,
however, that the officers of these companies and of the
staff of the regiment were gazetted.

The second city of the Kingdom was even in advance
of the capital in the matter of publicly bestirring itself
for defence, for on May 2, 1859, a letter signed "Pro

Bono Patriæ" appeared in 'The Glasgow Herald' advocating the formation of volunteer corps, and on the following day an advertisement was placed in the same newspaper asking those who were in favour of the formation of a volunteer rifle corps to communicate with "V.R.C., 'Herald' Office." The response was so satisfactory that "V.R.C." — Mr A. K. Murray — was able to call a meeting for May 4 at the Albion Hotel, 74 Argyle Street, which was attended by about a dozen gentlemen,[1] as a preliminary gathering, which was followed the same evening by a public meeting in the Royal Galleries, 123 St Vincent Street. At this latter meeting about 200 gentlemen put their names down as willing to join, and a committee was nominated to further the object and to communicate with the Secretary of State for War. After the issue of the circular of May 12, a second meeting was held, at which the Lord Provost occupied the chair, and at it, owing to the fact that no Government assistance in money or arms was promised by the circular, a discussion took place as to details, which caused the resignation of the first committee. A new one, under the presidency of the Lord Provost, and including the two Members of Parliament for Glasgow, the Sheriff of the County (Sir Archibald Alison, the historian of Europe), and others, was appointed, and a meeting was held in the Trades' Hall on July 12, when sub-committees were appointed in the northern, southern, eastern, western, and central districts of the city, and these at once set to work to enrol and organise all classes of the community,—clerks, warehousemen, shopkeepers, and artisans.

The
movement
in Glasgow.

---

[1] One of whom, Mr J. Carfrae Alston, served from 1859 to 1879 in the 1st Lanark R.V., from which he retired as major, and is now president of the "Boys' Brigade" in Scotland.

Meanwhile some gentlemen of the west end of Glasgow, impatient of the ponderous working of the official machine, had taken independent action, and immediately after the meeting on July 12 had drawn up and subscribed to a document offering their services to form "a volunteer rifle company, to be denominated the Glasgow Volunteer Rifle Corps, Western Section, No. 1," and further agreeing to supply their own arms and accoutrements, and to contribute to the extent of £2, 2s. per annum towards the expenses of the company. Much delay in the acceptance of their services was caused by the want of knowledge of procedure on the part of the promoters and the absence on the Continent of the Lord-Lieutenant, the Duke of Hamilton, but on August 5 the services of the company were offered, and on September 24 they were accepted, and the company numbered the first in the county of Lanark. It subsequently became "A" Company of the 1st Lanark V.R.C. Consequent on the above-mentioned delays, Lanarkshire, though one of the earliest afield, was only given the 25th place among the counties in order of precedence in the rifle volunteer force, Edinburgh City (11th), Renfrewshire (14th), and Stirlingshire (23rd) standing before it in Scotland. Other corps quickly followed the example of the 1st Western, and, without waiting for official sanction, the corps equipped themselves and began to drill with great enthusiasm. Two corps, the 2nd Western (University), later 2nd Lanark, and the 1st Southern, later 3rd Lanark, afterwards "A" Company 3rd Lanark V.R.C., claimed priority of origin to the 1st Western, but these claims were disallowed in the subsequent renumbering in seniority in the county.

During the initial stages of its development, the

Glasgow Central Committee, mentioned above, continued to watch over and help the movement. In the city, as throughout the country, money was raised by bazaars, fancy fairs, balls, &c., and professions, large employers of labour, and traders contributed handsomely to the funds of the corps organised from their members or employés, but it was thought that there were large numbers of merchants and manufacturers who could only be reached by public subscriptions. A public meeting was therefore summoned in the City Hall on 23rd November 1859, with the Lord Provost in the chair. It was addressed by Sir Archibald Alison, the Rev. Norman Macleod, and Sheriff Henry Bell, and so persuasive was their eloquence that in a short time £4000 was placed at the disposal of the Central Committee to assist in the formation of new corps. The usual contribution in artisan corps was for each man to pay £1 towards his uniform and an annual subscription of 10s. to the funds of the corps, and the Committee was thus enabled to subsidise corps requiring assistance to the extent of £1 per member. Twenty-four rifle and four artillery corps (companies) were thus assisted in Glasgow.

In the above summaries of the progress of the movement in the two principal centres of formation in Scotland, no mention has been made of important instructions which were issued from the War Office in the period under review.

The third War Office Circular of July 13, 1859.

The first of these was the circular of July 13, 1859, in which the Secretary of State for War announced that her Majesty's Government had decided to issue Enfield rifles free of cost for 25 per cent of the effective members of the force, and to undertake the armament of the whole force when called out for active service on certain conditions (see below), and had sanc-

B

tioned two officers or members of each corps proceeding
to the School of Musketry at Hythe (at their own
expense) to undergo a modified course of musketry
instruction.   Lieutenants of counties were urged to
specially encourage the formation of artillery rather
than rifle corps in coast towns, and a "memorandum
regarding the formation, organisation, establishment,
instruction, &c., of volunteer corps in Great Britain,
to be raised under the Act 44 Geo. III., cap. 54,"
was appended to the circular.

The principal provisions of this latter memorandum
were :—

In all cases of actual invasion or appearance of any
enemy in force on the coast of Great Britain, or of
rebellion or insurrection arising or existing within
the same, or the appearance of any enemy in force
on the coast, or during any invasion, but not otherwise, the services of the volunteer force were to extend to any part of Great Britain.

Before giving sanction to the formation of a rifle
corps, the Secretary of State required that a safe range
of not less than 200 yards should be obtained, that
safe storage should be provided for the arms, that
rules, binding on the members under legal penalties,
should be submitted and approved, and that the corps
should be subject to periodical inspection by a military
officer.   The uniform and equipment of all corps were
to be approved by the Lord-Lieutenant, and were to
be similar, for artillery and rifles respectively, throughout the county.

Artillery corps might be organised as companies of
not fewer than 50 or more than 80 effectives, with 1
captain, 1 lieutenant, and 1 2nd lieutenant, or as
subdivisions, with not fewer than 30 effectives, with
1 lieutenant and 1 2nd lieutenant, or as sections of not

fewer than 20 effectives under a lieutenant.   Rifle corps were to be organised as companies of not fewer than 60 or more than 100 effectives, with 1 captain, 1 lieutenant, and 1 ensign, or as subdivisions of not fewer than 30 effectives, with 1 lieutenant and 1 ensign.   In populous centres, where several such corps could be formed, in order to save expense by having one range and one armoury only, battalions might be formed, and where 8 companies, or a force not less than 500 strong, could be raised, sanction would be given to the appointment of a lieutenant-colonel, a major, and an adjutant (to be paid by the corps) for the battalion.   Supernumeraries beyond establishment, or honorary or non-effective members "willing to contribute towards the expenses of the corps," were to be permitted.

Artillery corps were to rank before rifle corps, and the whole volunteer force of a county was to take precedence throughout Great Britain according to the date of formation of the first company of their respective arms in the county, the several companies ranking, as artillery and rifles respectively, within their own counties in the order of their formation. Officers were to take precedence according to the dates of their commissions.

Artillery volunteers were not required to have small-arms, only side-arms.   Rifle volunteers were to have 25 per cent of their effective members supplied with rifles by Government, the remainder being purchased by the corps; and the equipment was to consist of a black or brown leather waist-belt, with sliding frog for the bayonet, ball-bag containing cap-pocket, and 20-round pouch.

Artillery ammunition for practice was to be issued free of cost in quantities to be determined later; and for rifle corps the allowance of ammunition laid down in the circular of May 25 was changed to 100 rounds of ball and 60 of blank cartridge, with 176 percussion caps and 20 caps for snapping purposes, annually to all qualified effectives, including recruits. Five targets per company were to be issued at cost price.

The eight days' drill in each four months required to make a volunteer "efficient" were not of necessity to be continuous, and it was to suffice if each attended on the prescribed number of days the ordinary drills laid down by the commanding officer.

Garrison gun-drill was to be taught by instructors of the Royal Artillery — the volunteer artillerymen, after preliminary instruction, being permanently told off to particular guns near their homes, of which they were to undertake the general service. All guns and stores were to be provided by Government and to remain in charge of the Royal Artillery, and a Volunteer Artilleryman's Manual' was prepared.

For volunteer riflemen a Manual was also prepared. As instructors, two serjeants of the permanent staff of the disembodied militia were to be told off to each volunteer company, and these men were to be asked to volunteer for the service, and were to be paid one shilling a-day each by the corps. It was hoped that, after a short time, the services of these non-commissioned officers could be dispensed with, the "most intelligent and zealous individuals" in each corps being then qualified to instruct the others. Musketry instructors were to be similarly supplied, and two members of each corps were to be permitted to proceed to Hythe at their own expense for a fourteen days' course of musketry instruction — the first class assembling there on Saturday, July 23, 1859.

In pursuance of the circular of July 13, draft model rules and regulations for volunteer corps were issued from the War Office on August 10, 1859. They had been drawn up by a committee of volunteers, of which the president was Viscount Ranelagh, and the representative Scottish member Mr R. Blackburn of the Edinburgh Rifles, and were recommended to volunteer corps for adoption as a model to be followed — modifications being, if necessary, made to suit the particular circumstances of corps. The rules were, summarily, as follows :—

Model rules for volunteer corps.

(1) Quoted the Act under which the corps was raised. (2) Defined effective, non - effective, supernumerary, and honorary members — the latter only contributing to the funds. (3) Subscriptions to be due on the 1st of each month. (4) Fixed the amount of monthly subscriptions, varying according to corps. (5) The commanding officer to propose gentlemen to the Lord - Lieutenant for commissions. (6) The commanding officer to appoint non-commissioned officers. (7) Candidates for admission to the corps to be proposed by three members, and admitted on approval of the commanding officer. (8) Each member to have uniform and equipment of the approved pattern ; and (9) to be responsible for all Government arms and property issued to him. (10) "Corps property" to be all articles purchased out of the funds. (11) When not on service, the commanding officer to be responsible for discipline, and to have the power of assembling a court of inquiry of two officers and two members to investigate irregularities. (12) The commanding officer to fix the time and place of parades. (13) The commanding officer to have the power to inflict fines, which might (14) be not less than—for

loading contrary to orders or shooting out of turn,
2s. 6d. ; for accidentally discharging the rifle, 5s. ;
for pointing the rifle, loaded or unloaded, at any
person without orders, 5s., &c. &c. ; absence from or
lateness on parade, speaking in the ranks, and other
sins of commission, had also penalties attached to them.
(15) All fines to be recorded, and (16) collected on
the 1st of each month.   (17) A committee to be
appointed to manage the corps' finances.   (18) An
abstract of the accounts to be laid before members.
(19) Payments for extra ammunition.   (20) Honorary
members not to interfere in military duties, and not
to be obliged to wear uniform, but (21) might use
the practice ground, and (22) must pay a donation
or annual subscription—the former generally £5, the
latter usually £1, 1s., but never less than that of
ordinary members.   (23) The system of musketry instruction to be that taught at Hythe.   (24) Members
to provide themselves with the Volunteer Manual and
a copy of Corps Rules.

These rules were adopted, in the spirit and the
letter, by all corps, and continued, with certain
modifications, to be the basis of volunteer discipline
till the force ceased to exist.

How little was expected of the volunteers of 1859,
as foreshadowed in the War Office circular of May 25,
quoted above, is exemplified by the 'Drill and
Rifle Instruction for Volunteer Rifle Corps,'
published in 1859, and compiled by Colonel
D. Lysons, C.B., Assistant Adjutant-General, a soldier
of the highest repute.   It was composed of extracts
from the infantry drill regulations for the regular
army.   It was familiarly known as the " Green
Book," from the colour of its binding, as compared
with the red of the parent volume.   Its price was

The first
Volunteer
Manuals.

sixpence, and, as its Preface stated, it contained "all the drill that volunteers need know," which was to be taught in six lessons. The first was on falling in and telling off a squad, position and attitude, standing at ease, facing, opening and closing the squad, dressing, and dismissing. The second was on marching, stepping out, marking time, the diagonal march, breaking off and reassembling, the double march, and wheeling. The third lesson comprised the manual exercise and piling arms, and the fourth the platoon (firing) exercise. The fifth lesson dealt with the formation of the squad in two ranks, telling off, firing, skirmishing, extending and closing from the halt and on the march, advancing and retiring in skirmishing order, inclining, changing front and firing in that order, and forming rallying squares. The sixth and last lesson treated of the formation and movements of the company, dispersing and assembling, advancing, retiring, and wheeling; the formation of columns of subdivisions or sections, company square, skirmishing, and bugle-calls. In the Preface it was added that "if, when they have been thoroughly drilled, volunteers have spare time, they may learn to form fours in the manner prescribed by the Manual," and in an appendix a short synopsis of musketry instruction was given.

It is perhaps hardly necessary to say that in a short time the volunteers outgrew their Manual, and adopted the drill regulations in force for the regular army.

A vexed and much debated question in the early days of the volunteer movement was that

County and corps precedence. of county and corps precedence, which was settled in the manner laid down in the War Office circular of July 13, quoted above. The counties were to rank, in the artillery or rifle volunteer force, according to the date on which the *first* company of each arm in the county was formed, which, as a matter of fact, resolved itself into the date on which the offer of the services of that company was received by the Secretary of State for War. Now this, again, depended, not on the date on which the original members first met and determined to offer their services as a volunteer corps, but on the celerity with which this offer was passed through the office of Lieutenancy of the county and arrived at the War Office. Counties in which the Lord - Lieutenant was an absentee were thus at a disadvantage, as was in several instances the case in Scotland, and in others traditional " canniness " delayed the offers of service until the conditions had been more clearly defined; but on the whole the Scottish counties obtained their due precedence in the two forces, and this was finally settled as follows:—

ORDER OF PRECEDENCE OF THE SEVERAL COUNTIES IN THE
ARTILLERY VOLUNTEER FORCE.

1. Northumberland	23. Ayrshire	44. Orkney
2. Hampshire	24. Argyll	45. Nairn
3. Devonshire	25. Gloucestershire	46. Sutherlandshire
4. Sussex	26. Pembrokeshire	47. Shropshire
5. Edinburgh (City)	27. Yorkshire (N. Rid.)	48. Yorkshire (W. Rid.)
6. Cornwall	28. Cheshire	49. Newcastle-on-Tyne
7. Mid-Lothian	29. Caithness	50. Somerset
8. Norfolk	30. Lincolnshire	51. Middlesex
9. Banff	31. Aberdeenshire	52. Suffolk
10. Kent	32. Berwickshire	53. Tower Hamlets
11. Forfarshire	33. Kirkcudbright	54. Monmouthshire
12. Essex	34. Inverness-shire	55. Surrey
13. Lancashire	35. Elgin	56. Anglesea
14. Kincardine	36. Stirlingshire	57. Isle of Man
15. Cinque Ports	37. Wigtown	58. Staffordshire
16. Renfrewshire	38. Dumbarton	59. Carnarvon
17. Dorsetshire	39. Berwick-on-Tweed	60. Bute
18. Fifeshire	40. Cumberland	61. City of London
19. Glamorganshire	41. Durham	62. Worcester
20. Haddington	42. Cromarty	63. Warwick
21. Lanarkshire	43. Ross-shire	64. Cardigan
22. Yorkshire (E. Rid.)		

ORDER OF PRECEDENCE OF THE SEVERAL COUNTIES IN THE
RIFLE VOLUNTEER FORCE.

1. Devonshire	33. Aberdeenshire	65. Wigtown
2. Middlesex	34. Roxburgh	66. Buteshire
3. Lancashire	35. Cinque Ports	67. Yorkshire (N. Rid.)
4. Surrey	36. Monmouthshire	68. Cumberland
5. Pembrokeshire	37. Cornwall	69. Herefordshire
6. Derbyshire	38. Ross-shire	70. Dumbartonshire
7. Oxfordshire	39. Worcestershire	71. Huntingdon
8. Cheshire	40. Inverness-shire	72. Carnarvonshire
9. Wiltshire	41. Warwickshire	73. Montgomeryshire
10. Sussex	42. Lincolnshire.	74. Orkney
11. Edinburgh (City)	43. Denbighshire	75. Carmarthen
12. Essex	44. Hampshire	76. Caithness
13. Northumberland	45. Somersetshire	77. Kirkcudbright
14. Renfrewshire	46. Forfar	78. Westmorland
15. Northamptonshire	47. Cambridgeshire	79. Fifeshire
16. Dorsetshire	48. Shropshire	80. Bedfordshire
17. Norfolk	49. London	81. Newcastle-on-Tyne
18. Staffordshire	50. Yorkshire (E. Rid.)	82. Linlithgowshire
19. Berkshire	51. Hertfordshire	83. Selkirkshire
20. Gloucestershire	52. Perthshire	84. Banffshire
21. Brecknockshire	53. Berwickshire	85. Radnorshire
22. Suffolk	54. Sutherland	86. Flintshire
23. Stirlingshire	55. Kincardineshire	87. Berwick-on-Tweed
24. Bucks	56. Haverfordwest	88. Clackmannan
25. Lanarkshire	57. Haddington	89. Tower Hamlets
26. Kent	58. Isle of Wight	90. Nairn
27. Glamorgan	59. Ayrshire	91. Peeblesshire
28. Nottinghamshire	60. Dumfries	92. Isle of Man
29. Merionethshire	61. Elgin	93. Kinross-shire
30. Yorkshire (W. Rid.)	62. Argyll	94. Anglesey
31. Leicestershire	63. Cardigan	95. Shetland
32. Mid-Lothian	64. Durham	

Within the counties, the precedence of corps was
settled by the date of the receipt of their offer of
service by the Lord-Lieutenant, and this in its turn
led to much rivalry, with the laudable desire of being
first in the field in the county and receiving therefore precedence and a lower number. As an instance
of this, Lieut.-Colonel T. R. Stuart, commanding the
late 1st Ayrshire and Galloway R.G.A.V., writes as
to his corps: "Irvine is the oldest battery or company in the regiment. In that connection I am informed that in 1859, at the start of the volunteer
movement, there was keen rivalry between Irvine and

Ayr for the honour of being premier battery. There was such a close run for it that the Irvine officers, on their return from Eglinton Castle for the purpose of offering their services to the Lord-Lieutenant, the Earl of Eglinton, actually met in the avenue of the Castle grounds the Ayr officers driving up post-haste on the same errand. Irvine thus won the distinction of being the 1st Ayrshire A.V., but only by the shortest of heads."

On the Lord-Lieutenant forwarding the offer of service to the War Office, he stated the date on which it was received, and on this the Secretary of State for War, when officially accepting the services of the corps in question, assigned to it a number in the county in its order of precedence. The gazetting of officers was proceeded with as soon as possible after the acceptance of the services of the corps; and throughout the records of units in Part II. of this work the date of first commission of the officers has been taken as that of the formation of the corps, as only in a few cases has it been possible to ascertain the dates of acceptance of services, and the number in order of precedence in the county is, with a few exceptions, sufficient to show the order in which the services of corps were accepted. The few exceptions are due to special circumstances, in which, on account of some informality in the offer, reference had to be made to the corps, the services of which were accepted later, although it retained its number in order of application. Such exceptions will be seen in the complete list of corps raised in Lanarkshire given in Appendix C.

In the matter of uniform the earliest volunteer riflemen frequently indulged their fancy or their taste in the wildest flights. Every shade of grey, green, and brown was adopted, and the uniforms were often richly

decorated with braid or lace, especially in the corps
equipped at their own expense. The usual uniform
Uniform, was a tunic long in the skirts, single-breasted,
equipment, and braided and laced, with trousers of the
and small-
arms. same, and a cap with a peak or a shako, the
latter frequently ornamented with cocks' feathers in
a plume. In Scotland the almost universal colour of
the uniform was some shade of grey, very few corps
only adopting the green which was much in favour
in England. The scarlet of the regular line infantry
was the only colour *not* at first adopted, probably
because the corps considered themselves "riflemen,"
as their name indicated, and no volunteer rifle corps
wore it at the date of the Royal Review in 1860.
The first corps to adopt scarlet at its inception was
the 4th Sutherland, formed at Rogart in the end of
1860, and the next was the 97th Lanarkshire, or
Glasgow Guards, formed in the middle of 1861. The
kilt was adopted by but few corps at first, and at the
Royal Review in 1860 the only corps which wore it
were the 1st and 2nd Highland Companies Edinburgh R.V., 10th and 11th Renfrew R.V., 60th and
61st Lanark R.V., 10th Forfar R.V., 3rd (three companies) Perth R.V., and 9th Argyll R.V. The belts
were generally of black-enamelled or brown leather,
and consisted of a pouch-belt, generally ornamented
with a badge for all ranks and a whistle with chain
for officers and serjeants, over the left shoulder, and
a waist-belt with cartridge-box or pouch and bayonet-
frog. Some few corps adopted knickerbockers and
leather leggings, but greatcoats were in use in hardly
any, and none provided themselves with haversacks,
water-bottles, knapsacks, or other equipment.

The artillery corps invariably adopted blue uniforms,
some of them a close copy of those of the Royal Artil-

lery, but they also frequently indulged in flights of fancy and embroidered their uniforms with braid. The engineer corps, formed later, closely copied the Royal Engineers, and the only mounted corps formed at first in Scotland, the Fife Mounted Rifles, adopted a uniform as nearly approaching to their red hunting-coats as possible.

Government, however, soon took up the question of volunteer uniforms, and a committee assembled at the War Office and issued a report on January 23, 1860, recommending a variety of patterns without deciding on any particular one, and leaving the matter to the choice of corps, subject to the approval of the Lord-Lieutenant. The uniform considered the best for rifle volunteers was brownish grey, of the pattern submitted by Lord Elcho (now the Earl of Wemyss) and adopted by the London Scottish, with peg-top trousers made to be worn with leggings, the tunic being quite plain, and only piped with the regimental colour and ornamented with an Austrian knot on the sleeve, a low cap of the same cloth with peak, brown leather belts, and a long cape with hood. For artillery the pattern recommended was the same, but of blue cloth with scarlet piping, and black belts. Sealed patterns were deposited at the War Office, and it was intimated that Government would issue to volunteers at cost price grey cloth in four shades (Elcho grey cloth, Elcho grey tweed, slate-grey cloth of Roxburgh Rifles pattern, and dark-grey cloth), rifle-green cloth, blue cloth for artillery, and scarlet cloth. The corps formed after the date of this pronouncement generally followed its advice, and the vagaries of fancy seen in the uniforms of the earlier (and perhaps richer) corps were not, as a rule, continued in those raised in 1860. The Austrian knot on the sleeve was almost universally adopted as the distinguishing mark of volunteer corps, and the badges of rank and patterns of lace of the officers conformed to those of the corresponding arms of the regular forces, with the exception that gold lace was not permitted to be worn.

The arms with which the rifle corps first equipped themselves were usually short Enfields with sword-bayonets, as used by rifle regiments of the regular army; but when Government took over the supply of arms the long Enfield rifle, as used in line regiments, with triangular bayonet, was issued, serjeants only retaining the short rifle and sword-bayonet. The artillery at first had smooth-bore, but afterwards rifled carbines, with sword - bayonets with steel scabbards, and the engineers were given the Lancaster oval-bored rifle with sword-bayonet.

During the autumn of 1859 the work of organising volunteer corps went on uninterruptedly in Scotland, as throughout Great Britain, and in October **Progress of the force in 1859, and the Queen's first Inspections of Scottish Volunteers.** portions of the Scottish volunteer force had the honour of parading before Her Majesty Queen Victoria. The first occasion was on Friday, October 14, when 382 of all ranks of the 2nd, 3rd, 4th, 5th, 7th, 8th, and 10th Lanark Rifle Corps, under Captain David Dreghorn of the 3rd Lanark, proceeded *via* Loch Lomond to Loch Katrine to form a guard of honour to the Queen, on the occasion of Her Majesty opening the City of Glasgow Water-works. This was the first public appearance of the volunteers in the west of Scotland, and the first of the Scottish volunteer corps Her Majesty had seen. It is on record that while the *Rob Roy*, in which the volunteers were embarked, was steaming down Loch Katrine, H.R.H. the Prince Consort questioned Captain Dreghorn as to the length of time the men had been drilled, and expressed his satisfaction at the appearance they made and the efficiency to which they had attained in such a short time.

The second occasion was on October 15, when the Edinburgh Rifle Volunteers were inspected by the Queen in Duke's Walk as Her Majesty drove from Holyrood to St Margaret's station, and the Lord Provost was commanded to inform them that Her Majesty had been "particularly struck and highly pleased with their appearance and fine soldierly bearing."

At the close of 1859 there had been organised in Great Britain 16 corps of artillery volunteers with 73 batteries, and 330 companies of rifle volunteers, and of these there were in Scotland, as shown in the monthly Army List of January 1860, 10 batteries and 1 subdivision of artillery, and 49 corps with 67 companies and 1 subdivision of rifles, as follows, the corps which had been authorised, but to which officers had not yet been gazetted, being shown in brackets :—

Artillery—

Edinburgh City . .	1st.
Mid-Lothian . .	(1st).
Banff	(1st), (2nd), (3rd), (1st subdivision).
Forfar	1st, 2nd, 3rd, 4th.
Kincardine . . .	(1st).

Rifles—

Edinburgh City . .	1st (16 companies).
Renfrew . .	1st, 2nd, 3rd, 4th, 5th, 6th.
Stirling . . .	1st.
Lanark . .	1st, 2nd, 3rd, 4th, 5th, 6th, 7th, 8th, 9th, 10th, 11th, 12th, 13th, (14th), 15th, (16th), (17th), 18th, (19th), (20th), 21st, (22nd), 23rd.

Rifles—

Aberdeen	. . .	(1st), 6th, 7th, 8th, 1st sub-division.
Roxburgh	. . .	1st.
Ross	. . .	(1st).
Inverness	. . .	1st.
Forfar	. . .	1st (5 companies), 2nd, 3rd, 4th, 5th.
Perth	. . .	1st, 2nd.
Berwick	. . .	1st.
Sutherland	. . .	1st, 2nd.

The national and patriotic character of the movement was acknowledged in the Queen's Speech from the Throne on the opening of Parliament in January 1860, in which Her Majesty said : "I have accepted with gratification and pride the extensive offers of service which I have received from my subjects. This manifestation of public spirit has added an important element to our system of national defence."

It will have been noticed that, in the earlier War Office circulars, no mention was made of the formation **Formation** of volunteer corps of other arms than artil- **of engineers and mounted** lery and rifles, but this defect in the com- **rifles.** position of the force, and in the utilisation for military purposes of all classes of the civil population in the arm of the service for which they were best suited, soon led to offers being made for the formation of engineer and mounted corps. The first meeting with a view to the formation of a military engineer corps in Scotland was held in Glasgow on November 28, 1859, when a number of civil engineers, architects, surveyors, and measurers agreed to offer their services as a "Military Engineer Volunteer Corps." This was the origin of the 1st Lanark Engineer Volunteers. A second corps or company was soon formed out of the overflow of the 1st, and

somewhat later a similar corps was formed in Edinburgh.   In the formation of engineer corps, Middlesex,
having led the way, was awarded the 1st place in
order of precedence, but Lanarkshire obtained 2nd,
and Edinburgh (City) 3rd.

The formation of mounted volunteers in Scotland
followed somewhat later, but for continuity's sake may
here be mentioned.   It was not until March 1860 that
a party of gentlemen in the smoking-room at Dysart
House, Fife, read of the volunteer levée on March 7,
and of the appearance of the officers of the Huntingdon
Light Horse.   Lord Loughborough (afterwards Lord
Rosslyn) said : " Why should we not have a cavalry
regiment in Fife ? " and asked Colonel Anstruther-
Thomson to undertake the organisation of one.   A
paper was drawn out and passed round in the hunting-
field and at markets, and, after 111 names had been
signed to it, on March 20 the Lord-Lieutenant was
addressed on the subject.   After correspondence with
the War Office, and the number of those willing to
join having increased to 135, on June 7 the War
Office approved of the formation of a " battalion " of
mounted rifles in Fife, to be composed of 4 corps
(companies).   The Earl of Rosslyn was appointed to
command, and all the four captains of corps had already
served in the regular army.   The men were mostly
well-to-do farmers, and the uniform adopted was as
like that of the Fife Hunt as possible.   Fife was
awarded No. 9 in order of precedence in the mounted
rifle volunteer force.   Such was the origin and composition of the mounted volunteer force in Scotland,
and it is worthy of note that it outlasted by many
years the corresponding force of light horse or mounted
rifles south of the Tweed.   Corps were raised in Elgin,
Roxburgh, Dumfries, and Forfarshire in succession,

and, though the Elgin corps had a merely ephemeral existence, the Dumfries corps lasted from 1874 to 1880, and the Roxburgh (Border) corps for twenty years, from 1872 to 1892, and when it was disbanded in the latter year the Fife and Forfar corps became the sole representatives of the mounted arm of the volunteers in Great Britain, and maintained an honoured existence and their efficiency, in spite of many adverse circumstances, until they were absorbed in the Imperial Yeomanry force in 1901, in which they became the Fife and Forfar Regiment.

On proof being afforded of the serious nature of the movement, further official aid was not withheld, **Progress of** and on December 20, 1859, an issue of Enfield **organisation** rifles, to bring the aggregate issue up to **early in** **1860.** 100 per cent of the effectives of the force, was authorised. On February 18, 1860, the attachment of non - commissioned officers of infantry and artillery as drill-instructors, for periods of three months at a time, at a rate of pay (from corps funds) of 2s. 6d. a-day, with lodging-money in addition, was sanctioned. In the same month adjutants were authorised for brigades of artillery or battalions of rifles, to be selected from officers who had served at least four years in the regular or East India Company's forces or embodied militia, who were to be paid (by Government) 8s. a-day, and 2s. for forage for a horse, all their other expenses being borne out of corps funds. These officers were appointed for an indefinite period, and it was only in 1872 that the system was changed, the former adjutants being compelled to retire on attaining sixty years of age, and all subsequent appointments to the position being made from the regular army for a period of five years, during which officers were seconded in their regiments.

On March 24, 1860, a circular was issued from the
War Office regulating the higher organisation of the
volunteers, which had become necessary on account
of the large and unforeseen number of independent
companies formed.   In towns where a number of
companies existed side by side, these might be consolidated into battalions, all the companies forming
one corps for all purposes, or they might be consolidated for drill and administrative purposes only, the
companies forming in themselves distinct and financially independent bodies.   In either case a major was
to be allowed for a battalion of 4, a lieutenant-colonel
for one of 6, a lieutenant-colonel and a major for one
of 8, and a lieutenant-colonel and two majors for one
of 9 to 12 companies, an adjutant being allowed in
all cases.   If of more than 12 companies, the corps
was to constitute a regiment and be divided into two
battalions, each with field-officers in the above proportions and an adjutant, the whole being commanded
by the senior lieutenant - colonel.   In rural districts
the corps were to be grouped together in "administrative battalions," to ensure unity of system in correspondence, drill, inspections, and returns, the corps
remaining distinct and financially independent.   To
such battalions ("brigades" of artillery) of 4 or 5
companies a major might be appointed, to those of
6, 7, 8, or 9 a lieutenant-colonel, and to those of 10,
11, or 12 companies a lieutenant-colonel and a major,
with an adjutant in all cases.   In forming an administrative battalion, the locality of the corps and
not their numerical seniority was to be considered,
and it was recommended that at the first renewal
of clothing a uniform colour, &c., should be adopted
for all corps in the same battalion.   Further instructions, defining the powers, duties, and responsibilities

of an officer commanding an administrative battalion (brigade), were issued on September 4, 1860, and they also emphasised the independence in matters of finance, corps rules, &c., of the corps composing it. In consequence of these circulars, the formation of the hitherto independent corps (companies or batteries) into consolidated battalions (brigades of artillery) in the cities, and into administrative battalions in the rural districts, was actively taken in hand, and towards the end of the year many new companies were formed to complete the battalion establishments, the individual small corps being all gradually absorbed in one or other of these higher organisations in their own county, or, in the case of small counties, in battalions or brigades of artillery formed of the corps of two or even more counties, as shown in Part II. in the records of the individual corps.

On July 7, 1860, the Secretary of State for War recommended to the General Commanding-in-Chief that general officers commanding districts should occasionally assemble and review the volunteers, and, on the 20th, instructions were given to them accordingly. Colonel W. M. S. Macmurdo, C.B., who had organised the Land Transport Corps in the Crimea, was appointed Inspector - General of the whole volunteer force, and took up his duties at the end of March 1860, and under him were appointed, as assistant-inspectors, field - officers of the regular army, one to each of ten districts, into which the United Kingdom was divided, whose duties were to carry out the annual detailed inspections of volunteer corps, to regulate the transmission of returns, and to see that all regulations as to the storage of arms, drills, and musketry, &c., were carried out. The 10th (South-west Scottish) District, headquarters at Glasgow, comprised the counties of Dumfries, Kirkcudbright, Wigtown, Ayr, Bute, Renfrew, Lanark, Argyll, and Dumbarton, the 9th (North-east Scottish), headquarters at Edinburgh, the rest of Scotland. To the 10th Major Young was appointed as assistant-inspector, to the 9th Lieut.-Colonel Douglas Jones.

In keeping with the sentiments expressed in her speech from the Throne in January 1860, the Queen held a levée for volunteer officers at St James's Palace on March 7. The announcement of Her Majesty's intention aroused tremendous enthusiasm throughout the country, and caused a redoubling of the efforts made to organise corps, so that the officers might have their commissions in time to appear before their sovereign. Railway companies allowed volunteer officers to travel to London and back for single fares, Lords-Lieutenant and members of Parliament invited the officers of their counties or constituencies to banquets in London, theatres were thrown open to them, and the citizens of London announced a grand banquet and ball in honour of the occasion. At the levée the Queen was accompanied by H.R.H. the Prince Consort and Their Royal Highnesses the Prince of Wales, Prince Alfred, the Duke of Cambridge, and Prince Frederick of the Netherlands. Three thousand two hundred volunteer officers from all parts of England and Scotland were presented to Her Majesty by their Lords-Lieutenant, or the Under-Secretary of State for War in his absence. The grand banquet, at which the Duke of Cambridge presided, was held the same evening in St James's Hall, when over 1000 volunteer officers were present, and hundreds were excluded for want of room. His Royal Highness proposed in glowing

The Queen and the volunteers. The Levée, Hyde Park Review, and National Rifle Association.

terms the health of "The Volunteer Service," and the banquet was succeeded by a grand ball in the Floral Hall of the Royal Italian Opera House.

The next honour done to the volunteer force by the sovereign was the review of the south of England corps by Her Majesty in Hyde Park, on Saturday, June 23, 1860. The only Scottish corps attending it was the 15th Middlesex (London Scottish), who were in the 1st Battalion, 4th Brigade (commanded by their colonel, Lord Elcho), 1st Division. The total number of volunteers reviewed was 20,890.

Closely following on this, on July 2 the Queen inaugurated the first great prize meeting of the National Rifle Association at Wimbledon by firing the first shot. This association had been formed for the purpose of encouraging the formation of rifle volunteer corps and the promotion of rifle-shooting throughout Great Britain, and was formally constituted at a meeting held at the Thatched House Tavern on November 16, 1859. The first president was Mr Sydney Herbert, Secretary of State for War, and the Queen headed the subscription list for prizes by giving £250 as an annual prize, the competition for which has always since been the great event of the meeting. The first shot was fired by the Queen from a Whitworth rifle, adjusted by Mr Whitworth himself, and the result was a bull's-eye at 400 yards.

On August 7, 1860, Her Majesty did the volunteers of Scotland the honour of reviewing them in their **The Royal Review in Edinburgh, August 7, 1860.** turn, the ground selected being Holyrood Park, the same on which their coming-of-age review in 1881 and the Royal Review of 1905 were subsequently held. The troops were conveyed to Edinburgh by rail, by road, or by sea, and accommodation and refreshment were liberally provided in Edinburgh for those from a distance, many of whom had to spend two to three days in coming and going. None but volunteers took part in the review, the ground being kept by the 13th Light Dragoons and 78th Highlanders, and the music for marching past supplied by the bands of the 29th and 78th Regiments and the 1st West York Rifle Militia. A grand stand had been erected, facing Arthur's Seat, for 4000 spectators, the central portion of which was draped with Royal Stuart tartan, and in front of this, and in rear of the saluting base, were drawn up the Royal Scottish Archers, the Queen's Bodyguard for Scotland. Spectators, variously estimated at from 200,000 to 300,000, covered the slopes of Arthur's Seat and crowded round the review ground on all sides, ·giving an enthusiastic reception to the various corps as they marched on to the ground.

The force was under the command of Lieut.-General Sir G. A. Wetherall, K.C.B., and the troops reviewed were as follows, the figures of strengths given being the official totals of all ranks :—

1ST DIVISION: MAJOR-GENERAL LORD ROKEBY, K.C.B.

1st Fife Mounted Rifle Volunteers, Major the Earl of Rosslyn   84

1st Artillery Brigade: Colonel Maclean, R.A.

1st Battalion : Lieut.-Col. Morris, R.A.
    1st City of Edinburgh (7 companies); 1st and 2nd (2 companies) Northumberland ; 1st Haddington; 1st, 3rd, and 4th (3 companies) Durham ; 1st Newcastle-on-Tyne; and 1st Berwick A.V.   .   .   .   869

2nd Battalion: Lieut.-Col. Sir J. G. Baird, 1st Mid-
Lothian A.V.

    1st (8 companies) and 2nd (2 companies) Mid-Lothian;
    1st, 2nd, 3rd, and 4th Cumberland; 1st Berwick-on-
    Tweed; and 1st Kirkcudbright A.V.   .   .   714

3rd Battalion: Lieut.-Col. Anderson, C.B., R.A.

    1st, 2nd, 3rd, 4th, 5th, 6th, and 7th Forfar; 1st
    Kincardine; 1st Caithness; and 4th Aberdeen A.V.   353

2nd Artillery Brigade: Colonel Gardiner, R.A.

1st Battalion: Captain A. Montgomery, 1st Ayr A.V.

    1st, 2nd, and 3rd Renfrew; 1st, 2nd, 3rd, and 5th
    Ayr; 1st and 3rd Argyll; 1st Wigtown; and 1st
    and 2nd Dumbarton A.V.   460

2nd Battalion: Captain W. H. Maitland Dougall, R.A.

    1st, 2nd, 3rd, 4th, 5th, 6th, and 8th Fife; 1st Inver-
    ness; 1st and 2nd Stirling; and 1st Nairn A.V.   .   652

3rd Battalion: Major J. Reid Stewart, Lanark A.V.

    1st, 2nd, 3rd, 4th, 5th, 6th, 7th, 8th, 9th, 10th, and
    11th Lanark A.V.   663

Engineers: Captain R. Johnstone, 1st Lanark E.V.

1st and 2nd Lanark and 1st City of Edinburgh E.V. .   198

RIFLE VOLUNTEERS.

1st Brigade: Lieut.-Col. D. Davidson, Edinburgh R.V.

1st Battalion: Captain E. S. Gordon, Edinburgh R.V.

    1st, 2nd, 3rd, 4th, 5th, 6th, 7th, 10th, 18th, and 1st
    Highland Edinburgh R.V.   .   .   .   706

2nd Battalion: Captain Sir G. Home, Bt., Edinburgh R.V.

    8th, 9th, 11th, 12th, 13th, 14th, 15th, 16th, 17th, and
    2nd Highland Edinburgh R.V.   .   .   .   655

3rd Battalion: Major Arnaud, 1st Mid-Lothian R.V.

    1st (5 companies), 2nd (2 companies), and 3rd (2
    companies) Mid-Lothian; 1st and 2nd Roxburgh;
    and 1st Selkirk R.V.   715

4th Battalion : Captain Hon. A. F. Cathcart, Berwick R.V.
1st, 2nd, 3rd, 4th, and 5th Berwick; 1st, 2nd, 3rd, 4th,
and 5th Haddington; 1st, 2nd, 4th, and 5th Kirkcudbright; and 1st Berwick-on-Tweed R.V. .   .   733

2nd Brigade: Lieut.-Col. Gordon, C.B.

1st Battalion : Captain G. L. Alison, 1st Forfar R.V.
1st (7 companies), 2nd, 3rd, 4th, 5th (2 companies),
8th, 9th, and 10th Forfar R.V.   .   .   835

2nd Battalion: Captain Sir T. Erskine, Bt., 3rd Fife R.V.
1st (2 companies), 2nd, 3rd, 5th, 7th, and 8th Fife R.V.   479

3rd Battalion : Major Potter, 1st Northumberland R.V.
1st (4 companies), 2nd, 3rd, and 5th Northumberland;
1st, 2nd, 4th, 5th, 6th, and 7th Cumberland R.V.   .   674

4th Battalion : Lieut.-Col. Sir J. Fyfe, 3rd Durham R.V.
3rd (4 companies), 6th, 7th (2 companies), 8th (2 companies), 11th, and 13th Durham, and 1st Newcastle-
on-Tyne (7 companies) R.V. .   .   .   820

3rd Brigade: Lieut.-Col. N. T. Christie, late 38th Foot.

1st Battalion : Major Elton, 22nd Depôt Battalion.
1st, 2nd, 3rd, 4th, 5th, 6th, 7th, 8th, and 9th Stirling,
and 1st (2 companies) and 2nd Clackmannan R.V. .   743

2nd Battalion : Major Pitcairn, 23rd Depôt Battalion.
1st (9 companies) and 7th Aberdeen; 1st Inverness
Administrative Battalion (1st, 2nd, 3rd, and 4th
Corps); 1st, 2nd, and 3rd Sutherland; and 1st
Nairn R.V.   901

3rd Battalion: Major Sir A. Gordon Cumming, Bt., 1st
Perth R.V.
1st (2 companies), 5th, 6th, 7th, 8th, 9th, 11th, and
12th Perth; 4th Kincardine; and 1st, 2nd, 3rd, and
4th Elgin R.V.   852

4th Battalion : Major the Marquis of Breadalbane, 3rd
Perth R.V.
3rd Perth (3 companies); 2nd, 3rd (2 companies), 7th,
9th, and 10th Argyll; and 1st, 2nd, and 3rd Linlithgow R.V.   859

2ND DIVISION: MAJOR-GENERAL CAMERON, C.B.

1st Brigade: Colonel Walter Hamilton, C.B.

1st Battalion: Major D. Latham, 1st A.B. Renfrew R.V.
    1st A.B. Renfrew R.V., consisting of 1st (4 companies),
    5th, 10th, 11th, and 22nd Corps   .   .   . 535

2nd Battalion: Lieut.-Col. J. Graham, 3rd A.B. Renfrew
R.V.
    2nd A.B. Renfrew R.V., consisting of 3rd, 6th, 9th,
    14th, 15th, 17th, and 24th Corps; and 3rd A.B.
    Renfrew R.V., consisting of 4th, 7th, 8th, 16th, 19th,
    21st, and 23rd Corps   446

3rd Battalion: Captain Hay Boyd, 3rd Ayrshire R.V.
    1st, 2nd, 3rd, 4th, 5th, 6th, 7th, and 8th Ayr R.V.   . 559

2nd Brigade: Lieut.-Col. Sir A. Islay Campbell, 1st Lanark R.V.

1st Battalion: Major Robertson, 1st Lanark R.V.
    1st Battalion 1st Lanark R.V., consisting of 1st, 9th,
    11th, 15th, 17th, 33rd, 39th, and 79th Corps   . 535

2nd Battalion: Major Macquorne Rankine, 1st Lanark R.V.
    2nd Battalion 1st Lanark R.V., consisting of 2nd, 18th,
    50th, 53rd, 63rd, 72nd, 76th, and 77th Corps   . 517

3rd Battalion: Major D. Reid, 19th (2nd Glasgow Northern)
L.R.V.
    19th Lanark R.V. (7 companies) [1]   .   .   . 592

4th Battalion: Major D. B. Macbrayne, 3rd Glasgow
Northern L.R.V.
    3rd Glasgow Northern Battalion (comprising 51st,
    67th, 74th, 80th, 81st, 83rd, 89th, and 91st Lanark
    R.V.) and 1st Bute R.V.   583

3rd Brigade: Lieut.-Col. J. Tennant, 4th Lanark R.V.

1st Battalion: Major J. F. Jamieson, 1st Glasgow Northern
L.R.V.
    4th Lanark (1st Glasgow Northern) (6 companies);
    60th and 61st Lanark R.V.   .   .   . 562

---

[1] Including the 85th Corps.

2nd Battalion: Lieut.-Col. W. Stirling, 7th Battalion
Lanark R.V.
 5th, 21st, 34th, 35th, 49th, 58th, 59th, 64th, 65th,
  66th, and 90th Lanark R.V. . . . 586

3rd Battalion: Major Rigby, 6th Battalion Lanark R.V.
 25th, 26th, 27th, 40th, 43rd, 48th, 68th, 69th, 70th,
  and 71st Lanark R.V. . . . 582

4th Battalion: Major A. Crum Ewing, 4th Battalion
Lanark R.V.
 29th, 30th, 31st, 32nd, 38th, 45th, 46th, 47th, 54th,
  75th, 84th, and 86th Lanark R.V.. . . 730

   4th Brigade: Lieut.-Col. J. M. Gartshore, 1st A.B.
      Dumbarton R.V.

1st Battalion: Major S. Simpson, 3rd Battalion Lanark R.V.
 16th, 42nd, 44th, 52nd, 56th, 57th, 37th, 55th, and
  73rd Lanark R.V. 765

2nd Battalion: Major Dawson, 1st A.B. Dumbarton R.V.
 1st A.B. Dumbarton R.V., consisting of the 1st, 2nd,
  3rd, 4th, 5th, 6th, 7th, 8th, 9th, and 10th Corps . 649

3rd Battalion: Major Walker, Inspector of Musketry.
 1st, 2nd, 3rd, 4th, 5th, 7th, and 8th Dumfries, and 1st,
  2nd, 3rd, and 4th Wigtown R.V. . . 495

4th Battalion: Lieut.-Col. the Hon. W. F. Scarlett, Scots
Fusilier Guards.
 3rd, 10th, 14th, 22nd, 78th, 82nd, and 87th Lanark R.V. 413

The total of all ranks on parade was 21,514, in 348
companies.

The Queen arrived in Edinburgh at 8 A.M. and
drove to Holyrood Palace, escorted by the 13th Light
Dragoons. After a visit in the forenoon to the
Duchess of Kent, her mother, at Cramond, near
Edinburgh, at 3.40 P.M. Her Majesty left Holyrood
for the review ground, again escorted by the 13th
Light Dragoons, and accompanied by Their Royal

Highnesses the Prince Consort, the Duchess of Kent, Princes Arthur and Leopold, and Princesses Alice, Helena, and Louise. The Prince Consort rode on the right of the Queen's carriage, the Duke of Buccleuch, Lord-Lieutenant of Edinburgh and Captain of the Bodyguard of Scottish Archers, on the left, and the Lords-Lieutenant of counties followed on horseback. The troops were formed up in line of quarter-columns along the base of Arthur's Seat, and Her Majesty drove along the line and took post at the saluting base, where the Royal Standard of Scotland was displayed. The march past was then carried out, after which the troops again formed into line of quarter-columns, advanced in review order, gave a royal salute, and finished up with three cheers, in which the spectators lustily joined. It was a proud moment for Scotland!

The day was hot and dusty, and the troops, un-accustomed as they were to long periods under arms, were highly tried, but that they acquitted themselves well is evident from the following Order, published by the Adjutant-General after the review :—

HORSE GUARDS, S.W., *August* 10, 1860.

The Adjutant-General has received the Queen's command to convey her thanks to the several corps of Artillery and Rifle Volunteers assembled at Edinburgh on the 7th inst., and to assure them of the satisfaction and gratification with which Her Majesty beheld the magnificent spectacle there presented to her.

Her Majesty could not see, without admiration, the soldier-like bearing of the different corps as they passed before her, and she finds in the high state of efficiency to which they have attained, in an incredibly short space of time, another proof that she may at all times rely on the loyalty and patriotism of her people for the defence, in the hour of need, of the freedom and integrity of the Empire.

By order,

J. YORKE SCARLETT, A.-G.

It is worthy of note that all the expenses attendant on this review were borne by the volunteers out of their own pockets or subscribed for from private sources.

On January 19, 1861, were published, by authority of the Secretary of State for War, the first ' Regula-The Regula-tions for the Volunteer Force,' which codified tions of 1861. and consolidated all previous circulars and orders and superseded them. The main features of these regulations, by clauses, were :—

Clause 6. The force is composed of light horse, artillery, engineer, mounted rifle, and rifle volunteers. Its objects (7) are to supplement the regular, militia, and other forces in the country.

8. The establishments of all ranks of enrolled volunteers for each arm are : Light horse troop, minimum 50, maximum 80, artillery battery 50-80, engineer or rifle company 60-100, mounted rifle company 43-70. The staffs of battalions (as laid down in the circular of March 24, 1860) to be included in the total establishments allowed for the companies of these units.

9 to 13. Offers for the formation of a corps are to be made through the Lord-Lieutenant of the county, and certain conditions as to numbers, headquarters, storehouse, and range must be complied with. An officer will then be detailed by the War Office to inspect all the proposed arrangements, and only if his report be satisfactory will the offer of service be laid before the sovereign for acceptance.

14. Engineer corps should be composed of engineers, masons, joiners, quarrymen, railway employés, &c.

16 to 19. Information required before the formation of an artillery corps is sanctioned.

20, 21. If an increase of a corps is projected, the proposed minimum establishment must have been attained (including those ready to be enrolled) before the increased establishment can be sanctioned, and, if the strength of a corps falls below its minimum, its establishment is liable to be reduced.

22 to 27. The volunteer force takes precedence after the militia, its arms ranking in the order given in clause 6. The precedence of counties in each arm is separate, and is arrived at in the manner explained on page 23. Officers rank according to date of commission in their rank and junior to militia officers of the same rank.

29 to 31. Corps are numbered in each arm and county according to their precedence, and special titles may be authorised in addition to the numbers. When a corps is disbanded or absorbed in a senior one, its number remains vacant.

32 to 39. Commissioned officers, except adjutants, are nominated by the Lords-Lieutenant and their names submitted for the sovereign's approval, resignations being similarly submitted. Certain fees have to be paid on officers' commissions. Officers on full pay are only eligible for honorary commissions.

40, 41. Two substantive commissions in the force cannot be held by one individual. If two corps have been raised by one person, he may be appointed commanding officer of both, but on actual service must resign the command of one of them.

42. Captains commanding corps of more than one company may be appointed captains-commandant.

43. Quartermasters and paymasters are not allowed, but supernumerary lieutenants may be enrolled to perform these duties.

44, 45. Officers holding 1st class musketry certificates may be appointed musketry instructors, but if they have not this certificate they may only be appointed acting instructors.

46 to 50. Honorary colonels, chaplains, assistant-surgeons, and veterinary surgeons may be appointed, but the two latter classes receive no pay.

51. Substantive officers must be effective members of their corps.

52 to 54. Non-commissioned officers, including lance-serjeants and lance - corporals, are appointed by the commanding officer, and may be reduced by him after investigation of their conduct by a court of inquiry.

55. No person below seventeen years of age may be enrolled as a volunteer, nor (56) any pensioner, without the consent of the Secretary of State, nor (57) any apprentice without that of his master.

58, 59. Enrolled members are classed as effective and non-effective. To be counted effective a member must have taken the oath of allegiance and attended, properly equipped, the prescribed number of drills.

60. Drills need not be on consecutive days, and one-half of them must be musters of the whole corps.

61. All members not complying with these conditions are counted as non-effective.

62, 63. Supernumerary members are not to be enrolled without authority, and are not entitled to the exemptions granted to volunteers by Act of Parliament. Honorary members are not included in the muster-roll, and may not interfere with the military duties of the corps, but they may wear its uniform.

64. Each corps must have an approved code of rules, which (65) must be certified by the Secretary of State.

66. Courts of inquiry may be assembled by Lords-Lieutenant to investigate any subject. They are not judicial bodies, and cannot administer oaths.

67 to 70. Small corps should be grouped into administrative battalions, regiments, or brigades, to receive uniformity of drill and to afford them the advantage

of the services of an adjutant; but this organisation is not to interfere with their constitution or financial arrangements, nor are they to be required to meet for united drill save with their own consent. Proposals for such grouping are to be made by the Lords-Lieutenant, and the corps are to be grouped by localities.

71. The staffs allowed for administrative battalions are as given in the circular of March 24, 1860 (page 34).

72. The administrative battalions, &c., in a county are to be numbered consecutively, and (73) headquarters assigned to them in addition to those of the corps composing them.

74. Four-company battalions, &c., are only to be formed when no more companies are available in the county, and (75) the adjutant of a corps administratively united with others will be recommissioned as adjutant of the administrative battalion.

76. Corps of adjoining counties may be united into an administrative battalion.

77. The field-officer commanding an administrative battalion has general charge of the drill and discipline of the several corps, inspects them occasionally, and is responsible that uniformity in drill is preserved. He commands any portion of his battalion assembled for drill.

78. No officer of a corps in an administrative battalion has any authority over those of others, but when assembled for combined drill the senior commands.

79 to 82. Contain regulations for the appointment of field-officers of administrative battalions.

83. An administrative battalion cannot have rules having legal force distinct from those of the corps composing it.

84 to 86. Small corps may be attached to others for drill or for the services of an adjutant.

87 to 91. The force may not assemble in greater strength than one brigade without the sanction of the Secretary of State, obtained through the Lord-Lieutenant.

92. Reviews of volunteers may be held from time to time by General Officers Commanding, but no volunteer corps can be compelled to attend. Volunteers may (93) be brigaded with other forces.

94. At shooting matches, &c., the senior officer present takes command and is responsible for the maintenance of order and discipline among the volunteers under arms.

95 to 97. Volunteer corps choose their own uniform and accoutrements, subject to the approval of the Lord-Lieutenant. No gold lace is allowed. The colour should be uniform in each county or in administrative battalions. The Dress Regulations of the Army are to be followed as to badges of rank.

98. Every volunteer should be provided with a service kit, in addition to the articles worn or carried on his person, and (99) the pouches of riflemen should hold sixty rounds.

100, 101. Officers and serjeants may wear side-arms when off duty. Neither standards nor colours are to be carried.

102 to 112. Instructions for the issue and care of the Government arms to be supplied gratuitously from stores for the full number of enrolled members of corps.

113 to 126. The proportion of ammunition to be issued to corps annually for each enrolled member is—

	GRATIS.			ON PAYMENT.		
1st Year of Service—	Ball.	Blank.	Caps.	Ball.	Blank.	Caps.
Light Horse . . .	70	10	98	50	...	55
Artillery . . .	70	10	98	50	...	55
Engineers and Rifles .	110	20	163	110	100	231
2nd and subsequent Years of Service—						
Light Horse . . .	50	...	55	70	...	77
Artillery . . .	50	...	53	70	...	77
Engineers and Rifles .	90	60	165	130	60	209

Artillery are allowed 80 shot and 20 shell of big-gun ammunition per battery, and £7, 13s. for the purchase of floating, or £2, 10s. for land targets. Guns are issued from store, and assistance is given in the construction of batteries, but the sites for these must be provided by the corps.

127 to 146. Adjutants are appointed under the Queen's commission on the recommendation of the Lord-Lieutenant. They must be under fifty years of age, and have previously served: for light horse, mounted rifles, or rifles, 4 years in the Imperial or Indian forces; for artillery, 2 years as an officer or 8 as a non-commissioned officer in the Royal, Indian, or Marine Artillery; for engineers, 2 years as an officer or 8 as a non-commissioned officer in the Royal or Indian Engineers; with certain exceptions in favour of officers who have served in the embodied militia, and reductions of the obligatory periods in the case of those who hold 1st class musketry certificates. Adjutants may not hold any other appointment or employment; their pay is 8s. a-day besides 2s. for the keep of a horse, and £4 per annum is allowed for every company in the battalion to cover contingent expenses, postage, &c. A special allowance of 2s. a-day in lieu of travelling expenses is given to adjutants of administrative battalions. Adjutants are not allowed to hold regimental commissions, nor to take

D

command in virtue of their rank when volunteer officers are present. They are subject to the Mutiny Act and Articles of War. Their duties are connected with the instruction of the corps and its military efficiency, but they are not to take part in its non-military or financial affairs. Special rates of pension are laid down for volunteer adjutants.

147 to 170. The serjeant instructors are under the adjutant, and are subject to the Mutiny Act and Articles of War. They are obtained by the transfer of non-commissioned officers of the regular army with at least 18 years' service, who are then borne as super-numeraries in their regiments until the time of their discharge occurs, and are provided in the proportion, for rifle corps, of 1 to corps of 1 to 3 companies, 2 for 4 to 7 companies, and 3 for 8 companies or upwards, and in similar proportions for the other arms. One of them may in each corps be appointed serjeant-major. The daily pay is 2s. 4d. if in receipt of a pension, 2s. 7d. if not, and 6d. extra if acting as serjeant-major. They may serve on after discharge from the army. Drill instructors may also be obtained under certain conditions from the permanent staff of the disembodied militia.

171 to 173. Volunteers may attend classes of musketry instruction at the School of Musketry for periods of fourteen working days, paying all their personal expenses, but having ammunition issued free.

174. A rifle-range must extend to 200, but it is desirable that it should extend to 900 yards.

175. Corps without adjutants may not fire blank or ball ammunition in military formation until the assistant-inspector of the district pronounces the members to be qualified to do so.

176. Only Government ammunition is to be used in testing the sights of Enfield rifles.

177 to 179. Refer to badges for good shooting (rifles embroidered horizontally on the sleeve, with 1, 2, or 3 stars above them according to proficiency).

180. Details the musketry practices to be performed, which vary with the length of the range.

181. The drill, &c., books to be used in the instruction of the volunteers are the same as those in use in the regular army.

182 to 184. Officers of volunteers may be attached for instruction to the regular army or militia for periods not exceeding one month.

185 to 195. Deal with correspondence and returns.

196 to 198. Deal with the appointment and duties of assistant-inspectors of volunteers (see page 35).

These regulations have been quoted at some length as they mark a distinct stage in the development of the volunteer force, and its final recognition as part of the defensive forces of the Crown. The former haphazard organisation is done away with, the small corps are combined into higher organisations provided with adequate staff, adjutants, and instructors, a system of inspection is provided for, a programme of drill and musketry laid down, and the drill regulations of the regular army are frankly adopted, the old idea of a very elementary course of instruction being sufficient for volunteers having become an exploded notion.

In Scotland the carrying into effect of the provisions of the new regulations as to the higher organisation of the force was actively pushed forward in 1861, and the extent to which consolidated corps in cities and administrative battalions or artillery brigades in the counties were formed may be seen from a comparison of Appendix E, which shows the composition and enrolled strength of the force on April 1, 1862, with the list of corps

The force in 1861-62.

already given as taking part in the Royal Review of August 7, 1860.

From the return of April 1, 1862, it will be seen that the force then consisted of—

Artillery.—3 consolidated city corps, 7 administrative brigades, and 35 small corps of from ¼ battery to 2 batteries,—in all, 107¾ batteries, with 6582 enrolled members.

Engineers. — 3 corps of 1 company each, with 235 enrolled members.

Mounted Rifles. — 1 corps of 4 troops, with 160 enrolled members.

Rifles.—11 consolidated city and 1 consolidated country (1st Sutherland) corps of 4 or more companies, 28 administrative battalions, and 34 small corps of from ½ company to 2 companies,—in all, 372 companies, with 27,263 enrolled members.

Total Force.—34,240 enrolled members.

The training and discipline of the force improved *pari passu* with its organisation : in shooting the volunteers took a leading part in the country, their marksmen even showing the way to the regular army, and through them a taste for rifle-shooting was developed throughout the country. Prize-lists were subscribed for in all corps ; local bodies, landowners, merchants, and the heads of great works and firms offered prizes or trophies for shooting, and provincial rifle associations, on the model of the National Rifle Association, sprang up all over the country. A healthy rivalry between corps was also established by the institution of matches, and the records of the volunteers of those days teem with descriptions of the interest which these excited, not only in the corps, but in the locality from which they were recruited.

These developments in the movement, and the organisation of the single corps into larger units, led, however, to fresh outlays. Larger drill-halls and stores were required, and regularly organised and equipped ranges were demanded, and thus expenses increased. The uniforms first obtained also began to wear out, and as the first enthusiasm abated the subscriptions both of members and of friends of the movement began to fall off. Some corps disappeared altogether or became amalgamated with others, and all sorts of expedients—bazaars, concerts, balls, &c.—were resorted to to raise funds; but it soon became evident that such sources of income were no longer to be relied upon. In all the large centres public meetings were held to urge upon Government that a money grant was absolutely necessary to the existence of the force. In Glasgow such a meeting was held, under the presidency of the Lord Provost, in the Merchants' Hall on January 9, 1861, and at it resolutions were passed that measures should be adopted for giving the force continuous national support, and that such measures should comprehend an annual pecuniary grant. The London commanding officers also took the matter in hand and invited the co-operation of their provincial brethren, and on February 23, 1861, similar resolutions were passed at a meeting at the Thatched House Tavern.

The War Office was quite alive to the difficulties of the force, and on January 13, 1862, a letter was addressed by the Inspector-General of Volunteers to the Assistant-Inspectors, calling for their opinions on various points. The replies

The Royal Commission of 1862.

showed such an unsatisfactory state of affairs to exist in the force that on May 16 a Royal Commission was issued to Colonel Viscount Eversley, A.D.C., Hants V.C.; the Earl of Ducie; Lieut.-Colonel Viscount Hardinge, 2nd A.B. Kent R.V.; Lieut.-Colonel Lord Elcho, 15th Middlesex R.V.; Lord Overstone; the

Right Hon. E. P. Bouverie, M.P.; Lieut.-Colonel Barttelot, 2nd A.B. Sussex R.V.; Lieut.-Colonel Sir A. Islay Campbell, Bt., 1st Lanark R.V.; Lieut.-General Sir G. A. Wetherall, K.C.B.; Major-General H. Eyre; Colonel W. M. S. Macmurdo, C.B. (Inspector-General of Volunteers); Lieut.-Colonel A. S. Gladstone, 5th Lancashire R.V.; and Major E. M. V. Hartcourt, 4th Cinque Ports R.V., "to inquire into the present condition of our Volunteer Force in Great Britain and into the probability of its continuance at its existing strength, and to report whether any measures should be adopted for the purpose of increasing its efficiency as an auxiliary means of national defence."

The Commission commenced its labours on May 27, and held its last meeting on July 15, between which dates it examined fifty-one witnesses, of whom the following represented Scotland: H. G. Bell, Esq., Sheriff-Substitute of Lanarkshire; Lieut.-Colonel Stirling Crawford, 1st Lanark A.V.; Lieut.-Colonel D. Dreghorn, 3rd Lanark R.V.; Captain Innes, 1st Kincardine A.V.; Captain M'Grigor and Ensign J. Lockhart, 1st Lanark R.V.; Captain Page (adjutant), Captain MacGregor, and Colour-Sergeant Pettie, London Scottish R.V.; Lieut.-Colonel Stirling, 5th Lanark R.V.; and Major Warrender, Haddington R.V. The Commission also issued a series of questions to all officers commanding corps. At the conclusion of its labours the Commission presented its report, which was published on October 29, 1862, and recommended that an annual capitation grant of £1 should be paid to the commanding officer of each rifle corps for every man who had attended nine drills in the year, six of which were to be battalion drills in the case of consolidated and three in that of administrative battalions; that a further grant of 10s. should be given for every rifleman who fired sixty rounds in class-firing and passed out of the 3rd class; and that for artillery corps the annual capitation grant should be 30s. for each efficient.

The recommendations of the Commission were considered by Government, and adopted almost in their entirety, the new state-supported character of the force being recognised by the passing by Parliament (July 21, 1863) of the "Volunteer Act, 1863," which to the end remained the controlling statute of the volunteer force. Its main provisions were that all volunteers had to take the oath of allegiance; that a volunteer, except when on actual military service, might quit his corps on giving fourteen days' notice, delivering up his arms and uniform in good order, and paying any arrears of money due from him under corps rules; that, "in case of actual or apprehended invasion," her Majesty might direct the Lords-Lieutenant to call out the volunteers for actual military service, when any one not responding to the call was liable to be dealt with as a deserter; and that any volunteer so called out should be entitled to the sum of £2, 2s. for necessaries, and should receive pay and relief for his wife or family, and be billeted or quartered the same as a militiaman. Volunteers were to be exempt from ballot for service in the militia. The conditions of volunteer efficiency were to be defined by an Order in Council, issued from time to time, and accordingly on July 23, 1863, such an Order was issued laying down these conditions, which were as above stated in the recommendations of the Commission, with the addition that recruits had to perform thirty squad, company, or battalion drills. It had to be certified that the volunteer possessed a competent knowledge of squad, company, and preliminary musketry drill, and had been present at the annual inspection of the corps, to enable him

The Volunteer Act of 1863.

to be classed as efficient.   For arms other than rifles
the conditions of efficiency were similar to the above.

On this Act and the Order in Council were based
the Volunteer Regulations of 1863, which replaced
The Volun- those of 1861.   The principal new provisions
teer Regula- were that for each efficient volunteer, as de-
tions of
1863. fined above, £1 of annual capitation grant
should be allowed, with, in addition, 10s. for each who
had fired twenty rounds each in the 1st, 2nd, and 3rd
periods of musketry instruction, and, in one of the
three, had passed into the 2nd class; also 4s. a-year
for each member of an administrative battalion belonging to corps at a greater distance than five miles from
headquarters, to cover the cost of attendance at united
drill.   Among the minor changes introduced by these
regulations was an order that all corps of an administrative battalion were to be dressed alike, and that
cloth for uniforms, cut out and basted, was to be issued
at cost price from the Army Clothing Depôt.   The pay
of adjutants was increased from 8s. to 10s. a-day, and
they were obliged to give security in their new capacity
as acting paymasters, for to them was now entrusted
the receipt and disbursement of the capitation allowances.   The formation of cadet corps attached to
volunteer units, and composed of boys of twelve years
of age and upwards, was sanctioned.   They were to be
officered by gentlemen holding honorary commissions,
and ten per cent of arms were to be issued to enable
those of sufficient age to carry on rifle practice.

The regulations of 1863 were followed by a marked
The force improvement in the volunteer force, which
from 1863 from that year began to increase in numbers
to 1871.
and efficiency.   The percentage of volunteers
to population was [1]—

---

[1] From Berry's ' History of the Volunteer Infantry.'

				In 1861.	In 1871.
England	.	.	.	·629	·655
Wales .	.	.	.	·655	·620
Scotland	.	.	.	1·119	1·316

—from which figures it is gratifying to note that the proportion of volunteers was in Scotland in 1861 nearly, and in 1871 more than, twice as great as in England or Wales.

The organisation of the force in Scotland was also rapidly pushed forward on the lines indicated above, and, as will be seen from the corps' records, by the close of the year 1863 all the smaller corps mentioned above as still independent on April 1, 1862, had been either organised into administrative battalions or, in a very few cases, attached to larger corps.

The reclothing of the force was carried out as laid down in the regulations, and it is noticeable how in Scotland the strong national military spirit asserted itself at this time in the matter of the assumption of national uniforms. In 1860 there had been little difference between the uniforms of the Scottish and English corps, but in 1863 and 1864, while the whole of the artillery and engineer corps adopted the uniform of their regular branches, there were few Scottish rifle corps which did not adopt either tartans, in the form of trews or kilts, or the diced band round their caps, and those which did not do so simply copied the uniforms of the regular line infantry or rifles. It is remarkable how many at this period assumed the traditional scarlet, no fewer than thirteen battalions, or nearly one-third of the then organised force, having adopted it in 1864, at a time when it was hardly worn at all south of the Border.

The cadet corps movement did not at all meet with approval in Scotland at first, and the only such corps formed before 1871 was that attached to the 3rd Edinburgh and formed by Captain John Hope in 1867 of teetotallers. The next raised was a school corps, at Glenalmond, in 1875, attached to the 1st Perthshire Administrative Battalion, and it was followed by a third, attached to the 1st Forfarshire R.V. in Dundee, formed in 1881; but these three were the only cadet corps existing in Scotland at the date of the coming-of-age review in the latter year.

There is little to chronicle in this period of steady development of the volunteer force; but the end of it was marked by the re-armament of the infantry portion of it with a breech-loading rifle, for on September 1, 1870, it was announced that the issue of Snider-Enfield rifles to the volunteers was sanctioned, and the corps received them in the following year.

In 1871 a most important change was made in the constitution of the volunteers, for in that year, by the "Regulation of the Forces Act, 1871," the "jurisdiction, powers, duties, command, and privileges" over the volunteers, hitherto vested in the Lords-Lieutenant, were transferred to Her Majesty, to be exercised by her through the Secretary of State; and in consequence of this the commissions of officers were henceforth issued by Her Majesty in the same manner as for officers of the regular forces, the Lords-Lieutenant only retaining the power of recommending candidates for first appointment. This Act also provided that, when any portion of the volunteer force was assembled for the purpose of being trained or exercised along with militia or regular forces, it should be subject to the Mutiny Act and Articles of War.

Transfer of the force from the Lords-Lieutenant to the Crown.

The lessons taught by the Franco-German War of

1870-71 were taken to heart in Great Britain, and

1872. one of the first results of their study was the institution of manœuvres of all arms on a large scale. These were first carried out near Aldershot in 1871, but in the following year were repeated on a more ambitious scale on Salisbury Plain, and in the latter manœuvres the Scottish volunteers, for the first time as formed bodies, made their appearance in the great training camps of the south of England. The 3rd Provisional Volunteer Battalion, formed to take part in these manœuvres, was commanded by Lieut.-Colonel J. H. A. Macdonald of the Queen's Edinburgh, and in the battalion was included a detachment of 6 officers and 100 men of his corps, who, it is recorded, "acquitted themselves creditably."

Another lesson learned was the necessity for improving the instruction of the officers of the force, and by "Auxiliary and Reserve Forces Circular" of May 28, 1872, various measures in this direction were ordered. An age limit of sixty years for officers was introduced, on attaining which they had to resign their commissions, five years' extension being allowed only in special cases. Officers were required within one year of first appointment or promotion to pass an examination for the rank to which they had been appointed or promoted, and those who failed to pass or who did not attend the number of drills required for efficiency were called on to resign. Schools of instruction for officers were opened at Shoeburyness for artillery, Chatham for engineers, Aldershot, London, Manchester, and Glasgow for rifles, with courses lasting a month, during which the officers attending were to receive 5s. a-day, together with quarters, fuel, light, and travelling expenses; and at the conclusion of the course, and on passing the

examination, each was to be given a certificate, and
" P.S." was to be entered after his name in the Army
List.   A special capitation allowance of £2, 10s. a-year
was granted to those who obtained this certificate,
and this was to continue as long as the officer was
certified proficient by his commanding officer.   Officers
might also be attached for instruction to the regulars
or militia for a month, and at the end might be
examined by a board of officers and granted a certificate of proficiency, in which case " P." was to be
placed after their names in the Army List.

Under the provisions of the same circular, measures
were also taken to improve the higher training of the
units.   To constitute a "battalion drill," it was laid
down that 100 of all ranks (including 16 officers and
serjeants) must be present.   If absent from inspection,
volunteers were required to perform two extra drills
to be classed as efficient, and rifle corps were required
to attend, with at least half their strength, one brigade
drill in the year of two hours' duration under a regular
officer, 1s. a-man being allowed for travelling expenses
—a great advance this, indeed, on the idea of 1859 of
the company being the highest volunteer unit !

" A portion " of the force was also allowed to form
regimental camps of exercise to last three clear days,
during which the annual inspection was to be made.
Travelling expenses were to be borne by the public,
and 10s. a-man was to be allowed for volunteers
remaining eight (of which six clear) days, and £1
for those doing thirteen clear days in camp.   Officers
were to receive 2s. 6d. a-day for field-officers, 1s. 6d.
for captains, and 1s. a-day for subalterns while in
camp, and greatcoats were to be *lent* from store to
all ranks while in camp.   Thus was inaugurated the
system of volunteer training in camp, which after-

wards received such great extension; but certain corps had already taken time by the forelock, and in 1869 the first volunteer camp had been held in Scotland, the 2nd Administrative Battalion Aberdeenshire R.V., afterwards the 2nd Volunteer Battalion Gordon Highlanders, having in that year gone into and been inspected in camp at Haddo House.

It was by this circular, as mentioned on p. 33, that the adjutants were directed to be appointed for five years only, and taken from captains of the army on full or half pay.

In the year 1873 a most important step was taken in the organisation of the volunteer force, which was the beginning of their closer association with the regular forces and the militia. By General Regulations and Instructions of July 24, 1873, there were brought into force the recommendations of the Localisation Committee of 1872. The United Kingdom was divided into seventy infantry sub-districts, each consisting of a certain area, to each of which were assigned for recruiting purposes, as a normal rule, two line battalions, two militia battalions, and the volunteers of the area. Of the line battalions, one was nominally to be stationed abroad, the other (which fed the foreign battalion in peace) at home, and two companies of each were to be permanently quartered at sub-district headquarters to form the brigade depôt. The depôt, the militia and volunteer battalions, and the army reserve men were constituted the "sub-district brigade," and were placed under the orders of the lieutenant-colonel commanding the sub-district brigade depôt, who was charged with the training and inspection of all the infantry of the auxiliary forces.

In the North British District (as the Scottish Com-

mand was then termed) the infantry sub-districts were
as follows :—

No. 55.—Counties of Orkney and Shetland, Sutherland, Caithness, Ross and Cromarty, Inverness, Nairn, and Elgin. Depôt
at Fort George.
> Regular Battalions—71st and 78th Foot.
> Militia   "   Highland Light Infantry and High-
> > land Rifles.
> Volunteers—1st A.B. Ross, 1st A.B. Inverness, 1st A.B.
> > Sutherland, and 1st A.B. Elgin.

No. 56.—Counties of Aberdeen, Banff, and Kincardine. Depôt
at Aberdeen.
> Regular Battalions—92nd and 93rd Foot.
> Militia   "   Royal Aberdeen (2nd battalion not
> > yet formed).
> Volunteers—1st Aberdeen R.V., 1st, 2nd, and 3rd A.B.
> > Aberdeen, 1st A.B. Kincardine, and 1st
> > A.B. Banff.

No. 57.—Counties of Forfar, Perth and Fife. Depôt at Perth.
> Regular Battalions—42nd and 79th Foot.
> Militia   "   Royal Perth (2nd battalion not yet
> > formed).
> Volunteers—1st Forfar R.V., 1st A.B. Forfar, 10th Forfar
> > R.V., 1st and 2nd A.B. Perth, and 1st
> > A.B. Fife.

No. 58.—Counties of Renfrew, Bute, Stirling, Dumbarton, Argyll,
Kinross, and Clackmannan. Depôt at Stirling.
> Regular Battalions—72nd and 91st Foot.
> Militia   "   Highland Borderers L.I., and Royal
> > Renfrew.
> Volunteers—1st, 2nd, and 3rd A.B. Renfrew, 1st A.B. Stir-
> > ling, 1st A.B. Argyll, 1st A.B. Dumbarton,
> > and 1st A.B. Clackmannan and Kinross.

No. 59.—County of Lanark. Depôt at Hamilton.
> Regular Battalions—26th and 74th Foot.
> Militia   "   1st Royal Lanark (two battalions).
> Volunteers—1st, 3rd, 4th, 16th, and 29th Lanark R.V.

No. 60.—County of Lanark.　Depôt at Hamilton.
　　Regular Battalions—73rd and 90th Foot.
　　Militia　　ₙ　　　2nd Royal Lanark (two battalions).
　　Volunteers—19th, 25th, 31st, and 105th Lanark R.V., and
　　　　　3rd A.B. Lanark.

No. 61.—Counties of Ayr, Wigtown, Kirkcudbright, Dumfries,
　　Selkirk, and Roxburgh.　Depôt at Ayr.
　　Regular Battalions—21st Foot (two battalions).
　　Militia　　ₙ　　　Scottish Borderers, and Royal Ayr
　　　　　and Wigtown.
　　Volunteers—1st A.B. Roxburgh and Selkirk, 1st and 2nd
　　　　　A.B. Ayr, 1st A.B. Dumfries, and 1st A.B.
　　　　　Galloway.

No. 62.—Counties of Edinburgh, Peebles, Haddington, Berwick,
　　and Linlithgow.　Depôt at Glencorse.
　　Regular Battalions—1st Foot (two battalions).
　　Militia　　ₙ　　　Edinburgh L.I. (2nd battalion not
　　　　　yet formed).
　　Volunteers—1st and 3rd Edinburgh R.V., 1st Mid-Lothian
　　　　　R.V., 1st A.B. Mid-Lothian, 1st A.B. Ber-
　　　　　wick, 1st A.B. Haddington, 1st A.B.
　　　　　Linlithgow.

For the command and training of the auxiliary
artillery, artillery sub-districts were similarly formed,
of which there were two in Scotland, each in charge
of a lieutenant-colonel of the Royal Artillery, who
commanded and inspected the corps of militia and
volunteer artillery and the army reserve of the
artillery in his sub-district. The 1st North British
Sub-district, headquarters at Edinburgh, comprised
the counties of Argyll, Ayr, Berwick, Bute, Clackmannan, Dumbarton, Dumfries, Edinburgh, Fife,
Haddington, Kinross, Kirkcudbright, Lanark, Linlithgow, Mid-Lothian, Peebles, Renfrew, Roxburgh,
Selkirk, Stirling, and Wigtown, and the 2nd, headquarters at Aberdeen, the rest (North) of Scotland.

The mounted volunteers of Scotland were placed for command and inspection under the lieutenant-colonel and inspecting officer of the 1st Cavalry District for Auxiliary Forces, headquarters at York, and the engineer volunteers were kept under the direct command of the Commanding Royal Engineer, North British District.

Thus the volunteers were for the first time brought into close organic connection with the other branches of the forces of the Crown, and in this same year a beginning was made with a scheme of mobilisation which, it must be confessed, existed at first only on paper, according to which definite duties in the defence of the country were told off to the various corps on the coast, which were formed into "local brigades" for its watching and defence, or as "detachments from corps" for the garrisoning of the fortresses.

No further changes in the organisation of the force are to be chronicled until the year 1878, in which were Regulations published new regulations, which superseded of 1878. those of 1863, and embodied all the changes Distinctions of uniform. and modifications, as indicated above, which had been introduced in the past fifteen years. The main feature in them not already mentioned was the obligatory introduction for the first time of distinctive marks on the uniform to distinguish volunteers from other branches of the service. Artillery volunteers were directed to wear scarlet, and engineer volunteers blue Austrian knots on the sleeves of the tunic and bands and buttons on the forage caps, the regulars having all these in yellow and the militia in white. Infantry battalions were to wear an Austrian knot on the sleeve, light green for those clothed in green, and of the colour of the facings (or blue in the case of scarlet facings) for those clothed in scarlet. In corps wearing the rifle busby, the lower portion of the plume was to be light green for those clothed in green, and of the colour of the facings for those in scarlet or grey. The initials of the county and the number of the corps (and of the administrative battalion or brigade, if included in such) were to be borne on the shoulder-straps. Silver officers' and serjeants' lace and white metal buttons were to be worn with scarlet or blue uniforms, and black lace and bronze buttons with those of green. Corps in blue or scarlet were to wear white belts and black pouches, those in green black, and those in grey brown or black belts and pouches. The infantry sash was not to be worn by officers or serjeants, and officers were to wear cross - belts and pouches. Where the corps of an administrative battalion were differently dressed, all had to conform to the approved pattern before April 1, 1879, or before five years had elapsed since their joining the battalion. With these exceptions, no alteration in the uniforms of the volunteer infantry was to be permitted except for the purpose of assimilation to that of one of the line battalions of the sub-district.

In 1879 the Martini-Henry rifle was first issued to the volunteers, but only to a limited extent. Its issue Re-arma- was not general till 1881, and it was not till ment of the 1885 that the Snider rifles and carbines were volunteers, 1879. withdrawn, and the force completely supplied with the army weapon.

In 1878 a committee had been appointed under the presidency of Viscount Bury, Parliamentary Under-Consolidation Secretary of State, to inquire into the finan-of the ad-cial state and internal organisation of the ministrative brigades and volunteer force, and its report was presented battalions, 1880. in January 1879. The committee bore testi-mony to " the generally sound and healthy condition

E

in which they found the volunteer force, which had increased from year to year in numbers, and had cheerfully responded to every call upon it for increased efficiency." The maximum authorised establishment of the force in 1863 was 226,156, of whom 113,511 were efficient out of 162,935 enrolled; while in 1878 the establishment was 244,263, of whom 194,191 were efficient out of 203,213 enrolled. The percentages of efficient to enrolled had thus risen from 69·66 in 1863 to 95·55 in 1878. The committee did not therefore propose any material changes in the composition of the force, but recommended its closer connection with the territorial brigades in the sub-districts, the consolidation of the independent corps still formed in administrative brigades and battalions with a view to increased economy and efficiency, and the assimilation of volunteer uniforms and equipment to those of the regular army. An increase in the capitation grant was not considered desirable, but more liberal camp and travelling allowances were recommended.

Action was taken on this report, and in the spring of 1880 all the administrative brigades of artillery and battalions of rifles were consolidated,[1] the newly-formed unit taking the number of the senior corps in it, and the batteries being numbered and the companies lettered consecutively in the brigade or battalion respectively. In counties with more than one battalion this led to a series of numbers with many blanks: thus in Lanarkshire there were the 1st, 3rd, 4th, 16th, 19th, 25th, 29th, 31st, 37th, and 105th Rifle Corps. In June 1880, therefore, a general re-numbering from 1 upwards of the

---

[1] This was not the earliest consolidation of country administrative battalions in Scotland, for the principle had been applied in 1873 to the 1st and 4th Administrative Battalions Lanarkshire R.V., which became the 16th and 29th Lanark R.V. respectively.

corps took place in each of such counties. The new numbers were generally allotted according to the former seniority, but in certain cases (*e.g.*, 3rd and 4th Lanark) corps preferred to retain their old numbers and permit junior corps to be placed in the vacant numbers above them (*e.g.*, 16th Lanark became 2nd).

The recommendations of the committee as to the assimilation of uniforms were carried out on April 1, 1881, when (in a new edition of the Volunteer Regulations) it was ordered that the badges of rank worn by regular and militia officers on the shoulder-cords and shoulder-straps should be adopted by the volunteers in place of the former ones on the collar; that non-commissioned officers' chevrons were to be worn on the right arm only, instead of on both, 1-, 2-, and 3-bar chevrons above the elbow, points down, and 4-bar chevrons below the elbow, points up, and that battery and company serjeant-majors and colour-serjeants were to wear 3 bars with a crown and badge (gun, colours, &c.), serjeants 3 bars and badge only, instead of 4 bars, badge and crown, and 3 bars, badge and crown, as formerly. Scarlet was to be the only colour to which infantry volunteers were to be permitted to change their uniform, and the facings then sanctioned were to be those of the senior regular battalion of the sub-district, with a black Austrian knot as a distinctive mark. Corps clothed in blue or scarlet were to wear buff belts and pouches.

The year 1881 was marked by a sweeping change in the organisation of the infantry, for in it were carried out the recommendations of a committee assembled in 1876 under Colonel Stanley to form territorial regiments. With this view, after certain changes had been made in their composition, the regular and militia battalions

Reorganisation into territorial regiments of the infantry in 1881.

belonging to the old sub-districts were formed into territorial regiments with distinctive titles, the old numbers being dropped, except that that of the senior regular battalion continued to be borne as that of the "regimental district," which term was substituted for "brigade sub-district," the regular battalions constituting the 1st and 2nd, the militia the 3rd (and 4th, if existing) battalions,[1] and the volunteer battalions were numbered in a separate sequence, from 1 upwards, in each regiment. The old facings were not retained, but it was laid down that all Scottish regiments were to have yellow facings [2] and thistle pattern lace, except royal regiments, which had blue facings, and the Scottish Rifles, which had green doublets and facings. The rearrangement of regimental districts in Scotland was mainly influenced by the desire to preserve the distinctive tartans of the old Highland regiments, and all Scottish infantry regiments were given doublets and tartan trews if not kilted. Volunteer battalions were to wear the uniform of the regiment and its badges, but not its battle honours.

The new organisation came into force by General Order 70 of 1881, on July 1, 1881, and under it the Scottish infantry were grouped into regiments as follows : [3]—

The Royal Scots (Lothian Regiment).
     Regimental District No. 1.—Glencorse.
          (1st and 2nd Battalions 1st Foot, and Edinburgh L.I. Militia.)

---

[1] The Cameron Highlanders had only one regular and one militia battalion, but in 1897 a second regular battalion was formed for it.

[2] In 1899 the old buff facings were restored to the Highland Light Infantry and Seaforth Highlanders.

[3] The titles of the regiments varied at first slightly from those given here, and shortly afterwards adopted—*e.g.*, "Scotch Rifles," "Sutherland and Argyll Highlanders."

Volunteers: 1st and 2nd Edinburgh, 1st and 2nd Mid-Lothian, 1st Berwick,[1] 1st Haddington, and 1st Linlithgow.

The Royal Scots Fusiliers.
Regimental District No. 21—Ayr.
(1st and 2nd Battalions 21st Foot, Scottish Borderers,[2] and Royal Ayr and Wigtown Militia.)
Volunteers: 1st Roxburgh and Selkirk,[2] 1st and 2nd Ayr, 1st Dumfries[2] and Galloway.[2]

The King's Own Borderers.[2]
Regimental District No. 25—Berwick-on-Tweed.
(1st and 2nd Battalions 25th Foot. No Militia or Volunteers.)

The Cameronians (Scottish Rifles).
Regimental District No. 26—Hamilton.
(26th and 90th Foot, 1st and 2nd Battalions 2nd Royal Lanark Militia.)
Volunteers: 1st, 2nd, 3rd, 4th, and 7th Lanarkshire.

The Black Watch (Royal Highlanders).
Regimental District No. 42—Perth.
(42nd and 73rd Foot, Perth Militia.)
Volunteers: 1st, 2nd, and 3rd Forfar, 1st and 2nd Perth, and 1st Fife.

The Highland Light Infantry.
Regimental District No. 71—Hamilton.
(71st and 74th Foot, 1st and 2nd Battalions 1st Royal Lanark Militia.)
Volunteers: 5th, 6th, 8th, 9th, and 10th Lanarkshire.

The Seaforth Highlanders (Ross-shire Buffs, Duke of Albany's).
Regimental District No. 72—Fort George.

---

[1] See note to King's Own Borderers.

[2] In May 1887 The King's Own Borderers were renamed The King's Own Scottish Borderers, and the Scottish Borderers Militia was transferred to it as 3rd (Militia) Battalion from the 21st Regimental District. At the same time the 1st Roxburgh and Selkirk, 1st Berwick, and 1st Dumfries R.V. were transferred to it as volunteer battalions from the 1st and 21st Regimental Districts, the Galloway Rifles being also transferred to it from the 21st in 1899.

(72nd and 78th Foot, Highland Rifle Militia.)
Volunteers: 1st Ross, 1st Inverness,[1] 1st Sutherland, and
1st Elgin.

The Gordon Highlanders.
Regimental District No. 75—Aberdeen.
(75th and 92nd Foot, and Aberdeen Militia.)
Volunteers: 1st, 2nd, 3rd, and 4th Aberdeen, 1st Kincardine and Aberdeen, and 1st Banff.

The Queen's Own Cameron Highlanders.
Regimental District No. 79—Inverness.
(79th Foot, and Highland Light Infantry Militia.)
Volunteers (see note to Seaforth Highlanders.)

Princess Louise's (Argyll and Sutherland Highlanders).
Regimental District No. 91—Stirling.
(91st and 93rd Foot, Highland Borderers, and Renfrew
Militia.)
Volunteers: 1st, 2nd, and 3rd Renfrew, 1st Stirling, 1st
Argyll, 1st Dumbarton, and 1st Clackmannan and
Kinross.

The closer connection with the regulars, and the
assimilation of uniforms, recommended for the volunteers by Lord Bury's Committee of 1878, and decreed
by the General Order forming the territorial regiments,
was only gradually carried out. It was not until
February 1884 (G.O. 12) that the volunteer battalions
affiliated to the Gordon Highlanders assumed the
designation of volunteer battalions of that regiment,
and they were followed in December 1887 only
(G.O. 161) by the bulk of the battalions of the Royal
Scots Fusiliers, King's Own Scottish Borderers, Scottish
Rifles, Black Watch, Highland Light Infantry, and
Seaforth, Cameron, and Argyll and Sutherland Highlanders, and in April 1888 (A.O. 144) by those of
the Royal Scots. Certain corps, seven in all, never
assumed the territorial regiment's designation. These

---

[1] This battalion was transferred to the 79th Regimental District in 1883.

were the 1st Roxburgh and Selkirk, Galloway Rifles, 1st, 3rd, and 9th Lanark, 1st Sutherland, and 1st Dumbarton.

The assumption of the uniforms of the territorial regiments proceeded even more slowly, partly owing to financial reasons and partly because certain corps desired to retain their original uniforms as volunteers, and by March 31, 1908, only 34 out of the 47 battalions in Scotland had so assimilated their uniform, with trews instead of kilts in certain cases, and with drab service-dress only in others. These, with the dates on which the uniforms were assumed, were :—

Royal Scots.—4th (1887), 5th (1890), 6th (1888), 7th (1904), 8th (drab, 1903), 9th (kilts, 1900).

Royal Scots Fusiliers.—1st (1888), 2nd (1898).

King's Own Scottish Borderers.—2nd (1884), 3rd (1888).

Scottish Rifles.—2nd (drab, 1902), 4th (drab, 1904).

Black Watch.—2nd (trews, 1882), 3rd (trews, 1882), 4th (trews, 1883; kilts, 1901).

Highland Light Infantry.—1st (1883), 2nd (kilts, drab, 1906), 3rd (1886), 9th Lanark (1883).

Seaforth Highlanders.—1st (1888), 3rd (trews, 1886; kilts, 1898).

Gordon Highlanders. — 1st (trews, 1879; kilts, 1895), 2nd (trews, 1875), 3rd (trews, 1885; kilts, 1903), 4th (kilts, drab, 1903), 6th (trews, 1891).

Cameron Highlanders.—1st (1893).

Argyll and Sutherland Highlanders.—1st (trews, 1889; kilts, 1899), 2nd (trews, 1898; kilts, 1903), 3rd (trews, 1889), 4th (trews, 1886), 5th (1883), 1st Dumbarton (trews, 1887), 7th (trews, 1888).

The month previous to the "Coming of Age Review" of the Scottish volunteers was signalised by increased demands on the force as regards efficiency being made, for on July 31, 1881, by an Order in Council, it was laid down that

New conditions of efficiency, 1881.

the following drills had to be performed to render a volunteer efficient :—

	YEARS OF SERVICE.			
	1st.	2nd.	3rd and 4th each.	Subsequent.
Light Horse and Mounted Rifles	19	19 (3 regimental)	9 (3 regl., 6 troop)	7
Artillery . .	{10 squad} {20 gun}	{10 squad} {20 gun}	12 gun	9 gun
Engineers . .	{24 squad} {12 technical}	{24 squad} {12 technical}	{9 squad} {6 technical}	{5 squad} {5 technical}
Rifles . .	30	{30} {(3 battalion)}	{6 company} {3 battalion}	7

In each year two extra drills had to be performed if the volunteer was absent from inspection, and all volunteers had to pass the regulation classes of volley and class-firing. Recruits were allowed to perform all the drills laid down for the first and second year in their first year of service, but in this case had to perform in addition, in their second year, the number of drills laid down for the third year. These requirements show a considerable advance on those in force in former years.

Thus organised, trained, equipped, and disciplined, the Scottish volunteer force, after an existence of twenty-one years, looked forward with con-fidence to the Review which was held by Her Majesty Queen Victoria, to celebrate its coming of age, on August 25, 1881, on the historical ground of Holyrood Park, where in its infancy it had paraded before her on August 7, 1860. The Queen had, on July 9, reviewed at Windsor 2286 officers and 49,954 men (total 52,240) of the English and Welsh volunteers, towards which force the 7th Middlesex (London Scottish) had con-tributed 23 officers and 477 men, and it was evident that the Northern Kingdom, with its total enrolled

The "Com-ing of Age Review" by Her Majesty, 25th August 1881.

force, could not equal this muster. Still, every effort had been made during the drill-season to recruit up and train the corps so as to parade before their sovereign a force worthy of the military traditions of Scotland.

The force reviewed was under the command of Major-General Alastair M'I. M'Donald, commanding the North British District, and consisted of 1654 officers and 37,819 other ranks, or a total of 39,473, of which 3739 all ranks belonged to English corps. The total was thus made up :—

Mounted troops	.	.	21 officers	189 other ranks.
Artillery .	.	.	359 "	7,517 " "
Engineers.	.	.	40 "	1,122 " "
Rifles	.	.	1,234 "	28,991 " "
Total	.	.	1,654 "	37,819 " "

The ground was kept by the 21st Hussars, which also supplied the escort for Her Majesty, and the 1st Battalion Royal Highlanders (42nd), and the music for the march past was furnished by the bands of the 1st Battalion Royal Highlanders (42nd), 1st Battalion Highland Light Infantry (71st), 2nd Battalion Royal Dublin Fusiliers (103rd), and 2nd Battalion Inniskilling Fusiliers (108th).

The organisation of the force was as follows :—

	Officers.	Other ranks.
Cavalry Brigade—Colonel The Hon. C. W. Thesiger.		
1st Fife Light Horse—Lt.-Col. J. A. Thomson . .	13	106
1st Forfar Light Horse—Captain P. A. W. Carnegy .	3	39
1st Roxburgh (Border) Mounted Rifles—Captain Viscount Melgund	5	44
Total Cavalry Brigade . . .	21	189

	Officers.	Other ranks.
1ST DIVISION—Major-General Sir A. Alison, Bt., K.C.B.		
1st Brigade—Colonel R. R. Jones, R.A.		
1st Forfar A.V.—Lt.-Col. F. Sandeman	31	831
1st Renfrew and Dumbarton A.V.—Lt.-Col. J. Scott	17	478
1st Argyll and Bute A.V.—Lt.-Col. F. Campbell	22	446
1st Caithness A.V.—Major J. Smith	6	123
1st Aberdeen A.V.—Lt.-Col. F. Campbell	19	461
1st Inverness A.V.—Lt.-Col. D. Davidson	24	479
2nd Brigade—Colonel S. A. Madden, C.B., 42nd Regtl. Dist.		
1st Forfar R.V.—Lt.-Col. W. Morrison	21	570
2nd „ „ Lt.-Col. J. Dickson	35	753
3rd „ „ Lt.-Col. R. Lamb	14	309
1st Perth R.V.—Lt.-Col. W. Colquhoun	21	525
2nd „ „ Lt.-Col. W. Macdonald	24	642
3rd Brigade—Colonel D. Macpherson, C.B., Royal High-landers.		
1st Stirling R.V.—Lt.-Col. C. King	33	625
1st Kincardine and Aberdeenshire R.V.—Lt.-Col. W. B. Ferguson	24	521
1st Sutherland R.V.—Lt.-Col. The Duke of Sutherland	17	433
1st Argyll R.V.—Lt.-Col. J. W. Malcolm	22	465
1st Dumbarton R.V.—Lt.-Col. H. Currie	31	790
1st Clackmannan and Kinross R.V.—Lt.-Col. A. Mitchell	28	542
4th Brigade—Colonel J. T. Dalyell, 1st Regtl. Dist.		
6th Lanark R.V.—Lt.-Col. A. Morrison	24	513
7th „ „ Lt.-Col. P. Forrest	24	654
1st Aberdeen R.V.—Lt.-Col. W. Jopp	28	621
1st Inverness R.V.—Lt.-Col. E. Macpherson, C.B.	28	735
1st Linlithgow R.V.—Lt.-Col. A. Gillon	24	551
Total 1st Division	517	12,067
2ND DIVISION—Major-General W. Cameron, C.B.		
1st Brigade—Colonel C. H. Ingilby, C.B., R.A.		
1st Northumberland A.V.—Lt.-Col. A. Potter, C.B.	24	481
2nd „ „ Lt.-Col. H. G. Earl Percy	13	267
1st Berwick-on-Tweed A.V.—Captain J. Allan	5	107
1st Berwick A.V.—Captain J. Johnston	3	49
2nd „ „ Captain R. Craig	2	51
1st Haddington A.V.—Captain J. Kelly	2	56
1st Edinburgh City A.V.—Lt.-Col. Sir W. Baillie, Bt.	31	515
1st Mid-Lothian A.V.—Major T. E. O. Horne	28	410
3rd Durham A.V.—Major J. Stevenson	4	132
1st Newcastle A.V.—Lt.-Col. J. R. Young	24	277
2nd Brigade—Colonel D. J. Baillie, 72nd Regtl. Dist.		
1st Fife A.V.—Lt.-Col. J. N. M'Leod	29	734
1st Fife R.V.—Lt.-Col. Sir C. T. Lindsay, Bt.	34	856
1st Ross R.V.—Major D. Davidson	27	556
1st Elgin R.V.—Lt.-Col. W. Culbard	21	533

	Officers.	Other ranks.
3rd Brigade—Col. G. G. Walker, 3rd Batt. Royal Scots Fus.		
1st Newcastle E.V.—Lt.-Col. C. M. Palmer	18	611
7th Middlesex R.V.—Lt.-Col. H. Lumsden	18	320
1st Mid-Lothian R.V.—Lt.-Col. W. Marjoribanks .	35	723
1st Cumberland R.V.—Lt.-Col. A. G. Thomson	37	846
4th Brigade—Colonel D. Davidson, C.B., 1st Edinburgh R.V.		
1st Edinburgh R.V. (2 batts.)—Lt.-Col. B. F. Primrose .	78	1495
2nd ,, ,, Lt.-Col. J. Hope	14	506
2nd ,, ,, Cadet Corps—Lt.-Col. D. M'Gibbon .	9	208
2nd Northumberland R.V.—Lt.-Col. H. F. Swan .	15	242
1st Haddington R.V.—Lt.-Col. A. Scott .	19	316
5th Brigade—Colonel W. P. Collingwood, C.M.G., 5th Regtl. Dist.		
1st Northumberland R.V.—Lt.-Col. J. Nicholson .	18	478
2nd Mid-Lothian R.V.—Lt.-Col. Sir G. D. Clerk, Bt. .	23	772
1st Roxburgh and Selkirk R.V.—Lt.-Col. Sir G. Douglas, Bt.	25	601
1st Berwick R.V.—Lt.-Col. Hon. R. Baillie Hamilton .	17	461
1st Newcastle R.V.—Lt.-Col. J. C. Earl of Durham	14	406
Total 2nd Division . . .	587	13,009
3RD DIVISION—Major-General Sir John MacLeod, K.C.B.		
1st Brigade—Colonel G. F. Herbert, 21st Regtl. Dist.		
1st Lanark A.V.—Lt.-Col. J. Kidston .	48	970
1st Ayrshire and Galloway A.V.—Lt.-Col. M. J. Stewart .	26	600
1st Lanark E.V.—Lt.-Col. D. Matheson, C.B. .	17	389
1st Aberdeen E.V.—Captain W. Hall .	5	122
1st Dumfries R.V.—Major W. E. Malcolm .	28	597
Galloway R.V.—Lt.-Col. J. Maitland .	21	586
2nd Brigade—Colonel M. de la P. Beresford, 91st Regtl. Dist.		
1st Renfrew R.V.—Lt.-Col. D. M. Latham .	31	744
2nd ,, ,, Lt.-Col. W. Carlile .	24	599
3rd ,, ,, Lt.-Col. R. King .	22	619
1st Ayrshire R.V.—Lt.-Col. J. Dickie .	26	521
2nd ,, ,, Lt.-Col. D. D. Whigham .	24	482
3rd Brigade—Colonel S. M. Wiseman-Clarke, 26th Regtl. Dist.		
1st Lanark R.V. (2 batts.)—Lt.-Col. J. N. Smith .	51	1,300
2nd ,, ,, Lt.-Col. R. E. S. Harington-Stuart .	26	767
5th ,, ,, Lt.-Col. J. M. Forrester .	27	679
9th ,, ,, Lt.-Col. J. S. Hamilton .	17	453
4th Brigade—Colonel A. Tisdall, 75th Regtl. Dist.		
3rd Lanark R.V.—Lt.-Col. J. Merry .	40	824
4th ,, ,, Lt.-Col. H. M. Hannan .	29	641
8th ,, ,, Lt.-Col. A. C. Campbell .	35	974
10th ,, ,, Lt.-Col. F. R. Reid .	32	737
Total 3rd Division . .	529	12,604
Grand total of the Force . .	1,654	37,819

The Review may best be described in the words of Field-Marshal H.R.H. The Duke of Cambridge, who wrote in his private diary, as given in vol. ii., p. 97, of 'George, Duke of Cambridge, a Memoir of His Private Life,' by Edgar Sheppard, C.V.O., D.D. (London, 1906) :—

Edinburgh, August 25.—At 11 rode with Arthur[1] and some of the Headquarters Staff to the several rendezvous; the town crowded, and nothing could exceed the loyal feeling of the public, and we were much cheered. At 2.40 left for Holyrood to attend the Queen to the Review. All the volunteers had arrived in proper time, and were in position on the ground as I rode down the line. At 3.45 the Queen started, I riding by the carriage with Alfred[2] and Arthur,[1] whilst Marie[3] and Beatrice[4] drove with the Queen. But for the dreadful downpour of rain which lasted the whole time of the Review, or rather increased in intensity as evening advanced, the sight would have been magnificent—all the hillside up to Arthur's Seat and on both flanks being crowded with spectators, all, alas! with umbrellas up, thus spoiling the *coup d'œil*; the troops very picturesquely placed at the bottom of the hills facing Holyrood. General A. M'Donald was in chief command, with Alison, Cameron, and M'Leod as generals of division, two with four and the centre with five brigades, the small mounted corps, which were excellently mounted, being under Thesiger. After driving down the entire line from left to right, the march past commenced, and went off, under the adverse condition of the weather, as well as it was reasonable to expect. About 40,000 men were on the ground, and their physique was very fine as a rule, better, I should say, than English corps in many cases, but the English regiments seemed to be better drilled and set, though it was difficult to judge, from the terrible condition of the marching-past ground, and the terrible discomfort of the continuous and pelting rain. The crowd, too, broke in at one point, coming down the hills in

[1] H.R.H. The Duke of Connaught.
[2] H.R.H. The Duke of Edinburgh.
[3] H.R.H. The Duchess of Edinburgh.
[4] H.R.H. Princess Henry of Battenberg.

dense masses to return to the town, and with great difficulty the rear battalions and brigades got through ; but they succeeded at last, after great exertions, and all passed with fairly maintained distances. The Queen returned with great ease through a temporary garden entrance to Holyrood ; and thoroughly drenched, though during the march past I had my waterproof on, by the Queen's permission, I reached home at six o'clock, had a hot bath, feeling very cold, and some brandy in my tea, and felt none the worse. At 8 drove with Macdonald [1] and Stephens [2] to dine with the Queen, being myself in plain clothes, happily, as my coat was soaking wet. There was a large dinner-party of 40, and the Queen seemed in excellent spirits. I handed her in and sat by her. We did not leave till 11.

From the same source is extracted the following letter from the Queen to the Duke of Cambridge :—

BALMORAL CASTLE, *August* 31.

I am anxious to take an early opportunity of telling you that I wish to confer the Order of the Thistle on you in remembrance of the Great Review of Volunteers in Edinburgh.

You have, I hope, not suffered from the wet, nor any of the officers, who must also have been saturated ! As for the poor volunteers, who had to go back wet through, I hear that they have really not materially suffered beyond great discomfort.

In connection with the last sentence of this letter, it may be noted that on August 26 the commanding officer of each corps received from the Major-General commanding the North British District the following telegram : " Her Majesty desires me to express her congratulations and great satisfaction with the bearing and conduct of your men, and wishes to be informed as to their safe return." It may be imagined what were the answers to this gracious message.

---

[1] Lieutenant-General Hon. J. W. B. Macdonald, C.B., 21st Hussars, Private Secretary.

[2] Colonel A. H. Stephens, h.p., late Rifle Brigade, Aide-de-Camp.

The following General Order was published by H.R.H. the Field-Marshal Commanding-in-Chief:—

EDINBURGH CASTLE, *26th August* 1881.

After an interval of twenty-one years the Queen has, for the second time, reviewed the volunteers of Scotland, but the corps which have now assembled for Her Majesty's inspection, including the volunteers from the Border counties of England, have amounted in number to 40,000, or nearly double the force brought together in 1860.

Although unhappily marred by continuous rain, the spectacle yesterday presented to Her Majesty was an admirable sequel to the great review recently held at Windsor, and the Queen has observed with much gratification that the same soldier-like bearing, progress in discipline, and uniform good conduct which distinguished the volunteers there assembled were conspicuous in a like degree on the present occasion.

Yesterday's review and the unavoidable discomfort attending the return of the troops to their homes, necessarily without change of clothing and after many hours of fatiguing delay, furnished a trial of endurance and discipline rarely called for; and Her Majesty, while deploring the cause, has learned with satisfaction that the conduct of her volunteers has been all that could be desired.

The Field-Marshal Commanding-in-Chief has been commanded by the Queen to express to the volunteers of all ranks her entire satisfaction with the appearance of the troops assembled; and his Royal Highness, in communicating Her Majesty's commands to the Forces, desires on his own part to convey his thanks to Major-General Alastair M'Donald, on whom devolved the duty of organising the Review and commanding the Force, as well as to the Army Corps, Divisional, Brigade, and Medical Staffs, through whose exertions this successful gathering of corps scattered throughout the kingdom into one united force has been most successfully accomplished.

By command,

C. H. ELLICE, A.-G.

Well might the Scottish volunteers of 1881 be content, as they were, with such encomiums!

Strength of
the force in
1881. The strength of the Scottish volunteer force in 1881, based on returns published officially in January 1882, was as follows :—

Establishment . . .	55,690 (and 121 super-	
		numeraries.)
Efficients	47,540	
Non-efficients . . .	1,396	
Total enrolled . . .	48,936	
Present at inspection .	40,519	

Details showing the strength of each corps are given in Appendix F, and it is interesting, as showing the progress realised in nineteen years, to compare them with those given in Appendix E for the same corps in 1862.

The five years following the great Review were un-
1882 to
1886.   eventful, and there were but few changes in the organisation of the force in Scotland. In 1882 the organisation of the artillery volunteers was made similar to that of the infantry, all the Scottish artillery corps being "affiliated" to the "Scottish Division" of the Royal Artillery, whose depôt was at Leith Fort, and whose 1st Brigade (of nine batteries) was composed of regular garrison artillery, the 2nd to 6th Brigades being composed of Scottish Artillery Militia. No change was, however, made in the designation of the corps, and the artillery sub-districts as formed in 1873 and the system of command were left unchanged. This "affiliation" continued till 1891, when, in consequence of a further reorganisation of the regular garrison artillery, the Scottish corps were "affiliated" to the "Southern Division Royal Artillery," headquarters at Portsmouth, with its second "sub-depôt" at Leith Fort, but this again caused no change in the command or

designation of corps, save that instead of "Artillery Volunteer Corps" they were now designated "Volunteer Artillery Corps."

In 1886 sanction was given for the formation of "cadet battalions" in the volunteer force, but this Submarine movement found no favour in Scotland, and miners. none have ever been raised. In the same year, by Clause 176 of Army Circulars, the formation of companies of volunteer submarine miners for the defence of commercial ports was authorised. These were to consist of 3 officers, 3 serjeants, 6 corporals, 2 buglers, and 49 sappers each, and were to undergo a period of 15 days' continuous training in camp each year, for which officers were to receive 10s. and men 5s. a-day each, and the corps a capitation grant of £5 for every efficient. Twenty per cent of the officers and non-commissioned officers might attend annually a course of instruction at Chatham of from 30 to 120 days' duration. Thus a class of paid volunteers was formed more approximating to the militia system, and the arrangement worked well, for these corps quickly attained to a high state of efficiency. The companies were organised later into "divisions," of which there were three in Scotland, called the "Clyde," "Forth," and "Tay," after the estuaries in which were situated the submarine defences they were designed to man. The variations in establishment of these "divisions" are given in Part II.

In 1886 a committee, presided over by Lord Harris, had been appointed to inquire into the money grants Increase of to the volunteeer force, and, in consequence the capita- of its recommendations, the following in- tion grant in creased capitation allowances were sanctioned 1887. by the new Regulations for the volunteer force issued in October 1887 :—

£1, 15s. for every rifle volunteer who attended the prescribed number of drills and passed into the second musketry class, and for officers of rifles who had attended the prescribed number of drills ; also the same sum for " efficients " of the other arms.

10s. for every volunteer who failed to pass into the 2nd musketry class, but who had fired 60 rounds and hit the target 12 times.

£2, 10s. for each officer or serjeant holding a proficiency certificate.

£1, 10s. for each officer holding a certificate for tactics or for signalling.

2s. for each volunteer in possession of a greatcoat.

£10 per battery of artillery to pay for store-houses and gun-sheds if required, and if it could be shown that £30 a-year had been already expended for this purpose.

By these same regulations of 1887 a step of honorary rank might be given to any field officer who had served 20 years as a commissioned officer,

Honorary rank for officers. or to a captain or surgeon who had served 15 years as such, either on continuing in the service or on retirement. Those who had served 15 years might be permitted to retain their rank and wear their uniform on retirement, as were also serjeants after 10 years' service as such.

Up to 1887 the medical *personnel* of the volunteer force had been confined to the medical officers belonging to corps, but in that year it was decided

Formation of the Volunteer Medical Staff Corps, 1887. to take advantage of the services of men trained in the medical or nursing professions to form a Medical Staff Corps, with officers of its own, for the volunteers. Companies were authorised to be formed of 3 surgeons, 1 quartermaster, and 96 other ranks, with 1 serjeant instructor, and these might be combined into "divisions" of 2 or more companies, for which a surgeon - commandant, a quartermaster, and an adjutant were allowed. The qualification for efficiency was 16 ambulance and 80

F

other drills in the 1st and 2nd years of service each,
and 8 ambulance and 9 other drills in subsequent years,
with 2 extra drills in each if absent from inspection.

In the formation of this new branch of the service
Edinburgh took the lead; indeed the Edinburgh company had been formed in 1886 before actual official
sanction had been given generally. Aberdeen followed
in 1889 and Glasgow in 1894, the nucleus of the men
of all the corps being formed by the medical students
of the universities of the three cities.

The year 1888 marked the commencement of a new
era for the volunteer force, for in it, besides several

1888-90.
Formation of
volunteer
brigades.
minor changes, a beginning was made with
an organisation of the force into units higher
than battalions, and mobile batteries of artillery were added to it. For some years work had been
actively pushed on at the War Office in the elabora-
tion of a general scheme of home defence, and it had
been decided that the available forces were to be
grouped into three bodies,—a mobile regular force for
active operations, a force for the defence of the capital,
round which a series of defensive positions had been
selected, and a force for coast and local defence. To
the two latter the volunteers were assigned, and out
of the Scottish infantry, by Army Orders 315 of July
and 408 of September 1888, there were formed five
brigades,—two for the London position, the " Highland "
and the "South of Scotland," and three for coast and
local defence, the " Forth," " Tay," and " Clyde " Brigades. These were composed as follows :—

Highland—4 battalions of Seaforth and Cameron Highlanders,
　　3rd, 5th, and 6th V.B. Gordon Highlanders = 7 battalions.
South of Scotland—3 battalions of K.O. Scottish Borderers,
　　Galloway V.R.C., 2nd and 5th V.B. Royal Highlanders = 6
　　battalions.

Forth—8 battalions of Royal Scots, 4th and 6th V.B. Royal
Highlanders, and 4th and 7th V.B. Argyll and Sutherland
Highlanders = 12 battalions.

Tay—1st and 3rd V.B. Royal, and 1st, 2nd, and 4th V.B. Gordon
Highlanders = 5 battalions.

Clyde—2 battalions Royal Scots Fusiliers, 5 each of Scottish
Rifles and Highland Light Infantry, 1st, 2nd, 3rd, and 5th
Argyll and Sutherland Highlanders, and 1st Dumbarton
V.R.C. = 17 battalions.

This distribution was speedily found to be too
cumbersome, especially in the local defence brigades.
Accordingly in 1890 (by Army Orders 207 of June
and 395 of December) the five brigades were increased
to seven, and the following brigading, more in consonance with the organisation of the territorial regiments,
was adopted :—

Aberdeen—1st, 2nd, 3rd, 4th, and 5th V.B. Gordon Highlanders.

Clyde—1st and 2nd V.B. Royal Scots Fusiliers, 1st, 2nd, 3rd, and
5th V.B. Argyll and Sutherland Highlanders, and 1st Dumbarton V.R.C.

Forth—8 battalions Royal Scots.

Glasgow — 10 battalions Scottish Rifles and Highland Light
Infantry.

Highland—1st and 3rd V.B. Seaforth, 1st V.B. Cameron and
6th V.B. Gordon Highlanders, and 1st Sutherland V.R.C.

South of Scotland—Border and Galloway V.R.C., 2nd and 3rd
V.B. K.O. Scottish Borderers.

Tay—6 battalions Royal Highlanders, 4th and 7th V.B. Argyll
and Sutherland Highlanders.

In 1891 (Army Order 258 of December) the 6th and
7th V.B. Royal Scots were transferred from the Forth
to the South of Scotland Brigade, and the latter was
given the title of "Scottish Border Brigade." In this
formation the volunteer infantry remained organised
till 1902.

To the command of each brigade a colonel, either in the army or in the volunteer force, was appointed, and he was given a staff composed of a brigade-major (either a retired army or a volunteer officer), an aide-de-camp, a staff officer for supply and transport duties, and a brigade-surgeon lieutenant-colonel. The only extra Government grant for this staff was an annual allowance of £100 to the brigade-major to cover all his office and travelling expenses, and for hire of a horse.

For each brigade were organised a supply detachment, a signalling detachment, and a bearer company. The supply detachment was composed of 1 captain as supply officer, with 1 non-commissioned officer as his assistant, 4 non-commissioned officers as issuers, and 1 non-commissioned officer and 3 men as butchers, and these were borne as supernumeraries to the establishment of one or other of the battalions of the brigade. For the brigade signalling detachment, each battalion furnished 2 non-commissioned officers and 6 men, and the whole were placed under 2 officers selected from the brigade. The brigade bearer company consisted of 3 medical officers, 7 staff serjeants and serjeants, 1 bugler, 6 corporals, and 47 privates, —64 of all ranks, and might be organised either as an independent unit or as supernumeraries to the establishment of one of the battalions of the brigade.

To the command of these brigades were appointed officers selected either for their services with Scottish regiments of the regular army, or with the volunteers. Colonel E. H. D. Macpherson of Cluny, ret. pay, late 93rd Highlanders, commanded the Highland Brigade, and Colonel the Right Hon. Sir J. H. A. Macdonald, K.C.B. (Lord Kingsburgh), of the Queen's Edinburgh Brigade, the Forth Brigade throughout their existences. The command of the South of Scotland (later Scottish Border) Brigade was assumed by Colonel G. J. Viscount Melgund, who had served in the Scots Guards, and had raised and commanded the Border Mounted Rifles, and he held it till 1899, when, on his appointment as Governor - General of Canada, he was succeeded by the officer commanding the 25th Regimental District. To the command of the Tay Brigade Colonel W. D. Viscount Stormont, late Grenadier Guards and Royal Perth Militia, was nominated, and he was succeeded in 1894 by the officer commanding the 42nd Regimental District. Colonel Sir W. J. M. Cunninghame, Bart., V.C., late Scots Guards, was appointed to the command of the Clyde Brigade, but, on the latter being divided into two, he retained that of the Glasgow Brigade, which he held till 1898, when the officer commanding the 26th-71st Regimental District took it over. On the formation of the new Clyde Brigade in 1890, its command was conferred on Colonel Sir D. Matheson, K.C.B., of the 1st Lanark Engineer Volunteers, who held it until his death in 1898, when he was succeeded by the officer commanding 91st Regimental District. Lastly, till 1892 the command of the Aberdeen Brigade was exercised by the officer commanding 75th Regimental District, when it was taken over by Major-General F. S. Russell of Aden, C.M.G., late Royal Dragoons, who retained the command till 1902.

To provide a proportion of mobile artillery to work with the infantry brigades, a number of volunteer artillery corps were invited to form "position" batteries. This was by no means the first attempt at volunteer field artillery in Scotland, for the 1st Lanark had had a 4-gun field battery since 1865, and the 1st Inverness and 4th Forfar had had

Formation of position batteries, 1889.

horsed field guns since 1867 ; but these were not recognised officially, and no extra allowances were drawn for them. By Army Order 204 of May 1888 the formation of "position batteries" was sanctioned, and in the following year 12 batteries of 16-pounder R.M.L. or 40-pounder R.B.L. guns were issued to the Scottish Artillery, two each to the 1st Edinburgh, 1st Mid-Lothian, and 1st Lanark, and one each to the 1st Aberdeen, 1st Ayr, 1st Fife,. 1st Forfar, Highland, and 1st Renfrew and Dumbarton. The conditions under which these batteries were formed, as laid down in the above quoted and modified or amplified by subsequent Army Orders, were that, in return for an annual allowance of £136 for each 40-pounder battery not supplied with waggons, £112 for each 40-pounder battery supplied with waggons, and £100 for each 16-pounder battery, the battery should be fully and efficiently equipped with horses, and turn out at least four times a-year on four separate days (one of which to be the annual inspection), the length of the drill to be at least two hours, that the corps undertook to produce, when required, the full transport necessary for a battery in the field, that provision was made for the safe custody of the stores and harness, and that the whole equipment should be kept at all times clean and efficient for service. Later (in 1895) a special extra allowance of £40 once in three years was granted to each battery in aid of expenses of hire of horses for duty when attending camps, marches, or field days fully horsed.

It was at first ordered that the horses should be agricultural horses with their everyday harness, the drivers leading them on foot, but this was soon modified, and part-worn artillery harness was issued and permission given to mount the drivers. The batteries were usually composed of 4 guns and 2 ammunition waggons each, and for the manning of each the *personnel* of two garrison batteries (1891 termed "companies") was required. The establishment of these remained unchanged, but it was permitted, always keeping within the total establishment, to appoint a veterinary surgeon, a farrier serjeant, a wheeler, 2 collar-makers, and 30 drivers, the last to be enrolled from men at least 5 ft. 4 in. in height and 33 in. round the chest, and the number of gunners being correspondingly reduced. For practice purposes, 100 rounds of service ammunition were allowed annually to each battery.

To provide in some measure for the absence of mounted troops in the volunteers, in 1888 authority

Cyclist sections and mounted infantry.

was given for cyclist sections, each consisting of 1 officer, 2 non-commissioned officers, and 13-21 men (including a bugler) to be formed in each battalion,—within its establishment, however. In certain corps sections or companies of mounted infantry were permitted to be formed, and this was done in the Queen's Edinburgh, 1st Lanark, and 1st Dumbartonshire corps, but of these only the first and the last continued to exist till 1908.

The period from 1890 to 1900 was marked by a steady and gradual increase, both in numbers and

1890 to 1900.

efficiency, of the force, and but few organic changes took place. The attention of the authorities was mainly directed to improving its interior efficiency and its training, and to bring up its fighting value to a higher standard. The latter desire found its expression in the abolition, in 1891, of the term "auxiliary forces," hitherto applied to the militia, yeomanry, and volunteers, and the substitution for it of the words designating the branch of the service

to which each belonged.   Improvement in efficiency
for field service was attained by the rearmament in
1896-7 of the infantry with the Lee-Metford rifle, the
issue of special capitation grants for equipment, by
paying off the debts of corps, increase of the allowances
for camps, and greater stringency in the regulations
for efficiency in drill and musketry.   Endeavours were
made to provide for better promotion for the officers,
and to lessen their expenses by granting an outfit
allowance; and finally rewards, in the form of decorations, were instituted for the force.

Prior to 1890, but few volunteer corps had been
provided with a suitable equipment for field-service,
Grants for   the utmost beyond the belt and pouches
equipment.   being a greatcoat and perhaps a haversack.
In 1866 efforts had been made, by means of funds
raised privately, to make good this deficiency, but the
result was only partially successful; so in 1890, by
Army Order 398 of December, it was ordered that
full capitation allowances were only to be paid for
volunteers who were fully efficient, and provided with
waist-belt with frog, water-bottle and strap, haversack,
mess-tin, and greatcoat with straps for all arms, and,
in addition for light horse, artillery, and engineers,
ammunition pouches or bandoliers to carry 20[1] rounds,
and for mounted infantry or rifles, braces and pouches
or bandoliers to carry 70[1] rounds.   To provide these
articles (other than greatcoats) a sum of 12s. was
granted once for all for each volunteer enrolled on
October 31, 1890, and an annual allowance of 1s. was
sanctioned for repairs.   Greatcoats were to be issued
free of cost from Government stores for all volunteers,
or a sum of 12s. a man if the corps was already
provided with greatcoats.   On the establishment of a

---

[1] Afterwards increased to 50 rounds for engineers and 100 for rifles.

corps being increased, 30s. was to be allowed per man for infantry and 23s. for the other arms to provide these essentials.

Many corps had in the course of years amassed debts for the construction of drill-halls, headquarters, &c., **Improvement** and the records of the force are full of **of financial** accounts of bazaars, public subscriptions, and **position of** **corps.** other private attempts to clear off these burdens and place the finances of corps in a satisfactory position. One great cause of complaint was that, while current expenses had to be met, the capitation grants were only paid in arrears—*i.e.*, after they had been earned. To in a measure obviate this and to assist in the clearing off of debts, by Army Order 76 of April 1896 a special extra issue of half the capitation grant (ordinary grant and special proficiency allowances) was made for all volunteers, in addition to the grant ordinarily payable on April 1, 1896, on condition that it was used in liquidation of any debt on the public funds of corps, and that steps were taken to place the public and private finances of corps in a satisfactory condition. Thanks to this liberal grant, the financial position of the force was greatly improved.

In 1889 the issue of camp allowances was increased to 2s. a-day for not less than three or more than four **Camp** clear days in camp, in addition to the actual **allowances.** travelling allowances; but in 1890, to encourage the spending of longer periods under canvas, the allowances were raised to 2s. a-day for each day of continuous attendance up to six, together with 4s. for travelling expenses for each volunteer attending camp for not fewer than three continuous days. If in camp along with regular troops, the allowance of 2s. might be continued for thirteen days. For a brigade camp allowances might be issued for seven days, but three battalions with at least 300 men each had to be present. Brigade camps became the rule, and were productive of much improvement in the training of the force.

In 1893, and again in 1899, the conditions of efficiency for earning the full capitation grant were **Increased demands for efficiency.** made more stringent, especially in the musketry qualification, both for trained volunteers and for recruits, but into the details of these it is unnecessary to enter, as the regulations then brought into force were superseded by those introduced after the war in South Africa. In 1896 (Army Order 178), a strict physical examination before the enrolment of volunteers was introduced, and a minimum physical standard was instituted of 5 ft. 6 in. height for artillery gunners and 5 ft. 4 in. for artillery drivers, the chest measurement being 33 in. for both, and 5 ft. 3 in. height with 32 in. chest measurement for light horse, engineers, infantry, and medical staff corps.

To provide for a suitable flow of promotion among officers, in 1896 (Army Order 206 of December) it was **Limitation of periods of command.** decided that the tenure of command of a volunteer corps should be for four years only, but extensions of four years more might be permitted, subject to the condition that officers were to be retired on attaining the age of sixty, unless specially granted an extension, which might be for two years at a time, and in no case beyond the age of sixty-seven.

With a view to lessening the necessary expenses **Outfit allowance for officers.** of volunteer officers, and at the same time to counteract the shortage of officers which, in certain corps, had been seriously felt, in 1896 (Army Order 123 of June) an outfit allowance for first equipment of £20 was granted, as a personal allowance, to officers on first appointment and after obtaining a satisfactory report after a month's instruction at a school or with the regular forces. If the officer did not serve for three years as an efficient or obtain the above report within two years, the allowance was to be refunded by him.

On August 3, 1892, Her Majesty Queen Victoria instituted the Volunteer Officers' Decoration (V.D.), to **Rewards for service in the volunteers.** be conferred upon those who had served for twenty years as officers in the volunteer force, years spent in the ranks to count as half-time towards the total service; and by Army Order 85 of June 1894 the "Volunteer Long-Service Medal" was instituted as a distinction for those who had served for twenty years in the ranks of the force. Both are worn on the left breast, along with war medals, and are suspended by a green ribbon, the officers' decoration being in the form of a gilt wreath with a crown and V.R. in the centre, and the medal being of silver and bearing on the obverse the head of Queen Victoria and on the reverse the inscription: "For Long Service in the Volunteer Force."

Before quitting this period of the history of the Scottish volunteers, it must be mentioned that the **The Queen's Diamond Jubilee, 1897.** force was largely represented at the great Jubilee festivities, probably the most striking popular and patriotic demonstration of loyalty in history, on June 22, 1887, when Her Majesty Queen Victoria drove in procession from Buckingham Palace to St Paul's Cathedral. Each corps was represented by an officer and twenty other ranks, and the Scottish Volunteer representatives, massed by brigades, were formed up in the Mall, and were passed in review by Her Majesty on her return journey to Buckingham

Palace. The officers commanding detachments received for this service the Jubilee Medal.

We now come to the most important and interesting years in the history of the volunteer force, those of the

1900-02. South African War, in which it was enabled, for the first time, to show its value on active service in the field alongside of its comrades of the regular army, militia, yeomanry, and colonial forces.

The reverses suffered by our arms in South Africa in December 1899 led to a call for more troops, and Volunteer to a great outburst of national warlike en- service companies thusiasm, and accordingly, on January 2, 1900, of infantry. a special Army Order was issued calling upon the volunteers to furnish their contingent of trained men to reinforce the army in the field. For each battalion serving in South Africa a selected company was directed to be raised from its affiliated volunteer battalions and sent out to serve with it, and to be placed under the orders of its commanding officer. Each company was to be composed of 1 captain, 2 subalterns, 1 serjeant-instructor as pay serjeant, 4 serjeants, 2 buglers, 5 corporals, 99 privates, and 2 stretcher-bearers, or 116 of all ranks, and an equal number of "waiting companies" was to be raised and maintained at home. Each volunteer battalion was to form a complete section at least. To surmount the difficulties of the Volunteer Act, the men were to be enlisted for the regular army for a period of one year or the duration of the war, those taken for the "waiting companies" being transferred to the reserve until required for service. The conditions of enlistment were that the men should be not under 20 or more than 35 years of age, 1st class (volunteer) shots, efficient in the years 1898 and 1899, of good character, medically fit, and, by preference, unmarried. They were to be paid, rationed, clothed, and equipped as soldiers of the regular battalions (though continuing to wear the designation of their volunteer battalions on their shoulder-straps), and were to be granted wound pensions as for the regular army. On completion of their term of service, they were to be granted £5 as a gratuity, besides any special gratuity issued for the war. The corps to which the men belonged was to be given a sum of £9 to cover the cost of equipment of each volunteer, and the men were to be borne as supernumerary to their corps and to be considered as " efficients," the corps continuing to draw the full capitation grant for them.

Needless to say, this call was met with alacrity in Scotland, and eleven special service companies were quickly formed, one for each regiment with one battalion in the field and two for the Gordon Highlanders, both regular battalions of which were at the seat of war, the London Scottish being affiliated with the local volunteer battalions of that regiment in the formation of the service companies. The companies sailed for South Africa in February or early in March 1900.

On January 25, 1901, before the year's service of the first companies had expired, a call for companies to replace those was made and responded to, and on March 3, 1901, the formation of 8 volunteer cyclist companies was called for, one of them to be furnished by the Scottish volunteers, of a strength of 1 captain, 4 subalterns, 1 serjeant-instructor as pay serjeant, 4 serjeants, 2 buglers, 5 corporals, 101 privates, and 2 stretcher-bearers, or 120 of all ranks. The conditions of enlistment were much the same as for the infantry companies, and cycles were to be supplied to the men on arrival in South Africa. Enlistment for this company was begun on March 21, and was conducted all over Scotland; on May 2 the company was concentrated at Berwick-on-Tweed, and in the middle of that month it embarked for South Africa.

Again, on January 9, 1902, a third call for service companies of infantry was made, and also responded to, though not in all cases to the same extent as in the first and second call; but it is noteworthy that many men who had served in the service companies of the first call, and had returned home with them, rejoined the third call companies and proceeded with them to South Africa.

On January 13, 1900, by a special Army Order, the War Office called upon the Volunteer Engineers to Special ser- form special service sections from each corps vice sections of Engineer of 1 subaltern, 1 serjeant, 1 corporal, 1 2nd Volunteers. corporal, and 22 sappers, or 26 of all ranks, to proceed to South Africa under the same terms as above detailed for the infantry. Of the Scottish corps, the section of the 1st Lanark was to be attached to the 9th (Field) Company of Royal Engineers, and that of the 1st Aberdeen was to be used as a reserve for disposal on arrival in South Africa, and was actually attached to the 47th (Fortress) Company of Royal Engineers. These sections embarked early in March 1900. A second call for similar sections was made on February 5, 1901, and was responded to by both corps to the fullest extent.

By Army Order 58 of March 1900, members of the Volunteer Medical Staff Corps and Bearer Companies Special ser- were invited to enlist into the Army Medical vice of the Medical Staff Staff Corps for one year, or the duration of Corps and Bearer Com- the war, under the same conditions as in the panies. infantry, and by Army Order 59 they were also invited to volunteer for six months' duty in the home hospitals. All the Scottish units of these services furnished their proportion of men for the duties required of them.

The nature of the war did not necessitate a call upon the services of the Volunteer Garrison Artillery as such, **Other branches of the force.** but it is on record that whole corps volunteered their services, and that many men served in units of other arms during the war. The Fife and Forfar Light Horse contributed a company (the 20th) towards the formation of the Imperial Yeomanry.

It is extremely difficult to arrive at any definite statistics as to the actual numbers of volunteers who **The contributions of the Scottish volunteers towards the South African War.** took part in the South African War, as many enlisted in the regular army, or colonial forces, or militia, or Imperial Yeomanry, and were consequently struck off the rolls of their corps and lost sight of by them. The only official figures available are those furnished to the War Office, details of which are given in the separate records of each corps, of the total number of all ranks of corps of volunteer infantry who, *while members of the corps,* took part in the war, and for the Scottish battalions these total up to (including the London and Liverpool Scottish) 4367 men. From another return, issued in September 1905, it appears that 147 of the Scottish Artillery, 161 of the Engineers, and 86 of the Medical Corps served in the war. There are no statistics available of the numbers of the Light Horse, but it is believed that if the total contribution of the Scottish volunteers be put at about 5000 men who, as volunteers, served in the war, it will be well within the mark. This represents about 10 per cent of the enrolled force.

Not only did the volunteer force provide a considerable number of men for active service **Increase of establishment and strength of the force.** during the war period, but it also increased at home in numbers and efficiency. The following tables showing the establishments and strength in detail of the Scottish volunteer force on

November 1, 1899, and November 1, 1900, are of interest as showing the actual results attained :—

Date.	Arm of the service.	Estab-lish-ment, all ranks.	Efficient.		Non-ef-ficients.	Total enrolled.	Present at inspec-tion.
			Officers.	Other ranks.			
1st November 1899.	Light Horse .	304	17	163	20	200	169
	Artillery . .	11,384	451	9,387	229	10,067	8,694
	Engineers .	1,515	42	1,283	108	1,433	1,227
	Do., Submarine Miners .	588	33	519	16	568	510
	Infantry . .	43,026	1423	34,200	982	36,605	31,545
	Medical Corps	534	17	420	12	449	372
	Total .	57,351	1983	45,972	1367	49,322	42,517
1st November 1900.	Light Horse .	304	12	119	41	172	120
	Artillery . .	11,869	476	10,623	190	11,289	9,891
	Engineers .	1,811	47	1,661	71	1,779	1,534
	Do., Submarine Miners .	777	37	684	19	740	650
	Infantry . .	55,163	1546	40,546	947	43,039	36,755
	Medical Corps	560	17	444	5	466	411
	Total .	70,484	2135	54,077	1273	57,485	49,361
Increase . .		13,133	152	8105	...	8,163	6,844

The figures for the year 1901 (see Appendix I) are slightly higher than those for 1900, and represent the maximum strength to which the force attained. They are—

Establishment .	.	.	.	.	.	70,374
Efficient—						
Officers	.	.	.	.	.	2,163
Other ranks	.	.	.	.	.	55,786
Non-efficients .	.	.	.	.	.	1,510
Total enrolled .	.	.	.	.	.	59,459
Present at inspection	.	.	.	.	52,384

The decrease in strength of the Light Horse is accounted for by the large numbers transferred to the Imperial Yeomanry in South Africa and by the suspension temporarily of enrolments in the force, which in May 1901 was transferred to the establishment of the Imperial Yeomanry in Great Britain.

No considerable increase of establishment took place in the artillery, as there were already more of that arm than was required to man the coast and other defences. The existing corps were, however, recruited nearly up to their full establishment, and their sphere of utility was enlarged by the issue, in 1901, of twelve more position batteries—eight to the 1st Lanark, two to the 1st Ayrshire and Galloway, and one each to the 1st Mid-Lothian and 1st Aberdeenshire,—thus bringing the total number of position (termed in 1902 " heavy ") batteries in Scotland up to twenty-four. The company of Garrison Artillery still remained fixed at an establishment of 80 of all ranks, the *personnel* of two such companies being allowed for each heavy battery.

The establishment of the Engineers was increased by three companies of fortress engineers (1st Lanark) and three companies of submarine miners, no change being made in the establishment of companies ; and these also attained a strength of close on their maximum establishment. It was not until 1903 that the formation of a new corps of fortress engineers, the 2nd Lanark, was sanctioned.

The greatest increase took place in the establishments and strength of the infantry. In the first place, the establishments of all companies were raised from 100 of all ranks, at which they had stood since 1859, to 100 *privates* and 116 of all ranks (see Appendix G). Then many corps, as will be seen from their individual records, received permission to raise new companies. Lastly, a new battalion—the 9th of the Royal Scots—was raised in Edinburgh in

G

July 1900, in the Shetland Islands a small battalion of three companies was organised (7th V.B. Gordon Highlanders) in December 1900, and in October 1900 the Scotsmen resident in Liverpool also formed a new battalion,—the 8th of the King's (Liverpool Regiment), —which, however, is not included in the figures given above.   Authority was also given (Army Order 93 of April 1900) to form cyclist companies in all battalions with an establishment of at least 600, each company of 5 officers and 95 other ranks; while battalions of lower strength might enrol sections of 1 officer and 15 to 23 other ranks,—an extra capitation grant of £2 being allowed for each efficient cyclist. It is doubtful, however, whether these measures added to the actual *strength* of the force, though they doubtless contributed to its efficiency.   It is noteworthy that, with all these measures, the strength of enrolled infantry in 1900 almost exactly equalled the establishment sanctioned for 1899, but fell short by nearly 20 per cent of that sanctioned for 1900.

Unconnected with the war, but falling in the same period, was the reorganisation of the volunteer artillery Higher organisation. sub-districts which was carried out in 1900. Their number was increased from two to three; each was placed under a lieutenant-colonel of Royal Artillery, who commanded and inspected the corps, and these latter were detailed to sub-districts as follows :—

1st. Leith Fort—1st Edinburgh City, 1st Mid-Lothian, 1st Fife, and 1st Berwick.

2nd. Aberdeen—1st Banff, 1st Forfar, 1st Caithness, 1st Aberdeen, The Highland, and 1st Orkney.

3rd. Glasgow—1st Lanark, 1st Renfrew and Dumbarton, 1st Argyll and Bute, and 1st Ayr and Galloway.

In 1902 a reorganisation of the volunteer infantry brigades was carried out, by which their formation was brought·more into consonance with the distribution of battalions to territorial regiments. Nine brigades (an increase of two) in all were formed as follows :—

Argyll and Sutherland Brigade — Seven battalions of that regiment.

Black Watch Brigade—Six battalions of that regiment.

Gordon Brigade—Seven battalions of that regiment.

Highland Light Infantry Brigade—Five battalions of H.L.I.

1st Lothian Brigade—Q.R.V.B., and 4th and 9th V.B. Royal Scots.

2nd Lothian Brigade—5th, 6th, 7th, and 8th V.B. Royal Scots.

Scottish Border Brigade—1st and 2nd V.B. Royal Scots Fusiliers, Border V.R.C., 2nd and 3rd V.B. King's Own Scottish Borderers, Galloway V.R.C.

Scottish Rifle Brigade—Four battalions of Scottish Rifles.

Seaforth and Cameron Brigade — 1st and 3rd V.B. Seaforth Highlanders, 1st Sutherland V.R.C., 1st V.B. Cameron Highlanders.

These brigades were placed under the command of the officers commanding the regimental districts (the Scottish Border Brigade being under the officer commanding the 25th Regimental District), with the exception of the 2nd Lothian and Scottish Rifle Brigades, to which retired army officers—Colonel W. Gordon, late Durham Light Infantry, and Colonel E. C. Browne, late Royal Scots Fusiliers — were respectively appointed. The same staffs and administrative services continued to be provided for the new brigades.

In the last year of the war, by special Army Order of March 4, 1902, was brought into force the new organisation of the army into six army corps, the first three of which were mainly regular troops, the last three mainly militia, yeomanry, and volunteers. The 6th Army Corps—consisting of the 16th, 17th, and 18th Divisions, a cavalry brigade, and corps troops— was assigned to Scotland, and in it were included, in addition to units which it was proposed to raise, the following volunteer infantry battalions :—

32nd Field Army Brigade, 16th Division, Edinburgh—
    A battalion of Q.R.V.B., Royal Scots.
    4th Vol. Bn. Royal Scots.
    5th Vol. Bn. Royal Scots.
    1st Roxburgh and Selkirk V.R.C.

34th Field Army Brigade, 17th Division, Glasgow—
    1st Vol. Bn. Royal Highlanders.
    1st Vol. Bn. Highland Light Infantry.
    3rd Vol. Bn. Highland Light Infantry.
    1st Vol. Bn. Gordon Highlanders.

Portion of 31st Brigade, 16th Division—
    9th Vol. Bn. Royal Scots.

Portion of 33rd Brigade, 17th Division—
    2nd Vol. Bn. Royal Scots Fusiliers.

These battalions were not removed from the command of the brigadiers of the volunteer infantry brigades to which they belonged in ordinary times, but when called out for training were placed under the command of selected officers—usually retired officers of the regular army. The period of training each year was thirteen clear days in camp, during which each battalion had to have present not less than 50 per cent of the establishment of a battalion at war strength—*i.e.,* 15 officers and 490 men,[1] — and higher allowances were granted to them than to other corps, as will be detailed below. This organisation continued until 1906, the battalions training in brigade camps at Stobs, Aldershot, or Barry Links, after which training season it was replaced by that in force till 1908.

[1] It is of interest to note that at the training of 1906 the battalions named above had the following numbers (all ranks) in camp for the full year—viz., Q.R.V.B., 749 ; 4th Royal Scots, 655 ; 5th Royal Scots, 702 ; Border, 512 ; 1st Royal Highlanders, 723 ; 1st H.L.I., 635 ; 3rd H.L.I., 906 ; 1st Gordon Highlanders, 551 ; and 2nd Royal Scots Fusiliers, 675.

Under the pressure of the war emergency, and in view of possible complications abroad arising out of the war, it was decided to give the whole **Emergency camps in 1900.** of the volunteer force a special extra training in the summer of 1900. With this view an appeal was made to the patriotism of the force, and, by a special Army Order of March 29, sanction was given for a camp to be formed for twenty-eight days by each volunteer infantry brigade, in which particular attention was to be paid to field training and musketry—a special course of the latter, during which sixty rounds were to be fired at 300 to 600 yards, being laid down. A special capitation grant of £2, 2s. was given for each volunteer attending the camp for fourteen clear days and firing the musketry course; and in addition officers and men received pay and field allowances at army rates, and the men drew separation allowances for their families. The special capitation grant was only issued, however, if 50 per cent of the enrolled strength of the corps complied with the conditions. The same training facilities were by subsequent orders extended to position batteries of Artillery, Engineers, Army Medical Corps, and Bearer Companies—the first receiving also £5 for the hire of each horse for the twenty-eight days, and each battery being allowed fifty rounds a gun for practice purposes. These camps were numerously attended in Scotland, and in the months of June and July the country presented the appearance of a vast camp—all the habitual training-grounds being filled to overflowing.

By an Order in Council of August 11, 1902, the **Increased demands for efficiency, 1902.** conditions of efficiency for volunteers were increased in strictness, and as these remained in force till 1908 (with certain modifications, which have been taken note of in the context) they are summarised here. It is to be noted that in all arms attendance at the annual inspection became obligatory, except in cases of certified sickness or of special leave granted by the commanding officer, and that corps might be exempted from obligatory camps by special authority, or individuals in cases of certified sickness. The 1st Orkney R.G.A. Volunteers and the 7th V.B. Gordon Highlanders were not obliged to attend camp, but were liable to the extra attendances instead.

ARM.	Year of service.	Recruit's training.	Company training.	Musketry.	Camp or attachment to regular forces.
Artillery	1st	45 attendances*	...	...	Obligatory for 6 clear and consecutive days, during which gun practice and inspection in manning works and fire discipline will take place.
	Subsequent	...	15 attendances*	...	
Fortress Engineers	1st	40 attendances†	...	Optional, as per musketry regulations	Obligatory for 6 clear and consecutive days, during which inspection in field duties will take place.
	Subsequent	...	10 attendances†		
Electrical Engineers	1st, and until qualified	18 attendances		...	Obligatory, either— (a) for 8 clear and consecutive days. (b) for 2 periods of 4 clear and consecutive days. (c) for qualified men, 6 clear and consecutive days.
	Subsequent, for qualified men who attend camp for 6 days only	18 attendances		...	
	In other cases	6 attendances		...	
Infantry	1st	40 attendances†	...	Obligatory, as per musketry regulations	Obligatory, as for fortress engineers.
	Subsequent	...	10 attendances		
R.A.M.C. and Bearer Companies	1st	45 attendances†	...	...	Obligatory, as for fortress engineers.
	Subsequent	...	15 attendances†	...	

* Six additional, including gun practice, if the corps is exempted from camp.
† Six additional if the corps is exempted from attending camp.

These new conditions, especially the prescription of obligatory attendance at camp, had in many cases an adverse effect upon the strength of volunteer corps, as may be seen from the returns in Appendix I, but less so in Scotland than elsewhere, and, if mere numbers fell off, the increase in efficiency was undoubtedly great.

By a special Army Order of March 20, 1901, a new

Increase in camp allowances in 1901. scale of camp allowances was introduced, which held good till 1908, the main provisions being as follows:—

	Daily allowance (representing ordinary pay, subsistence, &c.)		For a period in days.	Additional allowance to cover time occupied in joining and quitting.	
	Officers.	Others.		Officers.	Others.
CLASS I.	*s. d*	*s. d.*		*s. d.*	*s. d.*
Brigade camps . . .					
Camps with regular forces .					
Regimental camps (for garrison artillery and engineers)	8 0	2 6	6	16 0	5 0
Heavy artillery, medical corps, and brigade bearer companies . . .	8 0	2 6	6 or 13	16 0	5 0
SPECIAL.					
Infantry battalions and brigade bearer companies specially included in the field army . . .	11 6	5 0	13	23 0	10 0
CLASS II.					
Regimental camps (infantry and brigade bearer companies and medical corps)	8 0	2 6	6	...	...
CLASS III.					
Electrical Engineers . .	10 0	5 0	1 to 8	...	...

The allowances to officers were personal ones, and were drawn by commanding officers and paid to the officers. Travelling allowances to and from camp

were paid for Class I. and Special camps at the rate
of 1d. a mile from the headquarters of units to camp
up to a limit of 8s., and for Class II. camps up to a
limit of 4s. for each volunteer.   To qualify for Class I.
allowances in brigade camp, a battalion had to have
at least 300 members in camp for the regulated period ;
if not, it only drew the allowances for a Class II. or
regimental camp.   No allowances (except in the case
of electrical engineers) were granted to any volunteer who, before attending camp, had not completed
during the year at least, if a recruit, 20 attendances
at recruit training ; if a trained man, the battery or
company training required for efficiency.

Certain minor changes were made in 1901 and 1902
in the capitation allowances, and a summary of these

*Capitation
allowances,
1902.*

allowances may well find its place here to
supplement the efficiency and camping regulations given above.

The capitation allowances were—

£1, 15s. for every efficient officer and volunteer, except in the
electrical engineers, in which the allowance was £4.   If a
volunteer was exempted from camp, but otherwise qualified, he
earned the so-called " lower rate " of £1, 5s. only.

A special efficiency grant of 17s. 6d. a-head was made on an
increase of numbers in a corps.

£2, 10s. for every " proficient " officer or serjeant of artillery,
fortress engineers, infantry, or medical corps.

£1, 10s. for each officer of artillery who passed an examination
in artillery, or for each officer of engineers or infantry who passed
an examination in tactics.

£1 for each efficient cyclist in possession of a suitable cycle, or
for each efficient mounted infantryman in possession of suitable
horse equipment.

£1, 10s. for each efficient officer and serjeant in army service
corps companies or the transport section of the medical corps
who had been instructed in transport duties.

3s. annually for each volunteer under the rank of officer

for the maintenance of greatcoat, equipment, &c., and £1, 3s. each on increase of strength, for the first equipment of these ranks.

Into travelling and other allowances it would lead too far to enter here.

After the war, the volunteer force continued its work with fresh enthusiasm born of the consciousness The force in that it had not failed when called upon to 1903-1905. supplement the regular army, and that it had secured a definite place in the defensive system of the Empire. In spite of the fervour begotten of war at the gates having passed away, and of the effect of the more stringent regulations as to camping, numbers in Scotland were well kept up, the total of enrolled volunteers in 1905 being only 2589 fewer than in 1902, while the number of non-efficients had sunk from 2186 to 1657.

The only change in organisation which need be noted in this period is the redistribution of commands, introduced by special Army Order of January 6, 1905, by which the colonels commanding regimental districts were abolished and the depôts and the volunteer infantry brigades were placed under the orders of the Brigadier-General commanding the group of regimental districts (two in Scotland, "Highland" at Perth and "Lowland" at Hamilton), the volunteer artillery remaining as before under the lieutenant - colonels commanding artillery sub-districts, and the engineers under the Chief Engineer in the Scottish command. By a later Army Order (87 of May 1905), the Brigadier-General commanding the coast defences in Scotland was made responsible for the command and training of all units of artillery, engineers, and infantry allotted to these defences.

The review of Scottish volunteers in 1905, for which

there was no counterpart in England, was the outcome
of a proposal made by Sir Robert Cranston
shortly after his appointment as Lord Provost
of Edinburgh, and also as Colonel-Commandant of the Queen's Rifle Volunteer Brigade,
in the end of 1903, and in July 1905 Sir Robert
received an intimation that His Majesty would be
pleased to hold a review of Scottish volunteers at
Edinburgh on Monday, September 18.   The message
was received with the utmost enthusiasm throughout
Scotland; town councils voted money to help in the
expenses of their volunteers attending, Glasgow
contributing £750 and Edinburgh £500 in this way,
and schools, halls, and other public buildings in
Edinburgh were placed at the disposal of the military
authorities to accommodate the troops coming from a
distance, the entertainment of the majority of whom
was undertaken by their local friends settled in the
capital.   The ground selected was the same as that
on which the reviews of 1860 and 1881 had taken
place, — Holyrood Park, — and the general arrangements were similar, a grand stand to hold 5000 people
being erected, the bulk of the spectators finding places
as before on the slopes of Arthur's Seat.   Thanks to
the development since 1881 of the railway system,
it was possible to arrange for almost all the corps,
except those from the extreme north and west, to
be brought to Edinburgh and taken home again within
the twenty - four hours, and the plan of transport
worked without a hitch.   The Army Council granted
£4000 in aid of railway expenses, — an assistance
not granted in former reviews, — which sufficed to
pay about two-thirds of the expenses of travelling,
the remainder being met by the local contributions, and the whole expenses of the journey of

The Royal Review by His Majesty, September 18, 1905.

the Liverpool Scottish (8th V.B. The King's) were borne by Lord Strathcona, the honorary colonel of the corps.

The total strength of the force reviewed was, according to the parade state, 1744 officers and 36,639 other ranks, or a total of 38,383 ; and although this total was lower than that of the 1881 review, which amounted to 39,473, yet of the latter 3739 belonged to English corps, leaving the muster of Scottish corps at 35,734, so that the review of 1905 represented a record assemblage of Scots under arms in modern days. Although the Light Horse and Mounted Rifles of former days were no longer to the fore, the force yet showed a small body of mounted men, and the Naval Volunteer Reserves, the 42 horsed field-guns, the Submarine Miners, the Motor Volunteer Corps, and the Medical Corps represented arms of the service which had no existence in 1860 or 1881, and typified the progress made in the organisation and preparation for war of the force.   It was a force, too, which had a much greater resemblance to the regular army than its predecessors of 1860 or 1881, for it was difficult to distinguish at a short distance the uniforms of the bulk of the corps from those of the regular regiments to which they were affiliated and whose glorious names they bore, and that with a right now derived from close association with them on active service.

The troops reviewed were under the command of Lieut.-General Sir Charles Tucker, K.C.B., Commanding-in-Chief in Scotland, and were organised as follows :—

	Officers.	Other ranks.	Guns.
Naval Troops—Captain R. S. D. Cumming, R.N. R.N. Volunteer Reserve, Clyde and Tay—Commander The Marquess of Graham	30	670	3
Mounted Troops—Colonel Sir W. J. G. Baird, Bart. Lothian and Berwick I.Y. — Major Wauchope, D.S.O.	7	80	...
Q.R.V.B. Mounted Infantry—Major G. G. Watson .	4	63	...
Total mounted troops . . .	11	143	...
Royal Garrison Artillery Division—Brigadier-General Lord Playfair.			
Heavy Battery Brigade—Colonel A. B. Grant, V.D., 1st Lanark R.G.A.V.			
1st Mid-Lothian R.G.A.V. ⎱ Colonel J. A. Dalmahoy, ⎰	12	98	12
1st Forfar R.G.A.V. ⎰ V.D. ⎱	4	36	4
1st Lanark R. G. A. V. — Lieut.-Col. J. Taylor, V.D.	19	151	20
1st R.G.A. Brigade—Colonel T. W. Powles, R.G.A. 1st Edinburgh City R.G.A.V. — Lieut.-Col. E. Campbell	16	460	6
1st Mid-Lothian R.G.A.V. ⎱ Major C. L. Blaikie, ⎰	8	227	...
1st Berwick R.G.A.V. ⎰ V.D., 1st Mid- ⎱	2	34	...
1st Fife R.G.A.V. ⎰ Lothian R.G.A.V. ⎱	10	242	...
1st Fife R. G. A. V. — Colonel J. W. Johnston, V.D.	16	458	...
2nd R.G.A. Brigade—Colonel A. B. Purvis, R.G.A.			
1st Forfar R.G.A.V. ⎱ Colonel T. G. Luis, V.D., ⎰	25	429	...
1st Caithness R.G.A.V. ⎰ 1st Forfar R.G.A.V. ⎱	17	210	...
1st Aberdeen R.G.A.V. ⎱ Colonel G. Milne, V.D., ⎰	27	423	...
1st Banff R.G.A.V. ⎰ 1st Aberdeeen R.G.A.V. ⎱	17	257	...
The Highland R.G.A.V. ⎱ Colonel J. E. Baillie, ⎰	34	427	...
1st Orkney R.G.A.V. ⎰ Highland R.G.A.V. ⎱	15	165	...
3rd R.G.A. Brigade— Colonel A. Powell, D.S.O., R.G.A.			
1st Renfrew and Dum- ⎱ Lieut.-Col. C. C. Scott, ⎰ barton R.G.A.V. ⎰ V.D., 1st Renfrew ⎱	15	340	...
1st Argyll and Bute ⎱ and Dumbarton ⎰ R.G.A.V. ⎰ R.G.A.V. ⎱	32	549	...
1st Lanark R.G.A.V.—Lieut.-Col. A. McI. Shaw, V.D.	22	750	...
1st Ayr and Galloway R.G.A.V.—Lieut.-Col. T. R. Stuart	23	581	...
Total R.G.A. Division . . .	314	5837	42

	Officers.	Other ranks.	Guns.
Royal Engineer Brigade—Colonel R. L. Hippisley, C.B., R.E.			
1st Lanark R.E.V.—Colonel T. S. Park, V.D. .	22	421	...
1st Aberdeen R.E.V.—Colonel W. S. Gill, V.D. .	12	288	...
2nd Lanark R.E.V.—Lieut.-Col. A. Pearson .	35	805	...
Clyde Division Submarine Miners—Colonel D. F. D. Neill	10	175	...
Tay Division Submarine Miners—Lieut.-Col. F. S. Stephen	5	124	...
Forth Division Submarine Miners — Lieut.-Col. H. M. Cadell, V.D.	9	76	...
Total R.E. Brigade . . .	93	1889	...
1ST INFANTRY DIVISION—Brigadier-General A. Broadwood.			
1st *Lothian Brigade*—Colonel Sir R. Cranston, Kt., V.D.			
1st Bn. Q.R.V.B. Royal Scots — Colonel A. T. Hunter, V.D.	32	603	...
2nd Bn. Q.R.V.B. Royal Scots — Lieut.-Col. R. Clark, V.D.	32	633	...
3rd Bn. Q.R.V.B. Royal Scots—Colonel J. Gibb, V.D.	31	663	...
4th V.B. Royal Scots—Lieut.-Col. G. M'Crae, V.D.	27	822	...
9th V.B. (Highlanders) Royal Scots—Lieut.-Col. J. Clark	23	517	...
Bearer Company—Captain A. Macdonald . .	3	53	...
2nd *Lothian Brigade*—Brigadier-General W. Gordon.			
5th V.B. Royal Scots—Colonel Sir J. M. Clark, Bart., V.D.	20	1000	...
6th V.B. Royal Scots—Lieut.-Col. T. Rough, V.D.	18	515	...
7th " " Colonel R. M. Main, V.D. .	16	374	...
8th " " Lieut.-Col. C. Chalmers, V.D.	20	574	...
8th (Scottish) V.B. The King's (Liverpool Regiment) —Lieut.-Col. A. L. Macfie	20	480	...
Scottish Border Brigade—Colonel J. H. Campbell.			
1st V.B. Royal Scots Fusiliers—Lieut.-Col. J. Gow	20	610	...
2nd " " " Lieut.-Col. J. E. Shaw	22	501	...
1st Roxburgh and Selkirk (Border) V.R.C.—Colonel Sir R. J. Waldie-Griffith, Bart., V.D. . .	35	711	...
2nd V.B. K.O. Scottish Borderers—Colonel C. Hope	21	363	...
3rd " " " Colonel R. F. Dudgeon, V.D.	21	407	...
Galloway V.R.C.—Colonel J. M. Kennedy, V.D. .	14	635	...
Bearer Company—Surgeon-Captain G. R. Livingston	1	35	...
Total 1st Infantry Division . . .	376	9496	...

	Officers.	Other ranks.	Guns.
2ND INFANTRY DIVISION—Colonel J. W. Hughes-Hallett, C.B., D.S.O.			
Scottish Rifle Brigade — Brigadier - General E. C. Browne.			
1st Lanark V.R.C.—Colonel J. Macfarlane, V.D. .	49	833	...
2nd V.B. Scottish Rifles—Colonel T. B. Ralston, V.D.	32	800	...
3rd Lanark V.R.C.—Colonel J. B. Wilson, V.D. .	40	610	...
4th V.B. Scottish Rifles—Colonel F. J. Smith, V.D.	30	620	...
Highland Light Infantry Brigade—Colonel J. Stevenson, C.B., A.D.C.			
1st V.B. H.L.I.—Colonel R. C. Mackenzie, V.D. .	28	750	...
2nd ıı ıı Colonel J. D. Young, V.D. . .	25	500	...
3rd ıı ıı Colonel D. R. Graham, V.D. .	30	700	...
9th Lanark V.R.C.—Major J. Lancaster, V.D. .	14	344	...
5th (Glasgow Highland) V.B. H.L.I.—Lieut.-Col. P. W. Hendry, V.D.	30	770	...
Bearer Company—Surgeon-Major A. D. Moffat .	2	48	...
Argyll and Sutherland Brigade—Colonel J. M. Hunt.			
1st V.B. A. and S. Highlanders—Colonel W. U. Park, V.D.	28	622	...
2nd V.B. A. and S. Highlanders — Colonel J. Paton, V.D.	27	753	...
3rd V.B. A. and S. Highlanders — Lieut. - Col. J. M. Campbell	30	570	...
4th V.B. A. and S. Highlanders—Colonel R. Morton, V.D.	22	624	...
5th V.B. A. and S. Highlanders—Lieut.-Col. E. P. Campbell	27	583	...
1st Dumbarton V.R.C.—Lieut.-Col. H. Brock .	50	1,271	...
7th V.B. A. and S. Highlanders—Lieut.-Col. R. Haig	23	477	...
Bearer Company—Captain J. A. Boyd . . .	3	47	...
Total 2nd Infantry Division . . .	490	10,922	...
3RD INFANTRY DIVISION—Brigadier-General Forbes Macbean, C.B.			
Black Watch Brigade—Colonel E. G. Grogan, C.B.			
1st V.B. Black Watch—Lieut.-Col. H. Hill, V.D. .	19	581	...
2nd ıı ıı Colonel J. Davidson, V.D.	23	439	...
3rd ıı ıı Lieut. - Col. C. Batchelor, V.D.	20	350	...
4th V.B. Black Watch—Colonel Sir R. D. Moncrieffe, Bart., V.D.	24	434	...
5th V.B. Black Watch—Colonel Marquis of Breadalbane, K.G., A.D.C.	25	478	...
6th V.B. Black Watch—Colonel Sir R. W. Anstruther, Bart.	47	769	...
Bearer Company—Surgeon-Major W. Kinnear .	2	48	...

	Officers.	Other ranks.	Guns.
Gordon Brigade—Brigadier-General P. D. Trotter.			
1st V.B. Gordon Highlanders—Lieut.-Col. L. Mackinnon, V.D.	32	550	...
3rd V.B. Gordon Highlanders—Colonel R. Robertson, V.D.	20	295	...
4th V.B. Gordon Highlanders—Lieut.-Col. W. A. Mellis, V.D.	27	328	...
5th V.B. Gordon Highlanders—Lieut.-Col. A. H. Farquharson	21	308	...
6th V.B. Gordon Highlanders — Colonel J. G. Fleming, V.D.	16	271	...
7th V.B. Gordon Highlanders—Major J. C. C. Broun	5	75	...
London Scottish (7th Middlesex) V.R.C.—Colonel J. W. Greig, V.D.	20	240	...
Seaforth and Cameron Brigade—Colonel N. M'Leod.			
1st V.B. Seaforth Highlanders—Colonel A. R. B. Warrand	22	329	...
1st Sutherland V.R.C.—Colonel J. Morrison, V.D.	27	497	...
3rd V.B. Seaforth Highlanders — Colonel R. Urquhart, V.D.	24	446	...
1st V.B. Cameron Highlanders—Colonel D. Shaw, V.D.	19	453	...
Bearer Company—Captain J. Macdonald	3	50	...
Total 3rd Infantry Division	396	6941	...
Royal Army Medical Corps Volunteers—Lieut.-Col. Croly, R.A.M.C.			
Aberdeen Companies R.A.M.C.V. — Captain F. Kelly	9	157	...
Glasgow Companies R.A.M.C.V.—Lieut.-Col. G. T. Beatson, V.D.	21	429	...
6 War Ambulance Dogs—Major E. J. Richardson	...	...	...
Detachment Motor Volunteer Corps (10 cars)—Captain G. Macmillan.	...	10	...
Keeping Ground { Detachment 17th Lancers	1	40	...
Army Service Corps	1	40	...
Lothians and Berwick I.Y.	2	65	...
Grand total of force	1744	36,639	45
All ranks		38,383	
Horses		691	
Guns		45	
Motor cars		10	

The ground was kept by the 2nd Highland Light Infantry, and the music for the march past was supplied by the bands and pipers of the 2nd Scottish

Rifles, 1st Black Watch, and 2nd Highland Light Infantry. As a guard of honour in rear of the saluting base was drawn up the Royal Bodyguard of Scottish Archers, under the command of the Captain-General, the Duke of Buccleuch, K.T.; and in front of the grand stand were ranged 21 officers and 101 men, veterans of the Crimea and Indian Mutiny of Scottish regular regiments, and 1830 ex-volunteers, many of whom wore their old uniforms, who had taken part in the Reviews of 1860 and 1881, including 29 of the Loch Katrine Bodyguard of 1859. The weather was all that could be desired, cool and clear with occasional sunshine, very different from that of the 1881 review.

His Majesty, who had arrived in Edinburgh from Rufford Abbey in the morning, left Holyrood Palace on horseback at 11 o'clock, accompanied by Field Marshal H.R.H. the Duke of Connaught, and attended by the Marquis of Linlithgow, Secretary for Scotland, the Marquis of Tullibardine, and his Scottish aides-de-camp of the militia and volunteer forces, Colonel the Earl of Wemyss (London Scottish V.R.C.), Colonel Sir Reginald Ogilvy (Forfar and Kincardine R.G.A. Militia), Colonel the Earl of Kintore (3rd Gordon Highlanders), and Colonel the Marquis of Breadalbane (5th V.B. the Black Watch), a royal salute being fired on His Majesty entering the parade-ground by the 1st City of Edinburgh Artillery from their 4·7 inch guns. Their Royal Highnesses the Duchess and Princess Patricia of Connaught were seated in the grand stand. After inspecting the troops, who were formed up in line of quarter-columns round the King's Park and along the base of Salisbury Crags, and the veterans, His Majesty took post at the saluting base, and the march past began, the troops quitting the ground and proceeding straight to their temporary quarters after passing the saluting base, except the 1st Lothian Brigade, which lined the streets along which His Majesty subsequently passed from Holyrood to Waverley Station.   The march past was carried out with great precision, and the effect produced on the spectators may best be described in the words of His Majesty to some of the veterans: "Delighted to see you all; a grand show, wasn't it?"

At the luncheon in the City Chambers after the Review, H.R.H. the Duke of Connaught conveyed to the Lord Provost the following verbal message from the King: "Please tell the Lord Provost and Sir Charles Tucker how pleased I am with the splendid arrangements they have made to-day. I would have travelled double the distance to see the very fine sight that I have seen this day. I am thoroughly proud of the Scottish volunteers. I know they came here under great difficulties to themselves, many of them travelling all night, and yet there they were on parade, making a splendid show, and proving what great and true patriotism there is in Scotland."

In the evening the following telegram was received by Lieutenant-General Sir Charles Tucker from Colonel Davidson, Equerry-in-waiting to His Majesty :—

GLENQUOICH, INVERGARRY, 8.35 P.M.

The King commands me to convey to you, and to all ranks under your command, His Majesty's great satisfaction with the fine appearance of the Scottish volunteer force reviewed by him to-day.

The organisation by which so large a number of troops was conveyed from so many different quarters reflects the greatest credit on all concerned, and His Majesty fully recognises the patriotic spirit which has inspired the units of the force to come long distances, in many cases at great personal inconvenience, in order to be present at the Review.

His Majesty was greatly pleased with the physique and appear-

H

ance of the troops, and commands you to convey to all ranks his approval of their steadiness on parade and in marching past.

His Majesty highly appreciates the fine spirit which has resulted in the assembly of the magnificent force reviewed by him to-day, and heartily congratulates you on the success of the Review, to which your untiring energy has so largely contributed.

The Lord Provost of Edinburgh also received from the same source the following telegram :—

I am commanded by the King to convey to your lordship the expression of His Majesty's entire approval of the admirable arrangements (in which you have had so large a share) made in connection with the Review of the Scottish Volunteer Force held by the King. His Majesty wishes you to convey to the citizens of Edinburgh his appreciation of the loyalty and warmth of the reception accorded to him during his visit, which will always be a memorable one on account of the large number of Scottish volunteers assembled for inspection. His Majesty hopes that the extraordinarily fine appearance of the Scottish volunteers it was his pleasure to review to-day will act as an incentive to others to join a force whose patriotism is so greatly to be commended.—I remain, dear Lord Provost, yours sincerely,

ARTHUR DAVIDSON.

Little now remains to be chronicled of the last three years of the existence of the Scottish volunteer force as such, and in them only three changes of any importance were made.

1906-1908.

The first was the reorganisation of the infantry brigades, which, however, only affected the Scottish volunteers in so far as the Argyll and Sutherland Brigade, which was of unwieldy size, was split up into two from October 1, 1906, the "Argyll and Sutherland" comprising the 3rd, 4th, and 7th Volunteer Battalions, and the "Clyde" comprising the 1st, 2nd, and 5th Volunteer Battalions and the 1st Dumbarton V.R.C. As brigadiers were appointed colonels or

lieutenant-colonels from the retired or half-pay lists of
the regular forces or of the auxiliary forces, the latter
being given the temporary rank of colonel in the army.
These officers were to command the brigades in peace
or war, be responsible for their training, inspect the
battalions, and be the channel of communication between
the latter and the brigadiers-general commanding the
groups of regimental districts. Brigade-majors were to
be chosen either from retired regular or from qualified
volunteer officers, and both they and the officers commanding brigades were to hold their appointments for
five years, subject to an age limit of fifty-five for the
former and sixty-five for the latter. To the command
of brigades were appointed—

Argyll and Sutherland,	Colonel A. C. Duff, half-pay, June 1, 1906.
Black Watch .	Colonel E. C. Grogan, C.B., retired pay.
Clyde . . .	Colonel A. B. Purvis, half-pay, R.A., June 7, 1906. Colonel A. M. Carthew-Yorstoun, C.B., half-pay, June 23, 1907.
Gordons . .	Colonel J. W. Hughes-Hallett, C.V.O., C.B., D.S.O., retired pay, Aug. 6, 1906.
Highland Light Infantry . .	Colonel (temp. colonel in army) R. C. Mackenzie, V.D., late Lieut.-Colonel 1st V.B., H.L.I., June 8, 1906.
1st Lothian . .	Colonel (temp. colonel in army) Sir R. Cranston, Kt., K.C.V.O., late Lieut.-Colonel Queen's R.V.B., R.S., June 1, 1906.
2nd Lothian . .	Colonel A. C. Becher, retired pay, March 30, 1907.
Scottish Borderers .	Colonel P. D. Trotter, retired pay, June 1, 1906.
Scottish Rifles .	Colonel E. C. Browne, retired pay, June 1, 1906.
Seaforth and Cameron	Colonel H. H. L. Malcolm, D.S.O., half-pay, June 1, 1906.

The second change was the abolition of submarine
mine defences in all ports in 1907. The services of the

Submarine Mining Volunteers were consequently not required to anything like the same extent as before, and accordingly the Forth and Clyde Divisions were transformed into divisions of Electrical Engineers, and their numbers reduced to those necessary for working the electric lights in connection with the gun defences, and the Tay Division was disbanded.

Lastly, the rearmament of the volunteer heavy batteries is to be noticed. In 1907 the 15-pounder B.L. gun, transformed into a quick-firer, was issued to the 1st Lanarkshire R.G.A.V., in place of its 16-pounder R.M.L. guns, and the same course was ordered to be pursued with the other batteries armed with guns of the latter nature as transformed B.L.Q.F. guns became available.

The general development of the force, its changes in organisation, equipment, training, and uniform, its reviews by the Sovereign and the compliments paid to it, its progress in efficiency and military spirit, and its services in the field, have now been traced through the forty-eight years of its existence, and it now remains only to summarise its strength and composition at the time when it ceased to exist as the "Volunteer Force" and took its place as the nucleus of the more highly-developed "Territorial Army."[1]

The Scottish Volunteer Force in 1907.

The establishments of the force for the year ending March 31, 1908, are given in detail in Appendix G, and may be summarised as follows :—

The Royal Garrison Artillery Volunteers consisted of 14 corps (of which one was a one-company corps attached to a larger one), comprising altogether 24 heavy batteries and $99\frac{1}{2}$ garrison companies, with a total establishment of 509 volunteer officers and 11,329 volun-

---

[1] See Appendix J for the units of the Territorial Army, into which those of the Volunteer Force were transformed.

teers of other ranks, and a permanent staff of 14 officers and 97 other ranks of the regular forces.

The Royal Engineer Volunteers consisted of 3 corps of Fortress Engineers, with in all 27 companies, and 2 divisions (companies) of Electrical Engineers, with a total establishment of 101 volunteer officers and 2747 volunteers of other ranks, and a permanent staff of 3 officers and 14 other ranks of the regular forces.

The Volunteer Infantry (including the two Scottish battalions in London and Liverpool) numbered in all 50 battalions, of from 16 companies (1st Lanarkshire) down to 3 companies (7th V.B. Gordon Highlanders), the total being 476 companies, or an average of 9 to 10 per battalion, with an establishment of 1665 volunteer officers and 53,813 volunteers of other ranks, and a permanent staff of 49 officers and 298 other ranks of the regular forces. These included 1 company and 3 sections of mounted infantry, and 19 companies and 6 sections of cyclists.

The Royal Army Medical Corps Volunteers consisted of 8 companies and transport sections for 8 field hospitals and 3 bearer companies, and there were 5 volunteer brigade bearer companies, with a total establishment of 75 volunteer officers and 1321 volunteers of other ranks, and permanent staff of 1 officer and 11 other ranks of the regular forces.

Army Service Corps companies had been formed for seven out of the ten volunteer infantry brigades, but their *personnel* was borne as supernumerary to the establishment of one or more battalions of the brigade, and belonged to these battalions.

The return of strength and efficiency of the Scottish Volunteer Force on November 1, 1907, is given in detail in Appendix H, and its summary is as follows :—

Arms.	Establishment.	Efficients.		Non-efficients.		Total, all ranks.	Present at inspection, all ranks.	Mounted infantry included in foregoing.	Cyclists included in foregoing.
		Officers.	N.C.O. and men.	Officers.	N.C.O. and men.				
Artillery	11,951	427	9,069	11	294	9,801	4,857	...	...
Engineers	2,865	105	2,163	8	141	2,417	1,767	...	...
Infantry:— Highland Grouped Regimental Districts	26,289	753	16,816	26	351	17,946	10,276	128	693
Lowland Grouped Regimental Districts	27,672	757	19,047	29	425	20,258	12,049	75	900
Total Infantry	53,961	1510	35,863	55	776	38,204	22,325	203	1593
Royal Army Medical Corps	1,083	47	940	2	8	997	835	...	...
Volunteer Infantry Brigade Bearer Companies	585	10	290	1	9	310	237	...	...
Total, all arms	70,445	2099	48,325	77	1228	51,729	30,021	203	1593

II.

RECORDS OF THE SEVERAL CORPS WHICH HAVE CONSTITUTED THE SCOTTISH VOLUNTEER FORCE, 1859–1908.

NOTES.

THE "date of formation" of a corps is given throughout as that on which its first officers were commissioned, as shown in the monthly 'Army List.' This by no means corresponds with the date of acceptance of the services of the corps, but it is only in few cases that the latter can now be ascertained, and when this is known it is so stated.

In the lists of commanding-officers, all steps of honorary rank, orders, and decorations obtained by them during their period of command are shown.

The numbers of men given as having served in South Africa are those of officers and other ranks who, *while members of the corps*, took part in the war of 1899-1902.

LIGHT HORSE.

1st FIFE LIGHT HORSE.

(PLATE I.)

THE circumstances under which this corps was raised have been already detailed in Part I., on page 32.

It was originally formed as the 1st Fife Mounted

Rifles, with headquarters at Cupar, and four troops (companies), 1st at Cupar, 2nd at St Andrews, 3rd at Kirkcaldy, and 4th at Dunfermline, the date of acceptance of its services being June 7, 1860, and that of the first commissions of the officers July 11, 1860. The original uniform was scarlet tunics with blue piping, blue pantaloons with scarlet piping, Napoleon boots, black leather helmets with silver ornaments and spike, blue forage caps with scarlet band and top, and brown belts. White plumes for full dress were added to the helmets in 1864, and in 1879 silver-lace belts for full dress were adopted by the officers. The original armament was cavalry swords and short Enfield rifles, and the men rode their own horses and used hunting-saddles.

In 1870 the designation of the corps was changed to 1st Fife Light Horse, mainly on account of the difficulty of keeping up the minimum establishment of four companies of "mounted rifles," which was fixed at 172, while for "light horse" it was only 144. At the same time Westley-Richard carbines were substituted for the short Enfield rifles, which were very inconvenient to carry on horseback.

In 1876 the 1st Forfar Light Horse, one troop strong, was attached to the regiment for training and administration, and in 1883 a fifth troop was raised with headquarters at Perth.

On the formation of the Imperial Yeomanry for service in South Africa in January 1900, the Fife and Forfar Light Horse formed the nucleus of the 20th company, which was embodied in the 6th (Scottish) battalion, two of the officers of the Fife Light Horse, Lieutenants J. Gilmour and J. Simpson, proceeding to South Africa with the company.

In May 1901 the corps was amalgamated with the

1st Forfar Light Horse and transferred to the Imperial Yeomanry establishment under the title of "Fifeshire and Forfarshire Imperial Yeomanry," in which "A" squadron represented the old 1st, 2nd, and 3rd troops, "B" the 4th and 5th, and "C" the 1st Forfar Light Horse.

The commanding officers have been—

Major J. A. Earl of Rosslyn (Lieut.-General and Colonel 7th Hussars), July 11, 1860.

Lieut.-Colonel John Anstruther Thomson (hon. col.), late Captain 9th Light Dragoons, August 31, 1866.

Lieut.-Colonel Sir John Gilmour, Bart., V.D., October 30, 1895, till transfer to Imperial Yeomanry.

1st FORFAR LIGHT HORSE.

(Plate I.)

THE 1st Forfar Light Horse, one troop strong, was raised, with headquarters at Dundee, on July 5, 1876. Its uniform was the same as that of the 1st Fife Light Horse, to which it was attached for drill and administration from the date of its formation, and with which it was finally amalgamated on the transfer of both to the Imperial Yeomanry in May 1901.

Its commanding officer throughout its independent existence was—

Captain Patrick A. W. Carnegy (hon. major), V.D., late Captain 15th Hussars, July 5, 1876.

MOUNTED RIFLES.

1st ELGIN MOUNTED RIFLES.

THE 1st Elgin Mounted Rifles was formed, with the establishment of a company, at Elgin on January 9, 1869, and was attached to the 1st Administrative Battalion Elgin R.V.

The uniform was blue hussar tunics with white lace and red collars and cuffs, Bedford cord breeches with riding-boots, and busby with blue bag, and the armament was swords and short Snider-Enfield rifles.

The commanding officer was—

Captain J. Grant Peterkin, January 9, 1869.

The corps never attained its minimum establishment, and was only once inspected, when it mustered 17 men. It was disbanded on November 3, 1871.

1st ROXBURGH (THE BORDER) MOUNTED RIFLES.

(PLATE I.)

THIS corps was raised, with an establishment of one company, and headquarters at St Boswells, under the title of 1st Roxburgh Mounted Rifles, on February

13, 1872, and was attached to the 1st Roxburgh and Selkirk Administrative Battalion R.V. Its uniform was slate-grey, without facings, with five rows of broad black braid on the breast of the tunic, black piping and Austrian knot, and a double black stripe on the pantaloons, butcher boots, busbies with scarlet bag and black and white plume, and brown "Sam Browne" belts. The armament was a cavalry sword and short Snider-Enfield rifle, the latter carried in a "Namaqua" bucket on the off wallet, the muzzle under the man's right arm. The saddlery consisted of hunting-bridles and breastplates with head-collar and white head-rope, and hunting-saddles with white girths, the cloak being carried rolled in front of the saddle. The clothing cost £10, 4s. 6d., the belts £1, 10s., the head-collar and rope, Namaqua bucket, and cloak-straps £1, 1s., and spurs, &c., £1, 1s. 3d.,—in all, £13, 16s. 9d., which each man had to pay on joining, besides engaging to mount himself on a suitable horse. The corps assembled annually for eight days' training, as did the yeomanry of those days.

On January 22, 1880, the corps was granted the title of "The Border Mounted Rifles," and in that year grey helmets with silver star and the motto, "Wha daur meddle wi' me?" replaced the busbies, and silver-lace edging was added to the piping on the collars, shoulder-straps, and the Austrian knot. In the following year the Martini-Henry rifles replaced the short Snider-Enfield in the armament.

The corps acquired much fame in shooting competitions for its special arm, and in 1884 its teams were first and fifth, and in 1885 first and second, for the Lloyd-Lindsay competition at Wimbledon.

In 1886 the corps attained its highest strength, 57 members, and was then divided into two troops, "A" at

Hawick and "B" at Kelso, headquarters being moved to Hawick.

In 1888 bandoliers for 50 rounds were adopted in addition to the pouch for 20 rounds in front and that for 40 rounds in rear hitherto worn, and the sword was placed on the saddle. In the following year the corps was attached to the "South of Scotland" Volunteer Infantry Brigade, of which Viscount Melgund, who had till then commanded the corps, was appointed Brigadier, and it was supplied with four 1-horse carts as transport.

Unfortunately, agricultural depression had its effect on the corps, and the numbers gradually fell off. In 1891 the corps did not train, and on March 31, 1892, it was disbanded, after an honourable existence of twenty years.

The commanding officers were—

Captain G. J. Viscount Melgund (now the Earl of Minto), late Ensign and Lieutenant, Scots Guards, February 13, 1872.
Captain J. C. Earl of Dalkeith, November 27, 1889, till March 31, 1892.

1st DUMFRIES MOUNTED RIFLES.

(Plate I.)

The 1st Dumfries Mounted Rifles, with an establishment of one company and headquarters at Lockerbie, was formed on November 25, 1874, and was attached to the 1st Administrative Battalion Dumfries R.V. It was disbanded in 1880, numbers having fallen off on account of agricultural depression.

Its uniform was scarlet without facings, blue pantaloons with scarlet stripes, butcher boots, black leather helmets with silver ornaments, brown "Sam Browne" belts, and scarlet forage-caps with white (silver for officers) bands.   The armament, equipment, and saddlery were similar to those of the Border Mounted Rifles described above.

Its commanding officer throughout its existence was—

Captain Arthur Johnstone Douglas, late Ensign 42nd Foot, November 25, 1874.

ROYAL GARRISON ARTILLERY VOLUNTEERS.

NOTES COMMON TO ALL THE CORPS.

IN the following records of individual corps they have been placed in the order of their precedence in the whole force of Volunteer Garrison Artillery, which numbered sixty-eight corps, in the United Kingdom, namely :—

9. 1st Edinburgh (City).
11. 1st Mid-Lothian.
13. 1st Banff.
17. 1st Forfarshire.
30. 1st Renfrew and Dumbarton.
32. 1st Fife.
35. 1st Lanarkshire.
38. 1st Ayr and Galloway.
39. 1st Argyll and Bute.
43. 1st Caithness.
45. 1st Aberdeenshire.
46. 1st Berwickshire.
47. The Highland.
54. 1st Orkney.

The following changes of designation took place, and are common to all corps, so no mention of them has been made in the corps records:—

In 1882 all the Scottish artillery volunteer corps were "affiliated" to the "Scottish Division, Royal Artillery," but this involved no change in their titles.

By Army Order 166 of August 1891 the corps were termed "Volunteer Artillery Corps," and affiliated to the "Southern Division, Royal Artillery," but were not required to add the latter designation to their county titles. This affiliation to divisions was discontinued in 1901.

By Army Order 27 of February 1902 the corps were designated, *e.g.*, "1st Edinburgh (City) Royal Garrison Artillery (Volunteers)."

The "companies" of volunteer artillery first raised were in 1860 designated "batteries," and this title they continued to bear till 1891, when by Army Order 234 of November they were termed "companies," in accordance with the nomenclature adopted for the regular garrison artillery. When "position," afterwards called "heavy," batteries were formed in 1889, the *personnel* of two "garrison batteries" had to be combined to man each. This led to confusion, so in 1892 these position batteries were made independent units, and by Army Order 218 of November 1892 a numbering was ordered by which, in corps composed entirely of position batteries or garrison companies, these were numbered from 1 onwards, and in corps composed partly of position batteries and partly of garrison companies the former were numbered first—*e.g.*, 1st, 2nd, and 3rd,—the garrison companies being numbered in sequence, 4th, 5th, &c. Thus in the corps records the words "battery" and "company" are used before and after 1892 to designate the same unit, "position" or "heavy" battery being specially used to designate units of that nature. The "position" batteries were designated "heavy" by Army Order 120 of May 1902.

The uniform of the artillery volunteers has from the first been closely modelled on that of the Royal Artillery, therefore it has only been considered necessary to mention in the corps records the original uniforms of 1859-60, which varied considerably according to the fancy of individual corps, but always were dark blue. It was only in 1878 that the scarlet Austrian knot and cap-band were ordered to be worn as the badges to distinguish the volunteer from the militia and regular artillery, and silver lace for officers and white metal buttons for all ranks were from the first worn. As a head-dress, the busby of the Royal Artillery was universally adopted in the "early sixties," and this was replaced in 1880-81 by the helmet, at first worn with a spike and afterwards with a ball. At the "Coming of Age Review" in 1881 the 1st Edinburgh (City) and the 1st Renfrew and Dumbarton Artillery were the only corps which still wore the busby. The latter gave it up shortly afterwards, and the former was the only corps in Scotland which, till 1908, wore the head-dress it assumed on its first formation.

1st EDINBURGH (CITY) ROYAL GARRISON ARTILLERY (VOLUNTEERS).

(PLATE II.)

ORDER OF PRECEDENCE, 9.

Honorary Colonel—Sir L. M'IVER, Bt., December 2, 1896.

Headquarters—28 YORK PLACE, EDINBURGH.

THE 1st Edinburgh City Artillery Volunteers was formed as a brigade on September 13, 1860, from nine batteries raised in the city of Edinburgh : the 1st on 4th November 1859 ; 2nd on 10th, and 3rd on 28th January ; 4th on 6th, and 5th on 24th March ; 6th on 23rd May ; 7th on 6th June ; 8th on 13th August ; and 9th on 16th October 1860.   The 1st Battery was formed mainly of artists, its first commander being Joseph (later Sir Joseph) Noel Paton, and its first lieutenant John Faed.   The men of the 2nd and 4th Batteries were artisans ; but those of the others equipped themselves entirely, and the members of all paid subscriptions, which varied according to the rules of each battery : in No. 1, for example, members paid 10s. 6d., and honorary members £1, 1s. annually ; and in No. 9 officers paid £2, 2s., serjeants 10s., corporals 8s., bombardiers 6s., and gunners 4s. each year.

The first headquarters were at 21 Castle Street, and the corps used the Argyle Battery in the Castle, armed with 12-pounders, for drill, and a 32-pounder battery at Leith Fort for practice, carbine shooting being carried out at Hunter's Bog.

The original uniform was a dark blue single-breasted tunic, hooked in front, with blue collar and cuffs and flat black braid all round, the shoulder-cords and

Austrian knot on the sleeves being of black round lace. The trousers were blue, with a ½-inch red stripe with black braid on both sides of it, the belts of white (buff) leather, with black pouch, and the head-dress was the busby—a round forage cap without peak, with a badge varying for each battery, being worn in undress. The officers had silver lace on their collars only, and gold badges of rank, their sleeve lace being black.

In 1863 an alteration was gradually carried out, the cuffs and collars being changed to scarlet and the black lace to white (silver) cord, and a broad red trouser stripe being introduced (see Plate I.); but it was not till 1878 that the white cord was exchanged for red. The busby originally worn was always retained by this corps, the only one in Scotland which wore it throughout its existence (see Plate I.)

In February 1889 two position batteries of 16-pounder R.M.L. guns were issued to the corps, and were manned by the *personnel* of four garrison batteries, and in 1892 these position batteries were numbered 1st and 2nd, the five garrison companies remaining being numbered 3rd to 7th, which was the formation of the corps till 1908. In February 1903 the armament of the 1st and 2nd Batteries was changed to 4·7-inch B.L. guns.

The 1st Berwick R.G.A.(V.), a corps one company strong, at Eyemouth, was attached to the 1st Edinburgh City for administrative purposes from 1864 to 1908.

Great attention was always paid to gunnery in the corps: in 1907 its detachment won the King's Prize at the National Artillery Association meeting at Lydd, and at the Buddon camp of the Scottish National Artillery Association the corps won the

I

cup presented by Colonel Lord Playfair for general efficiency.

The corps possessed a commodious headquarters with drill hall, &c., at 28 York Place, Edinburgh, and for its musketry used the Queen's Rifle Volunteer Brigade range at Hunter's Bog. Its gun practice was carried out from the Inchkeith Batteries.

The lieutenant-colonels commanding the corps have been—

William M. G. M. Wellwood, late Captain 2nd Bengal Light Cavalry, September 13, 1860.

T. Bell, April 4, 1864.

Sir Wm. Baillie, Bt. (hon. col.), December 6, 1866.

Jas. Laing (hon. col.), July 26, 1884.

D. M. Potter (lieut.-colonel, retired pay) (hon. col.), August 11, 1888.

Jas. F. Mackay, V.D. (hon. col.), November 2, 1892.

Ewen Campbell, V.D. (hon. col.), February 6, 1904.

1st MID-LOTHIAN ROYAL GARRISON ARTILLERY (VOLUNTEERS).

(PLATE II.)

ORDER OF PRECEDENCE, 11.

Honorary Colonel—The Right Hon. A. P. EARL OF ROSEBERY, K.G., K.T., V.D., Jan. 7, 1903.

Headquarters—30 GRINDLAY STREET, EDINBURGH.

UNDER the title of the 1st Mid-Lothian Coast Artillery Volunteers this corps was formed on March 10, 1860, from six batteries raised at Leith (Nos. 1 to 6), two on September 16, two on November 17, 1859, and two, which at first constituted a separate corps, the 2nd Mid-Lothian, on February 28, 1860, and added to the 1st on June 4, 1860. The 7th and 8th Batteries were formed at Portobello and Musselburgh respectively on December 17, 1859, and February 28, 1860.

The original uniform of the corps was dark blue tunics and trousers, the latter with broad scarlet stripes. The tunic had a scarlet collar with silver grenades embroidered on both sides, blue cuffs, five rows of black cord lace on the breast, and black cord shoulder-cords and Austrian knot. The head-dress was a busby, a round forage-cap with red band being worn in undress, and the belts were black. The 2nd Mid-Lothian at first had scarlet cuffs and collar and white belts, but on amalgamation conformed to the dress of the 1st Corps. This uniform was worn down to the spring of 1881, when the corps changed to the regulation clothing.

In 1864 the 1st Haddington Artillery Volunteers, a corps of one battery at Dunbar, raised on January 20, 1860, was attached to the corps for administrative purposes.

In 1886 the corps obtained two 40-pounder R.B.L. guns on travelling carriages, and these, horsed by dray-horses from Messrs Youngers' and Messrs M'Ewan's breweries, appeared at all parades until 1889, when two batteries of 16-pounder R.M.L. guns were issued to the corps and manned by the *personnel* of four garrison batteries. The title of "Coast" artillery had been dropped in 1888, and in 1889 the headquarters of the corps were removed from Leith to Edinburgh.

In 1897 the 1st Haddington Artillery was amalgamated with the 1st Mid-Lothian, of which it became the 9th Company.

In 1901 a third "heavy" battery of 16-pounders was issued to the corps and manned by the two remaining garrison companies in Edinburgh, and two years later the three heavy batteries were numbered 1st, 2nd, and 3rd, the Portobello and Musselburgh companies being amalgamated as the 4th, and the Dunbar company becoming the 5th Garrison Company, which was the formation of the corps till 1908.

Lieut. A. H. M. Jamieson of the 1st M.R.G.A.V. served during the South African War as machine-gun commander with the 6th Battalion Imperial Yeomanry.

Since the institution of the Scottish National Artillery Association Camp at Buddon, the 1st Mid-Lothian was always well represented at it. In 1902 the King's Cup for heavy batteries was won by the 1st, and in 1905 by the 2nd Heavy Battery, in the latter year the other two batteries being respectively second and third in the competition.

The corps headquarters in Grindlay Street dated from 1888, and comprised two large drill-halls and all the necessary store-rooms and accessories. At Portobello and Musselburgh modern guns were available for drill, and in the latter the headquarters of the 4th Company were situated. The Dunbar Company had also a drill-hall, with orderly room, &c. The corps carried out its gun practice in camp, and its musketry at the Hunter's Bog range.

The following officers have commanded the corps as lieutenant-colonels :—

Sir Jas. G. Baird, Bt., late Captain 10th Hussars, Colonel, A.D.C., March 10, 1860.

Thos. E. O. Horne, July 18, 1883.

Chas. G. H. Kinnear (hon. col.), June 26, 1884.

David Whitelaw, V.D., December 29, 1894.

Jas. A. Dalmahoy, M.V.O., V.D. (hon. col.), June 8, 1898.

1st BANFF ROYAL GARRISON ARTILLERY (VOLUNTEERS).

(ABERDEEN, BANFF, AND ELGIN.)

(PLATE III.)

ORDER OF PRECEDENCE, 13.

Honorary Colonel—A. W. G. DUKE OF FIFE, K.T., G.C.V.O., V.D., March 15, 1884.

Headquarters—6 CASTLE STREET, BANFF.

ON October 22, 1861, the 1st Administrative Brigade Banff Artillery Volunteers was formed, with headquarters at Banff, and in it were included the following corps of one battery each, formed in the county :—

> 1st, Macduff, formed March 27, 1860.
> 2nd, Banff, formed April 5, 1860.
> 3rd, Banff, formed April 5, 1860.
> 4th, Portsoy, formed October 8, 1860.
> 5th, Cullen, formed January 18, 1861.

The original uniform of these corps closely followed that of the Royal Artillery, with silver (white) lace.

To the brigade were added in 1863 the 1st Elgin A.V., a battery formed at Lossiemouth on March 26, 1860, and in 1872 the 2nd Elgin A.V., also a battery strong, raised at Burghead on October 16, 1872. On account of numbers having fallen off, in 1864 the 2nd and 3rd Batteries at Banff were amalgamated into one, as the 2nd, and the No. 3 remained vacant until November 13, 1875, when a new 3rd Corps was formed at Gordonstown.

In 1876 a general reorganisation of the artillery volunteers of the north-east of Scotland took place, under which the Banff Administrative Brigade was broken up, the two Elgin batteries being added to the 1st Administrative Brigade Inverness A.V., and the five Banff batteries to the 1st Administrative Brigade Aberdeenshire A.V. When the latter was consolidated in May 1880, the Banff batteries were included in it, but in May 1882 they and batteries representing the former 1st and 5th Aberdeen Corps and 1st Elgin Corps were formed into the 1st Banff Artillery Volunteers, with headquarters at Banff. The 1st Aberdeen Corps had been formed at Peterhead on March 13, 1860, with a strength of two batteries, but had been reduced to one battery in 1864; and the 5th Aberdeen, of one battery, had been raised in Fraserburgh on February 15, 1860. The batteries of the new 1st Banff A.V. were numbered as follows :—

> No. 1, Macduff (late 1st Banff A.V.)
> No. 2, Banff (late 2nd Banff A.V.)
> No. 3, Gordonstown (late 3rd Banff A.V.)
> No. 4, Portsoy (late 4th Banff A.V.)
> No. 5, Cullen (late 5th Banff A.V.)
> No. 6, Peterhead (late 1st Aberdeen).
> No. 7, Fraserburgh (late 5th Aberdeen).
> No. 8, Lossiemouth (late 1st Elgin).

In this formation the corps continued until 1904, when the No. 3 Gordonstown Company was, for the second time in its history, disbanded, and the 4th to 8th Companies became the 3rd to 7th.

The corps had its headquarters in Castle Street, Banff, and was one of the few Scottish artillery corps which possessed a pipe band, which wore the Duff tartan of the honorary colonel of the corps. It latterly performed its annual practice in camp at Barry, and had five carbine ranges of its own near the headquarters of companies.

The commanding officers have been—

J. Cruikshank, Major, October 22, 1861; Lieut.-Colonel, August 14, 1863.

Jas. Moir, Lieut.-Colonel, December 29, 1865.

Francis W. Garden-Campbell, late Ensign and Lieutenant Scots Fusilier Guards (hon. col.), Lieut.-Colonel, November 8, 1873.

> [On amalgamation with the 1st Administrative Brigade Aberdeen A.V., Lieut.-Colonel Campbell was appointed second lieutenant-colonel therein, and in 1879 lieutenant-colonel commandant. On the 1st Banff being reformed in 1882, he assumed command of it.]

Pat. Jamieson, V.D. (hon. col.), Lieut.-Colonel, October 7, 1893.

> [The command was vacant from 1896 to April 18, 1900.]

Charles G. Masson (hon. col.), Lieut.-Colonel, April 18, 1900.

John James George, V.D., Lieut.-Colonel, April 18, 1907.

1st FORFARSHIRE ROYAL GARRISON ARTILLERY (VOLUNTEERS).

(PLATE III.)

ORDER OF PRECEDENCE, 17.

Honorary Colonel—G. J. LORD PLAYFAIR, C.V.O., Colonel R.A. (retired pay), December 12, 1903.

Headquarters—ALBANY QUARTERS, BELL STREET, DUNDEE.

IN 1859 and 1860 the following artillery volunteer corps were formed in the county of Forfar:—

1st, Arbroath, formed October 31, 1859, of one battery. Increased to two batteries April 18, 1865, and to three batteries in 1877. Its original uniform was a blue hooked tunic and trousers, the latter with broad red stripes, the former with scarlet collar and cuffs, black flat braid all round the front and skirts, and black cord Austrian knot, white belts, and busby.

2nd, Montrose, formed October 31, 1859, of one battery, increased to one and a half batteries June 23, 1866, and reduced to one battery 1875.

3rd, Broughty Ferry, ⎱ Both raised on December 5, 1879, and
4th, do. do., ⎰ amalgamated as the 3rd Forfar of two batteries in 1862. The original uniform of the 3rd Corps was a blue buttoned tunic with scarlet cuffs, collar, and piping, and black Austrian knot, the trousers with broad red stripes, a blue shako with red band and white plume of feathers, and black belts. The 4th Corps had the same uniform as the 1st.

5th, Dundee, formed January 16, 1860, ⎫ These corps, of one bat-
6th, do., formed April 24, 1860, ⎬ tery each, were amal-
7th, do., formed April 30, 1860, ⎭ gamated as the 4th
Corps of three batteries in 1862, which corps was raised to four batteries in 1867, to six in 1868, and to seven in 1879.

The seven Forfarshire corps were on December 14, 1860, united into the 1st Administrative Brigade Forfarshire A.V., the headquarters of which were at Dundee, but these were transferred in 1862 to Broughty Ferry, and in 1870 back to Dundee.

In 1876 the 2nd, 3rd, and 4th Kincardine Artillery Volunteers were attached to the brigade (see 1st Aberdeen R.G.A. (V.)

In March 1880 the brigade as then existing—four Forfarshire and three Kincardine corps—was consolidated as the 1st Forfar Artillery Volunteers, with headquarters at Dundee and sixteen batteries, but in May 1882 the Kincardine batteries were transferred to the 1st Aberdeen Artillery Volunteers, and the corps reduced thereby to thirteen batteries, namely :—

Nos. 1 to 7, Dundee (former 4th Corps).
Nos. 8 to 10, Arbroath (former 1st Corps).
No. 11, Montrose (former 2nd Corps).
Nos. 12 and 13, Broughty Ferry (former 3rd Corps).

In 1883 a fourteenth battery was formed at Perth.

The Dundee batteries of the corps had since 1868 had two batteries of four field-guns each, but these were only occasionally turned out, and were not officially recognised, and it was only in 1889 that a position battery of four 16-pounder R.M.L. guns was formed and manned by two of the Dundee garrison batteries. In 1892 this battery was termed the 1st Position Battery, and the remaining companies of garrison artillery were numbered, the Dundee companies becoming the 2nd to 6th, the Arbroath companies the 7th to 9th, the Montrose company the 10th, the Broughty Ferry companies the 11th and 12th, and the Perth company the 13th garrison company, which formation was maintained till 1908. The corps, along with the other Dundee corps, had its headquarters in the Albany Quarters, Bell Street, Dundee, and used Barry Links for its gun practice. It had a drill battery there, and a rifle range up to 500 yards at Monifieth Links for the Dundee and Broughty Ferry companies, and others at Eliot Links, near Arbroath, and near Montrose for the companies at these places.

The lieutenant-colonels commandant have been—

James E. Erskine, December 14, 1860.
Frank Stewart-Sandeman, V.D. (hon. col.), (lieutenant-colonel commanding 4th Forfar A.V., July 28, 1868), July 20, 1870.
Thomas Couper, V.D. (hon. col.), December 3, 1898.
William G. Thomson, V.D. (hon. col.), April 3, 1901.
Theodore G. Luis, V.D. (hon. col.), February 4, 1903.
James Lindsay Henderson, March 31, 1906.

1st RENFREW AND DUMBARTON ROYAL GARRISON ARTILLERY (VOLUNTEERS).

(PLATE IV.)

ORDER OF PRECEDENCE, 30.

Honorary Colonel—J. REID, June 17, 1905.

Headquarters—8 SOUTH STREET, GREENOCK.

THE following artillery volunteer corps were raised in 1860 in the counties of Renfrew and Dumbarton :—

1st Renfrew, Greenock,⎫ These were all formed on January 20,
2nd   do.,   do.,   ⎬   1860, and were amalgamated as the
3rd   do.,   do.,   ⎭   1st Renfrew of three batteries in
    1864, which corps was increased to four batteries in 1867.
    The original uniforms were blue tunics with scarlet cord on
    the cuff, scarlet collar with black edging, the company num-
    ber on the shoulder strap, silver buttons, blue trousers with
    scarlet stripe, blue cap with scarlet band and grenade or
    Prince of Wales' plumes in front, and black waist-belts.
1st Dumbarton, Helensburgh, formed February 9, 1860, as one
    battery.
2d Dumbarton, Roseneath, formed March 5, 1860, as one battery.
    Headquarters transferred to Kilcreggan in 1866.   Disbanded
    1871.   The original uniform of this corps was blue with
    scarlet facings and white belts.
3rd Dumbarton, Dumbarton, formed December 24, 1860, as one
    battery, and increased to two batteries on March 22, 1869.

These six corps were formed into the 1st Adminis-trative Brigade Renfrewshire A.V. on August 22, 1863, with headquarters at Greenock, and in May 1880 the brigade was consolidated as the 1st Renfrew and Dumbarton Artillery Volunteers, with headquarters at Greenock and seven batteries, namely—

Nos. 1 to 4, Greenock (late 1st Renfrew).
No. 5, Helensburgh (late 1st Dumbarton).
Nos. 6 and 7, Dumbarton (late 3rd Dumbarton).

In 1889 a position battery of 40-pounder Armstrong R.B.L. guns was issued to the corps and manned by two of the Greenock batteries, the headquarters of the other two being at the same time transferred to Port-Glasgow. In 1892 the position battery was numbered the 1st, the garrison companies taking the numbers 2 and 3 (Port-Glasgow), 4 (Helensburgh), and 5 and 6 (Dumbarton), which was the formation of the corps till 1908.

During the South African War seventy-two men of the corps volunteered their services, but only three were taken.

The drill batteries of the corps were at Greenock, and gun practice was carried out at Irvine. The corps had also a carbine range at Drumshantie, near Greenock.

The list of lieutenant-colonels commanding is—

John Scott, C.B., V.D. (hon. col.), August 22, 1863.
William Anderson, V.D. (hon. col.), June 11, 1892.
Robert Duncan (hon. col.), May 13, 1894.
Francis G. Gemmill, V.D. (hon. col.), May 18, 1898.
Charles C. Scott, V.D. (hon. col.), January 18, 1902.

1st FIFESHIRE ROYAL GARRISON ARTILLERY (VOLUNTEERS).

(Fife and Stirling.)

Plate IV.

Order of Precedence, 32.

Honorary Colonel—The Right Hon. V. A. Earl of Elgin and Kincardine, K.G., G.C.S.I., G.C.I.E., March 26, 1902.

Headquarters—Kirkcaldy.

On 27th November 1860 the 1st Administrative Brigade Fifeshire Artillery Volunteers, with headquarters at Kirkcaldy, was formed, and to it were attached, then or on their subsequent dates of formation, the following corps of Fifeshire Artillery Volunteers of one battery each, except the 8th, which at first had two :—

1st, Ferryport-on-Craig (Tayport), formed January 26, 1860.

2nd, Newport, formed April 13, 1860.

3rd, St Andrews, formed March 6, 1860. Uniform—blue long-skirted tunics with red collars and piping, four rows of black lace on the breast, and black Austrian knot, blue trousers with red piping, blue caps with turned-down peak, black band, and red piping, and white waist-belts. The officers had silver lace on their collars and silver shoulder-cords.

4th, Inverkeithing, formed March 3, 1860.

5th, Kirkcaldy, formed March 22, 1860. Uniform—blue long-skirted tunics bound with flat black braid, scarlet collars with silver grenade and black Austrian knot, blue trousers with black braid and red piping on both sides, caps like the 3rd Corps, with straight peaks, and brown pouch and waist-belts, the former with a badge of the Royal Arms, the latter with the Thane of Fife on the belt-plate.

6th, Burntisland, formed February 20, 1860.

7th, Elie, formed March 8, 1860; headquarters transferred to Anstruther in 1872.

8th, Leven, formed July 24, 1860, of two batteries. Uniform—
tunic as for 3rd Corps (with silver cord on the collar),
trousers, cap, and belts as for 5th Corps. Reduced to one
and a half batteries in 1866, and to one battery in 1875.

9th, Dysart, formed September 19, 1860.

10th, East Wemyss, formed January 16, 1862, out of the overflow
of the 8th. Uniform as for the 8th.

11th, Kinghorn, formed April 30, 1863.

The uniforms of the corps not mentioned above were
of the same type as that of the 5th; some had broad
red stripes on the trousers, some white and others
brown belts, and all wore the peaked cap.

In 1863 the following corps of Stirlingshire Artillery
Volunteers were added to the brigade :—

1st, Grangemouth, formed March 27, 1860. Uniform—long-
skirted blue tunic with four rows of flat black braid, red
collars with silver lace and black Austrian knot, blue
trousers with red stripes, round forage caps with red band
(piped with silver cord for officers), and brown belts.

2nd, Stirling, formed May 30, 1860, as one subdivision. Increased to one battery April 17, 1861. Uniform as for
the 1st, but with white belts.

In 1863 the whole brigade adopted the regulation
artillery tunic with scarlet cord, busby, and forage cap
with scarlet band, and brown belts, which were discarded
later for white. Helmets replaced the busby in 1881.

In 1861, headquarters of the brigade were transferred
to St Andrews, and in 1880 the brigade was consolidated as the 1st Fifeshire Artillery Volunteers, headquarters at St Andrews, with thirteen batteries, the Fife
batteries retaining their numbers as above, and the
Stirlingshire corps becoming Nos. 12 and 13 Batteries.
In 1882 the 7th Battery (Anstruther) was disbanded,
and in its place a new 7th formed at St Andrews out
of University students.

In 1889 a position battery of 16-pounder guns was

issued to the corps and manned by the 3rd (St Andrews) Battery, and an extra *personnel* specially raised. In 1892 this became the 1st Position Battery, the Tayport (1st) Company became the 2nd, and the 2nd (Kirkcaldy, transferred thither from Newport on March 3, 1888) became the 3rd. Lieutenant J. N. Hotchkis of the 1st Fife R.G.A.V. served with the 18th Battalion Imperial Yeomanry during the South African War.

On March 1, 1900, a new 14th Company was formed at Kirkcaldy, and in 1901 the 16-pounders of the position battery were replaced by 4·7 guns. In October 1906 headquarters were moved to Kirkcaldy.

The distribution of the corps till 1908 was, — 1st Heavy Battery and No. 7 Company, St Andrews; No. 2 Company, Tayport; Nos. 3, 5, and 14, Kirkcaldy; No. 4, Inverkeithing; No. 6, Burntisland; No. 8, Leven; No. 9, Dysart; No. 10, East Wemyss; No. 11, Kinghorn; No. 12, Grangemouth; and No. 13, Stirling. Gun drill and gun practice were carried out with 4·7-in., 5-in., and 6-in. Mark VII. B.L. guns at Kinghornness, and with 6-in. Mark VII. guns at Carlingnose. The corps had 10 carbine ranges, and held also the Pilmuir Links range, near St Andrews, conjointly with the 6th Volunteer Battalion, Black Watch.

The lieutenant-colonels commandant have been—

William Maitland M'Dougall of Scotscraig, Admiral, retired, Royal Navy, November 27, 1860.

John N. M'Leod, April 29, 1874.

R. Tod Boothby, late Major Forfar and Kincardine Artillery Militia, and from 1861 to 1879 Adjutant of the Brigade (hon. col.), June 28, 1882.

James William Johnston,[1] M.V.O., V.D. (hon. col.), November 19, 1892.

Robert C. Highet, September 30, 1907.

[1] Colonel Johnston is one of three volunteer officers who marched past at the Royal Reviews of 1860, 1881, and 1905, always in the same corps.

1st LANARKSHIRE ROYAL GARRISON ARTILLERY (VOLUNTEERS).

(Heavy Artillery.)

(Plate V.)

ORDER OF PRECEDENCE, 35.

Honorary Colonel—Sir C. W. Cayser, Bart., March 23, 1898.

Headquarters—8 Newton Terrace, Sauchiehall Street, Glasgow.

The 1st Administrative Brigade Lanarkshire Artillery Volunteers was formed, with headquarters at Glasgow, on March 6, 1860, and in it were included, then or on their subsequent dates of formation, the following corps, of one battery each, raised in Glasgow or its suburbs :—

No.	Local name.	Date of acceptance of services.	Date of commission of officers.
1st	...	Dec. 30, 1859	Dec. 30, 1859.
2nd	...	Dec. 30, 1859	Dec. 30, 1859.
3rd	...	Dec. 30, 1859	Dec. 30, 1859.
4th	1st Northern	Dec. 6, 1859	Dec. 24, 1859.
5th	2nd Northern	Dec. 27, 1859	Jan. 5, 1860.
6th	3rd Northern	Dec. 27, 1859	Feb. 6, 1860.
7th	1st Eastern, Gallowgate	Jan. 10, 1860	Feb. 13, 1860.
8th	Ironmongers	Jan. 10, 1860	Feb. 2, 1860.
9th	2nd Eastern	Jan. 30, 1860	Feb. 17, 1860.
10th	Calton Artisans	Feb. 16, 1860	Feb. 24, 1860.
11th	Maryhill Artisans	Mar. 5, 1860	Mar. 14, 1860.
12th	Western	May 12, 1860	Aug. 20, 1860.
13th	Hillhead and Dowanhill	July 24, 1860	Aug. 20, 1860.
14th	...	July 26, 1860	July 4, 1860.
15th	Partick	Nov. 2, 1860	June 20, 1860.

The 4th, 5th, 6th, 10th, and 11th were artisan corps, the men of which paid 2s. 6d. entry money, and 30s. for their uniforms, the remaining expenses being defrayed by outside subscriptions, and the first four being assisted from the Glasgow Central Fund. The 1st Corps was formed, it is said, at the suggestion of Prince Albert, made at the opening of the Loch Katrine Water-works on October 14, 1859, that Glasgow should form some artillery. Mr John Wilkie, a leading lawyer of the city, took the matter in hand, and so many members joined the corps that from the outset three batteries could be formed, which were numbered the 1st, 2nd, and 3rd. These were entirely self-supporting, the honorary members paying £5 each, on enrolment, to the funds, and the effective members subscribing 10s. each annually and buying their own uniform and belts at a cost of £4 a-head. The remaining corps were raised on similar principles.

The original uniform of all the corps was similar to that of the Royal Artillery, with busbies and white waist-belts, but with scarlet cuffs and forage caps with scarlet bands.

In 1862 the brigade was consolidated as the 1st Lanarkshire Artillery Volunteers of fifteen batteries, which retained their former numbers. Up to 1865 the only guns on which the batteries were drilled were 32-pounder smooth-bores, but in that year, on December 13, a sixteenth battery was raised, and equipped as a field-battery with four 6-pounder field-guns, but no extra allowances were drawn in consequence. The 17th Battery (garrison) was formed in 1868.

In 1889 two position batteries, each of four 16-pounder R.M.L. guns and two waggons, were issued to the corps, and manned by the *personnel* of four garrison batteries (including the former 16th); and in 1900 the corps was increased to the *personnel* for twenty companies, eight more 16-pounder R.M.L. batteries were issued to it, and the whole corps was reorganised into ten position batteries, numbered 1st to 10th, and divided into five brigades. The corps, being now composed entirely of position batteries, was in 1901 styled a "position artillery corps," and in 1902 "heavy artillery." With the new issue of equipment in 1900, harness was only given for three batteries, making five in all, but in 1905 harness for the remaining five was issued. In 1907-8 the 16-pounder guns were replaced by 15-pounder B.L. guns transformed into quick-firers. The corps was the only one in Scotland composed entirely of heavy batteries.

The orderly-room, officers' and serjeants' club, and headquarters were at 8 Newton Terrace, Sauchiehall Street, Glasgow, and the corps had five separate drill-halls in different parts of the city, each with harness-rooms, gun-sheds, &c., for two batteries, the Maryhill drill-hall, in addition, accommodating all the ammunition-waggons not in use in the batteries. For over thirty years the corps carried out its annual practice at Irvine, from Bogside Camp, and as a rifle-range it used that at Darnley belonging to the 1st and 3rd Lanark V.R.C.

In 1900 the whole corps volunteered its services for South Africa, but, artillery not being required as such, they were not accepted. Sixty-two members of the corps, however, including Lieut. J. C. Clark, served in various capacities in South Africa during the war.

The lieutenant-colonels commandant of the corps have been—

Wm. S. S. Crawford, February 7, 1861.
Jas. Reid Stewart, May 12, 1862.
John Kidston (hon. col.), March 10, 1875.
Robt. J. Bennett, V.D. (hon. col.), September 27, 1890.
Alexr. B. Grant, M.V.O., V.D. (hon. col.), January 2, 1895.
Archibald M'I. Shaw, V.D. (hon. col.), November 16, 1907.

K

1st AYRSHIRE AND GALLOWAY ROYAL GARRISON ARTILLERY (VOLUNTEERS).

(Ayr, Wigtown, and Kirkcudbright.)

(Plate V.)

Order of Precedence, 38.

Honorary Colonel—Sir M. J. Stewart, Bart., V.D., December 22, 1888.

Headquarters—Kilmarnock.

The 1st Administrative Brigade Ayrshire Artillery Volunteers, with headquarters at Irvine, was formed on December 19, 1860, and to it were attached the following corps :—

1st Ayrshire A.V., Irvine, formed December 22, 1859, as one and a half batteries; reduced to one battery, 1862.

2nd Ayrshire A.V., Ayr, formed January 31, 1860, as one and a half batteries; increased to two batteries, 1874.

3rd Ayrshire A.V., Largs, formed March 1, 1860, as one battery.

4th Ayrshire A.V., Ardrossan, formed March 3, 1860, as one battery.

5th Ayrshire A.V., Kilmarnock, formed July 12, 1860, as one battery; increased in 1864 to one and a half batteries.

The original uniform of the 1st and 2nd Ayrshire was blue tunics with red collars, cuffs, and piping, edged all round with black braid and with four rows of the same on the breast, blue trousers with black stripe with red piping, blue peaked caps with black lace band, scarlet piping, and silver grenade in front, and a black waist-belt. That of the other corps is said to have been the same.

To the brigade were added in 1863—

1st Kirkcudbright A.V., Kirkcudbright, formed February 2, 1860, as one battery.

1st Wigtown A.V., Stranraer, formed February 20, 1860, as one
battery.

2nd Wigtown A.V., Port Patrick, formed February 22, 1860, as
one battery.

And in 1867 the

3rd Wigtown A.V., Sandhead, formed May 4, 1867, as one
battery.

The original uniform of the 1st Wigtown was blue
with scarlet facings, white belts, and silver ornaments.

In 1863 brigade headquarters were moved from
Irvine to Ayr, and in May 1880 the brigade was
consolidated as the 1st Ayrshire and Galloway Artillery Volunteers, with headquarters at Ayr and eleven
batteries, viz.—

> No. 1, Irvine (late 1st A.A.V.)
> Nos. 2 and 3, Ayr (late 2nd A.A.V.)
> No. 4, Largs (late 3rd A.A.V.)
> No. 5, Ardrossan (late 4th A.A.V.)
> Nos. 6 and 7, Kilmarnock (late 5th A.A.V.)
> No. 8, Kirkcudbright (late 1st K.A.V.)
> No. 9, Stranraer (late 1st W.A.V.)
> No. 10, Port Patrick (late 2nd W.A.V.)
> No. 11, Sandhead (late 3rd W.A.V.)

In 1889 a position battery of 16-pounder R.M.L.
guns was issued to the corps and manned by the two
Kilmarnock batteries, and corps headquarters were
moved to Kilmarnock.

In 1892 the existing position battery took the
number 1, absorbing the 6th and 7th Companies, and
in 1901 two more batteries of 9-pounder R.M.L. guns
were issued to the corps, which took the numbers 2
and 3 and absorbed the Irvine and Ayr Companies,
and an extra *personnel* formed as a 6th Company at
Kilmarnock. The 8th to 11th Companies took the

numbers 7 to 10. In 1903 4·7-inch guns replaced the
R.M.L. armament of all three heavy batteries. The
formation of the corps till 1908 was in three heavy
batteries—No. 1 at Kilmarnock, Nos. 2 and 3 at Ayr—
and six garrison companies (Nos. 4, 5, 7, 8, 9, and 10 as
above), No. 6 being vacant, and accounted for by extra
personnel in the heavy batteries.

The corps carried out its gun practice at Irvine : it
used the Ayrshire Rifle Association range at Irvine for
the musketry of all but the 7th to 10th Companies,
which had ranges near their own headquarters.

In 1900 over 600 men of this corps volunteered their
services for the war in South Africa, but as artillerymen were not required they were not accepted.
Twenty-eight members actually served in South Africa
during the war.

The officers commanding the corps have been—

Major Sir E. Hunter-Blair, Bart., May 8, 1861.
Lieut.-Colonel Hon. G. R. Vernon, July 17, 1863.
Lieut.-Colonel Sir E. Hunter-Blair, Bart. (reappointed), September
    4, 1866.
(Vacant in 1872 and 1873.)
Lieut.-Colonel John Shand, May 6, 1874.
Lieut.-Colonel Sir Mark J. Stewart, Bart., V.D., February 5, 1879.
Lieut.-Colonel John G. Sturrock, V.D. (hon. col.), December 22,
    1888.
Lieut.-Colonel T. R. Stuart, April 5, 1905.

1st ARGYLL AND BUTE ROYAL GARRISON ARTILLERY (VOLUNTEERS).

(PLATE V.)

ORDER OF PRECEDENCE, 39.

Honorary Colonel—J. D. S. DUKE OF ARGYLL, K.T., K.C.M.G., V.D., July 18, 1900.

Headquarters—TARBERT, LOCH FYNE.

THE 1st Administrative Brigade Argyll Artillery Volunteers was formed with headquarters at Oban, on October 10, 1861, and to it were attached, then or on the date of their subsequent formation, the following corps of Argyll Artillery Volunteers of one battery each, except when otherwise stated :—

1st, Easdale, formed March 7, 1860, as two batteries.

2nd, Tarbert, formed April 12, 1860 ; disbanded 1862.

3rd, Oban, formed March 8, 1860.

4th, West Tarbert, formed April 12, 1860. Headquarters moved, 1864, to Dunmore, and, 1866, to Ronachan. Disbanded 1874.

5th, Ardgour, formed January 16, 1861, as one subdivision. Disbanded in 1865.

6th, Campbeltown, formed February 11, 1861. Increased to two batteries, 1870.

7th, Port Ellen, Islay, formed July 3, 1861.

8th, South Hall, formed September 10, 1861. Headquarters changed to Castle Toward, 1878.

9th, Tobermory, Mull, formed May 15, 1862. Reduced to a half-battery, 1874.

10th, Lochgilphead, formed May 15, 1862.

11th, Tarbert, formed February 13, 1866.

12th, Inveraray, formed April 2, 1867 ; recruited from men of the Furnace Quarries.

In 1863 the 1st Bute A.V., headquarters Rothesay, raised on March 20, 1862, and in 1867 the 2nd Bute

A.V., headquarters Millport, Cumbrae, raised on October 5, 1867, each one battery strong, were added to the brigade.

The original uniforms varied greatly. Colonel F. Campbell (commanding 1884-1903) writes: "The corps had their separate uniforms, which were tunics or Garibaldi shirts; caps with red, yellow, or white bands; belts brown, black, or white. The officers' dress was even more varied. They joined simply to encourage the movement, and wore much what they chose, utilising any old uniform that they might have worn some time or other, whether cavalry, infantry, or other. Swords of all patterns, perhaps presentations to their forefathers before and after Waterloo."

The 3rd Corps had in 1860 blue uniforms with scarlet facings, white pouch-belts, black waist-belts, and busbies; while the 4th Corps wore a jumper and trousers of blue flannel, and a broad Kilmarnock bonnet, such as are usually worn by Tarbert fishermen, of whom it was mainly composed.

In 1864 brigade headquarters were moved to Lochgilphead, and in 1870 to Rothesay.

In May 1880 the brigade was consolidated as the 1st Argyll and Bute Artillery Volunteers, with twelve and a half batteries, distributed as follows:—

> Nos. 1 and 2, Easdale (late 1st Argyll).
> No. 3, Oban (late 3rd Argyll).
> Nos. 4 and 5, Campbeltown (late 6th Argyll).
> No. 6, Port Ellen, Islay (late 7th Argyll).
> No. 7, Castle Toward (late 8th Argyll).
> No. 8, Rothesay (late 1st Bute).
> No. 9, Millport (late 2nd Bute).
> No. 10, Lochgilphead (late 10th Argyll).
> No. 11, Tarbert (late 11th Argyll).
> No. 12, Inveraray (late 12th Argyll).
> Half-battery, Tobermory, Mull (late 9th Argyll).

In 1887 the 12th Battery at Inveraray was disbanded, a new 12th being formed in its place at Rothesay, and in the following year the headquarters of the 8th Battery were removed from Castle Toward to Dunoon.

During the South African War, 211 men of the 1st Argyll and Bute volunteered their services, but only 8 were taken for active service.

The corps was one of the most scattered in the kingdom, for besides the headquarter detachments, No. 6 Company had detachments at Bowmore, Bridgend, and Ardbeg, and No. 12 one at Kingarth,—thus its men were spread over fifteen localities in every portion of the largest and least accessible county in Scotland. Owing to the varying natures of the occupations of the men, three-fourths of whom were Gaelic-speaking, no fewer than three camps had to be formed for training at different times of the year, and the corps had to keep up fifteen carbine-ranges. Still, many prizes have been gained by the corps, both in gun practices and repository exercises, at the Scottish National Artillery Association camps, and the King's Cup was won at Buddon in 1903 by the Easdale companies. The pipe band consisted of over thirty pipers.

The headquarters of the corps were transferred in March 1906 to Tarbert, Loch Fyne.

The lieutenant-colonels (commandant since 1866) of the corps have been—

J. Campbell, C.B., Major-General; Major, October 10, 1861; Lieut.-Colonel, July 23, 1863.

J. D. S. Marquis of Lorne, K.T., G.C.M.G., July 13, 1866.

Frederick Campbell, late Lieutenant R.A., C.B., V.D. (hon. col.), March 21, 1884.

John W. Stewart, V.D. (hon. col.), August 1, 1903.

Colin G. P. Campbell, late 2nd Lieutenant Scots Guards, February 17, 1906.

1st CAITHNESS ROYAL GARRISON ARTILLERY (VOLUNTEERS).

(CAITHNESS AND SUTHERLAND.)

(PLATE VI.)

ORDER OF PRECEDENCE, 43.

Honorary Colonel—Sir J. R. G. SINCLAIR, Bart., D.S.O., V.D. (hon. captain in the army), November 7, 1900.

Headquarters—THURSO.

IN 1863 the 1st, 2nd, and 3rd Caithness, 1st, 2nd, 3rd, and 4th Orkney, and 1st Ross Artillery Volunteer Corps were formed into the 1st Administrative Brigade Caithness Artillery Volunteers, with headquarters at Wick.

The Caithness corps which then, or on their subsequent formation, formed part of the brigade were—

1st, Wick, formed March 6, 1860, as one battery; increased to one and a half batteries in 1867, and to two batteries in 1870.

2nd, Thurso, formed April 24, 1860, as one subdivision; increased to one battery on December 28, 1860, and to two batteries in 1870.

3rd, Lybster, formed September 30, 1861, as one battery; disbanded 1873.

4th, Barrogill, Mey, formed December 1, 1866, as one battery.

5th, Castletown, formed December 1, 1866, as one battery.

6th, Thrumster, formed May 4, 1867, as one battery; disbanded 1878.

The first uniform of the Caithness corps was similar to that of the Royal Artillery, but with scarlet cuffs and white cord and piping. Busbies and white belts were worn. The officers had silver lace, and their tunics were piped all round with silver cord, and had silver lace on the skirts.

In 1867 the Orkney and Ross corps were withdrawn from the brigade, and to it were added the

1st Sutherland A.V., Helmsdale, formed April 26, 1860, which had since 1863 been attached to the 1st Inverness A.V. Its uniform was similar to that of the Caithness corps, but the busbies had chin-chains.

2nd Sutherland A.V., Golspie, formed February 18, 1867. This was a body of fishermen of wonderful physique. At its first parade the two flank men were each 6 ft. 6 in. The uniform was the same as the 1st Sutherland.

In 1880 the brigade was consolidated as the 1st Caithness Artillery Volunteers, headquarters at Wick, with eight batteries, viz. :—

> Nos. 1 and 2, Wick (late 1st Caithness).
> Nos. 3 and 4, Thurso (late 2nd Caithness).
> No. 5, Mey (late 4th Caithness).
> No. 6, Castletown (late 5th Caithness).
> No. 7, Helmsdale (late 1st Sutherland).
> No. 8, Golspie (late 2nd Sutherland).

In 1882 headquarters were transferred from Wick to Thurso. In 1894 the 1st and 2nd Companies ceased to exist, but in 1897 the 1st was resuscitated, since when the corps consisted of seven garrison companies, the 2nd being vacant.

The corps had a drill battery at each station, and possessed six carbine-ranges.

The lieutenant-colonels commanding have been—

Sir Robert S. Sinclair, Bart. of Murkle, October 10, 1864.
G. P. A. Earl of Caithness, June 17, 1882.
George R. Lawson (hon. col.), May 25, 1889.
Sir John R. G. Sinclair, Bart., D.S.O., of Dunbeath, July 2, 1892.
Alexander M'Donald, V.D. (hon. col.), May 9, 1900.
David Keith Murray, V.D. (hon. col.), April 5, 1905.

1st ABERDEENSHIRE ROYAL GARRISON ARTILLERY (VOLUNTEERS).

(ABERDEEN AND KINCARDINE.)

(PLATE VI.)

ORDER OF PRECEDENCE, 45.

Honorary Colonel—Right Hon. J. C. EARL OF ABERDEEN, G.C.M.G.,
January 14, 1888.

Headquarters—NORTH SILVER STREET, ABERDEEN.

ON October 24, 1860, the 1st Adminstrative Brigade Aberdeen Artillery Volunteers, with headquarters at Aberdeen, was formed, and to it, then or subsequently on date of formation, were attached the following corps formed in the county :—

1st, Peterhead, formed March 13, 1860, of two batteries, one of which for a short time bore the number 2nd Aberdeen. Reduced to one battery in 1864. The uniform was exactly the same as that of the Royal Artillery, with white (silver) lace (see Plate III.)

3rd, Aberdeen, formed May 2, 1860, as an artisan battery from the employés of Messrs Thomson, Catto, Buchanan, & Co., shipbuilders and ironfounders, who contributed largely to the funds of the corps. The uniform was that of the Royal Artillery, but the tunics had four rows of black lace on the breast, the Austrian knots were scarlet, the caps had scarlet bands, and the belts were brown.

4th, Aberdeen, formed April 14, 1860, as a citizens' battery, the members clothing and equipping themselves. The uniform was blue frockcoats with black braid all round, scarlet collars, and scarlet Austrian knots, blue trousers with black stripe edged with scarlet, blue caps with peaks and black band edged with scarlet, and black belts.

5th, Fraserburgh, formed February 15, 1860, as one battery.

6th, Aberdeen, formed February 9, 1860, as an artisan battery, from the employés of Messrs Blaikie Bros., shipbuilders and ironfounders. The uniform was the same as that of the 3rd Corps, except that the belts were black.

7th, Aberdeen, formed September 23, 1861, as one battery, and increased to two on July 19, 1865. The uniform was the same as that of the Royal Artillery, with white (silver) cord, busbies, and white belts.

In 1863 the following corps, raised in Kincardine-shire, were added to the brigade :—

1st, Stonehaven, formed January 10, 1860. Headquarters of this battery were moved to Cowie early in 1861, and to it was added in June 1861, as a 2nd Battery, the 5th Kincardine A.V. formed at Cowie on January 29, 1861. The two batteries were amalgamated in 1875. The 1st Battery originally wore Royal Artillery uniform (with white cord), the 2nd, being mainly composed of fishermen, a semi-naval dress.

2nd, Johnshaven, formed August 14, 1860, as a subdivision; increased to a full battery in 1869.

3rd, St Cyrus, formed July 30, 1860, as a subdivision; increased to a full battery in 1863.

4th, Bervie, formed October 29, 1860, as a subdivision; increased to a full battery in 1867.

The uniform of the 7th Aberdeen—namely, R.A. pattern, with white cord on the tunic, white band on the forage cap, busbies, and white belts—was adopted for the whole brigade in 1864, but it was long before the old patterns ceased to be worn, and only in 1875 that the pouch-belts were discontinued.

In 1874, under authority from the War Office dated September 4, the 3rd, 4th, 6th, and 7th Aberdeen A.V. were amalgamated into one corps of five batteries, designated the 3rd Aberdeen Artillery Volunteers, the former 3rd forming No. 1, 4th No. 2, 6th No. 3, and 7th Nos. 4 and 5 Batteries. A sixth battery was raised for this corps in September 1877, and a seventh was actually formed in 1877-78 but not officially sanctioned till 1880.

In 1876 the 2nd, 3rd, and 4th Kincardine were transferred to the 1st Administrative Brigade Forfar A.V., and the 1st, 2nd, 3rd, 4th, and 5th Banff Corps were added to the brigade (see 1st Banff R.G.A.V.)

The brigade as then constituted was consolidated in May 1880, under War Office authority of May 10, as the 1st Aberdeenshire Artillery Volunteers, with head-quarters at Aberdeen, and fourteen batteries as follows:—

> No. 1, Peterhead (late 1st Aberdeen A.V.)
> Nos. 2 to 7, Aberdeen (late 3rd Aberdeen A.V.)
> No. 8, Fraserburgh (late 5th Aberdeen A.V.)
> Nos. 9 to 13, in Banffshire (late 1st to 5th Banff A.V.)
> No. 14, Cowie (late 1st Kincardine A.V.)

At the end of 1880 the 14th Battery at Cowie ceased to exist, and a new 14th was formed at Aberdeen out of the 7th Battery, late 3rd A.A.V., mentioned above.

1882 brought another change in the composition of the corps, for by War Office authority of May 10, the 1st, 8th, and 9th to 13th Batteries were transferred to the newly-formed 1st Banffshire Artillery Volunteers (which see), and the batteries representing the former 2nd, 3rd, and 4th Kincardine were re-transferred back to the 1st Aberdeenshire, in which the 10 batteries were then renumbered as follows:—

Nos. 1 to 7, Aberdeen (the former 2nd to 7th and 14th Batteries).
No 8, Johnshaven (former 2nd Kincardine A.V.)
No. 9, St Cyrus (former 3rd Kincardine A.V.)
No. 10, Bervie (former 4th Kincardine A.V.)

In 1885 a new battery was raised in the University of Aberdeen which took the number 8, the 8th, 9th, and 10th becoming the 9th, 10th, and 11th respectively, and in December 1886 a new battery was formed at Stonehaven which was numbered the 12th.

On January 17, 1889, a position battery of 40-pounder

R.B.L. guns was issued to the corps and manned by the 5th and 8th Batteries, and on November 1, 1892, these two were amalgamated as the 1st Position Battery, the other Aberdeen garrison companies being numbered 2nd to 7th, Johnshaven the 8th, St Cyrus the 9th, Bervie the 10th, and Stonehaven the 11th Company.

In 1893 the Johnshaven and St Cyrus companies were amalgamated as the 8th, and the 10th and 11th became the 9th and 10th Companies.

On April 1, 1901, a second position battery of 40-pounders was issued to the corps, and a new *personnel* was raised for it. It took the number 2, the 2nd Company became the 8th, and the 8th, 9th, and 10th the 9th, 10th, and 11th. In 1902 both position batteries were rearmed with 4·7 - in. guns, and were termed " heavy " batteries.

Thus the latter-day composition of the corps, and the connection of the batteries and companies with the original corps, after these somewhat kaleidoscopic changes, were—

1st Heavy Battery, Aberdeen, original 2nd Battery of 7th Aberdeen and University Battery.

2nd Heavy Battery, Aberdeen, newly raised 1901.

3rd Garrison Company, Aberdeen, original 4th Aberdeen A.V. (Citizens).

4th Garrison Company, Aberdeen, original 6th Aberdeen A.V. (Artisans).

5th Garrison Company, Aberdeen, original 1st Battery of 7th Aberdeen A.V.

6th Garrison Company, Aberdeen, raised in 1877.

7th Garrison Company, Aberdeen, raised in 1880.

8th Garrison Company, Aberdeen, original 3rd Aberdeen A.V. (Artisans).

9th Garrison Company, Johnshaven, original 2nd and 3rd Kincardine A.V.

10th Garrison Company, Bervie, original 4th Kincardine A.V.

11th Garrison Company, Stonehaven, re-raised 1886.

During the South African war 13 men belonging to the corps served with various units in the field.

The corps headquarters in North Silver Street, Aberdeen, were erected in 1899 at a cost of upwards of £7000, and contained a drill-hall in which 5-in. and 6-in. guns were mounted for the training of the garrison companies, which carried out their practice from the Torry Point Battery, which had been rearmed with modern guns. The headquarters' batteries and companies used for their musketry the Seaton Links Rifle Range belonging to the 1st V.B. Gordon Highlanders, and the companies at outstations had carbine-ranges and drill batteries near their headquarters. The corps carried out its annual training and practice for the heavy batteries and garrison companies in camp at Buddon. In 1903 the 1st Aberdeen won the " Playfair " Cup for the smartest corps in camp, and in 1904 the garrison companies won the King's Cup at the Scottish National Artillery Association's camp at Buddon.

The lieutenant-colonels (commandant since May 1880) of the corps have been—

Wm. Cosmo Gordon of Fyvie, late Captain Madras Artillery, May 21, 1862.

Francis W. Garden-Campbell, transferred in 1876 from the 1st Adminstrative Brigade, Banff A.V., Lieut. - Colonel Commandant, 1st A.A.V., December 23, 1879 (retransferred to 1st Banff A.V., 1882).

Thomas A. W. A. Youngson, Lieut.-Colonel, March 3, 1880; Lieut.-Colonel Commandant, October 5, 1882.

James Ogston, V.D. (hon. col.), Lieut.-Colonel, October 26, 1887; Lieut.-Colonel Commandant, June 24, 1893.

Geo. Milne, V.D. (hon. col.), Lieut. - Colonel, May 15, 1901; Lieut.-Colonel Commandant, October 8, 1904.

1st BERWICK ROYAL GARRISON ARTILLERY (VOLUNTEERS).

(PLATE VI.)

ORDER OF PRECEDENCE, 46.

Headquarters—EYEMOUTH.

THIS corps was formed at Eyemouth on April 6, 1860, as one battery, and from 1864 was attached to the 1st Edinburgh (City) Artillery Volunteers.

A 2nd Berwick Artillery Volunteers, also of the strength of one battery, was formed at Coldingham in 1861, and was also attached to the 1st Edinburgh from 1864 until its disbandment in 1883.

The corps had a drill-battery and headquarters at Eyemouth and a rifle-range at Linkum, two miles from Eyemouth.

The captains commanding the 1st Berwick A.V. have been—

J. R. L'Amy, April 6, 1860; J. Gibson, February 1861 (vacant 1862 to 1867); P. Tod, November 14, 1867 (vacant 1876 to 1880); John Johnston, March 30, 1881; A. Johnston, January 9, 1889; D. Hume, February 1, 1898; G. J. Gibson, February 21, 1903; and Chas. M. Alexander, March 16, 1907.

THE HIGHLAND ROYAL GARRISON ARTILLERY (VOLUNTEERS).

(INVERNESS, CROMARTY, NAIRN, ROSS, AND ELGIN.)

(PLATE VII.)

ORDER OF PRECEDENCE, 47.

Honorary Colonel—W. FRASER, V.D., January 2, 1901.

Headquarters—INVERNESS.

THE first Artillery corps formed in the city of Inverness had its origin in a company of "Artisan Rifles," which was raised in consequence of a meeting held in the Trades' Hall on November 15, 1859. It was subsequently decided that this corps should become "Artisan Artillery Volunteers," and as such its services were accepted in January 1860 as the 1st Inverness Artillery Volunteers, of two batteries, the officers' commissions being dated February 4, 1860. So popular was the artillery arm in Inverness that on May 1, 1860, these batteries were doubled, the officers for the new 3rd and 4th Batteries being gazetted on June 23, 1860. In December 1864 a fifth, and in January 1865 a sixth, battery was added to the corps. The original uniform of the 1st Inverness A.V. was blue tunics with long skirts, scarlet collars and cuffs, black braid all round, five rows of black lace on the breast and black Austrian knot, blue trousers with scarlet stripe, a blue peaked cap with black band and scarlet piping, and a black waist-belt. Busbies were adopted in 1861, and in 1863 the uniform was assimilated to that of the Royal Artillery with white cord, white waist- and pouch-belts being also worn.

In 1863 the 1st Sutherland A.V. was attached to

the 1st Inverness, but was transferred to the 1st Administrative Brigade, Caithness A.V., in 1867.

In 1863, also, the 1st Cromarty and the 1st Nairn Artillery Volunteers were attached to the 1st Inverness. The former, a corps of one battery, with headquarters at Cromarty, had been formed on June 8, 1860. The 1st Nairn had been raised at Nairn on April 10, 1860, as one battery, but had been increased to two batteries on October 6, 1860. The original uniform was similar to that of the Royal Artillery, but with scarlet cuffs and white cord, and the head-dress was a peaked cap similar to that of the 1st Inverness, with an upright white horse-hair plume.

In December 1876 the 1st Inverness, 1st Cromarty, 1st Nairn, 1st and 2nd Elgin, and 1st and 2nd Ross Artillery Volunteers were formed into the 1st Administrative Brigade, Inverness-shire Artillery Volunteers, with headquarters at Inverness, the whole numbering thirteen batteries. The 1st Elgin, of one battery, had been formed at Lossiemouth on March 26, 1860, and the 2nd, also of one battery, at Burghhead, on October 16, 1872. These had been attached hitherto to the 1st Administrative Brigade, Banff A.V. The 1st Ross had been raised at Stornoway, as a corps of one battery, on April 13, 1860, and was in 1863 attached to the 1st Administrative Brigade, Caithness A.V. The 2nd Ross (Loch Carron) was formed on August 21, 1866, as one battery, and in 1867 the 1st and 2nd Ross had been formed into the 1st Administrative Brigade, Ross-shire A.V., which lasted till the above-mentioned reorganisation in 1876.

In May 1880 the brigade was consolidated as the 1st Inverness-shire Artillery Volunteers, with headquarters at Inverness, and thirteen batteries, but in 1882 the Lossiemouth (late 1st Elgin) battery was transferred to

L

the 1st Banff Artillery Volunteers, reducing the number of batteries to twelve, thus distributed—

> Nos. 1 to 6, Inverness (late 1st Inverness).
> No. 7, Burghhead (late 2nd Elgin).
> No. 8, Cromarty (late 1st Cromarty).
> No. 9, Stornoway (late 1st Ross).
> No. 10, Loch Carron (late 2d Ross).
> Nos. 11 and 12, Nairn (late 1st Nairn).

Since 1867 the 1st Inverness had had two 6-pounder brass field-guns, which were horsed by the corps when required, and in 1873 these were replaced by two 40-pounder Armstrong B.L. guns. No Government allowances were made for the horsing of these guns. In 1889 a position battery of 16-pounders was issued to the corps under the usual conditions, and was manned by the 1st and 2d Batteries ; in 1892 these two were amalgamated to form the 1st Position Battery (since 1902 1st Heavy Battery) at Inverness, and the 3rd to 12th garrison companies took the numbers 2 to 11 in their proper order, which was the formation of the corps till 1908—viz., one heavy battery and ten garrison companies.

In 1890, by General Order 45 of February 1, the corps received the title of "The Highland Artillery Volunteers," in substitution for that hitherto borne.

The corps had spacious headquarters, with drill-hall, stores, gun-sheds, &c., at Inverness. It carried out its training and gun practice from camp, and for its musketry used the range of the 1st V.B. Cameron Highlanders at Longman, near Inverness, and five carbine-ranges at the headquarters of outlying companies. In 1894 the 1st Position Battery won the Queen's Cup at the Scottish National Artillery Association's Camp at Buddon.

In 1900, 500 of the corps volunteered for South

Africa, but only 28 were taken for active service during the war.

The commanding officers have been—

Of 1st Inverness A.V.—

Major William Fraser Tytler of Ardrurie and Balnain, June 23, 1860; Lieut.-Colonel, January 24, 1865.

Lieut.-Colonel Eneas W. Mackintosh of Raigmore, November 13, 1869.

Of 1st Administrative Brigade, Inverness A.V., and later 1st Inverness and Highland A.V.—

Lieut.-Colonel Commandant Eneas W. Mackintosh of Raigmore, December 1, 1876.

Lieut.-Colonel Commandant Donald Davidson, January 14, 1880.

Lieut.-Colonel Commandant W. Fraser, V.D. (hon. col.), November 14, 1885.

Lieut.-Colonel Commandant James E. B. Baillie, M.V.O., V.D., of Dochfour (hon. col.), July 25, 1894.

1st ORKNEY ROYAL GARRISON ARTILLERY (VOLUNTEERS).

(Plate VII.)

Order of Precedence, 54.

*Headquarters—*Kirkwall.

The 1st Administrative Brigade, Orkney Artillery Volunteers, was formed on August 15, 1867, with headquarters at Kirkwall, and to it were attached, then or on subsequent date of formation, the following corps of Orkney Artillery Volunteers, of one battery each, except when otherwise stated :—

1st, Kirkwall, formed May 1, 1860.

2nd, Scar House, Sanday, formed June 23, 1863.

3rd, Balfour, Shapinshay, formed July 10, 1863.
4th, Stromness, formed June 23, 1863.
5th, Stronsay, formed August 17, 1865.
6th, Holm, formed November 28, 1866.
7th, Firth, formed October 31, 1868 as a half battery.   Disbanded
   in 1877.
8th, Evie, formed June 25, 1870.
9th, Rousay, formed December 13, 1874.
10th, Birsay, formed March 2, 1878.

The 1st to 6th Corps had since 1863, or date of formation, been attached to the 1st Administrative Brigade, Caithness A.V.

In March 1880 the brigade was consolidated as the
1st Orkney Artillery Volunteers, with headquarters at
Kirkwall, and nine batteries, numbered in the above
sequence, the 8th, 9th, and 10th Corps becoming the
7th, 8th, and 9th Batteries respectively.   In 1886 the
headquarters of the 8th (Rousay) Battery were transferred to Kirkwall, so that the latter-day constitution
of the corps in nine companies was—

> Nos. 1 and 8, Kirkwall (former 1st and 9th O.A.V.)
> No. 2, Sanday (former 2d O.A.V.)
> No. 3, Shapinshay (former 3rd O.A.V.)
> No. 4, Stromness (former 4th O.A.V.)
> No. 5, Stronsay (former 5th O.A.V.)
> No. 6, Holm (former 6th O.A.V.)
> No. 7, Evie (former 9th O.A.V.)
> No. 9, Birsay (former 10th O.A.V.)

The original uniform of the 1st Orkney A.V. was
frock-coats with blue cuffs and collars and five rows of
black lace on the breast, the men having scarlet and
the officers silver piping on the collar and Austrian
knots on the sleeves, blue trousers with red stripes,
blue peaked caps with black bands and scarlet piping,
with the Royal Arms in front, and white belts.   The

uniform of this corps was assimilated in 1863 to that of the Royal Artillery, which the other corps adopted from the outset.

The corps had erected commodious headquarters at Kirkwall, with drill-hall, stores, lecture and recreation rooms, officers' mess, &c., and had provided at each of its seven outstations a drill-hall with an armoury and a four-room cottage for the serjeant-instructor—all these the property of the corps and free from debt. There was a practice battery at each station, that at Kirkwall being of four and the others of two guns. These were, however, only armed with 64-pounder R.M.L. guns, and the principal practice was carried out in camp with modern ordnance. Each of the eight practice batteries had a carbine-range in its immediate vicinity.

The lieutenant-colonels commanding have been—

David Balfour, August 15, 1867 (became honorary colonel March 20, 1872, reappointed lieut.-colonel, December 7, 1872).

Fred W. Burroughs, C.B., Brevet-Colonel (half pay), late 93rd Foot, November 1, 1873.

J. W. Balfour, V.D., late Captain 7th D.G., October 9, 1880.

G. F. F. Horwood, late Captain 2nd Foot (hon. col.), March 27, 1895.

Richard Bailey, late Captain R.A., and formerly Adjutant of the corps (hon. col.), January 19, 1898.

Thomas S. Peace, V.D. (hon. col.), March 28, 1906.

ROYAL ENGINEER VOLUNTEERS.

1st LANARKSHIRE ROYAL ENGINEERS (VOLUNTEERS).

(PLATE VIII.)

ORDER OF PRECEDENCE, 2.

Honorary Colonel — General H. H. VISCOUNT KITCHENER OF KHARTOUM, G.C.B., O.M., G.C.M.G., Colonel-Commandant R.E., December 21, 1898.

Headquarters—21 JARDINE STREET, GLASGOW.

As already noted on page 31, the first meeting with a view to the formation of a Volunteer Engineer corps in Scotland was held in Glasgow on November 28, 1859, when a number of civil engineers, architects, surveyors, &c., agreed to offer their services as a "Military Engineer Volunteer Corps." The services of this company were accepted on February 27, but the commissions of its officers to the 1st Lanark Volunteer Engineers were dated February 11, 1860. From the overflow of this company and from artisans a second was shortly formed, the services of which, as the 2nd Lanark Volunteer Engineers, was accepted on May 9, 1860, the officers being gazetted on May 16. A third company, the 3rd Lanark, was formed on April 28, 1862, with headquarters at Cadder Hill, its services having been accepted in April 4, 1862, the men being mainly recruited in Kirkintilloch.

The original uniform of the 1st and 2nd Lanark E.V. was closely modelled upon that of the Royal Engineers, white cord (silver lace) being substituted for yellow (gold), and the belts being of white patent leather ; but while the 1st Company wore the busby with Garter blue bag and white plume, the 2nd wore scarlet shakos with a drooping white horse-hair plume. The 3rd adopted the same uniform as the 1st.

On July 30, 1861, the War Office had accepted the services of the 97th Lanark Rifle Volunteers, a four-company corps, formed of men of exceptional physique, and termed locally the " Glasgow Guards " (see Appendix C). The officers of this corps, the commandant of which was Major A. K. Murray, were gazetted on September 3, 1861, and the uniform was scarlet tunics with blue collars and cuffs, blue trousers with red piping, brown fur caps with a scarlet hackle on the right side, the cap being in the form of a Guards' bearskin, and white belts.

On May 19, 1863, the 1st, 2nd, and 3rd Lanark Engineers and the 97th Rifles were amalgamated as the 1st Lanarkshire Engineer Volunteers, of six companies, with headquarters at 115 West Campbell Street, Glasgow, the drill and practice ground being on the river Kelvin, above the bridge on the Great Western Road. The newly formed battalion adopted the uniform hitherto worn by the 1st Lanark E.V., and continued to wear it until 1876, when busbies of a new shape, with upright white horse-hair plumes in front and blue cord lace (the latter for officers only) were adopted, in conformation with the Royal Engineers. In 1878 the white Austrian knots on the sleeves of the tunics and the white band on the forage caps were changed to Garter blue in accordance with regulations, but in 1883 were similarly changed back to white, helmets being also taken into wear in the latter year.

In 1883 the establishment of the corps was increased

to 8 companies, and in 1885 a 9th (Submarine Mining) Company was raised for the Clyde submarine defences. A second submarine mining company was formed in 1888, but in the same year the bulk of both was detached to form the "Clyde Division" of Submarine Miners as an independent corps (see Clyde Division, Electrical E.V.), and in their place a new 9th (Railway) Company was formed. By Army Order 73 of March 1888, the title of the corps was changed to the "1st Lanarkshire Engineer Volunteers, Fortress and Railway Forces, Royal Engineers," and shortly afterwards headquarters were removed to 4 Albany Place, Glasgow, as a temporary measure pending the building of the more commodious headquarters at 21 Jardine Street, Kelvinside, which were occupied in 1894. The 9th (Railway) Company was disbanded in 1889, and in its place a new 9th Company was raised in Springburn.

On the call being made for special service sections for the war in South Africa, the 1st Lanarkshire fulfilled all requirements, and sent out two sections of the established strength to be attached to the 9th Field Company, Royal Engineers, the first being commanded by Captain (hon. major) J. Lang, and the second by Lieutenant J. H. Fleming. In all, 99 members of the corps served in various capacities during the war in South Africa.

In May 1900 the establishment of the corps was raised to twelve fortress companies, and in 1901 the title borne till 1908 was conferred upon the corps.

The headquarters of the corps comprised, besides a drill-hall, stores, &c., a practice ground on the bank of the Kelvin where bridging could be practised, and for its musketry it held, conjointly with the 1st and 2nd V.B.H.L.I., a range up to 1000 yards at Dechmont, nine miles from Glasgow. The 1st Lanarkshire R.E.V. attained to some fame as a shooting corps, and in 1889 Serjeant Reid won the Queen's Prize at the National Rifle Association Meeting.

The lieutenant - colonels commanding (since 1900 commandant) have been—

Ronald Johnstone, June 18, 1863.
Sir Donald Matheson, K.C.B., V.D., Colonel, November 25, 1865.
Herbert D. Robinson, V.D. (hon. col.), March 18, 1893.
Wm. R. Broadfoot, V.D. (hon. col.), April 18, 1896.
Ewing R. Crawford, V.D. (hon. col.), February 3, 1897.
Duncan Campbell, V.D. (hon. col.), November 29, 1899 ; (lieut.-colonel commandant) April 25, 1900.
J. Smith Park, M.V.O., V.D. (hon. col.) (lieut.-colonel commandant), May 28, 1904.

1st EDINBURGH (CITY) ENGINEER VOLUNTEERS.

THIS corps, which in order of procedure in the Engineer Volunteer force ranked immediately after the Lanarkshire Corps, was raised in Edinburgh, from the same classes as the Glasgow Engineer Corps, as a half-company on July 3, 1860, and on September 20 its establishment was increased to that of a full company. Its uniform was the same as that of the Royal Engineers, but with white (silver) cord, and instead of the busby it wore scarlet caps with peaks and green ball-tufts, with a badge of a lion rampant within a wreath. On the white patent-leather pouch-belts was a badge of a fortification.

The first commanding officer was Captain J. Millar

(September 20, 1861), but he resigned in 1862, and the establishment of the corps was reduced then to a half-company, which was attached to the 1st Lanark E.V. The command was exercised thenceforward by First-Lieutenant G. Cunningham until 1865, when the corps was disbanded.

1st ABERDEENSHIRE ROYAL ENGINEERS (VOLUNTEERS).

(PLATE IX.)

ORDER OF PRECEDENCE, 20.

Honorary Colonel—Sir A. H. GRANT, Bart. of Monymusk, August 2, 1890.

Headquarters—HARDGATE, ABERDEEN.

THE formation of the 1st Aberdeenshire Engineer Volunteers, a corps with an establishment of one company, was sanctioned on April 22, 1878, and the first officers were gazetted on June 29. For purposes of the capitation grant the corps was attached to the 1st Lanarkshire Engineer Volunteers. The uniform was that of the Royal Engineers, with helmets, the Austrian knot on the sleeve and band of the forage caps being Garter blue, but in 1883 these were changed to white.

On March 2, 1880, the corps was increased to two, and in 1883 to four, companies. In 1884 it was constituted an independent unit, no longer attached to the 1st Lanark, and in 1888 it was increased to six companies, all of them in the city of Aberdeen. In the latter year (Army Order 73 of March) its title was changed to " 1st Aberdeenshire Engineer

Volunteers, Fortress and Railway Forces, Royal Engineers"; and this nomenclature remained in force till 1901, when the title at the head of this record was assumed.

During the South African war the corps furnished two service sections, both of which were attached to the 47th (Fortress) Company, Royal Engineers. The 1st, consisting of 25 men under Lieutenant R. A. Duthie, left Aberdeen on March 4, 1900, the 2nd, also of 25 men, leaving on March 11, 1901. For their services with their sections Lieutenant Duthie, Serjeant J. Craig, Corporal W. Beveridge, and 2nd Corporal J. Stewart were mentioned in despatches. In all, 62 members of the corps served during the war in South Africa.

The corps had its headquarters in Hardgate, Aberdeen, which were specially erected for it, and first occupied in 1898, and a practice and drill ground in Torry of about 5 acres; its rifle-range was at Don Mouth, $2\frac{1}{2}$ miles from Aberdeen. The training was carried out in camp, at various places, and several times the whole corps trained at the School of Military Engineering, Chatham.

The commanding officers have been—

Captain William Hall, September 28, 1878 (Major, May 9, 1883; Lieut.-Colonel, August 4, 1888).

Lieut.-Colonel Robert H. Anstice (Major (retired pay), late Border Regiment), C.B. (hon. col.), January 28, 1891.

Lieut.-Colonel William S. Gill, V.D. (hon. col.), May 28, 1904.

2ND LANARKSHIRE ROYAL ENGINEER (VOLUNTEERS).

(PLATE IX.)

ORDER OF PRECEDENCE, 23.

Honorary Colonel—Col. A. C. Lord BELHAVEN and STENTON (retired pay), August 1, 1903.

Headquarters—COATBRIDGE.

THE formation of this corps was sanctioned on June 19, 1903, its commanding officer being gazetted on that date, and the remainder of the officers on August 1. The establishment was fixed at nine companies, with headquarters: A, B, and C, Coatbridge; D and E, Airdrie; F, Rutherglen; G, Motherwell; H, Bellshill; and K, Shettleston; and it is on record that within ten days of the date of sanction the corps was recruited up to over its establishment. Its recruiting district was practically that of the former 5th Volunteer Battalion Scottish Rifles, which was disbanded in 1897, and since then had supplied no volunteers. The men were drawn principally from the artisan class, and about one-fifth were miners.

The uniform was the service dress of the Royal Engineers (with red piping on the trousers and scarlet patch on the sleeve), drab felt hats, brown leather equipment, and grey putties. The officers wore the undress R.E. pattern caps and frock-coats.

The corps had a rifle range of its own up to 600 yards at Plains, near Airdrie, and the F to K Companies used the range of the 4th Volunteer Battalion Scottish Rifles.

The first commanding officer was—

Lieut.-Colonel Andrew Pearson, June 19, 1903.

ELECTRICAL ENGINEERS, ROYAL ENGINEERS (VOLUNTEERS).

THE CLYDE DIVISION.

ORDER OF PRECEDENCE, 4.

Honorary Commandant—Colonel E. D. MALCOLM, C.B., R.E. (retired pay), May 29, 1901.

Headquarters—GREENOCK.

THE Division had its origin in the 9th (Submarine Mining) Company, 1st Lanarkshire Engineer Volunteers, which was formed in 1885 to take charge of the submarine mining defences of the Clyde. In 1888 a second Submarine Mining Company was raised in the same corps, and on 1st February 1888 the two companies were formed into a separate corps, the "Clyde Division, Engineer Volunteers, Submarine Miners, Royal Engineers," and adopted the same uniforms as the regular submarine miners, with white cord on the tunic. The headquarters, stores, practice-ground, &c., were at Fort Matilda, Greenock.

In 1892 the establishment was increased to three, and in 1900 to four, companies. In 1901 the corps received the designation "Clyde Division, Submarine Miners, Royal Engineers (Volunteers)," and in 1903 its establishment was reduced to three companies.

In consequence of the abolition of submarine mines in all defended ports, by Army Order 130 of June 1907 the submarine miner volunteers were reduced to the numbers necessary to work the electric lights of the gun defences, and accordingly the Clyde Division became "Electrical Engineers, Royal Engineers (Volunteers)," and was reduced to an establishment of one company of four officers and seventy other ranks.

The commanding officers of the division have been—

Major A. E. Black, February 1, 1888.
Major W. W. B. Rodger, July 11, 1894.
Major Duncan F. D. Neill, December 22, 1897, Lieut.-Colonel (hon. col.), April 1, 1903.

THE FORTH DIVISION.

ORDER OF PRECEDENCE, 6.

Headquarters—14A QUEEN STREET, EDINBURGH.

THE Division was raised, with an establishment of two companies, at Leith, on March 31, 1888. Like the Clyde Division, it was increased to three companies in 1892 and to four in 1900; but was reduced to three again in 1903 and to one in 1907, undergoing also all the changes in designation detailed for the Clyde Division.

Its first headquarters were on board H.M.S *Dido*, off Leith, which was used as a storeship, &c.; but in 1905 a new practice-ground, with store-sheds, pier, &c., was completed at North Queensferry, and the headquarters were removed to Edinburgh.

The commanding officers have been—

Captain F. Grant-Ogilvie, March 31, 1888.
Major Theodore Salvesen, December 12, 1900, Lieut.-Colonel, April 1, 1903.
Lieut.-Colonel Hill M. Cadell, V.D. (hon. col.), January 28, 1905 (till 1906).
Captain Stephen Smith (hon. major), Captain, June 6, 1900.

THE TAY DIVISION, SUBMARINE MINERS, R.E. (VOLUNTEERS).

THIS Division was raised, with an establishment of one company and headquarters at Broughty Ferry, on March 17, 1888. In 1889, 1892, and 1900 it was increased successively to two, three, and four companies; but it was reduced to three in 1903, and finally disbanded on November 2, 1907. In changes of designation it followed the same sequence as the Clyde and Forth Divisions.

Its honorary colonel was A. FitzG. Lord Kinnaird, appointed October 10, 1903, and the commanding officers were—

Major William H. Fergusson, March 17, 1888, Lieut.-Colonel, April 1, 1903.

Lieut.-Colonel Frederick S. Stephens, May 28, 1904 (till November 2, 1907).

VOLUNTEER BATTALIONS OF TERRITORIAL REGIMENTS.

NOTE.

THE volunteer battalions of infantry are arranged in the following pages, not in the order of their precedence in the volunteer force, but in that of the Territorial Regiments to which they were affiliated, the number in the " Table of Precedence of Volunteer Rifle Corps " being given in the case of each.

To facilitate the identification at later dates of rifle corps raised in the early years in four counties—Aberdeen, Forfar, Lanark, and Renfrew—in which three or more battalions of rifle volunteers were formed, lists of these corps have been compiled, with the dates of the first commissions of their officers, and, where available, those of the acceptance of services of the corps, and these will be found in Appendices A to D. In the separate records of those battalions, to avoid repetition, these dates have, therefore, not been inserted.

THE QUEEN'S RIFLE VOLUNTEER BRIGADE, THE ROYAL SCOTS (LOTHIAN REGIMENT).

Regimental District No. 1.

(PLATE X.)

'SOUTH AFRICA, 1900-02." | ORDER OF PRECEDENCE, 78.

Honorary Colonels—

THE LORD PROVOST OF EDINBURGH for the time being.

Field-Marshal Rt. Hon. G. J. VISCOUNT WOLSELEY, K.P., G.C.B., O.M., G.C.M.G., V.D., April 24, 1889.

Colonel Rt. Hon. SIR J. H. A. MACDONALD, K.C.B., V.D., June 5, 1901.

*Headquarters—*FORREST ROAD, EDINBURGH.

THE circumstances attending the first formation of this, the premier corps of rifle volunteers in Scotland, have been already narrated in Part I., on page 13, and a graphic description of the enthusiasm in drill evinced by the corps in those days, from the pen of Colonel Sir J. H. A. Macdonald, has been quoted on page 12.

The City of Edinburgh adopted from the first the system of grouping the companies of riflemen raised by the efforts of individuals or corporations into one regiment for the city, consequently all the officers were gazetted, not to companies as elsewhere, but to the 1st City of Edinburgh Rifle Volunteer Corps, and the earliest dates of these commissions, for officers of the regimental staff, the 1st to 9th, and the 1st Highland companies, was August 31, 1859. This did not, however, prevent the companies from retaining, and from long maintaining, a peculiar individuality, and had the advantage of producing from the beginning a regi-

M

mental *esprit de corps* and a solidity of organisation which was necessarily wanting in units composed of companies grouped only by circumstances or chance.

The companies which were formed before the date (August 7) of the Royal Review of 1860, and which took part in it, were—

No. 1. Advocates, formed August 31, 1859.

No. 2. 1st Citizens, formed August 31, 1859.

No. 3. Writers to the Signet, formed August 31, 1859.

No. 4. Edinburgh University, formed August 31, 1859.

No. 5. Solicitors before the Supreme Court, formed August 31, 1859.

No. 6. Accountants, formed August 31, 1859.

> All the above were self-supporting companies—*i.e.*, the members paid for their own uniforms, equipment, and arms, and contributed a fixed sum annually towards the general expenses of the company.

No. 7. Bankers, formed August 31, 1859, from the clerks and employés of the various banks, which subscribed to provide uniforms, equipments, and arms for them.

No. 8. 1st Artisans, formed August 31, 1859.

No. 9. 2nd Artisans, formed August 31, 1859.

> These were the first artisan companies raised in Scotland. The men paid 30s. in the 8th and 45s. in the 9th, by instalments, for their uniform, and the rest of the expenses of the companies was defrayed by public subscription.

No. 10. Civil Service, formed October 7, 1859, a self-supporting company.

No. 11. 3rd Artisans, formed December 7, 1859, same as 8th and 9th.

No. 12. Freemasons, formed December 7, 1859. This company also formed the "Rifle Lodge, No. 405," but it soon dwindled in numbers and had almost ceased to exist when in 1861 Miss Catherine Sinclair announced her intention to provide funds for a Volunteer company. No. 12 was then reorganised and recruited chiefly from the Water of Leith district.

No. 13. 4th Artisans, formed December 7, 1859, same as 8th.

No. 14. 2nd Citizens, formed December 8, 1859, a self-supporting company.

No. 15. 1st Merchants, formed December 21, 1859. Uniformed,
equipped, and armed at the expense of members of the
Merchant Company, of which two firms—Messrs Cowan &
Co., and Messrs C. Lawson & Sons—paid all the expenses
of forty of their employés.

No. 16. Total Abstainers, formed February 29, 1860. Raised by
Mr John Hope, W.S., from members of the British Temper-
ance League. The company maintained its individuality
till 1867, when the 3rd Edinburgh R.V. (see 4th Vol. Batt.
Royal Scots) was formed and the majority of the members
transferred themselves to it. The company property, however, remained with it, and the 16th was re-constituted as
an artisan company.

No. 17. 2nd Merchants, formed May 11, 1860, from the overflow
of No. 15.

No. 18. High Constables, formed May 25, 1860, a self-supporting
corps.

No. 19. 5th Artisans, formed November 8, 1860, mainly from
operative tailors. Several houses in the clothing trade
subscribed £30, and the rest of the funds was found by
the members themselves. After 1873 it was recruited
from all trades.

1st Highland, formed August 31, 1859, the services of the company having been offered by the Highland Society of Edinburgh on June 13, 1859. The company was entirely self-
supporting.

2nd Highland, formed May 18, 1860, from the overflow of the
1st, and also entirely self-supporting.

From the beginning the corps was organised in two
battalions, and at the Royal Review on August 7,
1860, these were composed of: 1st Battalion, Nos. 1,
2, 3, 4, 5, 6, 7, 10, 18, and 1st Highland; 2nd Battalion, Nos. 8, 9, 11, 12, 13, 14, 15, 16, 17, and 2nd
Highland.

The 3rd Highland Company was formed of artisans

on July 23, 1860, but was not able to take part in the review.

On May 3, 1862, a company of Highland artisans was formed, mainly from the employés of Messrs W. D. Young's ironworks at Fountainbridge, and, contrary to the practice hitherto followed in the city of Edinburgh, it was constituted as a separate corps, designated the 2nd City of Edinburgh R.V., and was only "attached" to the 1st Edinburgh. On February 23, 1867, two more companies were formed for this corps, but on that same date all three were incorporated in the 1st Edinburgh as the 4th, 5th, and 6th Highland Companies.

The original uniform of the corps (except the Highland companies) was dark grey tunics, of a shade a little lighter than that later worn, with black braid, reaching almost to the knees, dark grey trousers with black braid, dark grey caps with black braid and a straight peak, and black patent leather belts, a badge (different for each company) being worn on the cap and pouch-belt. About 1862 a shako with a black ball-tuft replaced the cap, the tunic was assimilated in pattern to that of the Rifle Brigade, and piping replaced the braid on the trousers. The Highland companies wore dark grey doublets, with five rows of black lace on the breast and black piping, 42nd tartan kilts and belted plaids, goatskin sporrans with two grey horse-hair tails, green and black-diced hose, and belts as for the other companies. The 1st had a "Strathdon" and the 3rd a "Balmoral" bonnet, but the others adopted a plain blue glengarry, which afterwards became the head-dress for all the Highland companies.

In 1865 the corps was honoured by the conferring of the title "1st Queen's City of Edinburgh Rifle Volunteer Brigade," and in 1867 its establishment was fixed at 2500 volunteers of all ranks, divided into two battalions, or twenty-five companies. In 1868 the 1st (Advocates) and 3rd (Writers to the Signet) Companies ceased to exist, and to take their place two new companies were raised,—the 7th Highland, mainly formed from natives of Caithness resident in Edinburgh, on December 27, 1867, and the 20th, on March 19, 1869. The battalions were then reorganised, the 1st comprising Nos. 2, 4, 5, 6, 7, 10, 18, and the 1st to 7th Highland Companies, and the 2nd, Nos. 8, 9, 11, 12, 13, 14, 15, 16, 17, 19, and 20.

In January 1875 a busby with black plume and chin-chain replaced the shako, and was worn by the brigade until in 1895 it was replaced by the modern (soft) form of busby of Astrakhan fur. The pouch‑belt was abolished, greatcoats, worn rolled *en bandoulière* over the right shoulder, were issued, the cut of the tunic was assimilated again to that of the Rifle Brigade, and leggings were introduced. Orders were issued in the same year for the Highland companies to be clothed the same as the rest of the brigade, and this change was carried out in the years 1876-79.

A beginning was made in 1886 with the formation of a mounted infantry detachment, one man per company, or 25 all ranks, formed into a section, being in that year authorised.

By Army Order 144 of April 1888 the brigade was given the title of Queen's Rifle Volunteer Brigade, The Royal Scots, and at the same time it was divided into three battalions, the companies now giving up their old titles and numbers and becoming lettered companies of the battalions as follows :—

Company Letter.	A	B	C	D	E	F	G	H	I
1st Battalion	2nd	5th	6th	7th	10th	18th	1st Hd.	2nd Hd.	3rd Hd.
2nd Battalion	8th	9th	11th	12th	13th	14th	15th	16th	...
3rd Battalion	4th	17th	19th	20th	4th Hd.	5th Hd.	6th Hd.	7th Hd.	...

The South African War brought a large accession of numbers to the brigade, for not only was it recruited up to its full establishment, but in 1900 a new company was formed at Colinton as "I" Company, 3rd Battalion, a cyclist company attached to brigade headquarters was raised, and the mounted infantry were increased to three sections, or 105 all ranks. The brigade furnished its full contingent to the volunteer service companies of the Royal Scots, and in all 245 members served in South Africa during the war. Of these, Lieutenant R. G. W. Adams and 54 non-commissioned officers and men served with the 1st, Captain S. R. Dunn and 34 men with the 2nd, and Captain (hon. Major) S. Miller and 26 men with the 3rd Volunteer Service Company, Royal Scots. Of the 2nd Company, Corporal W. Spence died of disease and one private was wounded, and of the 3rd Major Miller and Private A. Blease were mentioned in despatches, the latter being promoted corporal for gallantry at Balmoral on April 5, 1902. Lieutenant R. W. D. Hewson and 13 privates served with the Scottish Volunteer Cyclist Company, and 12 members of the mounted infantry joined the City of London Imperial Volunteers Mounted Infantry, of whom 8 subsequently received commissions in the regular army and 1 in the Imperial Light Horse.

In the years 1900-01 a drab felt hat was worn with the dark grey uniform, but in 1902 this was prohibited, and a drab service dress with light green Austrian knot and trouser piping was authorised for marching and drill order, to be worn with a drab felt hat (with black plume and badge for mounted infantry, for whom it was the sole head-dress). The mounted infantry wore Bedford cord breeches and black putties.

The brigade was detailed to furnish one battalion to

the 32nd Field Army Brigade, to train for thirteen clear days annually, and this it did from 1902 to 1906, after which year this extra organisation ceased. The remainder of the brigade was included in the 1st Lothian Brigade.

The headquarters of the brigade in Forrest Road, which included a spacious drill hall, were acquired in 1872, and enlarged and reopened in 1905, and it shared, in common with the other Edinburgh corps, the rifle range up to 1100 yards at Hunter's Bog. Members of the brigade have won the Queen's (King's) prize at the National Rifle Association no fewer than four times — namely, in 1873, Serjeant (afterwards Major) A. Menzies; 1891, Lieutenant D. Dear; 1896, Lieutenant J. C. Thomson; and 1901, Private H. Ommundsen.

The battalion commanders and lieutenant-colonels commandant (a title now borne by the senior battalion commander) of the brigade have been—

The Rt. Hon. James, Lord Moncrieff, Lieut.-Colonel, August 31, 1859; Lieut.-Colonel Commandant, August 31, 1859, till 1873.

David Davidson, C.B., V.D., late major H.M. Indian Forces, Lieut.-Colonel, May 2, 1860; Lieut.-Colonel Commandant, June 4, 1873, till 1882.

Sir Alex. G. Maitland, Bt., Lieut.-Colonel, November 7, 1862, till 1864.

Rt. Hon. Sir John Hay Athol Macdonald, Lord Kingsburgh, K.C.B., V.D., colonel, Volunteer force, Lieut.-Colonel, May 10, 1864; Lieut.-Colonel Commandant, May 11, 1882, till 1892.

E. Strathearn Gordon, Lieut.-Colonel, November 29, 1867, till 1873.

Hon. Bouverie F. Primrose, Lieut.-Colonel, June 4, 1873, till 1882.

David MacGibbon, Lieut.-Colonel, May 11, 1882, till 1886.

William Taylor (hon. col.), July 29, 1882, till 1890.

Thomas W. Jones, V.D. (hon. col.), Lieut.-Colonel, April 11, 1885 ; Lieut. - Colonel Commandant, April 9, 1892, till 1894.

Robert Menzies, V.D. (hon. col.), Lieut.-Colonel, May 12, 1886 ; Lieut.-Colonel Commandant, June 23, 1894, till 1898.

Horatio R. Macrae, V.D. (hon. col.), Lieut.-Colonel, February 22, 1890 ; Lieut.-Colonel Commandant, February 3, 1898, till 1903.

Sir Robert Cranston, Kt., K.C.V.O., V.D., colonel, Volunteer force, Lieut.-Colonel, April 9, 1892 ; Lieut.-Colonel Commandant, December 3, 1903, till 1906.

James B. Sutherland, V.D. (hon. col.), Lieut.-Colonel 3rd Batt., August 15, 1894, till 1896.

L. Bilton, V.D. (hon. col.), Lieut.-Colonel 3rd Batt., February 5, 1896, till 1900.

G. W. Young, V.D. (hon. col.), Lieut.-Colonel 1st Batt., January 4, 1899, till 1901.

James Gibb, V.D. (hon. col.), Lieut.-Colonel 3rd Batt., March 14, 1900 ; Lieut.-Colonel Commandant, June 1, 1906, till March 31, 1908.

Alexander T. Hunter, V.D. (hon. col.), Lieut.-Colonel 1st Batt., March 9, 1901, till 1906.

Robert Clark, V.D. (hon. col.), Lieut.-Colonel 2nd Batt., February 16, 1904, till March 31, 1908.

A. Young, V.D., Lieut.-Colonel 1st Batt., June 3, 1906, till March 31, 1908.

4TH VOLUNTEER BATTALION THE ROYAL SCOTS (LOTHIAN REGIMENT).

Regimental District, No. 1.

(PLATE XI.)

" SOUTH AFRICA, 1901-02." | ORDER OF PRECEDENCE, 79.

Honorary Colonel—General H. H. Viscount KITCHENER OF KHARTOUM, G.C.B., O.M., G.C.M.G., August 19, 1905.

Headquarters—33 GILMORE PLACE, EDINBURGH.

THE 3rd City of Edinburgh Rifle Volunteer Corps was formed, as a corps of total abstainers, members of the British League, on May 27, 1867, by Captain John Hope, who had raised and commanded the 16th (Abstainers) Company of the Queen's Edinburgh. It consisted at first of two companies only, but was increased to three in 1868, to four in 1872, and to six companies in 1877. The original uniform was scarlet tunics with blue facings, blue trousers with a broad scarlet stripe, blue shakos with at first a red-and-white ball-tuft and later a scarlet upright horse-hair plume, and white belts. The corps for many years wore brass buttons and ornaments. To the corps was attached the British League Cadet Corps, formed in 1861, which consisted of four companies of boys, dressed in red Garibaldi shirts, blue forage-cap and knickerbockers, and brown canvas leggings.

In 1880 the corps was renumbered the 2nd Edinburgh Rifle Volunteers, and two years later it was constituted an independent unit, having till then been "attached" to the Queen's Edinburgh. In 1882 also, helmets replaced the shakos hitherto worn.

By Army Order 144 of 1st April 1888 it became the 4th Volunteer Battalion Royal Scots, and accordingly in that year adopted the uniform of the regiment, wearing the helmet with it till 1904, when the Kilmarnock bonnet was introduced for officers and the glengarry became the sole head-dress for other ranks. The uniform of the battalion has thus since 1888 been identical with that of the 5th V.B. (which see), and, as in it, the officers wore Hunting Stuart tartan trews in levée and mess dress only.

The battalion furnished in all 64 members for service in South Africa during the war, of whom 15 men served in the 1st, 12 in the 2nd, and 19 in the 3rd Volunteer Service Company of the Royal Scots. No casualties occurred among these contingents, but Drummer R. Robertson of the 3rd Company was mentioned in despatches (June 1, 1902), and promoted corporal for gallantry at Balmoral on April 5, 1902. Lieutenant W. B. Grey and 3 men served in the Scottish Volunteer Cyclist Company. The establishment of the battalion was in 1900 increased to eight companies, the new " G " Company being raised in Portobello, and " H " formed by students of the Church of Scotland Teachers' Training College.

From 1902 to 1906 the battalion belonged to the 32nd Field Army Brigade, and trained with it in camp for thirteen clear days annually, but in the end of 1906 this brigading was discontinued, and the battalion reverted to the 1st Lothian Brigade. Its musketry was carried out at the Hunter's Bog range, which it used in conjunction with other Edinburgh corps.

The commanding officers have been—

Captain John Hope (Captain 1st Edinburgh R.V., February 29, 1860), May 27, 1867; Major, March 30, 1872; Lieut.-Colonel, March 2, 1878.

Lieut.-Colonel Will. U. Martin, V.D. (hon. col.), June 27, 1883.

Lieut.-Colonel Stuart D. Elliot, V.D. (hon. col.), December 20, 1899.

Lieut.-Colonel George McCrae, V.D. (hon. col.), January 28, 1905.

5TH VOLUNTEER BATTALION THE ROYAL SCOTS (LOTHIAN REGIMENT).

Regimental District, No. 1.

(PLATE XII.)

"SOUTH AFRICA, 1900-02." | ORDER OF PRECEDENCE, 141.

Honorary Colonel—R. C. MACLAGAN, V.D. (hon. col.), August 20, 1892.

Headquarters—DALMENY STREET, LEITH WALK, LEITH.

ON August 6, 1859, the services of 153 gentlemen of Leith were offered to form two rifle companies which should pay all their own expenses and provide their own arms, and this offer was followed by that of two companies of Leith artisans, who paid a contribution of 30s. each, the rest of their expenses being defrayed by public subscription. These were accepted, and on December 6, 1859, officers were gazetted to the 1st Mid-Lothian (Leith) Rifle Volunteer Corps, of four companies. A brass band of 18 men was formed; a fifth company was added on May 28, 1860; a sixth on September 24, 1860; a seventh on March 18, 1861; and an eighth on May 28, 1861—all recruited in Leith. The original uniform of the corps was very dark grey tunic, trousers, and peaked cap, with black facings, leggings, and belts, but, to save expense, members were permitted to wear a plain blouse and trousers of any material, so long as the colour of the uniform was adhered to. The badge on the cap and pouch-belt was a lion rampant within a wreath.

In 1863 the 4th Mid-Lothian (Corstorphine) Rifle Volunteer Corps, which had been formed on November 26, 1860, and since then "attached" to the corps, was amalgamated with it as a 9th company, and in 1866 and 1868 a 10th and 11th companies were raised.

The uniform was in 1863 changed to scarlet tunics with black facings, blue trousers with scarlet piping, blue shakos with black horse-hair plumes, and black waist- and pouch-belts. This uniform was worn until 1878, when blue helmets with silver ornaments replaced the shakos, and in 1885 white (buff) belts with complete valise equipment, greatcoat, &c., were substituted for the black belts.

The establishment of the battalion was in 1884 reduced to ten companies, and in 1888 (Army Order 144 of April) it assumed its latest designation, as a consequence of which in 1890 it adopted the uniform of the Royal Scots, the helmet continuing to be worn till June 1905, when Kilmarnock bonnets with diced band and cock's-tail for officers, and glengarries with diced border for other ranks, became the head-dress. The battalion till 1908 wore the tartan first approved for the Royal Scots, officers only wearing in levée or mess dress the Hunting Stuart. The officers wore white pouch-belts till 1905, when they were replaced by claymore belts and sashes, which latter were worn by serjeants also. A drab service dress was approved in 1905.

During the South African War the battalion furnished 196 of its members for service, besides 94 who enlisted into the regular army. Of the former, Captain R. Wemyss Campbell and 19 men served with the 1st, 41 men with the 2nd, and 49 men with the 3rd Volunteer Service Company of the Royal Scots. Of the 1st Company, 2 men died of disease, and Captain Campbell and Corporal T. H. Greig were mentioned in Lord Roberts' despatch of September 4, 1901, the latter being awarded a medal for distinguished conduct in the field. Of the 2nd Company, 2 men were wounded, and of the 3rd, Private J. G. Lockhart was mentioned

in Lord Kitchener's despatch of June 1, 1902, and promoted corporal for gallantry at Balmoral on April 5,
1902. In addition, 32 non-commissioned officers and
men (of whom 1 was wounded) served in the Scottish
Volunteer Cyclist Company, 25 joined the Imperial
Yeomanry, 10 Baden-Powell's Police, and 19 the Scottish Horse.

In 1900 the establishment of the battalion was again
raised to eleven companies, but in 1901 it was reorganised into ten, of which one was a cyclist company.

The battalion formed part of the 32nd Field Army
Brigade during its existence from 1902 to 1906,
training in camp for thirteen days annually, and in
1906 its signallers made a record by securing 298
points at the examination out of a possible 300.

In 1877 a headquarters and drill-hall in Stead's
Place, Leith, which had been built at a cost of over
£3000, were occupied, but these were burned down in
1900, and in 1902 new headquarters and drill-hall in
Dalmeny Street, Leith Walk, were opened. The battalion had its own range, up to 1000 yards, at Seafield,
near Leith.

The commanding officers have been—

H. H. Arnaud, late H.E.I.C.S., Major, December 6, 1859.
Donald R. Macgregor, Major, July 27, 1861; Lieut.-Colonel,
    March 15, 1862.
Wm. Marjoribanks (hon. col.), Lieut.-Colonel, March 28, 1877.
Robt. C. Maclagan (hon. col.), Lieut.-Colonel, May 3, 1882.
Robt. S. Adam (hon. col.), Lieut.-Colonel, December 7, 1889.
Wm. I. Macadam, V.D. (hon. col.), Lieut.-Colonel, June 18, 1892.
Jas. R. Bertram, V.D. (hon. col.), Lieut.-Colonel, December 16,
    1896.
Johan T. Salvesen, V.D. (hon. col.), Lieut.-Colonel, January 2,
    1901.
Sir John M. Clark, Bart., V.D. (hon. col.), Lieut.-Colonel, February
    11, 1905.

6TH VOLUNTEER BATTALION THE ROYAL SCOTS (LOTHIAN REGIMENT).

Regimental District, No. 1.

(PLATE XIII.)

"SOUTH AFRICA, 1901." | ORDER OF PRECEDENCE, 142.

Honorary Colonel—Sir G. D. CLERK, Bart., V.D. (hon. col.), late Lieutenant
2nd Life Guards, February 4, 1899.

Headquarters—PEEBLES.

ON January 22, 1862, the 1st Administrative Battalion Mid-Lothian Rifle Volunteers, with headquarters at Dalkeith, was formed from the following corps :—

2nd Mid-Lothian R.V., Dalkeith, formed May 22, 1860, of two companies, increased to three in 1864, and to four in 1867. Its original uniform was medium grey with green facings and piping, grey shakos with plume of cock's feathers and badge of a huntsman blowing a horn, and motto, "Free for a blast," and brown belts.

3rd Mid-Lothian R.V., Penicuik, services accepted May 22, 1860, and officers gazetted June 4, 1860, of three companies—1st at Penicuik, 2nd at Valleyfield, 3rd at Roslin, which last was disbanded in 1864. The uniform was the same as the 2nd Corps, but with black patent-leather belts.

5th Mid-Lothian R.V., Musselburgh, formed April 19, 1861, of one company.

To this battalion were added in 1863—

1st Peebles R.V., Peebles, formed as one company, August 31, 1860, increased to two companies 1873.

2nd Peebles R.V., Broughton, formed as one company, August 31, 1860, disbanded 1873.

3rd Peebles R.V., Innerleithen, formed as one company, August 31, 1860.

There had also existed a 4th Peebles R.V., of one company, formed at Linton on October 16, 1860, but it had been disbanded in 1862. The uniform of all the Peebles corps was Elcho grey, with brown belts, the 1st having light blue facings.

In 1864 the battalion adopted scarlet tunics with black facings, blue trousers with scarlet piping, blue shakos with scarlet ball-tuft, and black belts, the forage cap being round, without a peak, and with red, white, and blue diced border. This uniform continued to be worn till 1875, when white belts replaced the black, and a black Austrian knot the white braid on the cuff. Officers wore white pouch-belts and the lace of the line infantry in silver.

In 1876 (April 29) the 6th Mid-Lothian R.V., at Loanhead, of one company, was raised and added to the battalion, and in April 1880 the battalion was consolidated as the 2nd Mid-Lothian and Peebles Rifle Volunteers, headquarters at Penicuik, with eleven companies, lettered as follows : A, B, C, and D, Dalkeith (late 2nd Mid-Lothian) ; E, Penicuik, and F, Valleyfield (late 3rd Mid-Lothian) ; G, Musselburgh (late 5th Mid-Lothian) ; H, Loanhead (late 6th Mid-Lothian) ; I and K, Peebles (late 1st Peebles) ; and L, Innerleithen (late 3rd Peebles). At the same time the shako was abolished, and a glengarry with red, white, and blue diced border adopted as the sole head-dress, which was worn until 1886, when blue helmets with silver ornaments were introduced.

In April 1888 (Army Order 144) the battalion became the 6th Volunteer Battalion of the Royal Scots, and accordingly in that year the uniform of the Royal Scots was adopted, the helmet being worn with it until 1900, when the glengarry again became the sole headdress. In February 1904 the Hunting Stuart tartan trews of the Royal Scots were taken into wear, sashes were introduced for officers and serjeants, and the former adopted the Kilmarnock bonnet with cock's-tail for review order dress.

The battalion furnished in all 36 members for service in South Africa during the war, of whom 13 non-commissioned officers and men served in the 1st, Lieutenant A. G. Ireland and 7 men in the 2nd, and 2 men in the 3rd Volunteer Service Company of the Royal Scots. Of the 2nd Company, Private T. Dickson died of disease. One private served in the Scottish Volunteer Cyclist Company, and the remainder in other corps.

About 1895 the headquarters of " D " Company were removed from Dalkeith to Bonnyrigg, and in February 1907 battalion headquarters were removed to Peebles, otherwise the battalion experienced no changes in interior organisation after 1880. It owned eight rifle-ranges near the headquarters of the various companies.

The lieutenant-colonels commanding have been—

Alex. Learmonth, late Lieut.-Colonel 17th Lancers, December 23, 1863.

Sir George D. Clerk, Bart., V.D. (hon. col.), late Lieutenant 2nd Life Guards, July 2, 1879.

Robert G. Wardlaw-Ramsay, V.D. (hon. col.), late Captain H.L.I., January 18, 1899.

Thomas Rough, V.D. (hon. col.), November 22, 1905.

7TH VOLUNTEER BATTALION THE ROYAL SCOTS (LOTHIAN REGIMENT).

Regimental District, No. 1.

(PLATE XIV.)

"SOUTH AFRICA, 1901." | ORDER OF PRECEDENCE, 190.

Honorary Colonel—H. R. LORD ELCHO, August 28, 1906.

Headquarters—HADDINGTON.

THE 1st Administrative Battalion Haddingtonshire Rifle Volunteers, with headquarters at Haddington, was formed on August 19, 1860, and included the following corps formed in the county:—

1st, Haddington, formed January 19, 1860, of one company, a self-supporting corps, providing its own arms.

2nd, Gifford, formed January 20, 1860, of one company, composed of agricultural labourers, principally from Lord Tweeddale's estates. It was disbanded in 1874.

3rd, Haddington, formed January 21, 1860, of one company, chiefly mechanics and artisans, and supported by local subscriptions.

4th, Aberlady, formed March 17, 1860, of one company, raised from Lord Wemyss's estates, and mainly supported by his subscription.

5th, East Linton, formed April 7, 1860, of one company.

6th, Dunglass, formed August 27, 1861, as one subdivision, the headquarters of which were transferred in 1873 to West Barns, near Dunbar.

7th, North Berwick, formed November 25, 1869, of one company.

The county of Haddington raised a general subscription to provide for the necessities of the battalion, and to this fund over £1000 was subscribed in the first two years of its existence.

The first uniform of the Haddington corps was Elcho grey, without facings, and brown belts; but about

N

1861, grey tunics with magenta cuffs and collars, with a black Austrian knot, grey trousers with a magenta stripe, and grey shakos with a magenta ball-tuft and badge of goat and thistle, were substituted for the former plainer uniform. In February 1864 the battalion adopted the rifle-green uniform with scarlet cuffs, collars, and piping, shakos with a black ball-tuft, and black belts of the 60th Rifles, and this continued to be worn until 1878, when the cuffs were changed, according to regulation, to dark green with red piping, black lace, and a light green Austrian knot.

In April 1880 the battalion was consolidated as the 1st Haddingtonshire Rifle Volunteers, with headquarters at Haddington, and six companies lettered: A and B, Haddington (late 1st and 3rd Corps); C, Aberlady (late 4th Corps); D, East Linton (late 5th Corps); E, West Barns (late 6th Corps); and F, North Berwick (late 7th Corps). The " E " Company had only the strength of a half-company, so in January 1881 a new " E " Company was formed at Tranent with a section at Prestonpans, the West Barns detachment being transferred to " D " Company at East Linton. In 1880, also, the shakos were replaced by helmets with a bronze Maltese cross as ornament, and these again were replaced in 1895 by Astrakhan fur busbies with red-and-black plumes, serges being also supplied to the battalion as undress in the same year.

In April 1888, by Army Order 144, the title of 7th Volunteer Battalion The Royal Scots was conferred upon the battalion; but it was not till January 1904 that the dress of the Royal Scots was assumed by it, and then only in the shape of the drab service doublet, worn with Hunting Stuart tartan trews, glengarries with red, white, and blue diced border, and brown leather equipment, the pipers wearing the white jacket, kilt, and shoulder plaid, and the drummers the scarlet doublet.

During the war in South Africa 30 members of the battalion saw active service, of whom Lieut. T. F. M. Williamson and 18 non-commissioned officers and men served with the 1st, 8 men with the 2nd, and 3 men with the 3rd Volunteer Service Company of the Royal Scots, and one man with the Scottish Volunteer Cyclist Company. Private D. Lambert of the 1st Service Company died of disease, and Colour-Serjeant H. Gray was mentioned in Lord Roberts' despatch of September 4, 1901.

In April 1906 the section of " E " Company at Prestonpans had so greatly increased in numbers that it was formed into a separate company and lettered " C," the detachment (formerly " C " Company) at Aberlady being added as a section to " A " Company. The battalion thenceforward was organised in six companies, viz. : A, Haddington, with a section at Aberlady; B, Haddington; C, Prestonpans; D, East Linton, with a section at West Barns; E, Tranent; and F, North Berwick. There was a rifle-range close to the headquarters of each company.

The commanding officers have been—

Sir George Warrender, Bart., late Captain 92nd Foot and Coldstream Guards, of Lochend and Bruntsfield; Major, September 19, 1860; Lieut.-Colonel, December 22, 1868.

Jas. W. H. Anderson, Lieut.-Colonel, June 1, 1872.

Alex. Scott, Lieut.-Colonel, June 25, 1879.

P. Dods (hon. col.), late Lieut.-Colonel Bombay Staff Corps, Lieut.-Colonel, May 31, 1882.

W. Guild, Lieut.-Colonel, September 5, 1894.

John D. Watson, V.D. (hon. col.), Lieut.-Colonel, May 1, 1898.

Robert Maxwell Main, V.D. (hon. col.), Lieut.-Colonel, February 20, 1904.

8TH VOLUNTEER BATTALION THE ROYAL SCOTS (LOTHIAN REGIMENT).

Regimental District, No. 1.

(PLATE XIV.)

"SOUTH AFRICA, 1901-02." | ORDER OF PRECEDENCE, 216.

Honorary Colonel—Rt. Hon. A. P. EARL OF ROSEBERY, K.G., K.T., V.D., April 18, 1874.

Headquarters—LINLITHGOW.

THE 1st Administrative Battalion Linlithgowshire Rifle Volunteers was formed on October 8, 1862, with headquarters at Linlithgow, and included the following corps, of one company each, raised in the county:—

1st, Linlithgow, raised March 19, 1860. Uniform—dark grey without facings and with scarlet piping, dark grey cap with ball-tuft, and brown belts with silver ornaments.

2nd, Bo'ness, raised March 19, 1860. Uniform—dark grey with scarlet facings, dark grey cap with ball-tuft, and brown belts with silver ornaments. Increased to one and a half companies in 1866.

3rd, Bathgate, raised April 25, 1860. Uniform as for 2nd Corps. Headquarters changed to Torphichen, 1864.

4th, Bathgate, raised August 9, 1862, mainly from the employés of Young's Chemical Works. Uniform as for 2nd Corps.

On May 18, 1863, the battalion adopted a rifle uniform of green with scarlet facings, and shakos, the same as that worn by the Haddington Battalion 1864 to 1878 (see 7th Volunteer Battalion), with which, however, the brown belts continued to be worn. The shakos were replaced by rifle busbies, with black-and-red plumes and bugle in front, on April 25, 1872.

On March 18, 1872, a 5th Corps, of one company, was formed at Uphall, and on April 17, 1878, a 6th, of one and a half companies, at West Calder.

On March 24, 1876, the lower part of the busby plume was changed to light green, and the cuffs of the tunic became rifle green, ornamented only by a light green Austrian knot.

In March 1880 the battalion was consolidated as the 1st Linlithgow Rifle Volunteers, headquarters at Linlithgow, with seven companies, lettered as follows: A, Linlithgow (late 1st Corps); B, Bo'ness (late 2nd); C, Torphichen (1881 Armadale) (late 3rd); D, Bathgate (late 4th); E, Uphall (late 5th); F, Addiewell (late half of the 6th); G, West Calder (late 6th).

In 1888, by Army Order 144 of April, the corps became the 8th Volunteer Battalion The Royal Scots, and in 1890 the Slade-Wallace equipment, with black belts, was adopted by the battalion. About the same time, the rifle serge with red piping on the collar and red crow's-foot on the cuff replaced the tunic, and the lower part of the busby plume was changed from green to red.

During the war in South Africa, 36 members of the battalion, including Captain M. W. Henderson and Lieut. P. W. Steuart, saw active service, principally with the Volunteer Service Companies of the Royal Scots. Captain Henderson commanded the 1st, and Lieut. Steuart served with the 2nd Volunteer Service Company, and of the latter Lance-Corporal A. Williamson and Private W. Earle died of disease.

As did other corps, the 8th V.B. increased its establishment during the war, an " H " Company being formed at South Queensferry and " I " at Kirkliston, the headquarters of " F " Company being at the same time (March 1900) transferred to Fauldhouse; but in 1906 " H " Company was disbanded again, and " I " relettered " H." In January 1903 authority was given for a drab service dress of Scottish pattern with red piping on the trousers, and glengarries with the Royal Scots badge and diced border, to be worn as the sole uniform of the battalion, along with buff belts and black leggings.

The distribution of the battalion in 1908 was—

A Company, Linlithgow.	E Company, Uphall.
B Company, Bo'ness.	F Company, Fauldhouse.
C Company, Armadale.	G Company, West Calder.
D Company, Bathgate.	H Company, Kirkliston.

The battalion had seven separate rifle-ranges.
The commanding officers have been—

R. H. J. Stewart, Major, October 21, 1862.

Andrew Gillon (hon. col.), Major, April 16, 1866; Lieut.-Colonel, April 28, 1870.

G. F. Melville, Lieut.-Colonel, June 17, 1888.

Thomas Hope of Bridge Castle, late Captain Bombay Staff Corps (hon. col.), Lieut.-Colonel, June 9, 1897.

Charles Chalmers, V.D., Lieut.-Colonel, July 11, 1903.

9TH VOLUNTEER BATTALION (HIGHLANDERS) THE ROYAL SCOTS (LOTHIAN REGIMENT).

Regimental District, No. 1.

(PLATE XI.)

"SOUTH AFRICA, 1901-02." | ORDER OF PRECEDENCE, 80.

Honorary Colonel—General SIR I. S. HAMILTON, K.C.B., D.S.O., August 31, 1901.

Headquarters—7 WEMYSS PLACE, EDINBURGH.

THIS battalion was raised in Edinburgh during the war in South Africa, its first commanding officer being gazetted on July 24, 1900. It was the out-come of the yearning of the Highlanders in Edinburgh to see a kilted battalion of volunteers recruited from the capital. The Queen's Edinburgh Rifle Volunteer Brigade had formerly included seven kilted companies in its ranks, but in 1875 these had been ordered to be clothed in the dress of the remaining companies of the Brigade (*q.v.*), and had by the subsequent reorganisation of the Brigade lost entirely their distinctively Highland character. The new battalion, which was formed at an establishment of eight companies, was at first designated "The Highland Battalion, Queen's Rifle Volunteer Brigade Royal Scots," but in 1901 it was constituted an independent unit as the 9th Volunteer Battalion of the Royal Scots.

The uniform, as approved on July 24, 1900, consisted of a scarlet doublet with blue facings, Hunting Stuart tartan kilts and belted plaids, white horsehair sporrans with two black tails, red - and - black diced hose, white spats, glengarries with red, white, and blue diced borders (feather bonnets with white hackle for officers), and white belts, service drab doublets being also authorised.

Young as the battalion was, 43 of its members found an opportunity of serving in South Africa during the war, of whom 22 men served in the 2nd and Lieutenant J. C. C. Broun and 2 men in the 3rd Volunteer Service Company of the Royal Scots, and 18 men in the Imperial Yeomanry. From 1902 to 1906 the battalion was included in the 31st Field Army Brigade, and trained accordingly for thirteen days annually during these years. It used the Hunter's Bog range for its musketry.

The lieutenant-colonels commanding have been—

James Ferguson, V.D. (hon. col.), July 24, 1900.
James Clark, December 17, 1904.

8TH (SCOTTISH) VOLUNTEER BATTALION, THE KING'S (LIVERPOOL REGIMENT).

Regimental District, No. 8.

(PLATE XI.)

" SOUTH AFRICA, 1902."

Honorary Colonel—Right Hon. D. A. LORD STRATHCONA AND
MOUNT ROYAL, G.C.M.G., February 12, 1902.

Headquarters—FRASER STREET, LIVERPOOL.

THE battalion was raised in Liverpool during the South African War, and was composed of Scotsmen resident in that city. Its first officers were gazetted on October 4, 1900, and the establishment of the battalion was fixed at eight companies. The uniform consisted of drab cloth doublets with scarlet collars, cuffs, and piping, and silver buttons, Forbes tartan kilts, grey sporrans with two black tails, red - and - black diced hose, drab spats, belted plaids, glengarries with red, white, and blue diced border and blackcock's tail, and brown belts and equipment.

During the war the Liverpool Scottish contributed a section, consisting of Lieutenant J. Watson and 22 men, to the 4th Volunteer Service Company of the Gordon Highlanders (see 1st V.B. Gordon Highlanders).

The lieutenant-colonels commanding have been—

C. Forbes Bell, V.D. (hon. col.), October 10, 1900.
Andrew L. Macfie, V.D. (hon. col.), July 26, 1902.

1st VOLUNTEER BATTALION THE ROYAL SCOTS FUSILIERS.

Regimental District, No. 21.

(PLATE XV.)

"SOUTH AFRICA, 1900-02." | ORDER OF PRECEDENCE, 192.

Honorary Colonel—R. M. McKERRELL, V.D. (hon. col.), April 23, 1904.

Headquarters—KILMARNOCK.

ON August 27, 1860, the 1st Administrative Battalion Ayrshire Rifle Volunteers was formed out of the 1st to 9th Corps, and to it were added in 1860 the 10th and 11th, in 1861 the 12th and 13th, and in 1862 the 14th Corps. The battalion having become inconveniently large, in March 1873 it was split up into two—the South Ayrshire corps forming the 1st Administrative Battalion, with headquarters at Ayr; the North Ayrshire the 2nd, with headquarters at Kilmarnock.

The corps comprising the 2nd Battalion were the

1st, Kilmarnock, formed January 14, 1860, as one company. Uniform — medium grey edged with black braid, black piping on trousers, and black patent leather belts.

2nd, Irvine, formed December 27, 1859, as one company. Uniform—medium grey with green facings and black braid, brown belts, bugle and thistle badge on cap, and arms of Scotland on the pouch-belt.

4th, Largs, formed February 27, 1860, as one company.

6th, Beith, formed February 15, 1860, as one company.

7th, Saltcoats, formed February 28, 1860, as one company, of which a detachment was at Stevenston.

9th, Kilmarnock, formed May 19, 1860, as one company. Uniform—medium grey with light blue facings.

11th, Dalry, formed December 4, 1860, as one company.

The uniforms of the corps not mentioned above were grey of various shades, and it was not until 1867 that the 1st Administrative Battalion, as then existing, was clothed uniformly in scarlet tunics with blue facings and trousers, blue shakos with dark green ball - tuft, white belts, and black leggings.

In the same year in which the 2nd Battalion was constituted, a new corps, the 15th, was raised at Darvel as one company on December 24, 1873, and on October 10, 1874, another one-company corps, the 17th, was formed at Galston, both being added to the battalion.   In 1875, however, the 9th Corps (Kilmarnock) was amalgamated with the 1st, thus leaving the battalion eight companies strong.

In June 1880 the battalion was consolidated as the 1st Ayrshire Rifle Volunteers, with headquarters at Kilmarnock, and eight companies lettered—A, Kilmarnock (late 1st Corps); B, Irvine (late 3rd); C, Largs (late 4th); D, Beith (late 6th); E, Saltcoats (late 7th); F, Dalry (late 11th); G, Darvel (late 15th); and H, Galston (late 17th).   At the same time blue helmets with silver ornaments replaced the shakos, and a black Austrian knot was added to the cuffs of the tunics.

By General Order 181, of December 1887, the battalion was designated the 1st Volunteer Battalion Royal Scots Fusiliers, and on the following 20th April it was authorised to adopt the uniform of that regiment, with volunteer distinctions, but without the raccoon skin cap, the diced glengarry remaining the sole head - dress.   Sashes were worn by serjeants only.

During the war in South Africa the battalion was represented by 94 of all ranks, of whom Captain C. G. Dickie, Lieutenant J. MacL. Frew, and 56 other ranks served with the 1st Service Company, and Lieutenant J. Alexander and 19 men with the 2nd Service Section (1902) of the Royal Scots Fusiliers, and Captain J. M. Hunter served with the Volunteer Cyclist Company. Of the 1st Service Company, Private Agnew was wounded, and Corporal T. Winton and Lance-Corporal J. Risk died of disease.

At home the battalion was increased in strength, for in 1900 two new companies, J and K, of which one was a cyclist company, were raised in Kilmarnock, and at the same time the headquarters of C Company were removed from Largs to Stewarton, and of H from Galston to Kilmarnock. The headquarters of the ten companies were, therefore, thenceforward—

A, H, J, K, Kilmarnock.
B, Irvine.
C, Stewarton.
D, Beith.

E, Saltcoats.
F, Dalry.
G, Darvel.

The headquarters range of the battalion at Irvine, up to 1000 yards, belonged to the Ayrshire Rifle Association, and D, E, F, and G Companies had their own separate ranges near their headquarters. The battalion had a good musketry record, and in 1888 it stood first in order of merit as regards musketry out of 212 rifle corps included in the War Office returns.

The lieutenant-colonels commanding since 1873 have been—

R. B. Robertson-Glasgow, March 26, 1873.
John Dickie, V.D. (hon. col.), September 16, 1874.
R. M. McKerrell, V.D. (hon. col.), May 10, 1895.
J. Gow, June 11, 1904.

2ND VOLUNTEER BATTALION THE ROYAL SCOTS FUSILIERS.

Regimental District, No. 21.

(PLATE XV.)

"SOUTH AFRICA, 1900-01." | ORDER OF PRECEDENCE, 193.

Honorary Colonel—R. P. ROBERTSON-GLASGOW (hon. col.), December 20, 1906.

Headquarters—AYR.

THE early history of this battalion, up to 1873, is identical with that of the 1st Volunteer Battalion (*q.v.*)

The original corps, which at the split of March 1873 remained constituting the 1st Administrative Battalion Ayrshire Rifle Volunteers, were the

3rd Ayr, formed January 19, 1860, as one company. Uniform— medium grey, with scarlet facings, black braid, and black patent-leather belts.

5th Maybole, formed February 27, 1860, as one company.

8th Colmonell, formed May 25, 1860, as one company.

10th Girvan, formed October 22, 1860, as one company.

12th Cumnock, formed January 14, 1861, as one company.

13th Sorn, formed March 18, 1861, as one company.

14th Ayr, formed April 14, 1862, as one subdivision, increased to a full company in 1871.

At the end of 1873 there was added to the battalion the 16th Corps, formed at Newmilns as one company on December 24, 1873.

The 8th Corps was disbanded in 1875, and in April 1880 the battalion was consolidated as the 3rd (numbered 2nd in June) Ayrshire Rifle Volunteers, headquarters at Ayr, with seven companies lettered A and B, Ayr (late 3rd and 14th Corps); C, Maybole (late 5th); D, Girvan (late 10th); E, Cumnock (late 12th); F, Sorn (late 13th); and G, Newmilns (late

16th). In this year also the uniform, which had hitherto been identical with that of the 2nd Administrative Battalion, was in so far changed that for the shako the glengarry with diced border was substituted, and was ever since the sole head-dress of the battalion. A black Austrian knot was also added to the cuff of the tunic.

In 1883 the headquarters of F Company were moved from Sorn to Catrine, in the same parish, and a new (H) company was raised at Troon.

In 1887 (General Order 181 of December) the battalion assumed the designation of 2nd Volunteer Battalion, The Royal Scots Fusiliers, but it was only on January 13, 1898, that it was authorised to be clothed in the doublet and trews of the regiment, the raccoon skin cap not being worn, and serjeants only wearing sashes.

A large number of men volunteered for the war in South Africa, and 2 officers and 62 men actually served, of whom Lieutenant G. D. Porteous and 54 other ranks belonged to the 1st Service Company and 4 men to the 2nd Service Section of the Royal Scots Fusiliers. Lieutenant R. M. M. Buntine was also attached to the line battalion. Of the 1st Service Company, Lance-Corporal J. M'Chesney and Privates R. Gilmore and J. M'Lean died of disease.

In 1900 I (Cyclist) Company was formed at Ayr, bringing the battalion up to an establishment of nine companies, viz. :—

A, B, and I, Ayr.	F, Catrine.
C, Maybole.	G, Newmilns.
D, Girvan.	H, Troon.
E, Cumnock.	

From 1902 to 1906 the battalion was detailed to the 33rd Field Army Brigade, and trained annually in camp for thirteen days. A, B, H, and I Companies used the range of the Ayrshire Rifle Association at Irvine, the other five having each their own range.

The lieutenant-colonels commanding the former 1st Administrative Battalion, or this corps, have been—

Archibald, Marquis of Ailsa, K.T., August 27, 1860.
Jas. G. Hay Boyd, late 20th Foot, January 8, 1862.
Right Hon. Sir J. Fergusson, Bart. of Kilkerran, late Lieutenant and Captain Grenadier Guards, December 10, 1879.
David D. Whigham, V.D. (hon. col.), August 21, 1890.
Robert P. Robertson-Glasgow of Montgreenan, late Lieutenant Durham L.I., March 29, 1896.
James E. Shaw, June 11, 1904, to February 10, 1908.

1st ROXBURGH AND SELKIRK (THE BORDER) VOLUNTEER RIFLE CORPS.

Regimental District, No. 25.

(PLATE XVI.)

"SOUTH AFRICA, 1900-02." | ORDER OF PRECEDENCE, 147.

Honorary Colonel—Sir R. J. WALDIE-GRIFFITH, Bart. (hon. col.), September 22, 1906.

Headquarters—MELROSE.

THE 1st Administrative Battalion, Roxburghshire Rifle Volunteers, was formed on November 9, 1861, with headquarters at Melrose, and including the 1st, 2nd, 3rd, 4th, and 5th Roxburgh Rifle Volunteer Corps. To it were added in 1862 the 1st and 2nd Selkirk Rifle Volunteer Corps. The individual details of the origin of these corps are as follows:—

1st Roxburgh R.V.C., Jedburgh. The corps, of one company, with a detachment at Denholm, which in 1863 was transferred to the 4th Corps when the latter raised a second company, was first sworn in on September 15, 1859, its officers being gazetted on November 17. The uniform was slate-grey tunics, trousers, and caps, the tunics hooked in front (buttoned for officers), and with scarlet collars and black piping and Austrian knot, the trousers and caps with black piping, and the latter with a crown and bugle ornament. Shakos with a black ball-tuft were adopted in 1862. The belts were brown leather, as for all corps of this battalion, the men wearing waist-belts only, officers and serjeants pouch-belts with chain and whistle.

2nd Roxburgh R.V.C., Kelso. The first public meeting to form this corps was held on May 27, 1859, but its services were not accepted till March 1860, the men being sworn in on the 26th, and the officers gazetted on the 29th of that month. The uniform (see Plate XVI.) was as for the 1st Corps, but the tunics were buttoned for all ranks, the trousers had broad black stripes, and the cap badge was a St Andrew on a red ground. The corps was of the strength of one company.

3rd Roxburgh R.V.C., Melrose. Raised on June 15, 1860, and men sworn in on July 15, 1860. Strength, one company. Uniform as for 2nd Corps.

4th Roxburgh R.V.C., Hawick. The first public meeting to form this corps, one company strong, was held on December 8, 1859. Its services were offered on March 6, and accepted on June 11, 1860, the officers being gazetted, along with those of the 3rd Corps, on June 15, 1860. Members paid for their uniform and equipment, and gave an annual subscription of 10s. at first. The first uniform (see Plate XVI.) was slate-grey, with red collars and black braid on the tunic, with four rows on the breast, and black Austrian knot, blue Kilmarnock bonnets, and brown waist-belts. This was shortly afterwards changed to the same uniform as the 2nd Corps, but with grey shako with black band and star badge in front and plume of cock's feathers. On December 1, 1863, the corps was increased to two companies, the detachment at Denholm, hitherto belonging to the 1st Corps, being incorporated in it.

5th Roxburgh R.V.C., Hawick, raised as one company on January 15, 1861, and disbanded in 1867.

1st Selkirk R.V.C., Galashiels. This corps, of one company, known as the " Gala Forest Rifles," was the outcome of a public meeting held on November 22, 1859. The officers were gazetted on March 27, 1860, and the corps was sworn in on April 9, 1860, there being then 85 effective and 38 honorary members. The cost of the uniform and equipment was £3, 10s. 7d., to which members were required to contribute a minimum of 30s., the balance being paid out of corps funds, which were formed by annual subscriptions of 10s. for each effective, and at least 21s. for each honorary member, and by public subscriptions. In 1861 the annual subscriptions for effective members were abolished, and the payment for uniform reduced to 15s. The uniform (see Plate XVI.) was slate-grey tunics, trousers, and caps, the tunics with scarlet collars and Austrian knots, bound all round with black braid, and with four rows of the same on the breast, the trousers with scarlet piping and two stripes of black braid, and the caps with a black band and scarlet piping. The shoulder- and waist-belts were of brown leather. The corps was increased to two companies on December 1, 1869.

2nd Selkirk R.V.C., Selkirk, known as the " Ettrick Forest Rifles," was raised on June 15, 1860, as one company, on the same conditions and with the same uniform as the 1st Selkirk. It was increased to two companies on November 1, 1879.

The title of " The Border Rifles " was conferred upon the battalion in 1868.

In 1863 the uniforms of all the corps were assimilated, the slate-grey colour being retained for tunics, trousers, and shakos. The tunics had scarlet collars with black braid, black piping, and black ring tracing on the cuff, the trousers black piping, and the shakos three rows of black braid, black and red ball-tuft, and bugle badge. Belts were of brown leather, and haversacks and greatcoats formed part of the equipment of the battalion. Blue Kilmarnock bonnets were worn in undress till 1885, when they were replaced by glengarries. In 1877 the red collar on the tunic was abolished, and in 1879 grey helmets, with a bronze Maltese cross on a black ground, were introduced.

Headquarters of the battalion were transferred on June 30, 1878, from Melrose to Newtown St Boswells, and on April 7, 1880, under War Office authority of March 24, the battalion was consolidated under the title of 1st Roxburgh and Selkirk (The Border) R.V.C., with 9 companies, lettered as follows :—

A, Jedburgh (late 1st R.R.V.), B, Kelso (late 2nd R.R.V.), C, Melrose (late 3rd R.R.V.), D and E, Hawick (late 4th R.R.V.), F and G, Galashiels (late 1st S.R.V.), H and I, Selkirk (late 2nd S.R.V.)

In 1887 (General Order 61 of May) the battalion was transferred from the 21st (Royal Scots Fusiliers) to the 25th (King's Own Scottish Borderers) Regimental District, and in the same year the headquarters of H Company were removed from Selkirk to Galashiels. On April 1, 1892, a tenth (K) Company was raised at Hawick.

During the South African war, the battalion contributed its contingent to all the volunteer service companies raised for the King's Own Scottish Borderers : Major A. Haddon, Lieutenant M. Craig-Brown, and 34 men serving in the 1st, Lieutenant J. Herbertson and 30 men in the 2nd, and 18 men in the 3rd Service Company. Eleven men served in the Scottish Volunteer Cyclist Company, and one man as a Royal Engineer telegraphist; making a total of 97 members of the battalion who served in the war. In 1901 the establishment of the battalion was raised to 12 companies, but in 1902 these new companies were again reduced, the headquarters were transferred to Melrose, and the cyclists of the whole battalion were formed into one company (L) with headquarters at Newcastleton. In this year the helmets were replaced by a grey felt hat with black and white feathers, turned up on the left side with a badge of the Douglas heart and crown and the motto, "Doe or die." In 1902 the battalion was included in the 32nd Field Army Brigade, and trained with it for thirteen days annually till 1906.

The latter-day distribution of the companies of the battalion was—

A, Jedburgh.
B, Kelso.
C, Melrose.
D, E, and K, Hawick.

F, G, and H, Galashiels.
I, Selkirk.
L (Cyclist) Newcastleton.

It possessed eight separate rifle - ranges near the headquarters of companies.

The lieutenant-colonels commanding have been :—

H. F. H. S. Lord Polwarth, November 9, 1861.

Sir George H. S. Douglas, Bart., Springwood Park, Kelso, late Captain 34th Foot (hon. col.), October 26, 1868.

Jas. Paton, of Crailing, late Major 4th Foot (hon. col.), February 6, 1886.

Wm. S. Elliott, of Teviot Lodge, Hawick (hon. col.), September 5, 1888.

Sir Richard J. Waldie-Griffith, Bart., of Hendersyde Park, Kelso (hon. col.), January 7, 1891.

Andrew Haddon, V.D. (hon. captain in army), December 27, 1900, to February 26, 1908.

2ND (BERWICKSHIRE) VOLUNTEER BATTALION, THE KING'S OWN SCOTTISH BORDERERS.

Regimental District, No. 25.

(PLATE XVII.)

"SOUTH AFRICA, 1900-02." | ORDER OF PRECEDENCE, 187.

Honorary Colonel—A. M. BROWN, late Captain R. A. (hon. col.), May 14, 1887.

Headquarters—DUNS.

ON November 19, 1863, the 1st Administrative Battalion, Berwickshire Rifle Volunteers, was formed, with headquarters at Duns, from the following corps :—

1st Duns, formed December 16, 1859, as one company. Uniform —dark grey tunic, trousers, and cap with black braiding, and black patent-leather belts.

2nd Coldstream, formed March 30, 1860, as one company. Uniform—medium grey tunic, with green cuffs and collar and black Austrian knot (for the men) and piping, medium grey trousers with green stripe, green cap with grey band and green ball-tuft, and brown waist-belts (pouch-belt also for officers and sergeants).

3rd Aytoun, formed May 11, 1860, as one subdivision ; increased to one company, August 20, 1860. Uniform the same as 1st Corps, but with red piping on the trousers.

4th, Greenlaw, formed February 24, 1860, as one company. Uniform the same as the 2nd Corps. Badge, the Marchmont crest (glaive in hand) and motto, "True to death."

5th Lauderdale, formed April 10, 1860, as one subdivision ; increased to one company, March 16, 1864. Uniform the same as the 2nd Corps, but all ranks had pouch-belts.

6th Earlston, formed June 5, 1863, as one company.

7th Chirnside, formed July 7, 1863, as one subdivision, increased to one company, August 5, 1868.

The 6th and 7th Corps adopted from the beginning the following uniform, which had been decided upon for the whole battalion at a meeting held on May 19, 1863 : Scarlet tunics with scarlet cuffs and collar, black braid all round, and Austrian knot, and for officers four "fern leaves" in black embroidery on the breast (abolished in 1865), dark grey (Oxford mixture) trousers with 1¼ in. scarlet stripes, dark grey shakos with red band, black piping, the Royal Arms in front, and a light green ostrich-feather plume (cock's feathers for officers), and brown waist- and pouch - belts.   In 1873 white haversacks were issued, and on April 1, 1875, the uniform was modernised, the black braid on the tunic being replaced by black piping, silver lace and buttons for officers and sergeants introduced, the trouser stripe replaced by piping, and the old shako replaced by a plain grey one, with green ball - tuft and bugle badge.   Blue helmets with silver star and crown badge replaced the shakos in February 1880.

The headquarters of the battalion were removed from Duns to Coldstream on November 1, 1876, and in April 1880 the battalion was consolidated as the 1st Berwickshire Rifle Volunteers, with seven companies lettered from A to G in the seniority of corps. On April 7, 1884, the battalion adopted the uniform of the Royal Scots (to which it was then affiliated), the helmet and brown belts continuing to be worn with it.   In 1885 headquarters were moved back to Duns, and in 1887 (General Order 61 of May) the battalion was transferred from the Royal Scots Regimental District to that of the King's Own Scottish Borderers, and assumed the title of 2nd Volunteer Battalion of that regiment (General Order 181 of December), serge doublets, with the new regimental badges, replacing at the same time those of cloth with blue cuffs hitherto worn. At that time the Royal Scots and the Scottish Borderers wore the same tartan. On April 1, 1891, a new company " H " was raised at Duns, bringing the establishment of the battalion up to eight companies.

During the South African war the battalion furnished its contingent to all the volunteer service companies of the King's Own Scottish Borderers, 80 members in all serving in South Africa. Of these, Lieutenant R. Stoddart and 34 men served with the 1st, Lieutenant R. C. Christie-Thomson and 27 men with the 2nd, and Captain J. E. Stevenson and 2 men with the 3rd Volunteer Service Company, 2nd Lieutenant D. H. Stewart and 11 men in the Imperial Yeomanry, 1 man in the Post Office Corps, and 2nd Lieutenant W. Home with the 4th (Militia) Battalion Argyll and Sutherland Highlanders. At home a cyclist section was formed, and a new company, " I," at Ladykirk raised, under War Office authority of May 29, 1900 ; but in 1905 " H " company was disbanded and " I " was re-lettered " H." In 1900 also the helmet was replaced by the glengarry with diced border as the sole head-dress, and the tartan of the trews was changed to Leslie. Sashes were permitted to be worn by serjeants.

The distribution of the battalion since 1905 was—

Headquarters and A Company, Duns.

B Company, Coldstream.

C Company, Ayton, detachment at Coldingham.

D Company, Greenlaw, detachment at Gordon.

E Company, Lauder, detachment at Stow.

F Company, Earlston.

G Company, Chirnside, detachment at Horncliffe.

H Company, Ladykirk, detachment at Swinton.

There were 10 ranges belonging to the battalion.

The lieutenant-colonels commanding have been—

Hon. A. F. Cathcart, Brevet-Lieutenant-Colonel, December 19, 1863.

Sir J. Marjoribanks, Bart., December 20, 1866.

Hon. Robert Baillie-Hamilton, late Major 44th Foot, February 9, 1881.

Alex. M. Brown, late Captain (R.A.), (hon. col.) January 18, 1882.

Charles Hope (late Captain King's Royal Rifle Corps), May 14, 1887, to March 30, 1908.

3RD (DUMFRIES) VOLUNTEER BATTALION, THE KING'S OWN SCOTTISH BORDERERS.

Regimental District, No. 25.

(PLATE XVIII.)

"SOUTH AFRICA, 1900-02." | ORDER OF PRECEDENCE, 194.

*Headquarters—*DUMFRIES.

ON January 4, 1862, the 1st Administrative Battalion, Dumfriesshire Rifle Volunteers, was formed, with headquarters at Dumfries, and to it were attached the following corps, all of one company each :—

1st, Dumfries, formed February 25, 1860,		{ increased to two companies, 1872.
2nd, Thornhill,	,,	February 28, 1860.
3rd, Sanquhar,	,,	Feburary 28, 1860.
4th, Penpont,	,,	February 29, 1860.
5th, Annan,	,,	June 14, 1860.
6th, Moffat,	,,	June 20, 1860.
7th, Langholm,	,,	June 1, 1860.
8th, Lockerbie,	,,	June 20, 1860.
9th, Lochmaben,	,,	February 18, 1861.

The original uniform of all corps was Elcho grey tunic and trousers, with scarlet collars, cuffs, piping, and Austrian knot, Elcho grey shakos with scarlet band and ball-tuft, with a bugle and crown badge and " 60 " (the county precedence number) in the centre of the bugle, and brown waist-belts. Some companies had at first blue facings, but these were changed to scarlet in 1862. The undress cap was a grey Balmoral bonnet, with blue, grey, and red diced border; but this was replaced in 1864 by a round grey forage cap with scarlet band. In 1876 this uniform was replaced by scarlet tunics with yellow facings and Austrian knot, blue trousers with scarlet piping, black busbies with yellow and black plume, with black lace and lines for officers, and white belts,—at first patent-leather, and afterwards of buff leather pipe-clayed.

In April 1880 the battalion was consolidated as the 1st Dumfriesshire Rifle Volunteers, with headquarters at Dumfries, and 10 companies, lettered—

A and B, Dumfries (late 1st Corps).
C, Thornhill (late 2nd).
D, Sanquhar (late 3rd).
E, Penpont (late 4th).
F, Annan (late 5th).

G, Moffat (late 6th).
H, Langholm (late 7th).
I, Lockerbie (late 8th).
K, Lochmaben (late 9th).

On March 23, 1885, the Penpont Company became a section of " C," and a new " E " Company was formed at Ecclefechan; and on December 7, 1888, the headquarters of " K " Company were removed from Lochmaben to Canonbie.

The battalion was removed, by General Order 61 of May 1887, from the 21st (Royal Scots Fusiliers) to the 25th (King's Own Scottish Borderers) Regimental District, and it assumed the title of 3rd Volunteer Battalion of the latter regiment by General Order 181 of December 1, 1887, consequent upon which, on February

29, 1888, the uniform of the King's Own Scottish Borderers was adopted, serge undress doublets (with scarlet cuffs) being worn.   The helmet was introduced with this uniform, and was worn until 1900, when the glengarry was adopted as the sole head-dress, and the trews were changed to Leslie tartan.   Sashes were worn by serjeants only.

During the war 1 officer and 72 men were contributed by the battalion to the volunteer service companies of the King's Own Scottish Borderers,— Lieutenant R. J. Cunningham and 32 men to the 1st, 24 men to the 2nd, and 16 men to the 3rd : in addition, 4 men joined the R.A.M.C., 3 the Scottish Volunteer Cyclist Company, 1 the Post Office Corps, 3 Colonial Corps, and 2 the Imperial Yeomanry,—making in all 86 members of the 3rd Volunteer Battalion who served in South Africa.

The distribution of the battalion was latterly as follows :—

A and B Companies, Dumfries.
C Company, Thornhill ; detachment at Penpont.
D Company, Sanquhar ; detachment at Kirkconnel.
E Company, Ecclefechan.

F Company, Annan.
G Company, Moffat ; detachment at Wanlockhead.
H Company, Langholm.
I Company, Lockerbie.
K Company, Canonbie.

The headquarters at Dumfries included a large drill-hall, the Annan Company had similar arrangements, and the battalion in all possessed 12 rifle-ranges.

The lieutenant-colonels commanding have been—

Lord H. J. M. Douglas-Scott, February 8, 1862.
J. S. D. Marquis of Queensberry, September 18, 1869.
John G. Clark, April 25, 1871.
Wm. E. Malcolm, August 15, 1881.
Robt. F. Dudgeon, V.D., late Captain R. Scots Fusiliers (hon. col.), May 22, 1886.

THE GALLOWAY VOLUNTEER RIFLE CORPS.

(KIRKCUDBRIGHT AND WIGTOWN.)

Regimental District, No. 25.

(PLATE XIX.)

"SOUTH AFRICA, 1900-02." | ORDER OF PRECEDENCE, 202.

Honorary Colonel—J. M. KENNEDY, M.V.O., V.D.(hon. col.), October 13, 1906.

Headquarters—MAXWELLTOWN.

THE Galloway Administrative Battalion of Rifle Volunteers was formed on June 30, 1860, with headquarters at Newton-Stewart, and to it, then or on their subsequent date of formation, were attached the following corps :—

1st Kirkcudbright R.V., Kirkcudbright, formed March 2, 1860, as one company. Uniform—steel grey, with green facings.

2nd Kirkcudbright R.V., Castle-Douglas, formed March 2, 1860, as one company.

3rd Kirkcudbright R.V., New Galloway, formed March 28, 1860, as one company.

4th Kirkcudbright R.V., Gatehouse, formed May 19, 1860, as a subdivision, disbanded in 1866.

5th Kirkcudbright R.V., Maxwelltown, formed June 1, 1860, as one company, increased to one and a-half companies in 1865 and to two companies in 1880.

6th Kirkcudbright R.V., Dalbeattie, formed June 23, 1869, as one company.

1st Wigtown R.V., Wigtown, formed February 24, 1860, as a subdivision, incorporated as a section in the 3rd Corps in 1874.

2nd Wigtown R.V., Stranraer, formed March 16, 1860, as one company.

3rd Wigtown R.V., Newton-Stewart, formed March 21, 1860, as one company.

4th Wigtown R.V., Whithorn, formed April 11, 1860, as a subdivision, disbanded in 1874.
5th Wigtown R.V., Drumore, formed November 23, 1860, as a
  subdivision, disbanded in 1866.

The original uniforms of the corps were steel or dark
grey, and varied greatly, not only between corps, but
also in the corps from year to year, one company
appearing one year with plumes of cock's feathers
and the next with shakos of Highland Light Infantry
pattern, &c.

Uniformity was first attained on December 5, 1873,
when the whole battalion was clothed in dark grey
tunics and trousers, with scarlet cuffs, collars, piping,
and Austrian knot (latter with black tracing all round),
dark grey shakos with black ball-tuft, and black belts.

On May 9, 1883, the shako was replaced by a plain
blue glengarry, but otherwise the 1873 uniform (which
remained till 1908 the regulation for officers in full dress)
was worn down to May 19, 1905, when drab service
dress with scarlet piping on the trousers, drab putties,
blue glengarry with regimental badge and red, white,
and blue diced border, and brown leather equipment
with bandolier, became the sole dress of the battalion.

In June 1880 the battalion was consolidated under
the title of the Galloway Rifle Volunteer Corps, with
headquarters at Newton-Stewart, and 8 companies,
lettered as follows :—

A, Kirkcudbright (late 1st K.R.V.)   E, New Galloway (late 3rd K.R.V.)
B, Castle-Douglas (late 2nd K.R.V.)   F and G, Maxwelltown (late 5th
C, Stranraer (late 2nd W.R.V.)   K.R.V.)
D, Newton-Stewart, detachments at   H, Dalbeattie (late 6th K.R.V.)
   Wigtown and Creetown (late
   3rd and 1st W.R.V.)

On March 21, 1885, headquarters were transferred to
Castle-Douglas, and in 1899, by Army Order 65, the
battalion was removed from the 21st (Royal Scots

Fusiliers) to the 25th (King's Own Scottish Borderers) Regimental District.

During the war 95 members of the battalion served in South Africa. Of these, 34 non-commissioned officers and men served with the 1st, Captain J. Blacklock and 26 men with the 2nd, and 20 men with the 3rd Volunteer Service Company of the King's Own Scottish Borderers. Of the 2nd company, Colour-Serjeant R. Grierson, Lance-Corporal J. M'Millan, and Private R. Dixon of the Galloway Rifles were mentioned for gallantry at the capture of Commandant Wolmarans and 30 Boers near Damhoek on August 10, 1901 (in Lord Kitchener's despatch of October 8, 1901), and the last two were specially promoted to corporal. In addition Lieutenant T. Shortridge and 2 men served in the Scottish Cyclist Company, Lieutenant E. S. Forde and one other as civil surgeons, 5 men served in the Imperial Yeomanry, 3 in Fincastle's Horse, and 1 in the South African Constabulary.

On September 6, 1904, battalion headquarters were removed from Castle - Douglas to Maxwelltown. The battalion possessed 14 separate rifle - ranges, one of which, at Conhuith, for F and G companies, was held conjointly with the 3rd Volunteer Battalion K.O.S.B.

The lieutenant-colonels commanding have been—

Wm. K. Lawrie, June 30, 1860.
John G. Maitland, January 6, 1872.
John M. Kennedy, M.V.O., V.D. (hon. col.), July 30, 1889.
John Lennox, V.D. (hon. col.), September 8, 1906.

1st LANARKSHIRE VOLUNTEER RIFLE CORPS.

Regimental District, No. 26.

(PLATE XX.)

"SOUTH AFRICA, 1900-02." | ORDER OF PRECEDENCE, 111.

Honorary Colonel—JAMES A. REID, V.D. (hon. col.), March 28, 1903.

Headquarters—261 WEST PRINCES STREET, GLASGOW.

THE origin of the 1st Lanarkshire Rifle Volunteer Corps, or Glasgow 1st Western, has already been indicated in Part I., on page 16. The first meeting of this corps for drill was held in the playground of the Glasgow Academy, Elmbank Street, July 27, 1859, and, after drill, the corps assembled in a class-room, under the presidency of Mr (afterwards Lieutenant) Charles Hutchison Smith,[1] and decided that Sir Archibald Islay Campbell, Bart. of Garscube, should be recommended to the Lord-Lieutenant for appointment as captain, Mr (afterwards Ensign) Ruthven Campbell Todd[2] being appointed treasurer. As already narrated, the services of this company were offered on August 5, 1859, and accepted on September 24, and on October 1, 1859, the first officers were gazetted.

On January 11, 1860, a meeting was held by the "1st Western" Corps, as a result of which the corps communicated with other companies with a view to forming a regiment, and, in consequence, on February 28, 1860, the 1st, 2nd, 9th, 11th, 15th, 17th, 18th, 33rd, 39th, 50th, and 53rd Corps of Lanarkshire Rifle Volunteers were formed into the "1st Lanarkshire Rifle Volunteer Corps," which was shown for the first time, eleven companies strong, in the Army List for April

---

[1] Afterwards Major 1st Lanark R.V. Retired 1872. Died July 13, 1904.

[2] Afterwards Lieut.-Colonel Commandant, and then Honorary Colonel 1st Lanark R.V. Resigned 1883. Died August 9, 1887.

1860, Sir Archibald Islay Campbell, the former captain of the 1st Western, having been gazetted lieutenant-colonel to command from March 6, 1860 ('Gazette,' March 9, 1860). During March and April 1860 the 63rd, 72nd, 76th, 77th, and 79th Corps of Lanarkshire Rifle Volunteers were added to it, bringing the total strength up to sixteen companies, and on June 1, 1860, the regiment was divided into two battalions.

The dates of acceptance of services and of first commissioning of officers of all corps are given in Appendix C. Each consisted originally of one company only, and the following notes show the first composition and uniform of the separate corps :—

1st Corps (1st Western), already mentioned. Uniform—dark grey tunics, trousers, and caps, first with five rows of black braid on the breast, and black patent leather waist- and pouch-belts. Badge, a Scottish lion on a shield. Motto, "Jus Patria." Arms, short Enfield and sword bayonet (all private property). The corps, as already indicated, was entirely self-supporting. Afterwards "A" Company.

2nd Corps (University of Glasgow). This corps, composed of professors, graduates, and students of the University, made a simultaneous offer of service with the 1st Corps, but the claims of the latter to priority of formation were allowed. Uniform said to have been much the same as for the 1st. The company fell off gradually in numbers, and on March 2, 1870, was amalgamated with "Q" Company (77th), which had a somewhat similar origin.

9th Corps (Bankers). Formed in consequence of a meeting on August 4, 1859, of tellers, clerks, &c., in the various Glasgow banks. Each bank, except the City of Glasgow and the Clydesdale, subscribed and paid for the armament and equipment of ten to fifteen men, £10 being the maximum expense for each man. The conditions of admission were afterwards extended, but have always been subject to a ballot of serving members, and the banks have always kept up their interest in the company by giving prizes for shooting, &c. Uniform as for the 1st Corps. Badge, St Andrew's Cross. Motto, "Semper Paratus." Afterwards "B" Company.

11th Corps (2nd Western). Formed at a meeting on October

4, 1859, as an overflow company of the 1st Corps, the formal offer of service being made on the 25th, and an officer (Lieut. C. H. Smith) of the 1st being elected captain. Uniform and armament the same as for the 1st, but of a slightly lighter (reddish) grey, and with a bugle and crown as a badge, and black piping instead of braid on the trousers.[1] In 1864 the 39th Corps (see below) was amalgamated with the 11th. Afterwards " C " Company.

15th Company (Procurators). Formed in consequence of a meeting held in the Faculty Hall on September 28, 1859, and composed of members of the legal profession, clerks, and apprentices. £105 was given by the Faculty towards the expenses of the corps, and the profession subscribed largely. Original uniform unknown, probably dark grey like 1st. Afterwards " D " Company.

17th Corps (Stockbrokers and Accountants). The offer of this corps' services was made on November 18, 1859, it having been formed in consequence of a meeting held on the 4th. The Stock Exchange contributed £150, and the Institute of Accountants and Actuaries £100, to its funds. Uniform, medium grey. Afterwards " E " Company.

18th Corps. Formed in consequence of a meeting on November 16, 1859, from the employés of the firm of Messrs Wylie & Lochhead, furnishers and undertakers, which subscribed £80 towards the funds, the rest of the cost of £4 per man being borne by the members or by outside subscriptions. Uniform—medium grey, with brown belts. The company maintained its distinctive character till 1881, when recruiting became general. Afterwards " L " Company.

33rd Corps (Partick). Formed after a meeting of the inhabitants of Partick held on October 6, 1859, its services being offered on December 8. It was a self-supporting corps, each member finding his own uniform and equipment, and paying £2, 2s. annual subscription. Uniform the same as the 1st Corps, with badge of bugle-horn and crown. Afterwards " F " Company.

39th Corps. Formed from employés of the shipping companies, which together contributed £334 to its funds. Its services were offered on December 13, 1859. Uniform unknown.

---

[1] A specimen of this uniform is to be seen in the Glasgow Art Galleries, Kelvingrove Park.

Numbers soon fell off, and in 1864 its remaining members were transferred to the 11th Corps.

50th Corps (1st Press). A meeting of newspaper employés and press-men was held on October 24, 1859, and the services of this corps, formed of these, were offered on December 28. So great were the numbers, that a second overflow company, numbered the 51st, was formed immediately, but this subsequently joined the 19th Lanark R.V. (1st V.B.H.L.I.) The uniform is unknown. The 50th corps fell off rapidly in numbers, and was broken up in 1863.

53rd Corps. Formed in consequence of a meeting held on November 29, 1860, from the employés of the firm of J. & W. Campbell, who gave £200 towards the funds of the corps. Its services were offered on December 29, 1860. The late Prime Minister, Sir H. Campbell-Bannerman, was at first lieutenant, and then, till 1867, captain of this company. In 1862, when the change of uniform was made, this officer paid £50, and the firm contributed £100, towards the expenses of the company. The uniform was Elcho grey, with knickerbockers, brown belts, and brown leggings. Afterwards "M" Company.

63rd Corps. Formed in consequence of a meeting held on December 7, 1859, out of members of the grain and provision trades and bakers, the various firms of which subscribed £450. Its services were offered on January 30, 1860. Uniform unknown. This corps formed an overflow company, numbered the 84th, which received half its funds and afterwards joined the 31st Lanark (see 3d V.B.H.L.I.) Afterwards "N" Company.

72nd Corps (Fine Arts). Formed of jewellers, watch and clock makers, silversmiths, engravers, &c., at a meeting held on December 7, 1859. Uniform—dark bluish grey, with light blue facings, small stiff bluish-grey shakos, plume of cock's feathers, and black belts. Badges, a silver wreath and crown on the shako, and a star with Minerva's head on the pouch-belt. The company fell off in numbers, and in 1863 its remaining members joined "P" Company (76th Corps).

76th Corps (Port Dundas). Formed in consequence of a meeting on February 13, 1860, of men employed in the distilleries, saw-mills, wharves, stores, and sugar-works at Port Dundas. The men are said to have been of quite exceptional physique. Uniform as for the 72nd Corps, but with ball-tufts on the shakos.

In 1863 the remains of the 72nd Corps were amalgamated with it. Afterwards " P " Company.

77th Corps (City Rifle Guard, or 2d University). This corps at first existed as a drill class, but at a meeting on February 10, 1860, it was resolved to form the class into a volunteer corps. The men were mostly of the mercantile community, but a university professor was captain, it drilled in College Green, and its headquarters were in the College. It never, however, recruited its ranks from the University till March 1870, when the remainder of the 2nd Corps (then " K " Company) was amalgamated with it. Uniform—dark green, with shakos and cock's feathers, and black belts. Afterwards " Q " Company.

79th Corps (3rd Western). Like the 77th at first a drill class which, at a meeting held on February 23, 1880, it was resolved to form into a volunteer corps. Uniform—Elcho grey, with green facings, brown belts, and bronze ornaments. Afterwards " G " Company.

When the regiment was divided into two battalions in June 1860, the corps were renumbered, but they appear to have continued to use their old numbers till the end of that year at least. It was not till 1864 that the companies were lettered, and by that time several of the original corps had ceased to exist. The following table shows how the re-numbering and re-lettering were carried out :—

	1st Corps became 1860	1st Company,	1864 "A" Company.
	9th ,, ,, ,,	2nd ,,	,, "B" ,,
	11th ,, ,, ,,	3rd ,,	,, "C" ,,
	15th ,, ,, ,,	4th ,,	,, "D" ,,
1st Battalion	17th ,, ,, ,,	5th ,,	,, "E" ,,
	33rd ,, ,, ,,	6th ,,	,, "F" ,,
	39th ,, ,, ,,	7th ,,	,, Amalgamated with C Coy.
	79th ,, ,, ,,	8th ,,	,, "G" Company.
	2nd ,, ,, ,,	9th ,,	,, "K" ,,
	18th ,, ,, ,,	10th ,,	,, "L" ,,
	50th ,, ,, ,,	11th ,,	Broken up 1863.
	53rd ,, ,, ,,	12th ,,	1864 "M" Company.
2nd Battalion	63rd ,, ,, ,,	13th ,,	,, "N" ,,
	72nd ,, ,, ,,	14th ,,	1863 Amalgamated with 15th Coy.
	76th ,, ,, ,,	15th ,,	1864 "P" Company.
	77th ,, ,, ,,	16th ,,	,, "Q" ,,

To do away with the sixteen varieties of uniform existing in the regiment, in November 1860 a ballot was taken, and the choice fell upon a Government (Elcho) grey uniform with blue facings, the wearing of which became obligatory in 1862. The 1st Lanark shade of grey was browner than the real Elcho grey, and this shade was throughout adhered to by the corps. The blue collar had grey cord lace, the blue cuff a grey Austrian knot, and the trousers blue piping. The cap was soft, of grey cloth with diced blue and white band, silver bugle in front, and straight peak. Brown pouch- and waist-belts. Yellow leggings with black band at the ankle.

In 1870 K Company was amalgamated with Q, and the regiment thus reduced to 12 companies, although the official establishment always remained at 16 companies. To remedy this, great exertions were made by Lieut.-Colonel R. C. Todd, then commanding, and in 1878 two new companies, which were lettered K and O, were formed. In 1881 similar efforts were made to recruit up for the Royal Review. The recently raised K Company became I, and two new companies, H and K, were formed, thus bringing the regiment up to its authorised establishment. Hitherto the post of lieutenant-colonel had remained vacant, but in 1881 an officer was appointed to this post to assist the lieutenant-colonel commandant, and command the 2nd Battalion. No change since then took place in the formation or designation of the corps, except that since 1900 K Company was recruited from University students, who were under special regulations. For a few years also a section of mounted infantry was maintained in the corps.

The uniform was changed very little. In 1872 grey busbies with blue lace and white plumes were adopted,

P

but these were discarded in 1876, and the cap alone worn till 1878, when grey helmets with bronze ornaments were adopted, the Austrian knot on the sleeve being replaced by a simple round loop of cord, and blue cloth shoulder-straps taking the place of the cord hitherto worn.   Elcho grey greatcoats were introduced in 1870, and were worn rolled "*en bandoulière*," but about 1890 these were replaced by the ordinary dark grey infantry greatcoat.   In July 1902 a drab service dress with green Austrian knot was approved for the corps, also a grey field cap with diced band as on the old cap, but of smaller pattern.   The loop of cord was removed from the cuff, and the cord from the collar of the tunic, and the shoulder-straps became grey with blue edges.

During the South African War the corps furnished 102 members who served in the field.   Of those Lieut. A. A. Kennedy and 33 other ranks served with the 1st, and Captain R. J. Douglas and 19 men with the 2nd Volunteer Service Company of the Scottish Rifles, of whom Private R. Pattman died of disease.   Thirty-six members served in the Imperial Yeomanry, and the rest in various corps.

A notable fact about the 1st Lanark R.V. is the large number of officers who have been supplied from its ranks to other volunteer corps, and it is on record that the A Company, the former 1st Western, between 1860 and 1881, furnished more than one hundred such, and that C Company, the former 2nd Western, or over-flow of the 1st, gave in the first year of its existence twenty-six officers to other volunteer corps.

The regiment first, in 1860, rented the Burnbank ground in the Great Western Road, and, in the years 1866-7, erected a drill-hall on it at a cost of £1250. When this ground became built over, it erected new headquarters at 261 West Princes Street, at a cost of £16,000, and acquired a new drill-ground at Yorkhill. Its first regimental shooting-range was at Possil, near Cowlairs, up to 900 yards, which it held in conjunction with the 19th Lanark Rifles and 1st Lanark Engineers, but this was closed in 1885, and in the following year a new range up to 1000 yards, at Darnley, which it held in conjunction with the 3rd Lanark V.R.C., was taken into use.

The lieutenant-colonels commandant and lieutenant-colonels commanding battalions have been—

Sir Archibald Islay Campbell, Bart. of Garscube, Lieut.-Colonel Commandant, March 6, 1860.

Sir George Campbell, Bart. of Garscube, late 1st Dragoons, Lieut.-Colonel Commandant, November 3, 1866.

Ruthven Campbell Todd (hon. col.), Lieut.-Colonel Commandant, May 4, 1874.

Joseph Newbigging Smith (hon. col.), Lieut.-Colonel Commandant, February 9, 1881.

Robert Easton Aitken, Lieut.-Colonel, December 3, 1881.

James A. Reid, V.D. (hon. col.), Lieut.-Colonel, March 3, 1888, Lieut.-Colonel Commandant, January 11, 1890.

Thomas A. Paul, V.D. (hon. col.), Lieut.-Colonel, February 8, 1890 till 1899.

H. A. Ker, V.D. (hon. col.), Lieut-Colonel, February 22, 1899 till 1902.

John Macfarlane, M.V.O., V.D. (hon. col.), Lieut.-Colonel, June 11, 1902, Lieut.-Colonel Commandant, February 21, 1903.

John A. Roxburgh, V.D. (hon. col.), Lieut.-Colonel, March 21, 1903, Lieut.-Colonel Commandant, March 31, 1906.

William A. Smith, V.D., Lieut.-Colonel, May 19, 1906.

2ND VOLUNTEER BATTALION, THE CAMERONIANS (SCOTTISH RIFLES).

Regimental District, No. 26.

(PLATE XXI.)

"SOUTH AFRICA, 1900-02." | ORDER OF PRECEDENCE, 112.

Honorary Colonel—A. D. DUKE OF HAMILTON AND BRANDON, November 6, 1895.

Headquarters—HAMILTON.

THE "3rd Battalion Lanarkshire Rifle Volunteers" appears for the first time in the June 1860 Army List as formed on May 8, 1860, and composed of the 42nd, 44th, 56th, and 57th Corps, and to these were added in June the 16th and 52nd Corps. In March 1861 the battalion became the 1st Administrative Battalion Lanarkshire Rifle Volunteers, with headquarters at Hamilton. The dates of acceptance of services and of commissioning of officers are given in Appendix C for the several corps, and the following were their composition and uniform :—

16th Corps, Hamilton, one company, originally self-supporting. Uniform—dark green, with black braid.

42nd Corps, Uddingston, one company, partly self - supporting, partly assisted by subscriptions. Uniform—medium grey, facings blue, brown belts.

44th Corps, Blantyre, one company, raised amongst the workers of Messrs Henry Monteith & Co., and assisted by the firm's subscriptions. Uniform—medium grey, facings blue, brown belts.

52nd Corps, Hamilton, one company, artisans, assisted by local subscriptions. Uniform—dark green, with black braid.

56th Corps, Bothwell, one company, partly self - supporting, partly assisted. Uniform—medium grey, facings blue, brown belts.

57th Corps, Wishaw, one company, partly self-supporting, partly assisted. Uniform—grey, facings scarlet, brown belts.

Soon after the formation of the 1st Administrative Battalion, in 1862-3, a uniform of 60th Rifles pattern —rifle-green, with scarlet facings and piping, green shakos with black ball-tuft, and black belts—was adopted, busbies with black and red plumes replacing the shakos in 1872.

In 1867 the 102nd (Motherwell) and 103rd (East Kilbride) Corps, of one company each, were raised and added to the battalion, in 1872 the 57th (Wishaw) Corps was increased to a strength of two companies, and in October 1873 the 106th (Strathaven) Corps, of one company, was raised and added.

In November 1873 the battalion was consolidated as the 16th Lanarkshire Rifle Volunteers (renumbered the 2nd L.R.V., in June 1880), with headquarters at Hamilton, and 10 companies lettered as follows :—

A and B, Hamilton (late 16th and 52nd).
C, Uddingston (late 42nd).
D, Strathaven (late 106th).
E, Bothwell (late 56th).

F and G, Wishaw (late 57th).
H, Motherwell (late 102nd).
I, Blantyre (late 44th and 103rd).
K, Motherwell (newly formed).

The scarlet facings were changed to rifle-green, with light green piping and Austrian knot, in 1876, and in the following year the battalion adopted a uniform of scarlet tunics, with blue trousers, facings, and Austrian knots, glengarries with red and white diced border, and white belts. Blue helmets with silver ornaments replaced the glengarries for full dress in 1881, in which year black leggings were adopted, and in 1891 brown leather equipment and leggings were obtained.

In 1892 a new company was raised at Larkhall, and lettered D, the existing D and K companies being combined as K, with headquarters at Strathaven; but in 1904 K was changed back to Motherwell, and D formed of half a company at Larkhall and half at Strathaven. L (Cyclist) company, with headquarters at Hamilton, was formed in 1899.

The battalion assumed the title of 2nd Volunteer Battalion, Scottish Rifles, in accordance with General Order 181 of 1st December 1887, and its companies had since 1904 their headquarters at: A, B, and L, Hamilton; C, Uddingston; D, Larkhall, Strathaven; E, Bothwell; F, Wishaw; G, Newmains, near Wishaw; H and K, Motherwell; I, Blantyre. On 6th May 1902 it was authorised to wear, as its sole uniform, a drab service dress, with green Austrian knot and piping on the trousers, brown belts and leggings, and drab felt hats turned up on the left side and fastened with a piece of Douglas tartan and the badge of the Scottish Rifles. Officers wore in full dress the uniform of the Scottish Rifles.

During the war in South Africa the battalion furnished in all 132 of its members for active service. To the 1st Volunteer Service Company of the Scottish Rifles it contributed 28 non-commissioned officers and men, with a reinforcing draft of Lieut. E. J. Heilbron and 10 men, to the 2nd Company, 39, and to the 3rd, 28 non-commissioned officers and men. Six men served in the Scottish Volunteer Cyclist Company, 12 with the Imperial Yeomanry, and the remainder with other corps. Privates J. Young and J. Muir, and Cyclist W. Gordon, died of disease.

The battalion headquarters, drill-hall, &c., were in Hamilton, close to the Depôt Barracks. Its central rifle-range, up to 600 yards, was at Cadzow, 1½ mile from Hamilton, and there were three local ranges for the use of D, F, and G Companies.

The lieutenant-colonels commanding the battalion have been—

Sam. Simpson, September 10, 1860.
J. Reid, August 23, 1869.
John Austine, April 10, 1875.

Robt. E. S. Harington-Stuart, late Captain Rifle Brigade, V.D.
(hon. col.), May 21, 1879.

Geo. Walker, V.D. (hon. col.), May 29, 1895.

Jas. Scott, V.D. (hon. col.), April 22, 1899.

Thos. B. Ralston, V.D. (hon. col.), June 13, 1903.

3RD LANARKSHIRE VOLUNTEER RIFLE CORPS.

Regimental District, No. 26.

(PLATE XXI.)

"SOUTH AFRICA, 1900-02." | ORDER OF PRECEDENCE, 113.

Honorary Colonel—SIR J. M. STIRLING-MAXWELL, Bart., January 13, 1894.

Headquarters—VICTORIA ROAD, GLASGOW.

THE 3rd Lanarkshire Rifle Volunteers first appear as a consolidated battalion (dating from 8th August 1860) in the November 1860 Army List, where it was shown as seven companies strong, formed by the 3rd, 10th, 14th, 22nd, 54th, 82nd, and 87th Corps. An eighth company was raised to complete the battalion, and is shown in the December 1860 Army List. In this corps also were absorbed what remained of the 78th Lanark Rifle Volunteers, or "Old Guard of Glasgow," concerning which see page 5.

The dates of acceptance of services and of commissioning of officers of the various original corps are given in Appendix C. Each was one company strong, and their compositions were :—

3rd Corps (Glasgow, 1st Southern) and 10th Corps (Glasgow, 2nd Southern) were raised in Glasgow, south of the Clyde, and were well endowed, £2000 having been raised in subscriptions for their equipment in the years 1859 and 1860, and the members paying for their uniforms and contributing an annual subscription. The 10th was an overflow company of the 3rd. The uniform of both was dark grey, without facings and with black braid, black piping on the trousers, dark grey caps with black braid, and black pouch- and waist-belts. The badges were a lion rampant on the cap and pouch-belt, and the arms of Glasgow on the clasp of the waist-belt.

14th Corps (South-Western) was partially self-supporting and partially equipped from subscriptions.

22nd Corps was raised chiefly among the workers of Messrs Cogan's spinning factory, and was liberally assisted by that firm.

54th and 82nd Corps were formed of total abstainers, the latter being of artisans, and receiving aid from the Glasgow Central Fund.

87th Corps was mainly formed out of the employés of Messrs Inglis & Wakefield's at Busby.

The eighth Company (which never received a county number) was recruited from the workmen of the Etna Foundry Company.

In 1861 the uniform of the consolidated 3rd Lanark became Elcho grey, with green facings and piping, light grey soft caps with green piping and straight peak, and brown belts. In 1864, scarlet tunics with blue collars and cuffs, the latter with an upright patch and three bars of white lace, blue trousers, blue shakos with red and white ball-tuft, and white belts, became the uniform.

The establishment was raised to twelve companies in 1877, and in 1902 a thirteenth (cyclist) company was formed, but with these exceptions no changes in formation were made during the existence of the corps.

The uniform also varied but little. In March 1878 blue helmets with silver ornaments replaced the shakos, the cuff was changed to a pointed pattern with a white crow's-foot of braid, and black leggings, dark grey greatcoats, and white haversacks, were issued. In 1891 brown ("Simplex") equipment replaced the white belts, and on July 12, 1902, as undress, a drab service dress, with green piping on the trousers, drab putties, and a brown felt hat, was authorised.

During the South African War the 3rd Lanark sent a total of 98 of its members on active service. Of these Lieutenant G. W. S. Clark and 31 men served with the 1st, Lieutenant J. B. Wilson and 25 men (of whom Private H. Burton died of disease) with the 2nd, and 4 men with the 3rd Volunteer Service Company of the Scottish Rifles. Two men served with the Scottish Volunteer (Cyclist) Company, and the others with various units.

The headquarters of the corps in Victoria Road, Glasgow, were new and commodious, comprising drill-hall, lecture-rooms, stores, armoury, &c. The corps recruited mainly from the South Side of Glasgow, and shared the range at Darnley with the 1st Lanark V.R.C. The 3rd always bore a high reputation for shooting, and two of its members gained the Queen's Prize at the National Rifle Association Meeting— Private Rennie in 1894 and Lieutenant Yates in 1898.

The lieutenant-colonels (commandant since 1877) have been—

David Dreghorn, August 28, 1860.
Wm. S. Dixon, October 27, 1863.
H. E. C. Ewing, May 3, 1865.
Jas. Merry (hon. col.), August 8, 1877.
H. J. M'Dowall, March 9, 1889.
Hugh Morton, V.D., September 19, 1894.
Robert Howie, V.D. (hon. col.), February 13, 1901.
John B. Wilson, V.D. (hon. col.), May 10, 1905.

4TH VOLUNTEER BATTALION, THE CAMERONIANS (SCOTTISH RIFLES).

Regimental District, No. 26.

(PLATE XXII.)

"SOUTH AFRICA, 1900-02." | ORDER OF PRECEDENCE, 114.

Honorary Colonel—W. R. MAXWELL, V.D., February 27, 1904.

Headquarters—149 CATHEDRAL STREET, GLASGOW.

By the 'London Gazette' of January 3, 1860, the 4th, 6th, 7th, 8th, 12th, and 13th Lanarkshire Rifle Volunteer Corps were formed, with effect from December 12, 1859, into the 4th Lanarkshire (Glasgow 1st Northern) Rifle Volunteer Corps, Lieut.-Colonel Tennant being gazetted to the command as from December 23, 1859. This was the first consolidated battalion formed out of the Lanarkshire corps. The companies were lettered in their proper order "A" to "F," and in July 1861 the 60th, 61st, and 93rd Lanarkshire, all Highland kilted corps, were added to the battalion as "G" "H" and "I" companies, thus bringing its strength up to nine companies, at which establishment it always remained, although one of the companies was in 1900 converted into a cyclist company. The dates of acceptance of services, &c., of these original corps are given in Appendix C. Their composition and uniforms were as follows :—

4th Corps (Glasgow, 1st Northern), a purely self-supporting corps, raised on the same principles as the 1st Lanark. Its uniform was dark grey, with green facings and black cord lace (five rows on the breast), dark grey caps, and black belts.

6th, 7th, and 8th Corps. Purely artisan corps, the members contributing £1 each to the funds, and the remainder being raised by public subscription, helped by the Central Committee for Glasgow. The uniform was dark grey for all, the

6th Corps having four rows of black braid on the breast of the tunic, grey shakos, cock's plumes, and black belts.

12th Corps (North-Eastern), a corps formed from the employés of Tennant's Wellpark Brewery, was partly self-supporting, and partly artisans as in the 6th, 7th, and 8th Corps. Uniform as for the latter.

13th Corps, an artisan corps raised in the St Rollox district on the same principles as the 6th, 7th, and 8th. Uniform as for the latter.

60th Corps (Glasgow, 1st Highland), an entirely self-supporting corps of Highlanders resident in Glasgow. The uniform was dark green doublets, with red piping and four rows of black braid on the breast, Celtic Society's tartan kilts, sporrans white with six black tassels for officers, grey goatskin with six black tassels for other ranks, black and green diced hose, plain blue glengarries, and black belts. Highland brogues, without spats, were worn.

61st Corps (Glasgow, 2nd Highland), an artisan corps, assisted from the Central Fund. The uniform was the same as that of the 60th.

93rd Corps (Glasgow, Highland Rifle Rangers), an entirely self-supporting corps, like the 60th. The uniform was the same, but with red and white diced hose.

In 1863 the corps assumed for the A to F companies scarlet tunics with green collars and cuffs, the latter with an upright patch and three bars of white lace, 42nd tartan trews, blue shakos with red-and-white ball-tuft, and white belts. G to I companies had scarlet doublets with green facings (as on the tunics), 42nd tartan kilts, white sporrans with three black tails, green-and-black diced hose, white spats, plain blue glengarries with blackcock's tail, and white belts. In 1868, when the 105th Lanark (Glasgow Highlanders) was raised, 187 men of G to I companies were transferred to it, and these latter, having lost their distinctively Highland character, were clothed in tunics and trews like the rest of the battalion. In 1876 blue trousers replaced the tartan trews, and in 1878 the shakos were exchanged for helmets, a green Austrian knot was added to the cuff, which became pointed, and dark grey greatcoats and black leggings were introduced.

In 1887, by General Order 181 of December 1, the battalion was entitled the 4th Volunteer Battalion, Scottish Rifles.

During the South African War the battalion contributed 73 of its members for service in the field. Of these, Captain J. B. Young and 31 non-commissioned officers and men joined the 1st, Lieutenant H. M. Hannan and 28 non-commissioned officers and men the 2nd, and 3 men the 3rd Volunteer Service Company of the Scottish Rifles, the remainder serving in various corps. Of the 1st Service Company, Privates W. M'Laren and J. Murray died of disease.

In April 1904 a drab service dress with scarlet piping on the trousers, grey putties, a brown felt hat turned up on the left side, with the Scottish Rifle badge and a black plume, and brown leather equipment was authorised as the sole uniform for the battalion. The officers alone wore the Scottish Rifle uniform in full and mess dress.

The battalion had its own headquarters and drill-hall at 149 Cathedral Street, Glasgow, and its own rifle-range up to 800 yards at Flemington.

The following is the list of lieutenant-colonels commanding the battalion :—

John Tennant, December 23, 1859.
Jas. Fyfe Jamieson, April 15, 1863.
Henry M. Hannan, March 18, 1874.
Alexander Mein (hon. col.), March 22, 1884.
Warden R. Maxwell, V.D. (hon. col.), January 26, 1889.
J. F. Newlands, V.D., December 12, 1894.
Frederick J. Smith, V.D. (hon. col.), January 2, 1901.

5TH VOLUNTEER BATTALION, THE CAMER-
ONIANS (SCOTTISH RIFLES).

(PLATE XXIII.)

Disbanded on April 1, 1897.

ON May 14, 1862, the 4th Administrative Battalion, Lanarkshire Rifle Volunteers, with headquarters at Airdrie, was formed from the 29th, 32nd, 43rd, 48th, and 95th Corps of Lanark Rifle Volunteers, of one company each. The 48th was increased to two companies on November 28, 1863, and the battalion thus brought up to six-company strength, entitling it to a lieutenant-colonel to command. The dates of formation, &c., of these corps are given in Appendix C. Their composition and uniforms were as follows :—

29th Corps, Coatbridge, a town corps, generally recruited, and supported by local subscriptions. Uniform—dark grey with black braid, green facings, dark grey cap with peak, black pouch and waist-belts.

32nd Corps, Summerlee, recruited from the workmen of Messrs Neilson's Iron Works. Uniform—dark grey.

43rd Corps, Gartsherrie, raised among the workmen of Messrs W. Baird & Co.'s Iron Works. Uniform—medium grey with black facings.

48th Corps, Airdrie, a town corps, locally supported. Uniform —dark grey with green cuffs and collar, black braid, and red piping on the trousers, grey cap with green band and plume, and black belts.

95th Corps, Bailliestown, a town corps, locally supported. Uniform, dark grey with green facings, cap with peak and ball-tuft, and black belts.

In 1863 the whole battalion adopted a uniform of dark grey tunics and knickerbockers, with black braid and without facings, dark grey shakos with black ball-tuft, black belts, and black leggings.

The battalion rapidly increased in numbers. In 1865 four corps of a company each—the 97th (second of that number in Lanarkshire, see Appendix C) at Woodhead, the 98th at Gartness, recruited from the Calderbank Iron Works and the Chapelhall Iron and Steel Works, the 99th at Clarkston (transferred in 1866 to Caldercruix, Airdrie), and the 100th at Calderbank (transferred also in 1866 to Caldercruix)—were raised and added to the battalion, followed in 1866 by the 101st at Newarthill, and in 1868 by the 104th at Holytown, Bellshill, recruited from Messrs Neilson's Mossend Works, thus bringing the total strength up to twelve companies. The headquarters of the 98th were changed in 1869 from Gartness to Wattstown, of the 97th in 1871 from Woodhead to Coltbridge, and of the 43rd in 1872 from Gartsherrie to Shotts.

In May 1871 the uniform of the battalion was changed to dark grey Norfolk jackets without facings, with light green piping on the collar and light green Austrian knot, Breadalbane tartan trews, black busbies with black and light green plumes, and black belts; and on September 19, 1873, the battalion was consolidated as the 29th Lanark Rifle Volunteers, with headquarters at Airdrie and twelve companies, lettered as follows :—

A, Coatbridge (late 29th).
B, Airdrie (late 32nd and 1st of 48th).
C, Shotts (late 43rd).
D, Airdrie (late 2nd of 48th).
E, Bailliestown (late 95th).
F, Coatbridge (late 97th).

G, Greengairs, near Gartness (late 98th).
H, Clarkston (late 99th).
I, Calderbank (late 100th).
K, Newarthill (late 101st).
L, Bellshill (late 104th).
M, Harthill and Benhar (overflow of 100th).

In 1875 a new company was formed at Cheyston and lettered "F," the former "F" being joined to

" E," and the headquarters of " E " transferred to Coatbridge. Numbers now began to fall off, and on October 4, 1877, the establishment of the battalion was reduced to eight companies, as under—

A, Coatbridge (late A).
B, Airdrie (late B).
C, Shotts (late C and M).
D, Airdrie (late D and L).

E, Coatbridge (late E).
F, Cheyston (late F).
G, Caldercruix (late G and H).
H, Newarthill (late I and K).

In March 1879 scarlet tunics with yellow collar-patches and cuffs and blue Austrian knot, blue trousers and helmets, and white belts became the uniform. In 1887, by General Order 181 of December 1, the corps became the 5th Volunteer Battalion, The Cameronians (Scottish Rifles), and on April 1, 1897, in consequence of strictures passed upon its discipline by the officer commanding 26th - 71st Regimental District, it was disbanded.

The lieutenant-colonels commanding were—

W. W. Hozier, late 2nd Dragoons—Major, May 19, 1862; Lieut.-Colonel, January 8, 1864.

Thos. Jackson, June 20, 1874.

Peter Forrest, November 23, 1878.

J. C. Forrest, August 6, 1887.

Peter Forrest (for the second time), May 12, 1894, to end of 1895.

1ST (CITY OF DUNDEE) VOLUNTEER BATTALION, THE BLACK WATCH (ROYAL HIGHLANDERS).

Regimental District, No. 42.

(PLATE XXIV.)

"SOUTH AFRICA, 1900-02." | ORDER OF PRECEDENCE, 171.

Honorary Colonel—The LORD PROVOST of DUNDEE for the time being.

Headquarters—ALBANY QUARTERS, DUNDEE.

THE first public meeting which led to the formation of the 1st Forfarshire Rifle Volunteers was held in Dundee on May 20, 1859, and drill began in the following month, although the services of the corps were not formally accepted until November. The officers were first commissioned on November 15, 1859, and the corps had an establishment of five companies. Two more were raised on February 17, and one on April 10, 1860, making eight in all, which continued to be the establishment of the battalion until 1900.

The original uniform of the corps was dark grey with five rows of black lace on the tunic and black stripes on the trousers, dark grey shakos with a plume of cock's feathers (replaced in 1860 by a black ball-tuft), and black belts. In 1861 a red Garibaldi shirt was adopted, and in 1862 the uniform was changed to scarlet tunics with blue facings and white Austrian knot, blue trousers, blue shakos with red, white, and blue diced band, black lace, and black ball-tuft (Highland Light Infantry pattern), and brown belts. In 1877 the Austrian knot on the sleeve was changed to blue, and busbies with blue plumes replaced the shakos. In 1881 helmets replaced the busbies, and in 1902 the black leggings hitherto worn were abolished, and (on December 9) a drab service dress with scarlet piping on the trousers, a field service cap, and drab puttees, were authorised. In 1904 the Austrian knot was removed from the tunic, and sashes were permitted to be worn by officers and serjeants.

In 1887, by General Order 181 of December 1, the corps assumed the title of 1st (Dundee) Volunteer Battalion, The Black Watch, but on February 2, 1889, "City of Dundee" was substituted for the word "Dundee."

During the war in South Africa, in 1900 the establishment of the battalion was increased to ten companies, of which one was a cyclist company, and it sent 4 officers (Captain A. Valentine, Lieutenants E. Tosh, A. B. Corrie, and C. E. C. Walker) and 66 men to the three volunteer service companies of the 2nd Black Watch, 97 members of the battalion in all serving actively during the war.

The headquarters and drill-hall of the battalion were, along with those of the other Dundee corps, in the Albany Quarters, Bell Street, Dundee, and its rifle-range, up to 600 yards, was at Monifieth Links, 7½ miles from Dundee.

From 1902 to 1906 the battalion formed part of the 34th Field Army Brigade, and trained in camp for thirteen clear days annually.

The lieutenant-colonels commanding have been—

Sir John Ogilvy, Bart., July 28, 1860.
G. L. Alison, October 10, 1865.
P. Anderson, January 10, 1870.
Peter Geddes Walker, April 22, 1874.
William R. Morrison (hon. col.), March 26, 1879.
George Mitchell (hon. col.), March 9, 1888.
James Rankin, V.D. (hon. col.), June 6, 1891.
Howard Hill, V.D. (hon. col.), March 13, 1901.

Q

2ND (ANGUS) VOLUNTEER BATTALION, THE BLACK WATCH (ROYAL HIGHLANDERS).

Regimental District, No. 42.

(PLATE XXV.)

"SOUTH AFRICA, 1900-02." | ORDER OF PRECEDENCE, 172.

Honorary Colonel—C. G. EARL OF STRATHMORE AND KINGHORNE, October 22, 1904.

Headquarters—ARBROATH.

ON May 3, 1861, the rifle corps existing in the county of Forfar, outside of the city of Dundee, were formed into two administrative battalions, the 1st (locally called the "Eastern"), with headquarters at Montrose, comprising the 3rd (Arbroath, two companies), 5th (Montrose, two companies), 7th (Brechin, one company), and subsequently (on June 4) the 13th (Friockheim, one company); and the 2nd (locally called the "Western"), with headquarters at Forfar, composed of the 2nd (Forfar, two companies), 8th (Newtyle, one company), 9th (Glamis, one company), 11th (Tannadice, one subdivision), 12th (Kirriemuir, one company), and subsequently (on August 16, 1865) the 15th (Cortachy, one company) Corps of Forfarshire Rifle Volunteers. The dates of formation of these companies are given in Appendix B, and their uniforms, so far as known, were as follows :—

2nd Corps, Forfar, Elcho grey.

3rd Corps, Arbroath, dark grey uniforms with black facings and plumed shakos, and badge of portcullis and abbot's head.

5th Corps, Montrose, steel grey uniforms with black facings and five rows of black braid on the breast of the tunic, grey caps with black braid, and black belts.

7th Corps, Brechin, light grey.

8th Corps, Newtyle, grey, with black facings.
9th Corps, Glamis, Elcho grey.
11th Corps, Tannadice, unknown.
12th Corps, Kirriemuir, Elcho grey.
13th Corps, Friockheim, unknown.

In 1864 the uniform of both battalions was changed to scarlet tunics with blue facings and white Austrian knot, blue trousers, blue caps with red band, blue ball-tuft, and silver star badge, and brown belts. In 1872 the officers adopted shakos the same as those then worn by the 1st Forfar (1st V.B. Black Watch), other ranks wearing only glengarries with red, white, and blue diced border, and the same badge as formerly on the caps.

In 1864 the 3rd Corps was increased to four companies, and in 1865 the 7th to two; but in 1869 the 11th and in 1872 the 15th Corps were disbanded. The 2nd Battalion being, by the loss of those two latter companies, reduced to five companies, was in 1874 amalgamated with the 1st Battalion, which then took the title "1st Administrative Battalion Forfarshire, or Angus, Rifle Volunteers," with headquarters at Friockheim by Arbroath, and consisting of the 2nd, 3rd, 5th, 7th, 8th, 9th, 12th, and 13th Corps—in all, fourteen companies.

In March 1880 the battalion was consolidated as the 2nd Forfar, or Angus, Rifle Volunteers, headquarters at Friockheim, the fourteen companies being lettered in succession of corps; and on October 31, 1882, it was authorised to wear the uniform of the Black Watch, but with plain glengarries and trews, the title "Angus" being borne on the shoulder-straps, and the brown leather belts continuing to be worn. This uniform was till 1908 regulation for the battalion, serjeants only wearing sashes.

In 1887 (General Order 181 of December 1) the battalion assumed the title of 2nd (Angus) Volunteer Battalion, The Black Watch, and soon afterwards headquarters were removed to Arbroath. In 1894 the fourth company at Arbroath was broken up and the companies at Newtyle and Glamis amalgamated, the twelve companies remaining being re-lettered: A and B, Forfar (late 2nd Corps); C, D, and E, Arbroath (late 3rd); F and G, Montrose (late 5th); H and I, Brechin (late 7th); K, Newtyle and Glamis (late 8th and 9th); L, Kirriemuir (late 12th); and M, Friockheim (late 13th), which was the distribution of the battalion till 1908.

During the war in South Africa, the Angus battalion sent out 2 officers (Captains—hon. majors—J. Buyers, V.D., and R. H. Millar, V.D., who commanded the 1st Service Company) and 54 other ranks to join the volunteer service companies of the Black Watch, and in all 72 members of the battalion served actively in the field.

There was a drill-hall at each of the out-stations, and the battalion had commodious headquarters and drill-hall at Arbroath. It possessed eight separate rifle-ranges in the vicinities of company headquarters.

The officers commanding have been—

1st Adm. Bn., 1861-74.	Lieut.-Colonel Thos. Renny Tailyour, late Major Bengal Engineers, June 4, 1861.
	Lieut.-Colonel Jas. Alex. Dickson, September 25, 1868.
2nd Adm. Bn., 1861-74.	Lieut.-Colonel John Kinloch, late Colonel on the Staff, May 3, 1861.
	Lieut.-Colonel the Earl of Airlie, March 14, 1865.
	Lieut.-Colonel G. H. Dempster, July 6, 1868.
	Major A. Black, November 20, 1872.

1st Adm. Bn., ⎰ Lieut.-Colonel Commandant J. A. Dickson (from
    1874-88. ⎱   1st Bn.), 1874.

Lieut.-Colonel Commandant Hon. Francis Bowes-Lyon, January
    14, 1888.

Lieut.-Colonel Commandant Wm. Alex. Gordon, V.D. (hon. col.),
    May 4, 1892.

Lieut.-Colonel Commandant Alex. M'Hardy, V.D. (hon. col.),
    September 9, 1903.

Lieut.-Colonel Commandant James Davidson, V.D. (hon. col.),
    September 3, 1904.

3RD (DUNDEE HIGHLAND) VOLUNTEER BATTALION, THE BLACK WATCH (ROYAL HIGHLANDERS).

Regimental District, No. 42.

(PLATE XXV.)

"SOUTH AFRICA, 1900-02." | ORDER OF PRECEDENCE, 173.

Honorary Colonel—Field-Marshal F. S. EARL ROBERTS, K.G., K.P., G.C.B.,
O.M., G.C.S.I., G.C.I.E., September 19, 1903.

Headquarters—THE ALBANY QUARTERS, DUNDEE.

ON April 10, 1860, there was raised at Dundee the
10th, and on June 14, 1861, the 14th Forfarshire
Rifle Volunteers, each one company strong, and from
October 1861 both were attached to the 1st Forfarshire
Rifle Volunteers. The original uniform of the 10th
was dark grey jackets with black facings, 42nd tartan
kilt and belted plaid, green-and-black diced hose, glengarry, and black belts with silver ornaments and badges,
and that of the 14th is said to have been the same.
In 1862 the uniform of both corps was changed to scarlet
doublets with blue facings, 42nd tartan kilts and belted

plaids, white sporrans with two black tails, red-and-black diced hose, white spats, glengarries with red, white, and blue diced border, and white belts.

On June 29, 1867, the two corps were increased to two companies each ; and on September 24, 1868, they were amalgamated as the 10th Forfar (Dundee Highland) Rifle Volunteers, with an establishment of six companies. In March 1880 the battalion was re-numbered 3rd Forfar, in 1887 (General Order 181 of December 1) it assumed the title of 3rd (Dundee Highland) Volunteer Battalion, The Black Watch, and in 1900 the establishment was raised to eight companies. In 1882 the kilt was replaced by trews of Black Watch tartan, with which the white spats continued to be worn, and helmets were introduced, but the latter were abolished in 1887 and replaced by the plain blue glengarry of the regular battalions. Sashes for serjeants were authorised later.

During the Boer War no fewer than 176 members of this battalion served in one capacity or another in South Africa, of whom 2 officers (Captains H. K. Smith and W. R. Smith) and 73 men served in the volunteer service companies of the Black Watch. Captain H. K. Smith was wounded at Retief's Nek on July 23, 1900.

The headquarters and drill-hall were, along with those of other Dundee corps, at the Albany Quarters, Bell Street, Dundee, and the battalion used for its musketry the War Department range at Barry Links.

The lieutenant-colonels commanding have been—

David Guthrie of Carlogie, September 24, 1868.
Robert Lamb, February 4, 1880.
Robert N. Reid, July 22, 1882.
William Smith, V.D. (hon. col.), November 27, 1886.
Charles Batchelor, V.D., May 19, 1906.

4TH (PERTHSHIRE) VOLUNTEER BATTALION, THE BLACK WATCH (ROYAL HIGH-LANDERS).

Regimental District, No. 42.

(PLATE XXVI.)

"SOUTH AFRICA, 1900-02." | ORDER OF PRECEDENCE, 185.

Honorary Colonel—DAVID R. WILLIAMSON of Lawers, V.D., late Ensign and Lieutenant Coldstream Guards, July 9, 1879.

Headquarters—PERTH.

THE 1st Administrative Battalion, Perthshire Rifle Volunteers, with headquarters at Perth, was formed on November 20, 1860, and to it then, or on the date on which they were subsequently raised, the following corps of Perthshire Rifle Volunteers were attached :—

1st, Perth, raised December 13, 1859, as one company.

2nd, Perth, raised December 13, 1859, as one company.

Of these corps the 1st was composed of "citizens," the 2nd of "artisans," and they were amalgamated as the 1st Perthshire Corps, of two companies, in June 1860. The uniform was medium grey hooked tunics and trousers, with scarlet collars and cuffs and black braid, grey peaked caps with scarlet bands and the arms of Perth, and black pouch-and waist-belts.

5th, Blairgowrie, raised March 16, 1860, as one company. Uniform, dark grey with red facings.

6th, Dunblane, services accepted December 13, 1859, officers commissioned May 3, 1860, as one company. Uniform, as for the 1st Perth, but with brown belts.

7th, Coupar-Angus, raised May 5, 1860, as one company. Uniform, dark grey with red facings.

8th, Crieff, raised May 5, 1860, as one company. Uniform, as for the 1st Perth, with black belts, and with the Ochtertyre badge in silver on the caps.

9th, Alyth, raised May 26, 1860, as one company. Uniform—dark grey with red facings.

11th, Doune, raised May 26, 1860, as one company. Uniform—as for the 1st Perth, with a bugle badge on the caps.

12th, Callander, raised May 26, 1860, as one subdivision. Disbanded in 1865.

13th, St Martins, raised August 22, 1860, as one company. Uniform—dark grey doublets with scarlet facings, Macdonald tartan kilts, plain glengarries, and black belts.

14th, Birnam, raised November 10, 1860, as one company. Uniform—dark grey doublets with scarlet facings, Royal Stuart tartan kilts, plain glengarries, and black belts.

15th, Auchterarder, raised December 4, 1860, as one company. Uniform—light grey tunics and trousers with scarlet facings, low grey shakos, and brown belts.

16th, Stanley, raised January 21, 1861, as one company. Disbanded in 1864.

17th, Bridge of Earn, formed in April 1863 as one subdivision, and disbanded in June 1863. No officers were appointed to it.

18th (Highland), Perth, raised May 8, 1863, as one company. Uniform—dark grey doublets with scarlet cuffs and collars and four rows of black lace across the breast, Atholl (Murray) tartan trews, plain glengarries with blackcock's tail, and black pouch- and waist-belts.

19th (Highland), Crieff, services accepted as one company December 7, 1868, officers commissioned December 11, 1868. Uniform—dark green doublets with Royal Stuart tartan kilts and plaids, red-and-green diced hose, and Balmoral bonnets with feather. Absorbed in the 8th Corps in 1878.

In 1868 a general uniform was adopted for the battalion, consisting of dark grey buttoned tunics and trousers with scarlet facings and piping, dark blue shakos with red, white, and blue diced borders, bugle badge, and ball-tuft black below and red above, and black belts; but the 13th, 14th, and 19th Corps continued to wear their Highland dress, and the 18th only modified theirs in so far as to adopt the shako, but with a ball-tuft red below and white above. The 8th Corps was permitted to wear the same uniform as the 18th, but with Black Watch trews.

In 1869 the 5th, 7th, 9th, 13th, and 14th Corps were transferred to the 2nd Administrative Battalion (see 5th Volunteer Battalion), and as the 12th Corps had been disbanded in 1865 and the 16th in 1864, and the 17th had only lasted two months, the 1st Battalion was left composed of the 1st, 6th, 8th, 11th, 15th, 18th, and 19th Corps, with in all eight companies. In July 1875 a 21st Corps, of one company, was raised at Comrie, but it was disbanded in March 1876, and in 1878 the 19th Corps was amalgamated with the 8th. In 1878 a busby, with a black-and-red plume and bugle badge, was adopted by the whole battalion.

On March 13, 1880, the battalion was consolidated as the 1st Perthshire Rifle Volunteers, headquarters at Perth, with seven companies, lettered A and B, Perth (late 1st Corps); C, Dunblane (late 6th); D, Crieff (late 8th); E, Doune (late 11th); F, Auchterarder (late 15th); and G, Perth (late 18th); and on April 24, 1883, authority was given for the adoption by the battalion of the uniform of the Black Watch —scarlet doublets with blue facings, trews with brown leggings, plain glengarries, and white belts. On March 21, 1885, the battalion was increased to eight companies by the formation of "H" Company at Bridge of Allan, and in 1887, by General Order 181 of December 1, the battalion became the 4th Volunteer Battalion, The Black Watch.

During the South African War the battalion contributed 22 men to the 1st, Captain R. M. Christie and 17 men to the 2nd, and 6 men to the 3rd

Volunteer Service Company of the Black Watch, all three of which were attached to the 2nd Battalion. In all, 2 officers (including Surgeon-Major R. Stirling, M.D., who was mentioned in despatches November 29, 1900) and 72 members of the battalion took part in the war, and Sergeant J. B. Deas and Private J. Chalmers, both of "A" Company, were killed in action. Recruiting became very brisk at home, "I" and "K" Companies being raised at Perth under War Office authority of March 17, 1900, and "L" (Cyclist) Company, also at Perth, under that of May 26, 1900; but after the war it was found impossible to maintain them, and "I" Company was reduced in 1902 and "K" and "L" in 1905, thus leaving the battalion with eight companies, including a cyclist section.

On October 17, 1901, Black Watch kilts with red-and-black diced hose, white spats, and white sporrans with five black tassels were introduced, sashes for serjeants being at the same time authorised.

Battalion headquarters, with drill-hall, were in Tay Street, Perth, and six rifle-ranges at the headquarters of companies served the battalion.

The lieutenant-colonels commanding have been—

Sir William Keith Murray, Bart. of Ochtertyre, late Captain 42nd Foot, November 20, 1860.

George, 6th Duke of Atholl, late Lieutenant 2nd Dragoons, November 22, 1861.

James Wedderburn Ogilvy of Rannagulzion, late Captain 25th Foot, March 7, 1864.

David R. Williamson of Lawers, late Ensign and Lieutenant Coldstream Guards, July 23, 1873.

William C. Colquhoun of Clathick, late 15th Foot, August 16, 1879.

Patrick Stirling of Kippendavie, late 92nd Foot, March 22, 1884.

Sir Robert D. Moncreiffe, Bart. of Moncreiffe, V.D. (hon. col.), late Lieut. Scots Guards, April 15, 1893.

5TH (PERTHSHIRE HIGHLAND) VOLUNTEER BATTALION, THE BLACK WATCH (ROYAL HIGHLANDERS).

Regimental District, No. 42.

(PLATE XXVI.)

"SOUTH AFRICA, 1900-02." | ORDER OF PRECEDENCE, 186.

*Headquarters—*BIRNAM.

THE 3rd Perthshire (Breadalbane) Rifle Volunteer Corps, four companies strong, was raised in the end of 1859, and its officers were commissioned on February 29, 1860, the major-commandant being John, second Marquess of Breadalbane, K.T. Headquarters were at Taymouth Castle, and those of its four companies: 1st at Kenmore, 2nd at Aberfeldy, 3rd at Killin, and 4th at Strathfillan. The uniform was plain dark green doublets, without facings, and with black buttons marked " BV," Breadalbane Campbell kilts and belted plaids, round deerskin sporran with three tassels, black and red twisted "moggans" with black spats, "Rob Rorison" bonnets with badge and sprigs of heather and bog myrtle, and black belts. To this corps was attached, for administrative purposes, the 10th Perthshire Rifle Volunteer Corps, of one company, with headquarters at Strathtay, raised on May 19, 1860. Its first uniform was rifle-green coatees with short tails and brass buttons marked " SV," without facings, 42nd tartan trews, plain glengarries, and black belts, but soon the uniform was assimilated to that of the 3rd Corps, black and red diced hose, white goatskin sporrans without tassels, and white spats being worn.

On November 12, 1861, the 2nd Administrative Battalion Perthshire Rifle Volunteers, with headquarters at Taymouth, was formed, comprising the 3rd and 10th Perth and the 9th Argyllshire Rifle Volunteers, the latter a corps of one company, with headquarters at Glenorchy, raised on April 12, 1860, from the Breadalbane estates in Argyllshire, and wearing grey doublets with green facings, and kilts and belted plaids òf Breadalbane Campbell tartan.

In 1865 the 9th Argyllshire was transferred to its own county battalion (see 5th V.B. Argyll and Sutherland Highlanders). In 1869 the 3rd Perthshire was reduced to two companies and split into two corps of one company each, the 3rd (Breadalbane) at Aberfeldy and the 4th (Breadalbane) at Killin, and at the same time the 5th (Blairgowrie), 7th (Coupar-Angus), 9th (Alyth), 13th (St Martins), and 14th (Birnam) Corps were transferred to the 2nd from the 1st Administrative Battalion Perthshire Rifle Volunteers, and the strength of the battalion was raised to nine companies by the formation of the 20th Corps at Pitlochry on May 27, 1869. Battalion headquarters were at the same time moved to Birnam. The uniform of the battalion was authorised to be dark grey doublets with scarlet collars, cuffs, and piping, and black lace across the breast, plain glengarries (with blackcock's tail for officers), and black belts. The 3rd, 4th, and 10th Corps wore Breadalbane Campbell, the 13th Macdonald, the 14th Royal Stuart, and the 20th Atholl (Murray) kilts and belted plaids, while the 5th, 7th, and 9th Corps wore Atholl (Murray) tartan trews, which they only exchanged for kilts of the same tartan in 1881.

In 1873 the 10th Corps was disbanded, and in the following year the title "Perthshire Highland" was conferred upon the battalion, which in March 1880 was consolidated as the 3rd (re-numbered 2nd in April 1880) Perthshire (Perthshire Highland) Rifle Volunteers, with headquarters at Birnam, and eight companies lettered : A, Aberfeldy (late 3rd Corps); B, Killin (detachments at Crianlarich, Lochearnhead, and Kenmore) (late 4th); C, Blairgowrie (late 5th); D, Coupar-Angus (late 7th); E, Alyth (late 9th); F, St Martins (late 13th); G, Birnam (late 14th); and H, Pitlochry (late 20th). In 1883 the whole battalion adopted the uniform worn ever since, namely, dark grey doublets with scarlet collars, cuffs, and piping, 42nd tartan kilts and belted plaids (shoulder plaids for officers), white sporrans with two black tails, green and red diced hose (black and red for officers), white spats, plain glengarries (with blackcocks' tails for officers), and black belts. Drab service doublets and khaki spats for marching order were authorised in 1902.

By General Order 181 of December 1, 1887, the title of 5th (Perthshire Highland) Volunteer Battalion, The Black Watch, was conferred upon the battalion.

During the South African War 94 members of the battalion served in the field, of whom 23 non-commissioned officers and men joined the 1st, Lieutenant F. B. Buchanan-White and 31 men the 2nd, and Lieutenant T. Ferguson and 10 men the 3rd Volunteer Service Company of the Black Watch, the remainder serving in various other corps. One man was wounded and 3 died of disease.

In 1899 the headquarters of F Company were transferred from St Martins to New Scone, and in the same year two new companies, at Blairgowrie and Birnam, were added to the establishment of the battalion, but these were reduced again in 1904 and 1905 respectively. The battalion in 1907 possessed 17 separate rifle-ranges.

The lieutenant-colonels commanding the battalion have been—

John, 2nd Marquess of Breadalbane, K.T., November 12, 1861 to 1862.
William M. Macdonald of St Martins (hon. col.), March 7, 1864.
Sir Robert Menzies of Menzies, Bart., V.D. (hon. col.), February 28, 1885.
Gavin, 3rd Marquess of Breadalbane, K.G., A.D.C., Colonel, February 17, 1897.

6TH (FIFESHIRE) VOLUNTEER BATTALION, THE BLACK WATCH (ROYAL HIGHLANDERS).

Regimental District, No. 42.

(PLATE XXVII.)

"SOUTH AFRICA, 1900-02." | ORDER OF PRECEDENCE, 213.

Honorary Colonel—Sir FF. W. ERSKINE, Bt., V.D., August 11, 1900.

Headquarters—ST ANDREWS.

THE 1st Administrative Battalion Fifeshire Rifle Volunteers, with headquarters at St Andrews, was formed on September 21, 1860, and to it were attached the following corps of Fifeshire Rifle Volunteers :—

1st, Dunfermline, raised in consequence of a meeting held on November 14, 1859, when 104 names were put down to join. The public subscription list was headed by one of £300 from Mr James Kerr of Middlebank. Members paid £2 entrance money, and many equipped themselves. The services of the corps, of two companies, were accepted on February 25, 1860, and the officers were commissioned on March 6, 1860. The uniform was medium grey with scarlet facings and brown belts, the officers wearing five rows of black lace on the breast of the tunic, and having cock's feathers in their caps.

2nd, Cupar, raised March 6, 1860, of two companies.

3rd, Kilconquhar, later East Anstruther, raised April 25, 1860, as one company.

4th, Colinsburgh, raised April 20, 1860, as one company.

5th, St Andrews, raised April 23, 1860, as one company. Uniform—medium grey tunic with buttons in a fly, scarlet collar and piping, and black Austrian knot, grey trousers with black stripe, grey cap with black band and scarlet piping, to which was afterwards added a scarlet ball-tuft, and brown belts.

6th, Strathleven, raised August 25, 1860, as one company. In 1872 the corps was increased to two companies, the headquarters of the 1st being placed at Leslie and of the 2nd at Falkland, but the latter was not officially recognised till 1880.

7th, Kirkcaldy, raised April 23, 1860, as one company.

8th, Auchterderran, raised April 20, 1860, as one company; headquarters transferred to Lochgelly in 1870.

9th, Newburgh, raised July 28, 1860, as one subdivision, increased to one company June 2, 1862.

In June 1861 the 1st Kinross Corps was attached to the battalion, but was transferred to the 1st Clackmannan and Kinross Administrative Battalion in 1873.

With the exception of the 1st and 5th Corps, the details of the original uniform are not known, but at a meeting held at Cupar early in 1860 it was decided that all the corps of the county should be clothed in medium (slate) grey with brown belts. Slight differences between corps existed, and two of them had no red collars and black lace across the breast of the tunic. In 1863 the whole battalion was clothed in loose scarlet blouses with purple collars, cuffs, and piping, and "79" (the county precedence number) on the shoulder-straps, and blue shakos with front and rear peaks and green ball-tuft. The medium grey trousers were continued, but with red piping, and also the brown belts, the ornaments on which were changed from bronze to white metal. Officers had silver lace and Austrian knots. In 1875 scarlet tunics with blue facings and blue trousers with red piping were adopted, and for the shako was substituted a plain blue glengarry, which was worn till 1880, when a dark green helmet took its place for full dress. In 1878 a blue (in 1880 black) Austrian knot was adopted and worn on the cuff till 1905. The brown belts (with pouch-belts with whistle and chain for officers and serjeants) have been worn throughout. On January 15, 1903, drab service dress, with scarlet Austrian knot and trouser piping and brown felt hat, was authorised as undress.

In April 1880 the battalion was consolidated as the 1st Fifeshire Rifle Volunteers, with headquarters at St Andrews, and twelve companies lettered as follows : A and B, Dunfermline (late 1st); C and D, Cupar (late 2nd); E, East Anstruther (late 3rd); F, Colinsburgh (late 4th); G, St Andrews (late 5th); H, Leslie (late 1st of the 6th); I, Falkland (late 2nd of the 6th); K, Kirkcaldy (late 7th); L, Lochgelly (late 8th); and M, Newburgh (late 9th). In 1887, by General Order 181 of 1st December, the title of 6th (Fifeshire) V.B., The Black Watch, was assumed by the battalion.

Sixty-seven members of the battalion, none of officer's rank, served in South Africa during the war. At home certain interior changes only were carried out in the battalion, the headquarters of "C" and "D" Companies being changed to Kirkcaldy and of "K" to Cupar on March 12, 1900, the number of volunteers in the latter having fallen off while that in Kirkcaldy had much increased. A new "O" (Cyclist) Company was formed at Dunfermline on January 2, 1901. In 1906 the headquarters of F Company were changed from Colinsburgh to Leven, so that the distribution of the companies of the battalion then became : A, B, and O, Dunfermline ; C and D, Kirkcaldy ; E, East Anstruther ; F, Leven ; G, St Andrews ; H, Leslie ; I, Falkland ; K, Cupar ; L, Lochgelly ; M, Newburgh. The battalion had ten rifle ranges, one of which, at Pilmuir Links, near St Andrews, was held conjointly with the 1st Fife R.G.A. Volunteers.

The list of lieutenant-colonels commandant is—

Sir Thomas Erskine, Bt. of Cambo, September 21, 1860.
Sir Coutts T. Lindsay, Bt., late Lieutenant and Captain Grenadier Guards, September 6, 1864.
Sir ff. W. Erskine, Bt., late Lieut.-Colonel Scots Guards, V.D. (hon. col.), August 16, 1884.
Sir Ralph W. Anstruther, Bt. of Balcaskie, late Captain R.E. (hon. col.), May 16, 1900.

1st VOLUNTEER BATTALION, THE HIGHLAND LIGHT INFANTRY.

Regimental District, No. 71.

(PLATE XXVIII.)

" SOUTH AFRICA, 1900-02." | ORDER OF PRECEDENCE, 115.

Honorary Colonel—General Sir ARCHIBALD HUNTER, K.C.B., D.S.O., June 24, 1907.

Headquarters—24 HILL STREET, GARNETHILL, GLASGOW.

THE services of the 19th Lanark (Glasgow, 2nd Northern) R.V.C., a one-company corps, were accepted on December 5, 1859, and on December 30 its officers were commissioned. In the February 1860 Army List the 23rd, 24th, 28th, 36th, and 41st Corps are shown as amalgamated with it. To these were added in the

R

September 1860 List the 51st, 67th, 74th, 80th, 81st, 83rd, and 89th Corps (of which the first six had for a short time formed the 5th Administrative Battalion Lanarkshire R.V.), and in the November 1860 List the 85th and 91st,—the 19th Lanarkshire (Glasgow, 2nd Northern) R.V.C. being shown in the latter list as composed of 15 companies.

In the 'Glasgow Directory' of June 1861 the corps is termed the "2nd Regiment Lanarkshire Rifle Volunteers," but there is no mention of this title in any Army List. The two battalions into which it was divided were locally termed the 2nd and 3rd Northern (the 4th Lanark R.V. being reckoned the "1st Northern"), but this again was not officially recognised.

The dates of acceptance of services and of first commissions of officers of the various corps are given in Appendix C. All the corps were of one-company establishment, and their origins were as follows:—

2ND NORTHERN BATTALION.

19th Corps (Glasgow, 2nd Northern), artisans, in the Western and Clyde Engineering Works, helped by the Central Fund.

23rd Corps (Warehousemen), an entirely self-supporting body raised among the large drapery establishments of the city.

24th Corps (North-Western), raised in the Cowcaddens district.

28th Corps (Railway), formed from employés of the Edinburgh and Glasgow Railway, the directors of which contributed towards the expenses of its equipment.

36th Corps, formed from the men of Messrs Edington & Co.'s Phœnix Ironworks, Port Dundas. Besides being most liberally aided by the firm, this corps was helped from the Central Fund.

41st Corps (North-Western Artisans) consisted chiefly of masons, and was assisted in its equipment by subscriptions and out of the Central Fund.

89th Corps (Manufacturers), a self-equipped corps raised among the employés of the textile manufacturers of Glasgow.

3RD NORTHERN BATTALION.

51st Corps (2nd Press), an overflow corps of the 50th (see 1st Lanark V.R.C.), raised in the newspaper offices of the city, and assisted by the Central Fund.

67th Corps, raised among the workmen of Messrs D. Laidlaw & Sons, of the Alliance Foundry, and assisted from the Central Fund.

74th Corps (Grenadiers), a self-equipped corps of superior physique, accepting no recruits under 5 ft. 9 in.

80th Corps, composed of the workmen of Messrs M'Gavin & Co., ironworkers, Windmill Croft, who subscribed liberally, the corps being also assisted from the Central Fund.

81st Corps (Northern Artisans), raised mainly from the workers in Messrs Law & Co.'s Iron Foundry, Port Dundas, who subscribed to the funds, which were augmented from the Central Fund.

83rd Corps (Northern Artisans), composed chiefly of joiners, and aided from the Central Fund.

85th Corps (2nd North-Eastern), raised among the iron-workers of the North-Eastern and St Rollox districts.

91st Corps (3rd Abstainers' Artisans), raised among the workers of certain total abstainer firms.

Very little is on record of the uniforms worn by these corps at first, except that they were mostly grey, that the 74th had tall shakos with cock's feathers, and that the 89th had a "handsome dark green uniform with shako and plume." Shortly after consolidation the corps adopted a medium grey uniform, without facings, with black lace and piping, medium grey cap with black piping, and black belts. In 1863, however, its uniform was changed to rifle-green with light green facings, piping, and Austrian knot, rifle-green caps with light green and black diced band, and black belts.

In 1864 the establishment of the corps was reduced to twelve companies,[1] and it was formed into one

---

[1] The 89th Corps became No. 2 Company and the 51st No. 10.

battalion, at which strength it ever since then remained. It was re-numbered the 5th Lanark Rifle Volunteers in June 1880, and in 1887, by General Order 181 of 1st December, it assumed the designation of 1st V.B. Highland Light Infantry.

The uniform underwent many changes. In 1870 rifle-green doublets with light-green collars and cuffs, yellow piping, and silver buttons, Breadalbane Campbell tartan trews, rifle-green shakos with black lace, light green and yellow diced band and green and yellow ball-tuft, and black waist-belts became the uniform, officers wearing lines and shoulder-plaids. This, however, only lasted till 1874, when the uniform of the 90th Light Infantry (included in the 60th Sub-District Brigade, to which the 19th Lanark then belonged) was adopted—namely, scarlet tunics with buff facings (worn with a white Austrian knot as volunteers), blue trousers, dark green shakos with black ball-tuft, and white belts. This gave way on May 23, 1883, to the uniform of the Highland Light Infantry, the officers alone wearing shakos and the men glengarries, the yellow facings at first worn being changed to buff on April 20, 1903, when sashes for serjeants were also introduced. On January 4, 1905, a drab service dress, to be worn with the glengarry, was authorised in addition to the full dress.

The battalion contributed to all the volunteer service companies of the Highland Light Infantry, sending to the 1st Captain D. S. Morton, Lieutenant J. Kelso, and 27 men; to the 2nd, Lieutenant T. L. Jowitt and 22 men; and to the 3rd, 5 men. In all, 70 members of the battalion served in South Africa. Private J. Jamieson died of disease, and Captain D. S. Morton was mentioned in despatches. In 1902 the battalion was placed in the 34th Field Army Brigade, and trained for thirteen clear days annually with it until 1906, when the brigade was broken up.

The first headquarters of the corps were at 179 West George Street, Glasgow, its drill-hall and drill-field being in Parliamentary Road, but in July 1876 headquarters were changed to 13 Renfrew Street, and in July 1879 a new drill-hall in Ark Lane, Dennistoun, was purchased. This latter was blown down in the great gale on 25th December 1879, and the Crown Halls, 98 Sauchiehall Street, were rented, until in 1885 new headquarters and drill-hall at 24 Hill Street, Garnethill, were built and purchased, the cost being finally cleared off by a bazaar held in 1891. In 1886 a new range at Dechmont, near Cambuslang, up to 1000 yards, which was held conjointly with the 1st Lanark R.E.V. and 2nd V.B.H.L.I., was opened and taken into use.

The lieutenant-colonels commandant have been—

John Middleton, December 7, 1860.
Robert Robson, December 17, 1873.
John M. Forrester, September 16, 1874.
James Mactear, June 22, 1881.
John A. Sillars, February 27, 1886.
Edmund H. B. Lysons, late lieut. R.M.L.I. (hon. col.) (formerly adjutant of the corps, December 1, 1869 to May 21, 1888), May 21, 1888.
Robert C. Mackenzie, V.D. (hon. col.), February 27, 1892.
James Outram, V.D. (hon. col.), June 8, 1906.

2ND VOLUNTEER BATTALION, THE HIGHLAND LIGHT INFANTRY.

Regimental District, No. 71.

(PLATE XXIX.)

"SOUTH AFRICA, 1900-02." | ORDER OF PRECEDENCE, 116.

Honorary Colonel—Sir T. J. LIPTON, Bt., K.C.V.O., November 21, 1900.

Headquarters—YORKHILL STREET, GLASGOW.

THE "6th Battalion Lanarkshire Rifle Volunteers" appeared for the first time in the Army List for July 1860, as consisting of the 25th, 26th, 27th, 40th, 68th, 69th, 70th, and 71st Corps, of one company each, the dates of acceptance of services and of commissioning of officers of which are shown in Appendix C. The battalion was locally known as the "Clyde Artisans," the corps having been all formed from the employés of the great Clyde shipbuilding and engineering yards as follows :—

25th Corps, Messrs Barclay, Curle, & Co.
26th Corps, Messrs R. Napier & Sons, Govan.
27th Corps, Messrs R. Napier & Sons, Engineering Department.
40th Corps, various smaller yards.
68th Corps, Messrs Neilson & Co.'s Locomotive Works.
69th Corps, Messrs J. & G. Thompson's.
70th Corps, Messrs A. & J. Inglis, and Todd and MacGregor's.
71st Corps, Lancefield Forge and the Anderston Foundry.

All these corps were liberally subscribed to by the firms from whose workers they were raised, the 25th alone being aided from the Glasgow Central Fund. The original uniforms were dark grey, with black or red facings according to corps (black for the 25th), and black lace, grey caps with a plume of cock's feathers for officers, and black belts.

In April 1861 these eight companies were consolidated as the 25th Lanark Rifle Volunteers, headquarters at Kelvinhaugh Road, Glasgow, the companies being lettered : A, 26th; B, 68th; C, 71st; D, 40th; E, 70th; F, 27th; G, 69th; and H, 25th Corps. At the same time the uniform was changed to rifle-green with scarlet cuffs, collars, and piping, rifle-green shakos with black ball-tufts, and black belts. This uniform was worn till 1873, when scarlet tunics with black facings and Austrian knot, blue trousers, blue shakos with red and white ball-tufts, and white belts were adopted, leggings not being worn.

In June 1880 the corps was re-numbered the 6th Lanark, and blue helmets with silver ornaments replaced the shakos. In 1882 the establishment was increased to ten companies (at which it remained till 1908, one having been since 1900 a cyclist company), and in 1887 the battalion assumed the designation of 2nd V.B. The Highland Light Infantry (Army Order 181 of 1st December). In 1898 brown leather equipment was provided, and leggings introduced.

During the Boer War the battalion contributed Lieutenant J. Shearer and 24 men to the 1st, 21 men to the 2nd, and 11 men to the 3rd Volunteer Service Company of the Highland Light Infantry. Of these Serjeant W. Black was drowned in the Orange River, and Private R. A. M'Gilvray died of disease. Captain T. K. Gardner served with the 3rd Battalion Scottish Rifles, and in all 79 members of the battalion saw active service in South Africa.

In 1904 the facings were changed to blue, but in 1906 (January 10) a complete change of uniform was sanctioned, a drab service doublet of H.L.I. pattern,

Mackenzie tartan kilt, black sporran with three white tassels, red and white hose, drab spats, blue Balmoral bonnet with red, white, and blue diced border and eagle's feather, and brown equipment being adopted as the sole dress. Officers wore Highland Light Infantry doublets and mess uniforms, with buff facings.

The battalion had its own spacious and recently built headquarters and drill‑hall, with underground range, in Yorkhill Street, Overnewtown, Glasgow, and shared since 1886 the range at Dechmont, near Cambuslang, with the 1st Lanark R.E.V. and the 1st V.B.H.L.I.

The lieutenant-colonels commanding have been—

William Rigby, retired pay (major July 28, 1860), Lieut.-
    Colonel, April 23, 1861.
Walter M. Neilson, January 5, 1863.
Adam Morrison (hon. col.), October 10, 1874.
Peter W. Hall, V.D. (hon. col.), May 9, 1887.
John D. Young, V.D. (hon. col.), July 3, 1897.
Hugh D. D. Chalmers, V.D. (hon. col.), December 13, 1905.

3RD (THE BLYTHSWOOD) VOLUNTEER BATTALION, THE HIGHLAND LIGHT INFANTRY.

Regimental District, No. 71.

(PLATE XXX.)

"SOUTH AFRICA, 1900-02." | ORDER OF PRECEDENCE, 117.

Honorary Colonel—Colonel A. C. LORD BLYTHSWOOD, A.D.C., V.D., late Lieut.-Colonel Scots Guards, May 28, 1902.

Headquarters—69 MAIN STREET, BRIDGETON, GLASGOW.

THIS battalion represents two corps which had a separate existence up to 1873, and were known as the 5th and 31st Lanark Rifle Volunteers. The former was absorbed in the latter, so the 31st is the parent corps of the 3rd V.B. Highland Light Infantry.

The "4th Battalion Lanarkshire Rifle Volunteers" was formed on the 4th July 1860 out of the 30th, 31st, 38th, 45th, 46th, 47th, 75th, and 84th Corps. In March 1861 the 86th and 96th Corps were added to it, and the battalion was termed the "2nd Administrative Battalion Lanarkshire Rifle Volunteers," the 88th Corps being added to it in October 1861, making in all twelve companies, each corps consisting of one company only, except the 96th, which had two. The dates of acceptance of services and of commissioning of officers of these corps is given in Appendix C. Their origin and composition were as follows :—

30th Corps (1st Central) was raised in the East Central district, and comprised a good number of artisans.

31st and 75th Corps, the latter an overflow company of the former, were raised in the leather trade and assisted from the Central Fund.

38th Corps (Rifle Rangers) was raised in the Central district among better class mechanics, and assisted from the Central Fund.

45th, 46th, and 47th Corps were raised among the grocers of the city, the firms of which subscribed upwards of £1000 towards their equipment.

84th Corps was raised in the grain and provision trade out of the overflow of the 63rd (see 1st Lanark V.R.C.)

86th Corps was raised among the tailors, and was assisted out of the Central Fund, the members making their own uniforms.

88th Corps was formed from men employed in the fleshers' trade.

96th Corps was a mixed self-supporting corps of citizens, raised as one company and afterwards increased to two.

The original uniform of the 30th Corps was light grey with no facings and scarlet piping, that of the 31st, 38th, and 75th Corps, dark grey with red collars and cuffs and black lace, dark grey caps with red piping, and black belts, and that of the 45th, 46th, 47th, and 84th Corps, a lighter shade of grey. The 86th Corps wore green without braid, with red collars and cuffs and black Austrian knot, green caps, and black belts, and the 96th Corps had a green uniform with red facings and brown belts, which only cost 22s. 6d. a man. In July 1861 the battalion adopted a uniform dress of rifle-green with scarlet collars and piping, rifle-green shakos with a black ball-tuft, and black belts.

In 1864 the 88th, and in 1865 the 30th Corps were disbanded, and on 10th May 1865 the battalion was consolidated as the 31st Lanark Rifle Volunteers, of ten companies, with headquarters in North John Street, Glasgow. Locally the battalion was called the "Central Battalion," but there is no official trace of this title, and it was only in June 1869 that the name "Blythswood Rifles" was added to the title of the battalion in compliment to its commanding officer, Lieut.-Colonel Campbell of Blythswood.

———

The "7th Battalion Lanarkshire Rifle Volunteers" appears for the first time in the September 1860 Army List, as composed of the 5th, 34th, 35th, 58th, 59th, 64th, 65th, 66th, and 90th Corps, and in October the 21st is added to them. The dates of acceptance of services and of commissioning of officers of these corps, which consisted of one company each, are given in Appendix C. Their composition was as follows :—

5th Corps (1st Eastern). An entirely self-supporting corps, the members providing their own arms and equipment. Uniform—dark grey with black facings and lace, and black belts.

21st Corps (Parkhead Artisans). ⎫ Artisan corps raised in the
34th Corps (1st Rifle Rangers). ⎪ eastern district of Glas-
35th Corps (2nd Rifle Rangers). ⎪ gow, and, with the ex-
58th Corps (Eastern Artisans). ⎬ ceptions of the 34th and
59th Corps (Eastern Artisans). ⎪ 90th, assisted from the
66th Corps (Eastern Rifle Rangers). ⎪ Central Fund. Uniforms
90th Corps (Whitevale). ⎭ generally similar to that
of the 5th, some having cock's plumes in their caps. The 58th had five rows of black braid on the breast of the tunic, no facings, black lace on the cuff, and black cord shoulder-straps.[1]

64th Corps (1st Rutherglen). ⎫ Corps raised in Rutherglen, and
65th Corps (2nd Rutherglen). ⎭ liberally assisted by subscriptions in the district. Uniform—Elcho grey with scarlet collars and black lace, grey caps with black band and scarlet piping, and brown belts.

———

[1] A specimen of this uniform is to be seen in the Glasgow Art Galleries, Kelvingrove Park.

In the January 1861 Army List the above ten companies were shown as amalgamated, dated November 27, 1860, as the 5th Lanark Rifle Volunteers, with an establishment of twelve companies; so presumably two new companies were formed for it.   On consolidation the corps adopted a rifle-green uniform with black facings and scarlet piping on the trousers, rifle-green shakos with black ball-tuft, and black belts; in 1869 black haversacks were adopted, and in 1872 black busbies with black plumes were taken into wear.   The corps was reduced to ten companies in 1864, and its numbers gradually fell off until, in September 1873, it was amalgamated with the 31st Lanark Rifle Volunteers.

Its lieutenant-colonels commanding had been—

William Stirling, July 28, 1860.
John Boag, April 3, 1863.
James Farie, February 21, 1868.
James R. Reid, October 12, 1869, till September 16, 1873.

The amalgamation of the remains of the 5th Lanark, then under Major Thomas Glen, with the 31st Lanark, brought to the latter no increase of establishment, but in 1874 the uniform was changed to scarlet tunics with blue facings and trousers, blue glengarries, and white belts, helmets being issued in 1878 and a blue Austrian knot added to the cuffs.   In 1877 the establishment was increased to twelve companies; on June 20, 1880, the battalion was re-numbered the 8th Lanarkshire R.V. (The Blythswood), and in 1887, by General Order 181 of December 1, the title of 3rd (The Blythswood) V.B. The Highland Light Infantry was assumed.   The full uniform of the Highland Light

Infantry, with white metal ornaments and brown belts, was authorised to be worn on May 14, 1886, officers wearing white belts in full dress, and officers and serjeants were authorised to wear sashes in 1904. The facings remained the original yellow adopted in 1886.

Sixty-one members of the battalion took part in the war in South Africa. Of those, 24 men served in the 1st, 21 in the 2nd, and 11 in the 3rd Volunteer Service Company of the Highland Light Infantry, of whom Serjeant J. Cooper died of wounds and Private A. Dobie of disease; Private H. Paterson was wounded at Vecht Kop. Surgeon-Major R. Pollok served with the R.A.M.C., and Lieutenant W. H. Youden with the 3rd Battalion Argyll and Sutherland Highlanders. A cyclist section was formed in 1900, and from 1902 to 1906 the battalion formed part of the 34th Field Army Brigade, training thirteen clear days in camp annually.

The headquarters and drill-hall of the battalion, at 69 Main Street, Bridgeton, were erected in 1902 at a cost of £12,000, and it possessed its own rifle-range, up to 900 yards, at Gilbertfield, near Cambuslang.

The lieutenant - colonels (commandant since 1887) have been—

Alexander Cowan Ewing, September 20, 1860.

John Campbell of Possil, late Captain 7th Dragoon Guards, December 1, 1864.

Archibald Campbell Campbell (afterwards Lord Blythswood), A.D.C., V.D., Colonel, late Lieutenant-Colonel Scots Fusilier Guards, July 25, 1867.

William Clark, V.D. (hon. col.), January 13, 1897.

Robert S. Murray, V.D. (hon. col.), April 17, 1901.

R. Barclay Shaw, V.D. (hon. col.), March 19, 1904.

David Runciman Graham, V.D. (hon. col.), July 26, 1905.

Francis J. Stevenson, V.D. (hon. col.), February 10, 1906.

9TH LANARKSHIRE RIFLE VOLUNTEER CORPS.

Regimental District, No. 71.

(PLATE XXXI.)

"SOUTH AFRICA, 1900-02." | ORDER OF PRECEDENCE, 118.

Headquarters—LANARK.

THE "8th Battalion Lanarkshire Rifle Volunteers" appears for the first time in the January 1861 Army List as having been formed on December 9, 1860, when it was composed of the 37th (Lesmahagow), 55th (Lanark), 73rd (Carluke), and 94th (Douglas) Corps of one company each, the dates of offer of services and of commissioning of officers of which are given in Appendix C. The uniform of the 37th Corps was Elcho grey tunics and knickerbockers, with scarlet piping and scarlet and black Austrian knots, small grey shakos with a blackcock's tail on the left side, scarlet piping, and bugle and crown badge, yellow leather leggings, and brown belts. Those of the 55th and 73rd Corps are given as "grey, facings scarlet," and are stated to have been similar to that of the 37th. In March 1861 the battalion became the 3rd Administrative Battalion Lanarkshire Rifle Volunteers, with headquarters at Lanark. Locally it was, and continued to be, known as the "Upper Ward Battalion." In 1862 the battalion adopted a scarlet tunic with blue facings and white Austrian knot, blue trousers with red piping, blue shakos with red piping and black ball-tuft, and brown belts.

In 1863 the 62nd Corps (Biggar), which had had an ephemeral existence in 1860 (see Appendix C), was revived and added to the battalion, and in 1875 the

107th Corps (Leadhills) was formed, thus bringing the establishment of the battalion up to six companies.

In March 1880 the battalion was consolidated and numbered the 37th, but in June 1880 it was re-numbered the 9th Lanarkshire Rifle Volunteer Corps. The companies were lettered — A, Lesmahagow (late 37th); B, Lanark (late 55th); C, Biggar (late 62nd); D, Carluke (late 73rd); E, Douglas (late 94th); and F, Leadhills (late 107th). In the same year blue helmets took the place of the shakos, white belts replaced the brown, and for the tunic was substituted a red serge frock with blue collar, red cuffs, and white Austrian knot. On June 27, 1883, sanction was given for the adoption of the scarlet doublet with yellow facings and Mackenzie tartan trews of the Highland Light Infantry, with black leggings. The helmet was re-tained until 1904, when it was replaced by the diced shako of the H.L.I. for officers and a glengarry for the other ranks. In 1904, also, the facings were changed from yellow to buff.

In 1894 the headquarters of "E" Company were transferred to Forth, and in 1901 those of "F" Company were moved to Law, the Leadhills de-tachment becoming a section of "C" Company. The battalion possessed five rifle-ranges.

During the South African War 96 members of the battalion — including Captain J. Gray, who was attached to the Scottish Volunteer Cyclist Company, and was mentioned in despatches—saw active service. Of these, 25 men served with the 1st, 22 with the 2nd, and 18 with the 3rd Volunteer Service Company of the Highland Light Infantry, of whom Lance-Corporal J. Walker and Private A. Gray died of disease, and Private A. Wilson was wounded at Retief's Nek; 26 men served with the Imperial Yeomanry.

The commanding officers of the battalion have been—

Major James T. Brown, December 12, 1860.
Major Hugh Mossman, July 15, 1868.
Major James Stevenson Hamilton, late Captain 12th Lancers, September 21, 1872.
Lieut. - Colonel J. Stevenson Hamilton (afterwards James Stevenson), A.D.C., C.B., V.D., Colonel, May 26, 1875.
Lieut.-Colonel W. Bertram, Major (retired pay), late Manchester Regiment, December 20, 1905, to March 10, 1908.

5TH (GLASGOW HIGHLAND) VOLUNTEER BATTALION, THE HIGHLAND LIGHT INFANTRY.

Regimental District, No. 71.

(PLATE XXXI.)

"South Africa, 1900-02." | Order of Precedence, 119.

Honorary Colonel—J. D. S. Duke of Argyll, K.T., G.C.M.G., G.C.V.O., V.D., June 21, 1899.

Headquarters—81 Greendyke Street, Glasgow.

As the outcome of a desire expressed by many Highlanders resident in Glasgow that a Highland volunteer battalion should be formed, a meeting was held in Glasgow for the purpose on April 24, 1868, and at this it was announced that 200 men had already given in their names as ready to join. Six hundred men joined that evening, and the services of the corps, as the 105th Lanarkshire (Glasgow Highland) Rifle Volunteers, of twelve companies, were accepted on July

21, 1868, the commissions of the first officers being dated October 19. 187 officers and men transferred their services to it from the Highland companies of the 4th Lanarkshire (see 4th V.B. Scottish Rifles). "C" Company was originally recruited from residents of Partick, "E" from those of Crosshill, "F" from natives of Islay, "G" from natives of Argyllshire, and the other companies had general recruiting. The uniform, sanctioned on September 28, 1868, was modelled on that of the 42nd Highlanders, and consisted of scarlet doublets with blue facings, 42nd tartan kilts and belted plaids, white sporrans with three black tails, red-and-black diced hose, white spats, glengarries with blackcock's tail, and white belts. The cap and sporran badges were St Andrew with his cross within a garter, inscribed "Clanna nan Gaidheal ri guelibh a cheile" ("Highlanders, shoulder to shoulder").

The first public appearance of a portion of the corps was on October 8, 1868, when H.R.H. the Prince of Wales laid the foundation-stone of the new University buildings.

In June 1880 the battalion was re-numbered the 10th Lanarkshire Rifle Volunteers, and in 1877, by General Order 181 of December 1, it received the title of 5th (Glasgow Highland) V.B., The Highland Light Infantry. In 1885 the "set" of the tartan (which had been smaller) was changed to that worn by the Black Watch, the badges of the latter were adopted, the sporran received five black tassels instead of the three long tails, the blackcocks' tails were removed from the glengarries, and "G.H." was substituted for "10 Lk." on the shoulder-straps. In 1902 the officers were permitted to wear feather bonnets with scarlet and white hackles, and sashes for serjeants were issued. At the same time drab service

s

doublets and drab spats were authorised as undress and service dress.

134 members of the Glasgow Highlanders saw active service in South Africa during the war. Of these, Lieut. J. R. Leisk and 30 men served with the 1st, Major P. W. Hendry, Lieut. G. Wingate, and 24 men with the 2nd, and 9 men with the 3rd Volunteer Company of the Highland Light Infantry, of whom Private D. M. Rose died of disease, and Colour - Serjeant F. Willis and Private W. Duncan were wounded, the former at Vecht Kop, the latter at Retief's Nek. Captain C. C. Murray and 37 men served in the Imperial Yeomanry, and the remainder of the number in various units.

A thirteenth (cyclist) company was added to the battalion in 1900.

Of recent years, "A" Company was recruited from Highland residents of Springburn, "B" from White-inch, "C" from Partick, "E" from Queen's Park, "M" from Hillhead, and "F," as always, from natives of Islay. The headquarters and drill-hall of the battalion were at 81 Greendyke Street, Glasgow, and it shared with the 3rd V.B., Argyll and Sutherland Highlanders, a rifle-range up to 900 yards at Patterton.

The following is the list of lieutenant-colonels commandant :—

Francis Robertson-Reid, late Captain Royal Renfrew Militia (hon. col.), May 7, 1869.

James Todd Stewart, V.D. (hon. col.), May 10, 1890.

Charles M. Williamson, V.D. (hon. col.), May 15, 1895.

Thomas Ramsay, V.D. (hon. col.), July 18, 1903.

William I. Mackenzie, V.D., February 25, 1905.

Patrick W. Hendry, V.D. (hon. captain in the army) (hon. col.), September 16, 1905.

Alexander Birrell, V.D. (hon. col.), December 1, 1906.

1st (ROSS HIGHLAND) VOLUNTEER BATTALION, SEAFORTH HIGHLANDERS (ROSS-SHIRE BUFFS, THE DUKE OF ALBANY'S).

Regimental District, No. 78.

(PLATE XXXII.)

"SOUTH AFRICA, 1900-02." | ORDER OF PRECEDENCE, 154.

Honorary Colonel—J. A. F. H. STEWART-MACKENZIE of Seaforth, Brevet-Colonel (retired pay), late 9th Lancers, November 28, 1903.

Headquarters—DINGWALL.

THE 1st Administrative Battalion, Ross-shire Rifle Volunteers, was formed, with headquarters at Dingwall, on September 30, 1861, and the following corps, of one company each, raised in Ross-shire, were incorporated with it on that date :—

1st, Invergordon, raised February 15, 1860. Uniform—medium grey tunic, trousers, and cap with black braid, no facings, brown waist-belt. Headquarters removed, 1869, to Tain.

2nd, Dingwall, raised February 15, 1860. Uniform the same as the 1st Corps, but with black leggings and a black plume in the cap.

3rd, Avoch, raised February 17, 1860. Uniform—grey tweed loose jacket, knickerbockers, and cap, brown leggings and brown waist-belt. Headquarters changed in 1876 to Fortrose, a mile from Avoch.

4th, Knockbain, services accepted March 22, 1860; officers commissioned April 12, 1860. Uniform—light grey tunics with red facings, light grey trousers with black braid, light grey cap with deer's-head badge, black patent-leather waist- and shoulder-belts, and black leggings. Headquarters transferred in 1876 to Munlochy, in the parish of Knockbain.

5th, Alness, raised May 20, 1861. Uniform—grey. Headquarters transferred in 1865 to Ullapool.

6th, Alness, raised as one subdivision on May 21, 1861. Uniform—grey. Increased to one company, and headquarters transferred to Invergordon in 1871.

In 1864 it was decided to clothe the battalion in scarlet hooked tunics with blue facings, white cord on the collar and cuffs, and black braid down the front, blue trousers with red piping, blue shakos with red band, deer's-head badge, and white horse-hair plume, and white patent-leather waist- and pouch-belts, and this uniform was adopted in the following years by all the above companies with the exception of the 3rd, which adopted scarlet doublets with blue facings, Mackenzie tartan kilts, and plain glengarries, and wore this uniform till 1876.

Subsequently to 1864 the following corps were raised and added to the battalion :—

7th, Evanton, raised May 12, 1866.   Uniform for a short time— grey tunics, 42nd tartan trews, and plain glengarries; but in the end of 1866 the company adopted scarlet doublets with blue (later buff) facings, Mackenzie tartan kilts, heather mixture hose with green tops, no spats, grey goat-skin sporrans without tassels or badge, plain glengarries with deer's-head badge, and white patent-leather belts.

8th, Moy, near Dingwall, raised August 11, 1866, from men of the Brahan estate.   Uniform—scarlet doublet with white facings; otherwise the same as the 7th.

9th, Gairloch, raised February 23, 1867. Uniform—scarlet doublet with blue facings; otherwise the same as the 7th.

On November 1, 1875, a new uniform was approved for the battalion.   It consisted of a scarlet doublet with blue collar and cuffs, the latter with black Austrian knot and blue piping, Mackenzie tartan trews, glengarries with diced border and deer's-head badge, and white belts.   This uniform was adopted by the whole battalion, the 3rd, 7th, 8th, and 9th Corps discontinuing the wearing of the kilt.

In June 1800 the battalion was consolidated as the 1st Ross-shire (Ross Highland) Rifle Volunteers, with headquarters at Dingwall, and nine companies, lettered as follows: A, Tain (late 1st Corps); B, Dingwall (late 2nd); C, Fortrose (late 3rd); D, Munlochy (late 4th); E, Ullapool (late 5th); F, Invergordon (late 6th); G, Evanton (late 7th); H, Moy (late 8th); and I, Gairloch (late 9th). In 1887 the title of 1st (Ross Highland) V.B. Seaforth Highlanders was conferred upon the battalion by General Order 181 of December 1, and about this time the headquarters of G Company were moved to Dingwall, with a detachment at Alness, and of H Company to Fairburn, close to Moy, on the Brahan estate.

After 1880 the battalion had been gradually reverting to the kilted uniform, H Company having resumed it in 1881 and A in 1883; but it was only on October 31, 1888, that authority was given for the adoption by the battalion of the full dress of the Seaforth Highlanders, the diced glengarry being substituted for the feather bonnet. Yellow facings were then worn, but these were changed to buff in 1903, in which year also brown belts were substituted for the white hitherto worn. On June 14, 1902, drab service doublets and drab spats were authorised for marching and drill order dress.

During the war in South Africa the battalion furnished 110 of its members for active service. Of these, 43 men joined the 1st, 26 men the 2nd, and Lieutenant W. M. Macphail and 3 men the 3rd Volunteer Service Company of the Seaforth Highlanders. The remainder, including Lieutenant J. O. Black, served in various corps.

Headquarters of the battalion were at Dingwall, and those of companies were—

A, Tain.
B, Dingwall.
C, Fortrose.
D, Munlochy.
E, Ullapool.

F, Invergordon.
G, Dingwall, with detachment at Alness.
H, Fairburn (Brahan).
I, Gairloch.

The battalion had fourteen separate rifle-ranges.

In 1865 Captain Ross of the battalion won the Queen's Prize at Wimbledon.

The commanding officers have been—

Keith W. Stewart-Mackenzie of Seaforth, late Lieutenant 90th Foot, Major, September 30, 1861; Lieut.-Colonel, May 26, 1865.

Duncan H. C. R. Davidson of Tulloch (hon. col.), Lieut.-Colonel, August 17, 1881.

Alexander J. C. Warrand, V.D. (hon. col.), Lieut.-Colonel, March 29, 1889.

Alexander R. B. Warrand, Captain (retired pay), late Seaforth Highlanders (hon. col.), Lieut.-Colonel, July 1, 1897.

1st SUTHERLAND (THE SUTHERLAND HIGHLAND) VOLUNTEER RIFLE CORPS.

(SUTHERLAND, ORKNEY, AND CAITHNESS.)

Regimental District, No. 72.

(PLATE XXXIII.)

"SOUTH AFRICA, 1900-02." | ORDER OF PRECEDENCE, 188.

Honorary Colonel—HIS MAJESTY THE KING.

Headquarters—GOLSPIE.

THE first meeting which led to the formation of the 1st Sutherland Rifle Volunteers was held in Golspie Inn on June 6, 1859, the chair being taken by Mr Charles Hood of Inverbrora, and at it a number of gentlemen enrolled themselves. On October 17 intimation was received that the services of the Golspie company had been accepted, and shortly afterwards similar sanction was given to companies at Dornoch

and Brora. These three formed the 1st Sutherland
Rifle Volunteers, a corps of three companies, the dates
of commission of the officers being: 1st, Golspie,
December 2, 1859; 2nd, Dornoch, December 2, 1859;
3rd, Brora, January 3, 1860,—the date of formation
of the three into one corps being January 1861. The
uniform of the corps was medium grey tunics and
trousers with blue facings and piping, grey shakos
with band of Sutherland tartan and black horse-hair
plume, and brown belts. The clothing, &c., for the
three companies cost £1000, of which the Duke of
Sutherland paid £800, the rest being raised by subscriptions in the county. A fourth company for the
corps was formed at Rogart, the first meeting having
been held on October 13, 1860, and its officers were
commissioned in January 1861. Its uniform was
scarlet doublets with yellow collars, Sutherland tartan
kilts and belted plaids, grey goat-skin sporrans, black-
and-red diced hose, plain glengarries, and white belts,
with a plate on the pouch-belt bearing the inscription
"Duchess Harriet's Company, Rogart." It is believed
that this was the first rifle volunteer corps in Scotland
to adopt the national scarlet uniform. In 1863 the
1st, 2nd, and 3rd Companies adopted the same doublet
as the 4th, with Sutherland tartan trews and white
belts, and all four companies adopted glengarries with
red, white, and blue diced borders.

In Caithness three companies were at first formed,
the 1st at Thurso on April 10, 1860, the 2nd at Wick
on February 16, 1861, and the 3rd at Halkirk on
April 11, 1861. Their uniform was light grey tunics
with red piping, darker grey trousers with red piping,
a grey shako with bugle and crown badge and red-and-
white horse-hair plume (feathers for officers), and brown
belts.

In Orkney and Shetland a small corps, the 1st, was raised at Lerwick as one subdivision on April 24, 1860, and increased to full-company strength on August 24, 1866.

On January 4, 1864, the 1st Administrative Battalion, Sutherland Rifle Volunteers, with headquarters at Golspie, was formed out of the above corps, the 1st Sutherland being broken up into four independent corps, which resumed their former numbers in the county, the battalion thus consisting of the 1st, 2nd, 3rd, and 4th Sutherland, 1st Orkney and Shetland, and 1st, 2nd, and 3rd Caithness Corps. To these were added on September 25, 1867, the 4th Caithness Corps of one company, formed at Watten, and on August 6, 1868, the 5th Sutherland Corps of one company, formed at Bonar Bridge. The Orkney and Caithness corps in 1864 adopted a uniform of scarlet tunics with blue facings, dark grey trousers with red piping, and blue shakos with red band and red-and-white plume, and two or three years later exchanged their brown belts for white. In 1870-74 the shoulder-belts were abolished and the plume replaced by a ball-tuft, and in 1879 the shakos gave way to blue helmets with star and crown badge in silver. The Sutherland companies were, in 1867, all provided with Sutherland tartan kilts and belted plaids, with grey goat-skin sporrans, red-and-green diced hose (with white spats from 1870), and glengarries with red-and-white diced borders, the 5th Corps receiving this uniform on its first formation.

In September 1866 H.R.H. the Prince of Wales reviewed the battalion at Dunrobin and was appointed honorary colonel of it, which His Majesty continued to be till 1908.

In June 1880 the battalion was consolidated as the

1st Sutherland Highland Rifle Volunteers, headquarters at Golspie, with ten companies, lettered as follows : A, Golspie (late 1st Sutherland) ; B, Dornoch (late 2nd Sutherland) ; C, Brora (late 3rd Sutherland) ; D, Rogart (late 4th Sutherland) ; E, Bonar Bridge (late 5th Sutherland) ; F, Lerwick (late 1st Orkney and Shetland) ; G, Thurso (late 1st Caithness) ; H, Wick (late 2nd Caithness) ; I, Halkirk (late 3rd Caithness) ; K, Watten (late 4th Caithness).

The 1st Sutherland was always remarkable for the fine physique of its men, and it is on record that at the Royal Review in Edinburgh, in 1881, in the leading company the flank men were each 6 ft. 3 in. and the centre man 5 ft. 10 in. 'The Times' correspondent wrote : " Splendid men the Duke's corps are, reminding some of the spectators of the 93rd in its Crimean days. They marched also as well as they looked."

The year 1883 was marked in the annals of the battalion by one of its members, Colour-Serjeant R. Mackay, winning the Queen's Prize at the National Rifle Association Meeting. In this year also the Caithness companies began to conform to the dress of the rest of the battalion, and " G," " I," and " K " Companies adopted the kilt and doublet, " H " Company following suit in the following year. In 1884 the " F " (Lerwick) Company was disbanded and a new " F " Company raised in its place at Lairg, in Sutherland. Brass bands were abolished in the battalion in 1883, and a band of thirty pipers, besides drummers, formed, the pipers wearing green doublets, Sutherland kilt, Royal Stuart shoulder-plaid, and plain glengarries with blackcock's tail. In 1890 a new Caithness company (L) was raised at Wick, and in 1901 a sixth (M) at Reay, thus bringing the battalion up to a strength of twelve companies—six in Sutherland (A to F) and six in Caithness (G to M). In 1899 two white tassels for the men and three for the officers were added to the sporrans, and on February 19, 1906, a drab service doublet was authorised to be worn in undress and marching order. The officers' glengarries had been plain blue since 1880, and they wore red-and-white hose in levée dress.

Eighty-seven members of the 1st Sutherland served during the South African War. Of these, Lieutenant R. G. Campbell and 34 men served with the 1st, Captain W. C. Ross, Lieutenant J. Brims, and 18 men with the 2nd, and 2 men with the 3rd Volunteer Service Company of the Seaforth Highlanders, of whom 1 man (transferred to the Scottish Horse) was killed and 3 died of disease. Sixteen men served in Lovat's Scouts and 9 in other corps of Imperial Yeomanry, 3 in the South African Constabulary, and 1 in a volunteer service company of the Black Watch. Surgeon-Captain J. K. Tomory served in a medical capacity.

Owing to the scattered nature of the battalion, each company had its own rifle range or ranges, there being thirteen in all. The headquarters range at Golspie, up to 1000 yards, belonged to the "Sutherland Rifle Association."

The commanding officers of the battalion have been—

G. G. W. Duke of Sutherland, K.G., Major, January 30, 1860; Lieut.-Colonel, January 4, 1864.

C. Marquis of Stafford, late Lieutenant 2nd Life Guards, Lieut.-Colonel, April 26, 1882.

C. G. Sinclair, younger of Ulbster, Lieut.-Colonel, June 13, 1891.

D. Menzies of Blarich, Rogart, Lieut.-Colonel, June 10, 1893.

J. Mackintosh, V.D., Lieut.-Colonel, August 30, 1899.

John Morrison, V.D. (hon. col.), Lieut.-Colonel, November 2, 1901; Lieut.-Colonel Commandant, October 31, 1903.

3RD (MORAYSHIRE) VOLUNTEER BATTALION, SEAFORTH HIGHLANDERS (ROSS-SHIRE BUFFS, THE DUKE OF ALBANY'S).

Regimental District, No. 72.

(PLATE XXXIV.)

" SOUTH AFRICA, 1900-02." | ORDER OF PRECEDENCE, 195.

Honorary Colonel—CHARLES J. JOHNSTON, V.D. (hon. col.), November 22, 1902.

Headquarters—ELGIN.

THE first public meeting with a view to the formation of this corps was held in Elgin on June 20, 1859 ; but though much enthusiasm was displayed, nothing was done until November 28, when the master tradesmen of Elgin held a meeting, at which it was resolved to form a rifle corps, and on December 5 a public meeting was held at which the formation of two companies was decided upon. These became the 2nd and 3rd Elgin, the 2nd being composed of citizens, the 3rd of artisans. In Forres a meeting had been held on January 4, 1860, the outcome of which was the 1st Elgin Corps at Forres, which gained the first place in precedence in the county by the expedition displayed in the offer of its services.

The 1st Administrative Battalion, Elgin Rifle Volunteers, with headquarters at Elgin, was formed on May 4, 1860, and to it were attached, at that time or on the subsequent date of their formation, the following corps of Elgin Rifle Volunteers :—

1st, Forres. Services accepted January 11, 1860, as one company. Officers commissioned January 3, 1860. Uniform—dark grey (dark green according to one authority) with black facings and scarlet piping, black shakos, and brown belts. Increased to two companies May 22, 1867.

2nd, Elgin (citizens). Services accepted January 31, 1860, as one company. Officers commissioned February 24, 1860. Uniform—Elcho grey with scarlet facings and piping, black caps with peak, and black belts.

3rd, Elgin (artisans). Services accepted February 20, 1860, as one company. Officers commissioned March 6, 1860. Uniform—Elcho grey with scarlet facings and piping, black shakos with black horse-hair plume, and black belts.

4th, Rothes, formed May 28, 1860, as one company. Uniform—Elcho grey with black facings and piping, black caps with peak, and black belts.

5th, Fochabers, formed April 10, 1861, as one company. Uniform—dark grey with black facings and scarlet piping, and black belts.

6th, Carr Bridge, formed August 26, 1861, as one company. Uniform—Elcho grey with scarlet facings and piping, black caps with peak, and black belts.

7th (The Duff), Lhanbryde, afterwards Urquhart. Formed April 15, 1863, as one company. Increased to one and a half companies May 12, 1863.

8th, Garmouth, formed December 2, 1867, as one company.

9th, Grantown, formed January 9, 1871, as one company.

In 1862 the uniform of the whole battalion was changed to scarlet tunics with blue facings and white Austrian knot, blue trousers, blue shakos with black ball-tuft, and black belts. The 7th, 8th, and 9th Corps adopted this uniform on their formation, except that the 7th had a band of Duff tartan round the shako. The 6th Corps had scarlet doublets with blue facings, Grant tartan kilts, green-and-black hose, goat-skin sporrans, glengarries, and black belts, but did not wear spats till 1878. In 1879 blue helmets were substituted for the shakos, and white belts replaced the black hitherto worn.

In March 1880 the battalion was consolidated as the 1st Elgin Rifle Volunteers, headquarters at Elgin, with ten companies, lettered as follows: A and H, Forres (late 1st Corps); B and C, Elgin (late 2nd and 3rd);

D, Rothes (late 4th); E, Fochabers (late 5th); F, Carr Bridge (late 6th); G, Urquhart, with a half company at Pluscarden (late 7th); I, Garmouth (late 8th); and K, Grantown (late 9th).

On January 11, 1886, the battalion was authorised to wear scarlet doublets with yellow facings, Mackenzie tartan trews, glengarries with diced red, white, and blue border, and white belts; and in 1887, by General Order 181 of December 1, the title of 3rd (Morayshire) V.B., Seaforth Highlanders, was conferred upon it. The headquarters of F Company were at this time changed to Abernethy, and in 1897 the half company of G at Pluscarden was raised to a full company and lettered " L," its headquarters being moved thence to Alves in 1904. In 1905 the headquarters of " G " Company were moved back to Lhanbryde, their original station.

On May 21, 1898, the kilt, sporran, hose, and spats of the Seaforth Highlanders were authorised to be worn by the battalion; on June 14, 1902, drab doublets and drab spats were authorised for service dress, and in 1905 the facings were changed from yellow to buff.

The battalion contributed in all 193 of its members for service in South Africa during the war. Of these, there joined the volunteer service companies of the Seaforth Highlanders, — 1st contingent, Captain C. Ernest Johnston and 48 others (including 6 reservists); 2nd, Lieutenant W. C. Reid and 9 others; 3rd, 64 men; 4th, 24 men,—in all, 2 officers and 145 other ranks. Of the 1st contingent, Corporal A. Paterson was wounded at Heilbron; and of the 2nd, Corporal J. Dow received a commission in the 2nd Scottish Horse, and was killed on 21st December 1901.

The distribution of the battalion from 1905 onwards was: A and H Companies, Forres; B and C, Elgin; D, Rothes, with a detachment at Archiestown; E,

Fochabers; F, Abernethy; G, Lhanbryde; I, Garmouth; K, Grantown, with a detachment at Cromdale; and L, Alves. The headquarters occupied a commodious building in the Cowper Park, Elgin, and there were two headquarter ranges at Garmouth, twelve miles from Elgin, for B, C, G, and I Companies, and nine ranges in other parts of the county for the others.

The lieutenant-colonels commanding have been—

Sir A. P. Gordon-Cumming, Bart. of Altyre, Major, May 4, 1860; Lieut.-Colonel, June 12, 1861.
Hon. James Grant, late Lieutenant 42nd Foot, October 24, 1866.
William Culbard, September 25, 1880.
Felix Calvert Mackenzie, V.D. (hon. col.), May 28, 1884.
Charles J. Johnston, V.D. (hon. col.), September 23, 1893.
Robert Urquhart, M.V.O., V.D. (hon. col.), September 13, 1902.
Sir George A. Cooper, Bart., V.D., December 9, 1907.

NOTE.

The 1st Nairn Rifle Volunteer Corps was raised at Nairn as one company on April 14, 1860. It was reduced to a subdivision in 1861, and disbanded in 1862.

1st VOLUNTEER BATTALION, THE GORDON HIGHLANDERS.
Regimental District, No. 75.

(PLATE XXXV.)

"SOUTH AFRICA, 1900-02." | ORDER OF PRECEDENCE 143.
Headquarters—ABERDEEN.

WITH a view to forming rifle corps in the city of Aberdeen, a preliminary meeting was held on May 28, 1859, the Lord Provost in the chair, and this was followed by a public meeting on May 30. There were formed the following corps (see Appendix A) :—

6th. Raised November 19, 1859; a self-supporting corps of one company.

7th. Raised November 19, 1859; a self-supporting corps of one company.

8th. Raised November 26, 1859; a corps of one company, composed of employés of Aberdeen merchants, and aided by the contributions of the latter. A second company was formed for it on December 30, 1859.

9th. Raised December 30, 1859, as one company.

11th. Raised January 13, 1860, as one company; composed of artisans, who paid £1 towards the cost of their equipment.

12th. Raised January 27, 1860, as two companies; composed of artisans, as in the 11th.

13th. Raised January 21, 1860, as one company; mainly recruited from the employés of the Scottish North-Eastern Railway.

These corps were consolidated on March 16, 1860, as the 6th Aberdeenshire Rifle Volunteers, the companies being numbered in the order of the first commissions of their captains as follows :—

No. 1 Coy. (late 6th Corps).
No. 2 Coy. (late 7th Corps).
No. 3 Coy. (late 1st of the 8th Corps).
No. 4 Coy. (late 2nd of the 8th Corps).
No. 5 Coy. (late 9th Corps).

No. 6 Coy. (late 11th Corps).
No. 7 Coy. (late 13th Corps).
No. 8 Coy. (late 1st of the 12th Corps).
No. 9 Coy. (late 2nd of the 12th Corps).

On July 19, 1860, in consequence of the general re-numbering throughout the county (see Appendix A), the corps became the 1st Aberdeenshire Rifle Volunteers. Its uniform was dark grey with black braid and four rows of black lace on the breast, grey caps with peak, and black patent-leather belts. On November 10, 1860, a tenth company was added, which wore grey doublets with black facings, Forbes tartan trews and shoulder-plaids, and glengarries. On May

4, 1861, the 1st and 2nd Companies were amalgamated
as the 1st, the others took the next higher number, and
a new No. 10 Company was raised, which wore green
doublets with black piping, 42nd tartan kilts, green-and-
black diced hose, grey sporrans with three white tassels,
Balmoral bonnets with eagle's feather, and black belts.
The 9th Company were disbanded on November 24, 1861,
as they had declined to change their uniform to conform
to that of the rest of the battalion, and had been insub-
ordinate in the matter ; and the same fate befell the
10th (kilted) Company in 1862, when (on June 27) a
rifle-green uniform was adopted by the battalion.   This
consisted of a hooked tunic with five rows of black lace
on the breast and black braid on the cuffs, trousers with
black braid stripe, rifle-green shakos with black ball-
tuft, and black patent-leather belts.   In 1870 a company at Woodside, beyond the city boundary, was
added to the corps, bringing it up to nine companies,
at which strength it continued until 1895, although
throughout its official establishment was eleven companies.   On June 25, 1880, the companies were lettered
A to I.

On December 8, 1879, authority was given to change
the uniform to one of scarlet doublets with yellow facings, Gordon tartan trews, blue helmets, brown belts,
and black leggings, the officers to wear shoulder-plaids,
white sword-belts, and dirks on white waist-belts, and
in 1884, by General Order 12 of February 1, the title
of 1st Volunteer Battalion, Gordon Highlanders, was
conferred upon the battalion.   The full uniform of the
Gordon Highlanders (less the feather bonnet, which was
replaced by the glengarry with red, white, and blue
diced border), with white belts, was authorised on
October 30, 1895, but the change was carried out
gradually, a new company, " L," formed in that year

being the first to be kilted, and the whole battalion being completely re-clothed only by 1901. Drab service doublets were authorised for undress on July 9, 1902, and sashes to be worn by serjeants in full dress.

A cyclist section was formed for the battalion in 1890; in 1898 "H" Company was broken up and a new company, "U," formed from university students, and in 1905 D and I Companies were amalgamated as "D," and E and L as "M." The official establishment of the battalion was reduced from eleven to nine companies in 1903, but only eight actually existed since then, and these represented the following units of earlier existence :—

A Coy. (former 6th and 7th Aberdeen).

B Coy. (former 1st of the 8th Aberdeen).

C Coy. (former 2nd of the 8th Aberdeen).

D Coy. (former 9th Aberdeen and Woodside Company).

F Coy. (former 13th Aberdeen).

G Coy. (former 1st of the 12th Aberdeen).

M Coy. (former 11th Aberdeen and L Coy. of 1895).

U Coy., university company.

During the South African War 128 members of the battalion served in the field. To the 1st Volunteer Service Company it contributed Captain J. B. Buchanan, Lieutenant F. J. O. Mackinnon, and 57 other ranks. This company left Aberdeen on February 16, 1900, served with the 1st Battalion of the Gordon Highlanders, and returned to Aberdeen on May 4, 1901. It distinguished itself at the action of Doornkop, near Johannesburg, on May 29, 1900, and there Captain Buchanan, Lieutenant Mackinnon, and 5 other ranks of the 1st Volunteer Battalion were wounded, and Lance-Serjeant W. Simpson and Private G. W. Middleton were killed. In the action at Leehoek, near Krugersdorp, on July 11, one man of the 1st Volunteer Battalion, and on September 30, at Komati Poort, two more men of the battalion, were wounded.

T

To a draft sent out from Aberdeen on May 18 to strengthen this company, the battalion contributed Captain W. O. Duncan and 14 other ranks.

The 3rd Volunteer Service Company left Aberdeen on March 15, 1901, and joined the 2nd Battalion in South Africa, returning to Aberdeen on July 6, 1902. To it the 1st Volunteer Battalion contributed Lieutenant R. A. Henderson and 34 other ranks, of whom one private (C. V. Hutchison) died of disease. The 4th Volunteer Service Company, which left Aberdeen on March 2, 1902, joined the 1st Battalion, and returned to Aberdeen on July 14, 1902, included 2nd Lieutenant G. A. S. Chedburn and 18 other ranks of the 1st Volunteer Battalion.

Captain J. B. Buchanan was mentioned in despatches for his services in South Africa.

In 1902 the battalion was attached to the 34th Field Army Brigade, and trained in camp for thirteen clear days annually until 1906, when the brigade was broken up.

The rifle-range of the battalion, up to 900 yards, was at Seaton Links, two and a half miles from Aberdeen.

The lieutenant-colonels commanding the battalion have been—

Napier Turner Christie, late Major 38th Foot, March 5, 1860.
Henry Knight - Erskine of Pittodrie, late Captain 33rd Foot, January 13, 1862.
William Jopp (hon. col.), December 24, 1870.
Douglass Duncan, V.D. (hon. col.), September 20, 1890.
George Cruden, V.D. (hon. col.), September 20, 1900.
Lachlan Mackinnon, V.D. (hon. col.), December 10, 1904.
D. B. D. Stewart, V.D. (hon. col.), November 19, 1906.

2ND VOLUNTEER BATTALION, THE GORDON HIGHLANDERS.

Regimental District, No. 75.

(PLATE XXXVI.)

"SOUTH AFRICA, 1900." | ORDER OF PRECEDENCE, 144.

Headquarters—OLD MELDRUM.

IN June 1861 the 2nd Administrative Battalion, Aberdeenshire Rifle Volunteers, was formed from the then existing 2nd (Tarves, of three companies), 5th (New Deer, of one subdivision), 6th (Ellon, of one company), and 19th (New Deer, of one company) Corps of Aberdeenshire Rifle Volunteers, headquarters being at Tarves. In November 1861 the 5th and 19th Corps were amalgamated as the 5th Corps of one company, which in 1862 was transferred to the 3rd Administrative Battalion (afterwards 3rd V.B., *q.v.*), and in the latter year the 13th (Turriff), 15th (Fyvie), and 16th (Meldrum) Corps, hitherto unattached, and each of one company, were added to the battalion. The 2nd Administrative Battalion, therefore, then consisted of the 2nd, 6th, 13th, 15th, and 16th Corps, the dates of formation of which are given in Appendix A. Their original uniforms were as follows :—

2nd Corps, dark green, with black patent-leather belts.
6th Corps, Elcho grey with scarlet piping, caps with scarlet piping and ball-tuft, and brown belts.
13th Corps, Elcho grey.
15th Corps, Elcho grey.
16th Corps, Elcho grey ; but in 1863 this corps adopted dark green uniforms with black facings and belts.

In 1864 a new 12th Corps was raised at Udny to replace the former 12th Corps (headquarters at Old

Aberdeen, raised July 21, 1860, and hitherto unattached), which had been disbanded the previous year,
and was added to the battalion; and in this same year,
1864, the battalion, with the exception of the 16th
Corps, adopted an Elcho grey uniform with scarlet
collars, piping, and Austrian knot, and black braid on
the collar and round the cuff, grey shakos with black
ball-tuft, and brown belts. The 16th Corps continued
to wear its dark green uniform, assumed in 1863, until
1875.

In the beginning of 1867, headquarters of the 12th
Corps were transferred to Newmachar, and on June 11
of that year the 2nd Corps, which had been reduced
from three to two companies in 1862, was divided into
two, of which the first retained the name 2nd Corps
and had its headquarters at Methlie, while the second,
with headquarters at Tarves, became the 18th Corps.
In 1868 the headquarters of the battalion were removed from Tarves to Old Meldrum, and in 1877 to
Aberdeen, about which time also the headquarters
of the 12th Corps were moved from Newmachar to
Newburgh.

In May 1875 the whole battalion was authorised
to wear scarlet doublets with yellow facings, Gordon
tartan trews, blue helmets, and white belts, but in
1880 the helmets were replaced by glengarries with
red, white, and blue diced border, and brown belts
were reintroduced. This uniform continued to be worn
till 1908, drab service doublets, to be worn with the
glengarry and tartan trews in undress and marching
order, having been sanctioned in 1906.

The battalion was consolidated in May 1880 as the
2nd Aberdeenshire Rifle Volunteers, with headquarters
at Aberdeen, and seven companies, lettered as follows:
A, Methlie (late 2nd Corps); B, Ellon (late 6th); C,

Newburgh (late 12th); D, Turriff (late 13th); E, Fyvie (late 15th); F, Old Meldrum (late 16th); and G, Tarves (late 18th).

In 1884, by General Order 12 of February 1, the battalion became the 2nd Volunteer Battalion Gordon Highlanders, and since then the only changes in its formation were the raising of a cyclist section in 1890, and the removal of headquarters from Aberdeen to Old Meldrum in 1899.

During the South African War the battalion furnished 27 of its members for active service, of whom 22 joined the 1st Volunteer Service Company, 1 its reinforcing draft, and 1 the 4th Service Company of the Gordon Highlanders (see 1st Volunteer Battalion). Of the members of the battalion in the 1st Company, 2 were wounded on May 29, 1900, at Doornkop, 2 on July 11 at Leehoek, and 1 on September 30 at Komati Poort, and Privates J. A. Gordon and W. Geddes were mentioned in Lord Roberts' despatch of September 4, 1901.

The battalion possessed eleven separate rifle-ranges.

The lieutenant-colonels commanding have been—

Sir W. C. Seton, Bart. of Pitmedden, May 14, 1863.
J. Ramsay, June 24, 1871.
Henry Wolrige-Gordon of Esslemont (hon. col.), June 14, 1873.
James Mackie, V.D. (hon. col.), May 30, 1891.
John Rae, V.D. (hon. col.), February 10, 1894.
John Marr, V.D. (hon. col.), March 12, 1902.
John L. Reid, June 2, 1906.

3RD (THE BUCHAN) VOLUNTEER BATTALION, THE GORDON HIGHLANDERS.

Regimental District, No. 75.

(PLATE XXXVII.)

" SOUTH AFRICA, 1900-01." | ORDER OF PRECEDENCE, 145.

Honorary Colonel—C. G. EARL OF ERROL, K.T., C.B., Colonel (retired pay), late 2nd Life Guards, May 28, 1892.

Headquarters—PETERHEAD.

THE 3rd Administrative Battalion, Aberdeenshire Rifle Volunteers, with headquarters at Peterhead, was formed in January 1862 from the following corps, the dates of formation of which are given in Appendix A :—

5th, New Deer, one company. Uniform—dark grey with red piping, and black belts. Caps with sloping peak, black band, red piping, and red-and-white badge on left side.

9th, Peterhead, two companies. Uniform—medium grey with red piping and black cord lace, caps with black band and red piping, and black belts.

17th, Old Deer, two companies. Uniform—Elcho grey with blue piping, cap with black band and blue piping, and brown belts.

20th, Longside, one company. Uniform—dark grey with black piping and cord lace, caps with black band, and black belts.

On August 18, 1863, the whole battalion adopted tunics and knickerbockers of Elcho grey with black piping (and cord lace for officers), grey stockings, grey caps with black-and-white diced border, and black belts, but this uniform was changed in 1868 to rifle green tunics and trousers with scarlet collars and piping, green shakos with green ball-tuft, and black belts, the same as worn by the 4th V.B. from 1869 to 1887 (see Plate XXXVIII.); and on May 22, 1872, the rifle busby with red-and-black plume was sanctioned for the battalion.

In 1867 the 24th Corps (St Fergus, one subdivision), in 1868 the 25th Corps (New Pitsligo, one company), and in 1872 the 26th Corps (Cruden, one company), were formed and added to the battalion, which was granted the title "The Buchan," in 1868. In September 1875 the 24th Corps was amalgamated with the 9th, which still retained an establishment of two companies, and a new 24th Corps of one company was formed at Fraserburgh.

On May 23, 1880, the battalion was consolidated as the 5th Aberdeen (The Buchan) Rifle Volunteers, but in June was re-numbered the 3rd. Headquarters were at Old Deer, and the nine companies were lettered: A, New Deer (late 5th Corps); B, Peterhead (late 1st of 9th); C, St Fergus (late 2nd of 9th); D, Old Deer (late 1st of 17th); E, Strichen (late 2nd of 17th); F, Longside (late 20th); G, Fraserburgh (late 24th); H, New Pitsligo (late 25th); and I, Cruden (late 26th).

In 1883 Gordon tartan trews replaced the trousers and glengarries with red and dark green diced border the busbies, the headquarters of "H" Company were moved from New Pitsligo to Fraserburgh, a new "K" Company was formed at Boddam, and the headquarters of the battalion were transferred to Peterhead. In the following year the battalion assumed the title of 3rd (The Buchan) V.B. Gordon Highlanders (General Order 12 of February 1), and in 1885 it was authorised to wear the uniform and badges of the Gordon Highlanders, but with trews and glengarries with red, white, and blue diced borders, the officers wearing a shoulder-plaid, claymore, and dirk, and buff belts, the men black belts, the men's uniform being identical with that worn by the 2nd Volunteer Battalion from 1880 to 1907 (see Plate XXXVI.) In 1885 also the headquarters of " C " Company were transferred from St Fergus to Crimond, but in 1888 were moved to Lonmay with a detachment at Aberdour, the headquarters of " K " Company being also in this year transferred from Boddam to Peterhead. Brown leather equipment replaced the black belts in 1891.

The battalion contributed 21 of its members for active service during the South African War, of whom Lieutenant A. W. Robertson and 19 men formed the reinforcing draft for the 2nd Volunteer Service Company (see 7th Middlesex V.R.C.), and left Aberdeen on May 19, 1900, and one man proceeded with the draft for the 1st Service Company (see 1st Volunteer Battalion). Of the 2nd Service Company, 1 private was wounded at Rooikopjes on July 24, and 3 at Lydenburg on September 8.

On November 23, 1900, " I " Company was broken up, and on March 8, 1901, " C " (Lonmay) and " E " (Strichen) were amalgamated as " E," with headquarters at Strichen, and " K " Company became " C." The battalion was thus reduced to eight companies, and after 1901 was distributed as follows, the numbers of the original corps being inserted to enable their descent to be traced : A, New Deer (5th); B and C, Peterhead (1st of 9th and late K); D, Old Deer (1st of 17th); E, Strichen (2nd of 9th and 2nd of 17th); F, Longside (20th); G and H, Fraserburgh (24th and 25th). The battalion had seven separate ranges.

In 1903 the battalion was authorised to wear the full dress of the Gordon Highlanders except the feather bonnet, and a drab service doublet was permitted for undress and marching order, to be worn with drab spats. Belts and equipment were brown.

The lieutenant-colonels commanding have been—

J. Russell of Aden, June 2, 1862.
John Ferguson, December 30, 1876.
Alexander D. Fordyce, late Captain 71st Foot, V.D. (hon. col.),
    July 24, 1880.
Robert Robertson, M.V.O., V.D. (hon. col.), October 3, 1900.
Robert Scott, V.D. (hon. col.), March 28, 1906.
William M'Connachie, V.D., November 2, 1907.

4TH (DONSIDE HIGHLAND) VOLUNTEER BATTALION, THE GORDON HIGHLANDERS.

Regimental District, No. 75.

(PLATE XXXVIII.)

"SOUTH AFRICA, 1900-01." | ORDER OF PRECEDENCE, 146.

Headquarters—28 GUILD STREET, ABERDEEN.

THE 1st Administrative Battalion, Aberdeenshire Rifle Volunteers, with headquarters at Inverurie, was formed in May 1860, and included the following corps (shown by the numbers assigned to them at the general re-numbering in the county in July 1860, see Appendix A):—

3rd, Cluny, one company. Uniform—light grey tunic and trousers with scarlet piping; light grey shako with black horse-hair plume; black patent-leather waist-belt.
4th, Alford, one company. Uniform—grey tunic and trousers with scarlet piping and bronze buttons; grey shakos with black horse-hair plume; brown waist and pouch belts.
7th, Huntly, one company. Uniform—silver grey tunic and trousers with grey braid, piped with blue, and four rows

of grey cord lace on the breast of the tunic; grey caps with blue piping, blue ball-tuft, and thistle badge; black waist-belt.

8th, Echt, two companies. Uniform—grey.

10th, Inverurie, one company. Uniform—medium grey tunic and trousers with light blue piping and Austrian knot (light blue facings for officers); grey cap with light blue piping and bugle badge; brown waist-belts and black leggings.

11th, Kildrummy, one subdivision. Uniform — Elcho grey tweed tunic, trousers, and cap, all with scarlet piping, and brown waist-belts.

The dates of formation of all corps are given in Appendix A.

To these were added in October 1860 the 14th Corps (Tarland, one subdivision, increased to one company in May 1861), in 1862 the 21st (Aboyne, one company) and 23rd (Lumphanan, one company, headquarters changed in 1864 to Torphins), and in 1863 the 22nd Corps (Auchmull, one company, uniform dark grey tunic and trousers with black braid and trouser stripe and lace on the breast, dark grey shako with black braid, bugle badge, and plume of black feathers, and black patent-leather belts with badge of St Andrew within a wreath of thistles).

In 1864 the whole battalion adopted a uniform of Elcho grey tunics and trousers with scarlet piping, and brown belts. The shakos were grey with red piping round the top, the 10th Corps having red cord lace like the Highland Light Infantry, and were at first worn with a black horse-hair plume, which was replaced by a black ball-tuft in 1865.

In 1866 the 8th Corps was reduced to an establishment of one company, but in the following year the 11th Corps was increased from a subdivision to a full

company, and a new 19th Corps at Insch was formed
and added to the battalion, which thus attained a
strength of eleven companies. Headquarters were
moved to Aberdeen in 1868. On April 1, 1869, the
uniform was again changed to rifle green with scarlet
collars and piping, green shakos with green ball-tuft,
and black belts, which uniform continued to be worn
till 1887.

In 1871 the 21st Corps was increased to two companies; the headquarters of the 3rd Corps were transferred from Cluny to Kemnay in 1875; and in 1876 the
8th, 14th, 21st, and 23rd Corps were transferred to the
1st Administrative Battalion Kincardine Rifle Volunteers (see 5th Volunteer Battalion). In April 1880 the
battalion was consolidated as the 3rd (re-numbered 4th
in June) Aberdeenshire Rifle Volunteers, with headquarters at Aberdeen, and seven companies, lettered as
follows: A, Huntly (late 7th); B, Kildrummy (late
11th); C, Insch (late 19th); D, Alford (late 4th); E,
Inverurie (late 10th); F, Kemnay (late 3rd); and G,
Auchmull (late 22nd).

The title of the battalion was changed to 4th Volunteer Battalion, The Gordon Highlanders, by General
Order No. 12 of February 1, 1884, but it was not till 1893
(Army Order 26 of February) that the title " Donside
Highland " was added. On April 22, 1887, the uniform
was changed to rifle green doublets with light green
piping, Gordon tartan trews, glengarries with red-and-
black diced border, and black belts and leggings. In
1897 a new " H " Company was formed at Auchmull,
and in 1899 the headquarters of " B " Company were
moved to Strathdon, a new " K " Company was formed
at Kintore, and a new " L " Company at Kildrummy,
thus bringing the establishment up to ten companies.

During the South African War the battalion contributed Lieutenant H. Forbes and 28 other ranks to the 1st Volunteer Service Company, 4 privates to its reinforcing draft, and 1 serjeant, 1 drummer, and 3 privates to the 3rd Service Company of the Gordon Highlanders (see 1st Volunteer Battalion). Of the 1st Service Company Private J. M. Meldrum was killed and Lieutenant Forbes and 2 privates wounded at Doornkop on May 29, 1900; one private was wounded at Komati Poort on September 30, and Private W. Bennet died of disease at Johannesburg on June 8. Of the 3rd Service Company Private J. Copland died of disease at Petersburg on May 26, 1901. Lieutenant H. Forbes received the Distinguished Service Order and Serjeant J. R. Campbell the medal for Distinguished Conduct, both having been mentioned in Lord Roberts' despatch of September 4, 1901.

In 1903 the kilt, sporran, hose, and glengarry of the Gordon Highlanders were authorised for the battalion, with drab service doublet and spats (the green doublets being abolished), and black belts as hitherto worn. In this year also a cyclist section was formed, and the name of the headquarters of "G" and "H" Companies was changed from Auchmull to Bucksburn. In 1906 "B" and "C" Companies were amalgamated as "B," with headquarters at Kildrummy, although the battalion was till 1908 still shown in estimates as having an establishment of ten companies. The distribution in 1908 of the companies was (the numbers of the original corps being shown, where necessary, for reference): A, Huntly (7th); B, Kildrummy (11th); C, Insch (19th); D, Alford (4th); E, Inverurie (10th); F, Kemnay (3rd); G and H, Bucksburn (22nd); and K, Kintore. The battalion had fourteen rifle-ranges.

The lieutenant-colonels commanding have been—

F. Fraser of Castle Fraser, June 25, 1861.

Sir William Forbes, Bart. (afterwards Lord Sempill), July 9, 1868.

J. Allardyce of Colquoich, late Colonel Madras S.C. (hon. col.), February 26, 1887.

George Jackson, V.D. (hon. col.), May 4, 1892.

William A. Mellis, V.D. (hon. col.), February 7, 1903.

5TH (DEESIDE HIGHLAND) VOLUNTEER BATTALION, THE GORDON HIGHLANDERS.

Regimental District, No. 75.

(PLATE XXXVI.)

"SOUTH AFRICA, 1900-02." | ORDER OF PRECEDENCE, 189.

Honorary Colonel—C. G. MARQUIS OF HUNTLY, February 23, 1876.

Headquarters—BANCHORY.

THE 1st Administrative Battalion, Kincardineshire Rifle Volunteers, with headquarters at Stonehaven, was formed on May 14, 1861, from the following corps of Kincardineshire Rifle Volunteers :—

1st, Fetteresso, raised January 10, 1860, as one company. Uniform—Elcho grey, with peaked cap. Headquarters removed to Stonehaven 1867, disbanded October 1870.

2nd, Banchory, raised January 28, 1860, as one company. Uniform—Elcho grey.

3rd, Laurencekirk, raised February 1860 as one subdivision, increased to a company May 23, 1860. Uniform—dark grey with black braid, and shako. Amalgamated with 5th Corps, 1873.

4th, Fettercairn, raised March 13, 1860, as one subdivision. Uniform—dark grey without facings. Amalgamated with the 5th Corps, February 1871.

5th, Auchinblae, raised June 9, 1860, as one company. Uniform
    unknown. Headquarters changed in June 1878 to Laur-
    encekirk.
6th, Netherley, raised May 7, 1860, as one company. Uniform—
    Elcho grey. Headquarters removed, May 1869, to Portlethen.
7th, Durris, raised February 13, 1861, as one company. Uniform
    unknown.

In 1864 the uniform of the whole battalion became
Elcho grey with scarlet collars, piping, and Austrian
knot, grey shakos with red ball-tuft and lace, and black
belts.

In 1869 the battalion was joined by the 8th Kincardine Corps, formed at Maryculter and Peterculter on
October 21, 1869.

By 1876 the strength of the battalion had been
reduced to five companies—*i.e.*, the 2nd, 5th, 6th, 7th,
and 8th Corps—and it was accordingly decided to recon-
stitute it. On February 23, 1876, headquarters were
transferred to Banchory, the 8th (Echt, one company),
14th (Tarland, one company), 21st (Marquis of Huntly's
Highland, Aboyne, two companies), and 23rd (Torphins,
one company) Corps of Aberdeenshire Rifle Volunteers
(see Appendix A) were transferred to it from the 1st
Administrative Battalion, Aberdeenshire Rifle Volunteers, and on November 13, 1876, the title of " Deeside
Highland " was added to that of the battalion. The
Aberdeen corps had followed all the changes of uniform
of their battalion (see 4th Volunteer Battalion), and on
May 5, 1876, the following uniform was approved for
the reconstituted battalion, and was worn till 1908 :
rifle green doublet, with collar and cuffs of the same,
and light green piping, Gordon tartan kilt (for all
except the Ballater company, which, being mainly composed of Braemar men from the Invercauld estate, wore
Farquharson tartan kilts), heather mixture hose with

white spats, white sporrans with two black tails, glengarry with red-and-black diced border, and black belts.

On March 15, 1880, the battalion was consolidated as the 2nd (on May 19 re-numbered 1st) Kincardine and Aberdeen or Deeside Highland Rifle Volunteers, with headquarters at Banchory, and ten companies lettered as follows : A, Banchory (late 2nd K.R.V.) ; B, Laurencekirk (late 5th K.R.V.) ; C, Portlethen (late 6th K.R.V.) ; D, Durris (late 7th K.R.V.) ; E, Maryculter (late 8th K.R.V.) ; F, Echt (late 8th A.R.V.) ; G, Tarland (late 14th A.R.V.) ; H, Aboyne (late 1st of 21st A.R.V.) ; I, Ballater (late 2nd of 21st A.R.V.) ; and K, Torphins (late 23rd A.R.V.) The title of 5th (Deeside Highland) Volunteer Battalion, The Gordon Highlanders, was assumed on January 17, 1884 (General Order 12 of February 1).

On November 28, 1883, " K " Company was amalgamated with " A " and a new " K " formed at Stonehaven, and on May 13, 1885, " G " Company was amalgamated with " H." Battalion headquarters were removed to Aberdeen in May 1886, but back to Banchory in July 1894. The headquarters of " E " Company were changed to Peterculter on March 21, 1887, and of " F " to Skene on March 22, 1891. The distribution of the battalion since then was therefore in nine companies : A, Banchory (detachment at Kincardine O'Neil) ; B, Laurencekirk ; C, Portlethen ; D, Durris ; E, Peterculter ; F, Skene ; H, Aboyne ; I, Ballater ; and K, Stonehaven. The battalion had thirteen rifle-ranges for the various companies.

Seventy - eight members of the battalion served actively in South Africa during the war. Of these, 6 men joined the 1st Volunteer Service Company (see 1st Volunteer Battalion), Lieutenant W. A. Duguid and

31 other ranks the 2nd Volunteer Service Company (see 7th Middlesex V.R.C.), 16 men the 3rd, and 13 men the 4th Service Company of the Gordon Highlanders, the others serving in various corps. Of the 1st Company, one man was wounded at Komati Poort on September 30, 1900 ; of the 2nd, two were wounded at Rooikopjes on July 24, and Private P. Stuart killed at Lydenburg on September 8 ; and of the 3rd, one private was wounded while escorting a train at Nylstrom on August 10, 1901.

The majors or lieutenant-colonels commanding the battalion have been—

William M'Inroy, late Major 91st and 69th Foot; Major, May 14, 1861.

William Black Fergusson, Major, August 3, 1870 ; Lieut.-Colonel, February 23, 1876.

James Ross Farquharson of Invercauld, late Captain and Lieut.-Colonel Scots Fusilier Guards, Lieut.-Colonel, November 19, 1881.

Alexander Cochran, V.D. (hon. col.), Lieut.-Colonel, May 20, 1882.

James Johnston, V.D. (hon. col.), Lieut.-Colonel, January 6, 1894.

James M. Duff, V.D. (hon. col.), Lieut.-Colonel, January 2, 1901.

Alexander H. Farquharson of Invercauld, late Lieutenant 10th Hussars, Lieut.-Colonel, February 11, 1905.

6TH VOLUNTEER BATTALION, THE GORDON HIGHLANDERS.

Regimental District, No. 75.

(PLATE XXXIX.)

"SOUTH AFRICA, 1900-02." | ORDER OF PRECEDENCE, 217.

Honorary Colonel—G. S. GRANT, V.D. (hon. col.), February 5, 1902.

Headquarters—KEITH.

THE 1st Administrative Battalion, Banffshire Rifle Volunteers, with headquarters at Keith, was formed on August 12, 1861, and to it were attached, then or on their subsequent date of formation, the following corps of Banffshire Rifle Volunteers :[1]—

2nd, Banff, raised April 18, 1860, of one company. Re-numbered 1st in 1862.

3rd, Aberlour, raised September 29, 1860, of one company. Re-numbered 2nd in 1862.

4th, Keith, raised November 2, 1860, of two companies. These were separated as the 3rd and 4th Corps in 1862, but on July 26, 1866, were amalgamated as the 3rd Corps, of one company.

5th, Buckie, raised March 12, 1863, of one company.

6th, Minmore, Glenlivet, raised April 19, 1867, of one company.

7th, Dufftown, raised May 1, 1868, of one and a half companies.

The separate corps had originally grey uniforms of various patterns, but in 1861 the battalion adopted a uniform of medium grey with black cuffs, collars, and broad trouser stripes with white piping and Austrian knot, grey shako with black band with white piping and black ball-tuft, and black belts, the officers having silver lace and a silver band on the shako. In 1870

---

[1] A 1st Corps of one subdivision at Macduff is shown in the 1860 and 1861 Army Lists, but it never had any officers appointed to it.

U

the wearing of the shoulder-belt and cartridge-box was discontinued.

The battalion was consolidated in June 1880 as the 1st Banffshire Rifle Volunteers, with headquarters at Keith, and six and a half companies, lettered as follows : A, Banff (late 1st) ; B, Aberlour (late 2nd) ; C, Keith (late 3rd) ; D, Buckie (late 5th) ; E, Glenlivet (late 6th) ; and F, Dufftown (one and a half companies, the half company at Glenrinnes, late 7th). In the same year the white piping was removed from the collars, trouser stripes, and shoulder-straps, and replaced on the tunic by black piping and Austrian knot.

In 1884 (General Order 12 of February 1) the battalion was entitled 6th V.B. The Gordon Highlanders ; in 1887 grey helmets with silver ornaments were adopted ; on January 17, 1891, scarlet doublets with yellow facings, Gordon tartan trews, glengarries with red, white, and blue diced border, and white belts became the uniform ; in 1899 a new "G" Company, at Aberchirder, was formed ; and in 1902 a drab service doublet, for undress and marching order, to be worn with the glengarry and trews, and sashes, to be worn by serjeants in full dress, were authorised.

Eighty-five members of the battalion in all served in South Africa during the war. Of these, Lieutenant A. M. Robertson and 25 other ranks joined the 2nd Volunteer Service Company, Gordon Highlanders (see 7th Middlesex V.R.C.), and 1 corporal and 2 privates the reinforcing draft of the 1st Service Company. Of the former, 1 private was wounded on July 24, 1900, at Rooikopjes, and Private D. B. Stuart (the same who was wounded on July 24) was killed and 1 lance-corporal was wounded on September 8 at Lydenburg. Colour-Serjeant Instructor E. J. Reynolds and Lance-Serjeant J. Margach were mentioned in

Lord Roberts' despatch of September 4, 1901. To the 3rd Volunteer Service Company of the Gordon Highlanders the battalion contributed 34 non-commissioned officers and men (of whom Colour-Serjeant Instructor J. Craib died of disease on May 4, 1901), and to the 4th Company 18 privates. In addition to the above, Lieutenant B. M'Kerrol of the battalion went out early in the war, joined the Imperial Light Infantry (Natal), and was killed at Spion Kop.

The headquarters of the battalion, with drill-hall, &c., were at Keith; drill-halls existed for the outlying companies, and the battalion had nine rifle-ranges.

The commanding officers have been—

T. Adam, Major, August 12, 1861.

W. Thorburn, Major, July 17, 1866; Lieut.-Colonel, May 1, 1868.

William G. Gordon-Cumming, Lieut.-Colonel (retired pay) Bombay S.C. (hon. col.), Lieut.-Colonel, January 27, 1872.

John G. Smith (hon. col.), Lieut.-Colonel, January 8, 1890.

George S. Grant, V.D. (hon. col.), Lieut.-Colonel, March 5, 1892.

John G. Fleming, V.D. (hon. col.), Lieut.-Colonel, May 9, 1900.

Alfred B. Whitton, Lieut.-Colonel, May 26, 1906.

7TH VOLUNTEER BATTALION, THE GORDON HIGHLANDERS.

Regimental District, No. 75.

(PLATE XXXIX.)

ORDER OF PRECEDENCE, 222.

Headquarters—LERWICK (attached to 1st Volunteer Battalion).

THIS battalion was raised in Shetland on December 19, 1900, at an establishment of three companies, there having been no volunteers in these islands since the disbandment of "F" Company 1st Sutherland V.R.C.

(Lerwick) in 1884. Battalion headquarters were at Lerwick, but only an acting-adjutant was allowed, the battalion being attached for administration to the 1st Volunteer Battalion. The headquarters of A and B Companies were at Lerwick, and their range, up to 600 yards, at Ness of Sound, while those of C Company were at Scalloway and its range at Asta.

The uniform, as approved on February 14, 1901, consisted of drab service dress with red piping on the trousers and patch on the upper arm, grey felt hats, brown belts and equipment, and brown leather leggings.

The commanding officers have been—

Captain-Commandant Alexander Moffatt, December 19, 1900.
Major-Commandant J. C. C. Broun, June 10, 1905.

1ST (INVERNESS HIGHLAND) VOLUNTEER BATTALION, THE QUEEN'S OWN CAMERON HIGHLANDERS.

Regimental District, No. 79.

(PLATE XL.)

"SOUTH AFRICA, 1900-02." | ORDER OF PRECEDENCE, 157.

*Headquarters—*INVERNESS.

THE 1st Administrative Battalion, Inverness - shire Rifle Volunteers, with headquarters at Inverness, was formed on June 18, 1860, and to it were attached, then or on their subsequent date of formation, the following corps of one company each, raised in the county—

1st, Inverness, a self-supporting corps, raised November 18, 1859, as a result of a meeting held under the presidency of the Provost on May 21, 1859. Uniform—very dark grey with facings and caps of the same, flat black braid on the breast, front, and skirts of the tunic, on the trousers, and round the cap, and black patent-leather belts. The serjeants had silver cord on the collar and round the chevrons, and the officers had silver cord shoulder-straps.

2nd, Fort-William (Lochaber), raised April 9, 1860. Uniform almost identical with that of 1st Corps, but with a band of Erracht Cameron tartan round the cap in place of the black braid.

3rd, Inverness (Merchants), raised March 26, 1860. Uniform—medium (slate) grey tunics and trousers with green collars and cuffs, grey caps with green band and bugle badge, and black belts.

4th, Inverness (Clachnacuddin), raised May 3, 1860. Uniform—Elcho grey tunics, trousers, and caps, scarlet collars and cuffs, black belts.

5th, Inverness (Celtic), raised July 16, 1860. Uniform—medium (slate) grey double-breasted doublet with green collar and piping and silver diamond buttons, Celtic tartan kilts and plaids, grey goatskin sporrans, green-and-red mixed hose with green tops, plain glengarries with blackcock's tail, and black belts.

6th, Kingussie (Badenoch), raised June 3, 1861. Uniform—Elcho grey tunics with bronze buttons, green cuffs and collars, grey piping on the latter, and black Austrian knot, grey trousers with black stripes, grey cap with peak and black band and badge of wreath and crown with V.R. in centre, and black patent-leather belts.

7th, Beauly, raised July 1, 1861. Uniform—Elcho grey doublets with green facings, Fraser tartan trews, plain glengarries, and black belts.

In 1863 the uniforms of the various companies were assimilated, that adopted for all being Elcho grey doublets with green collar and piping, plain glengarries with company badge and without black-cock's tail, and black waist-belts (except the 1st, which till 1872 wore pouch-belts also). The 1st Corps wore trews, all the others kilts and belted plaids, the tartans being 42nd for the 1st, 3rd, 4th, and 5th, Cameron of Erracht for the 2nd, Hunting Macpherson for the 6th, and Fraser for the 7th. The sporrans were grey goatskin (white for officers), and the hose red-and-green mixture with green tops (except the 2nd Corps, which had red-and-green (79th) diced hose).

In 1865 the battalion received the title "Inverness Highland," and in the following year Private Angus Cameron of the 6th Corps won the Queen's Prize at Wimbledon, a performance which he repeated in 1869.

The following companies were added to the battalion about this time, all kilted and dressed in the above uniform :—

8th, Portree, raised July 20, 1867. Tartan—Macdonald of the Isles. Increased to one and a half companies, February 7, 1868.

9th, Campbeltown, Ardersier, raised November 12, 1867. Tartan —42nd.

10th, Roy Bridge, raised February 11, 1869. Tartan—Mackintosh.

On February 16, 1880, sanction was given for the battalion to change its uniform to scarlet doublets with buff facings (it being then affiliated to the 71st and 78th Highlanders), 42nd tartan kilts (for all companies), grey goatskin sporrans (white for officers), red-and-black diced hose, white spats, plain glengarries, and white belts.

In June 1880 the battalion was consolidated as the 1st Inverness-shire (Inverness Highland) Rifle Volunteers, with headquarters at Inverness, and ten companies, lettered : A to D, Inverness (late 1st, 3rd, 4th, and 5th Corps) ; E, Fort-William (late 2nd) ; F, Kingussie (late 6th) ; G, Beauly (late 7th) ; H, Portree (late 8th) ; I, Ardersier (late 9th) ; and K, Roy Bridge (late 10th). The only change in distribution which since then took place was on September 30, 1903, when the headquarters of K Company were transferred to Fort-Augustus, with a section at Drumnadrochit to serve Glen Urquhart. The battalion had eight separate rifle-ranges.

In 1887 the title of 1st (Inverness Highland) Volunteer Battalion, The Cameron Highlanders, was conferred upon the battalion by General Order 181 of December 1, and on October 20, 1893, it was authorised to adopt the uniform of the Cameron Highlanders. The officers wore the feather bonnet in full dress, the men having only the glengarry, and sashes were not worn by officers or serjeants.

During the South African War, the battalion furnished no fewer than 245 men for service, which is the record proportion for Scotland. Of these, Captain A. D. Mackinnon, Lieutenant J. Burn, Lieutenant J. Campbell, and 75 men served in the only Volunteer Service Company sent out to the Cameron Highlanders. Of this company, Serjeant A. G. Mackintosh, Private A. M'Kay, and Private D. M'Lennan died of disease, Lieutenant J. Campbell was wounded, and Serjeant P. Stuart was mentioned in Lord Roberts' despatch of September 4, 1901. Major S. J. Lord Lovat, 2nd Lieutenant E. G. Fraser Tytler (both mentioned in despatches, September 4, 1901, and March 1, 1902, respectively : D.S.O. for Lord Lovat), and 80 men served in Lovat's Scouts, of whom Private MacLaren was killed in action on September 20, 1901, and the remainder joined the Imperial Yeomanry or other corps.

The lieutenant-colonels commanding the battalion have been—

Ewen Macpherson of Cluny, late Captain 42nd Foot, June 3, 1861.
Charles A. Earl of Dunmore, November 2, 1882.
Alexander Macdonald, V.D. (hon. col.), July 22, 1896.
David Munro, V.D., December 13, 1899.
Duncan Shaw, V.D. (hon. col.), July 26, 1902.
James Leslie Fraser, September 8, 1906.

1st (RENFREWSHIRE) VOLUNTEER BATTALION, PRINCESS LOUISE'S (ARGYLL AND SUTHERLAND HIGHLANDERS).

Regimental District, No. 91.

(PLATE XLI.)

"SOUTH AFRICA, 1900-02." | ORDER OF PRECEDENCE, 87.

Honorary Colonel—Sir H. SHAW STEWART, Bart., March 12, 1904.

Headquarters—GREENOCK.

THE 1st Administrative Battalion, Renfrewshire Rifle Volunteers, with headquarters at Greenock, was formed on August 1, 1860, from the following corps of Renfrewshire Rifle Volunteers, the dates of raising, &c., of which are given in Appendix D :—

1st, Greenock, four companies. Uniform—dark grey tunic, trousers, and cap, with black braid.

5th, Port Glasgow, one company. Uniform—grey.

10th, Greenock, Highlanders, one company ; and

11th, Greenock, Highlanders, one company. Uniform of both companies—green doublets with five rows of black braid on the breast, green cuffs and collars, and black piping, 42nd tartan kilts and belted plaids, grey sporrans with three white tails, green-and-black diced hose, buckled brogues, Balmoral bonnets, and black belts. The officers wore pouch-belts, the claymore and dirk being carried on the waist-belt.

22nd, Gourock, one company. Uniform—medium grey.

Soon after the formation of the battalion, a county uniform was adopted for Renfrewshire (shown in the figures in Plates XLI. and XLII. for the 2nd and 3rd Volunteer Battalions) of medium grey tunics and trousers, with scarlet cuffs, collars, and piping on the trousers, grey shakos with black ball-tufts, and black belts, the 1st Battalion alone differing in that the officers had grey lace on the breast of the tunic. The two Highland companies continued to wear the uniform described above until 1889, with the exception that in 1877 glengarry bonnets (with blackcock's tail for officers), black sporrans with six white tassels (and badger's head for officers), and white spats were adopted.

In 1863 the 10th and 11th Corps were amalgamated as the 10th Corps of two companies, and the 1st Buteshire Rifle Volunteer Corps, headquarters Rothesay, which had been formed on January 19, 1860, as one company, was added to the battalion.

In March 1880 the battalion was consolidated as the 1st Renfrewshire Rifle Volunteers, headquarters at Greenock, with nine companies, lettered as follows: A, B, C, and D, Greenock (late 1st R.R.V.); E, Port Glasgow (late 5th R.R.V.); F and G, Greenock (Highlanders) (late 10th R.R.V.); H, Gourock (late 22nd R.R.V.); and I, Rothesay (late 1st Bute R.V.) In 1881 grey helmets with bronze ornaments were adopted by the battalion.

In 1887, by General Order 181 of December 1, the corps became the 1st (Renfrewshire) V.B. Argyll and Sutherland Highlanders, and on December 13, 1889, sanction was given for a change of uniform to scarlet doublets with yellow facings, Sutherland tartan trews, glengarries with red-and-white diced border, and white belts, the Highland companies conforming but continuing to wear their kilts and hose, until on September 18, 1899, authority was given for the whole battalion to assume the kilts, sporrans, hose, and spats of the regular battalions, to be worn with the glengarry with red-and-white diced border. A drab service doublet for undress and marching order was authorised in 1903.

Of the battalion, Lieutenant A. E. Stewart and 18 men served with the 1st, 18 men with the 2nd, and

Lieutenant J. M. Lamont and 34 men with the 3rd Volunteer Service Company, Argyll and Sutherland Highlanders, in the war in South Africa, of whom Corporal D. K. Aitken (1st Company) died of enteric. In addition, 10 men served in the Scottish Horse, 22 in the Imperial Yeomanry, 3 in the Scottish Cyclist Company, 11 in the South African Constabulary, 1 in the R.A.M.C., and 3 in local corps, making in all a contribution of 2 officers and 120 men from the battalion. Of the 22 men serving in the Imperial Yeomanry, 2 were officers who served as troopers— Lieutenant R. E. Wilson (who was mentioned in despatches) and Lieutenant N. Rae; Trooper G. R. Benson died of wounds and Troopers F. L. R. Laurent and A. Scorgie of enteric, and Trooper R. Calderhead was drowned.

In 1900 a cyclist company was formed, but this did not entail an increase of establishment except on paper, for the "I" (Rothesay) Company had long been dwindling away, and in 1906 it finally ceased to exist.

The headquarters of the battalion were at 37 Newton Street, Greenock. It had a headquarter range, up to 800 yards, at Hole Farm, 1½ mile from Greenock, and E and H Companies had their own ranges near their headquarters.

The lieutenant-colonels commanding the battalion have been—

Sir Michael R. Shaw Stewart, Bart., August 1, 1860.
David M. Lathom, late Captain Royal Renfrew Militia, May 13, 1869.
William Ross (hon. col.), October 4, 1884.
William Orr Leitch (hon. col.), February 8, 1890.
William Lamont, V.D. (hon. col.), October 29, 1892.
William U. Park, M.V.O., V.D. (hon. col.), December 12, 1903.
Abram Lyle, V.D., January 28, 1908.

2ND (RENFREWSHIRE) VOLUNTEER BATTALION, PRINCESS LOUISE'S (ARGYLL AND SUTHERLAND HIGHLANDERS).

Regimental District, No. 91.

(PLATE XLI.)

"SOUTH AFRICA, 1900-02." | ORDER OF PRECEDENCE, 88.

Honorary Colonel—Sir THOS. G. GLEN-COATS, Bart., V.D. (hon. col.), June 13, 1903.

Headquarters—PAISLEY.

THE 2nd Administrative Battalion, Renfrewshire Rifle Volunteers, with headquarters at Paisley, was formed on June 2, 1860, of the 3rd, 6th, 14th, and 24th Corps (Paisley), 9th Corps (Johnstone), 15th Corps (Kilbarchan), 17th Corps (Lochwinnoch), and 20th Corps (Renfrew) of Renfrewshire Rifle Volunteers, of one company each. The dates of formation of these corps are given in Appendix D.

The original uniforms of the 3rd, 6th, 14th, and 24th Corps were dark grey with black braid, that of the 20th dark grey with scarlet facings, but in 1862 the battalion adopted the county uniform of medium grey, as described for the 1st Volunteer Battalion, and wore it until 1875, when (on November 27) scarlet tunics with blue facings and Austrian knot, blue trousers, blue shakos with ball-tuft, and white belts became the uniform. Blue helmets replaced the shakos in 1881.

In March 1880 the battalion was consolidated as the 3rd (re-numbered 2nd in June) Renfrewshire Rifle Volunteers, headquarters Paisley, with eight companies, lettered : A, B, D, and H, Paisley (late 3rd, 6th, 14th, and 24th Corps) ; C, Johnstone (late 9th) ; E, Kilbarchan (late 15th) ; F, Lochwinnoch (late 17th) ; and

G, Renfrew (late 20th). In 1884 a new company, "I," was formed at Paisley, and dressed in scarlet doublets with blue facings, Sutherland kilts, and the glengarry, sporran, hose, and spats of the regular battalions of the regiment. By General Order 181 of December 1, 1887, the title of 2nd (Renfrewshire) V.B. Argyll and Sutherland Highlanders was conferred upon the battalion, and on April 18, 1898, it was authorised to wear scarlet doublets with yellow facings, Sutherland tartan trews, glengarries with red-and-white diced border, and white belts (the same as shown in Plate XX. for the 3rd V.B., 1889-1908), the kilted company retaining its special dress, but changing its facings to yellow. Helmets, however, continued to be worn by the non-kilted companies till 1903.

During the South African War 59 members of the battalion saw active service, mostly with the volunteer service companies of the Argyll and Sutherland Highlanders. Captain J. Cook commanded the 1st Service Company. Lieutenant J. L. Jack served with the 2nd Service Company, and on its departure for home he remained behind attached to the 2nd Scottish Horse, and was mentioned in Lord Kitchener's despatch of June 23, 1902. Second Lieutenant Foulds served in the Scottish Cyclist Company.

In 1900 a cyclist company was formed at Paisley and lettered "K." In 1903 "E" Company was disbanded, and the headquarters of "F" moved to Elderslie, with detachments at Howwood, Kilbarchan, and Lochwinnoch, but officially the establishment of the battalion remained till 1908 at ten companies. On November 17, 1903, the adoption of the full uniform of the Argyll and Sutherland Highlanders was sanctioned for the whole battalion, except that the glengarry with red-and-white diced border took the place of the feather bonnet, and was worn with a blackcock's tail by officers. A drab service doublet and drab spats were worn in marching order.

The battalion possessed very fine headquarters, with a drill-hall and Morris-tube range, in High Street, Paisley, and a rifle-range up to 800 yards at Foxbar on the Gleniffer Hills. The former was completed and the latter acquired in 1901, at a total cost of £11,000, which was covered by public subscriptions.

The lieutenant-colonels commanding have been—

William Mure of Caldwell, late Captain and Lieut.-Colonel Scots
    Fusilier Guards, December 17, 1860.
William Carlisle, December 15, 1880.
Andrew Millar (hon. col.), November 21, 1885.
Sir Thomas G. Glen-Coats, Bart., V.D. (hon. col.), May 28, 1887.
James Paton, V.D. (hon. col.), June 13, 1903.
James Cook, V.D. (hon. captain in army), December 18, 1906.

3RD (RENFREWSHIRE) VOLUNTEER BATTALION, PRINCESS LOUISE'S (ARGYLL AND SUTHERLAND HIGHLANDERS).

Regimental District, No. 91.

(PLATE XLII.)

"SOUTH AFRICA, 1901-02." | ORDER OF PRECEDENCE, 89.

Honorary Colonel—R. KING (hon. col.), October 14, 1903.

Headquarters—POLLOCKSHAWS.

THE 3rd Administrative Battalion, Renfrewshire Rifle Volunteers, with headquarters at Barrhead, was formed on August 4, 1860, from the 4th (Pollockshaws), 7th and 21st (Barrhead), 8th (Neilston), 16th (Thornlie-

bank), 19th (Hurlet), and 23rd (Cathcart) Corps of
Renfrewshire Rifle Volunteers, of one company each,
and the 25th (Thornliebank) Corps was added in 1862.
The dates of formation of these corps are given in
Appendix D.

The original uniforms of these corps were mostly
Elcho grey, but in 1862 the county uniform of medium
grey, described for the 1st Volunteer Battalion, was
adopted and was worn till 1874, when scarlet tunics
with blue facings, blue trousers, glengarries, and white
belts became the uniform.

In 1880 the battalion was consolidated as the 4th
(re-numbered 3rd in June) Renfrewshire Rifle Volunteers, with headquarters at Barrhead (1881, Pollockshaws) and eight companies, lettered: A, Pollockshaws
(late 4th); B and F, Barrhead (late 7th and 21st); C,
Neilston (late 8th); D and H, Thornliebank (late 16th
and 25th); E, Hurlet (afterwards Newton-Mearns, late
19th), and G, Cathcart (late 23rd).

The title of 3rd (Renfrewshire) V.B. Argyll and
Sutherland Highlanders was conferred upon the
battalion by General Order 181 of December 1, 1887;
and on January 29, 1889, sanction was given for the
adoption of scarlet doublets with yellow facings,
Sutherland tartan trews, glengarries with red-and-
white diced borders, white belts, and black leggings
as the uniform. To this was added on December 17,
1900, a drab service dress with red piping on the
trousers, grey felt hats, and putties, for use in undress
and marching order.

Forty-six members of the battalion served actively in
the South African War. Of these, 14 men served in
the 1st, Captain J. Paton and 11 men in the 2nd, and
8 men in the 3rd Volunteer Service Company of
the Argyll and Sutherland Highlanders. Private J.

Campbell (1st Company) was killed at Rustenburg on October 1, 1900, and Private C. Clanachan (3rd Company) at Kaal Spruit on March 14, 1902. Private J. Gilmour (2nd Company) died of disease, and Private G. Williams (3rd Company) of wounds received at Driekuil, April 3, 1902.

In 1900 " I " and " K " (Cyclist) Companies were formed at Barrhead, but in 1903 the former was disbanded and the battalion then reduced to its latter-day establishment of nine companies (one of them a cyclist company). The battalion shared a rifle-range up to 900 yards at Patterton, near Thornliebank, with the 5th Volunteer Battalion Highland Light Infantry. In 1892 Major Pollock of this battalion won the Queen's Prize at Bisley.

The lieutenant-colonels commanding the battalion have been—

John Graham (afterwards J. Barns-Graham), August 4, 1860.
Alexander Crum, April 10, 1875.
Robert King (hon. col.), June 18, 1881.
Z. J. Heys, V.D. (hon. col.), May 29, 1889.
David Hamilton (hon. col.), April 27, 1898.
John M. Campbell, May 28, 1904.
J. Menzies, March 31, 1906.

4TH (STIRLINGSHIRE) VOLUNTEER BATTALION, PRINCESS LOUISE'S (ARGYLL AND SUTHERLAND HIGHLANDERS).

Regimental District, No. 91.

(PLATE XLII.)

" SOUTH AFRICA, 1900-02." | ORDER OF PRECEDENCE, 108.

Honorary Colonel—C. M. KING, V.D. (hon. col.), May 5, 1897.

Headquarters—STIRLING.

THE 1st Administrative Battalion, Stirlingshire Rifle Volunteers, with headquarters at Stirling, was formed on June 9, 1860, and to it, then or on their subsequent date of formation, were attached the following corps, all of one company, except the 8th, which was only one subdivision strong :—

1st, Stirling, formed October 14, 1859. A citizen corps. Uniform—dark grey, facings black.

2nd, Stirling, formed February 3, 1860. An artisan corps. Uniform—dark grey, facings black.

3rd, Falkirk, formed March 27, 1860. Uniform—medium grey with black braid, scarlet cuffs and collars, grey caps with red-and-white diced band, and brown belts.

4th, Lennoxtown, formed March 6, 1860. Uniform—Elcho grey, facings black with red piping.

5th, Balfron, formed May 1, 1860. Uniform—Elcho grey, facings black with red piping. Disbanded 1879.

6th, Denny, formed April 11, 1860. Uniform—Elcho grey, facings black.

7th, Lennox Mill, formed May 1, 1860. Uniform—Elcho grey, facings green.

8th, Strathblane, formed May 25, 1860, as one subdivision. Uniform—Elcho grey, facings green. Disbanded in 1863.

9th, Bannockburn, formed May 21, 1860.   Uniform—dark grey,
  facings black.
11th, Stirling, formed December 6, 1860.
12th, Carron, formed February 10, 1862.
13th, Kilsyth, formed July 19, 1866.

As a county badge all the Stirlingshire corps wore a
band of Graham tartan (that of the Duke of Montrose,
the Lord-Lieutenant) round their caps at the Royal
Review in 1860, but this was discontinued after the
review, except in the case of the 2nd Corps, which
wore it in the form of a St Andrew's Cross in front
of their caps.

There existed a 10th Stirlingshire (Highland) Corps
at Stirling, formed on November 10, 1860, and disbanded in 1864, but it never formed part of the administrative battalion, and the 14th Stirlingshire
Corps, raised at Alva on October 17, 1868, formed from
that date portion of the 1st Administrative Battalion,
Clackmannan R.V. (see 7th Volunteer Battalion).
The 1st and 2nd Clackmannan Corps were from 1862
attached to the Stirlingshire Battalion, but in 1867
were formed into an independent battalion (see 7th
Volunteer Battalion).

In 1862 all the Stirlingshire rifle corps adopted
trews of Graham tartan, continuing to wear their old
tunics, but on November 12, 1863, the battalion
assumed a uniform of rifle-green tunics with scarlet
collars and cuffs with black Austrian knot, Graham
tartan trews, green shakos with red, white, and green
diced band and black ball-tuft, and brown belts.
The officers wore tunics with black lace of rifle pattern,
lines, and lace on their shakos like the Highland Light
Infantry.

In March 1880 the battalion was consolidated as the

1st Stirlingshire Rifle Volunteers, with headquarters at Stirling, and ten companies, lettered : A, B, and F, Stirling (late 1st, 2nd, and 11th Corps); C, Falkirk (late 3rd); D, Lennox Mill (afterwards Falkirk, late 7th Corps); E, Lennoxtown (late 4th); G, Denny (late 6th); H, Bannockburn (late 9th); I, Carron (late 12th); and K, Kilsyth (late 13th).   In 1882 the cuffs and collars of the tunics were changed from scarlet to rifle-green, and the piping and Austrian knot to light green, and on November 15, 1886, the uniform was changed to scarlet doublets with yellow facings, Sutherland tartan trews, glengarries with red-and-white diced borders, and brown belts, sashes being worn by serjeants only.   In 1887 (General Order 181 of December 1) the battalion assumed the title of 4th (Stirlingshire) V.B. Argyll and Sutherland Highlanders.

Fifty - seven members of the battalion served in the field during the South African War. Of these, Lieutenant J. Hunter (who died of enteric fever) and 18 men served with the 1st, 13 men with the 2nd, and 5 men with the 3rd Volunteer Service Company of the Argyll and Sutherland Highlanders.

In 1904 the headquarters of " H " and " I " Companies were transferred from Bannockburn and Carron to Stenhousemuir, and in 1906 those of " F " Company to Falkirk, so that the distribution of the battalion after 1906 was : A and B Companies, Stirling ; C, D, and F, Falkirk ; E, Lennoxtown ; G, Denny ; H and I, Stenhousemuir ; and K, Kilsyth.   The battalion range, which extended up to 1000 yards, was at Greenhill, and "E" Company had its own range, up to 600 yards, at South Brae, near its headquarters.

In 1878 Private Rae of the 11th Stirlingshire won the Queen's Prize at the National Rifle Association meeting.

The lieutenant-colonels commanding the battalion have been—

J. Dundas, May 29, 1861.
Alexander Wilson, V.D., October 26, 1872.
Charles M'I. King, February 21, 1880.
Alexander Nimmo (hon. col.), May 27, 1885.
Donald MacFadyen, V.D. (hon. col.), March 10, 1888.
John W. King, V.D. (hon. col.), May 2, 1900.
Robert Morton, V.D. (hon. col.), January 2, 1904.
Ebenezer Simpson, V.D. (hon. col.), November 8, 1906.

5TH VOLUNTEER BATTALION, PRINCESS LOUISE'S (ARGYLL AND SUTHERLAND HIGHLANDERS).

Regimental District, No. 91.

(PLATE XLIII.)

"SOUTH AFRICA, 1900-02." | ORDER OF PRECEDENCE, 196.

Honorary Colonel—J. D. S. DUKE OF ARGYLL, K.T., G.C.M.G., G.C.V.O., V.D., September 20, 1902.

Headquarters—DUNOON.

THE following corps of rifle volunteers were raised in the county of Argyll :—

2nd,[1] Inveraray, formed May 4, 1860, of one company.
3rd, Campbeltown, formed April 16, 1860, of two companies.
5th,[1] Mull, formed December 6, 1860, of one company; disbanded 1862.
6th, Melfort, formed April 22, 1860, of two companies; disbanded 1864.

---

[1] No trace can be found of a 1st or 4th Corps. Such never appeared in an Army List.

7th, Dunoon, formed March 28, 1860, of one company.

8th, Cowal, formed June 4, 1860, of two companies. Headquarters changed to Glendaruel 1862, reduced to one company 1864.

9th, Glenorchy, formed April 12, 1860, of one company. Headquarters changed to Dalmally 1869, disbanded 1870.

10th, Tayvollich, near Ardrishaig, formed June 4, 1860, by Campbell of Inverneill, from men of the Ross estate, as one company. It had medium grey uniform with green facings and piping, shakos with a band of Argyll (Cawdor) Campbell tartan, and brown belts. Disbanded in 1869, the Ardrishaig detachment joining the 14th Corps.

11th, Oban, formed July 7, 1860, of one company; disbanded 1865.

12th, Bridgend, Islay, formed June 7, 1861, of one company; disbanded 1865.

13th, Ballachulish, formed August 31, 1867, as one company; increased to two companies 1873.

14th, Kilmartin, formed January 15, 1868, of one company.

Except the above description of the uniform of the 10th Corps, and statements that the 9th Corps wore grey doublets with green facings and kilts of Breadalbane Campbell tartan, and that the uniforms of all the other corps originally were " dark grey with trousers," nothing is known of the uniforms first worn.

In July 1861 the 1st Administrative Battalion, Argyllshire Rifle Volunteers, with headquarters at Oban, was formed. It included the 2nd, 3rd, 7th, and 11th Corps, to which the 6th and 10th were added in 1862, the 12th in 1863, and the 8th in 1864. The 6th Corps was disbanded in 1864, and the 11th and 12th in 1865, but in the latter year the 9th Corps, which since December 1860 had been attached to the 3rd Perthshire or 2nd Administrative Battalion Perthshire Rifle Volunteers, was transferred to the battalion, and in 1867 the 13th and in 1868 the 14th Corps were added to it. The 10th Corps was disbanded in 1869 and the 9th in 1870. Battalion headquarters were in 1866 moved to Ardrishaig, and in 1867 to Dunoon. The scattered nature of the battalion may be gathered from the fact that, on the 6th August 1868, the 2nd, 3rd, and 7th Corps assembled for battalion drill and inspection at Rothesay (not in the county !), and that this was the first occasion since the formation of the battalion in which any two of its corps had met for drill.

In 1863 or 1864 the battalion adopted a uniform of green doublets with scarlet collars, cuffs, and piping, Argyll (Cawdor) Campbell tartan kilts and belted plaids, white sporrans with three black tails, heather mixture hose, Highland brogues, glengarries with badge of bugle and crown with a boar's head in the centre (Balmoral bonnets with blackcock's tail for the 2nd Corps), and black belts. There were minor differences among corps—*e.g.*, the 13th and 14th Corps had square cuffs with upright patch, while the others had gauntlet pattern, and the 14th had grey goatskin sporrans. Brown spats were adopted in 1870. In 1867 the 2nd Corps changed its uniform to scarlet doublets with green facings, Argyll (Cawdor) Campbell kilts, black sporrans with three white tails, red-and-black diced hose, white spats, glengarry with blackcock's tail, and white belts. The 9th Corps until its disbandment retained its grey uniform with green facings and Breadalbane Campbell kilts.

On March 23, 1874, authority was given for the whole battalion to wear scarlet doublets with yellow facings, Argyll (Cawdor) Campbell tartan kilts, white sporrans with two black tails, red-and-black diced hose, white spats, plain glengarries with the badge hitherto worn, and white belts, and this change was finally carried out by April 1, 1879.

On March 26, 1880, the battalion, then reduced to the 2nd, 3rd, 7th, 8th, 13th, and 14th Corps, was consolidated as the 2nd (re-numbered 1st in September) Argyllshire Highland Rifle Volunteers, with head-quarters at Dunoon, and eight companies, lettered as follows : A, Inveraray (late 2nd) ; B and C, Campbeltown (late 3rd) ; D, Dunoon (late 7th) ; E, Glendaruel (late 8th) ; F and G, Ballachulish (late 13th) ; and H, Kilmartin (late 14th). The year 1880 is also noted in the annals of the battalion, as in it Private Ferguson won the Queen's Cup at the National Rifle Association meeting.

On December 1, 1882, the headquarters of G Company were moved from Ballachulish to Southend, near Campbeltown, and on February 21, 1883, the tartan of the kilts was changed to that worn by the Argyll and Sutherland Highlanders, and the glengarry with red-and-white diced border replaced the plain one hitherto worn. In 1887, by General Order 181 of December 1, the battalion assumed the title of 5th V.B. Argyll and Sutherland Highlanders.

Sixty-one members of the battalion served in South Africa during the war. Of these, Lieutenant A. J. Macarthur and 15 men served with the 1st, 15 men with the 2nd, and Captain and Honorary Major G. H. Black and 23 men with the 3rd Volunteer Service Company of the Argyll and Sutherland Highlanders. Corporal W. Gillespie of the 1st Company was killed at Commando Nek on October 1, 1900, this being the only casualty among the men of the 5th V.B. Surgeon-Captain J. P. Brown and Captain J. Pender also served in the war, the former as a civil surgeon, the latter in the remount department.

In 1900 a new company, " I," was formed at Carradale, also a cyclist company, " K," with headquarters at Campbeltown, but recruited from all over the battalion area. On June 18, 1902, a blue Kilmarnock bonnet with red - and - white diced band and red tuft was adopted as the full head-dress, the glengarry being retained for undress.

The distribution of the battalion from 1900 onwards was as follows:—

A Company, Inveraray ; detachments at Dalmally and Furnace.

B, C, and K (Cyclist) Companies, Campbeltown.

D Company, Dunoon.

E Company, Glendaruel ; detachments at Strachur, Tighnabruaich, and Lochgoilhead.

F Company, Ballachulish.

G Company, Southend; detachments at Kilkenzie and Glenbar.

H Company, Kilmartin, with detachment at Ardrishaig.

I Company, Carradale, with detachment at Tayinloan.

Corresponding to its scattered distribution, the battalion had nineteen rifle-ranges.

The lieutenant-colonels commanding the battalion have been—

C. A. Stewart, Major, December 9, 1861; Lieut.-Colonel, September 4, 1862.

Archibald Campbell of Glendaruel, late 42nd Foot, May 31, 1867.

John W. Malcolm of Poltalloch (afterwards Lord Malcolm), late Captain Kent Artillery Militia, C.B., V.D. (hon. col.), March 30, 1872.

Duncan Campbell of Inverneill, late Captain 89th Foot (hon. col.), December 8, 1897.

Edward P. Campbell of South Hall, Major (retired pay), late Royal Highlanders (hon. col.), May 10, 1905.

1st DUMBARTONSHIRE VOLUNTEER RIFLE CORPS.

Regimental District, No. 91.

(PLATE XLIV.)

"SOUTH AFRICA, 1900-02." | ORDER OF PRECEDENCE, 208.

Honorary Colonel—J. McA. DENNY, V.D. (hon. col.), February 7, 1903.

Headquarters—HELENSBURGH.

THE 1st Administrative Battalion, Dumbartonshire Rifle Volunteers, with headquarters at Balloch, was formed May 7, 1860, and in it were included, then or on their subsequent date of formation, the following corps of rifle volunteers (of one company each, except where otherwise stated) raised in the county :—

1st, Row, raised February 18, 1860. Headquarters changed January 1, 1873, to Helensburgh.

2nd, East Kilpatrick, raised February 8, 1860. Uniform—slate-grey tunics with black collars, black braid all round and on the cuff, grey trousers and cap, both with black braid, and brown belts. Headquarters changed to Maryhill and corps increased to one and a half companies in 1868.

3rd, Bonhill, raised February 8, 1860.

4th, Jamestown, raised February 8, 1860.

5th, Alexandria, raised February 8, 1860.

6th, Dumbarton, raised February 8, 1860. Uniform—slate-grey tunics with double black braid all round and in four rows on the breast, black collar with red piping, black braid with red piping on the cuff, grey trousers with red piping, grey cap with red-and-grey diced band, and brown belts. Increased to one and a half companies in 1878.

7th, Cardross, services accepted November 11, 1859; officers commissioned March 15, 1860.

8th, Gareloch, raised February 16, 1860, as one subdivision. In-

creased to one company 1863, and amalgamated with the
1st Corps on June 24, 1865.

9th, Luss, raised February 8, 1860, as one subdivision. Increased
to one company on August 28, 1868.

10th, Kirkintilloch, raised March 5, 1860. Increased to one
and a half companies 1874. Uniform—slate-grey, facings
scarlet.

11th, Cumbernauld, raised June 13, 1860.

12th, Tarbert (with a detachment at Arrochar), raised as one
subdivision March 7, 1861 ; disbanded 1869.

13th, Milngavie, services accepted August 9, 1867 ; officers commissioned August 23, 1867.

14th, Clydebank, Dalmuir, services accepted May 18, 1875 ;
officers commissioned June 23, 1875.

The uniforms of the first twelve corps were all slate
grey, and shortly after the formation of the battalion
they were dressed uniformly in tunics, trousers, and
shakos of that colour with scarlet facings and piping,
grey - and - scarlet diced band and scarlet ball-tuft on
the shakos, and brown waist and pouch belts. This
uniform was worn till 1864, when it was replaced by
a rifle-green one with scarlet collars and piping, and
black braid on the cuffs, green shakos with black ball-
tuft and red - and - black diced band, and black belts.
Busbies with black and light green plumes replaced the
shakos in 1874 (when also a double red piping was
added to the cuffs) and were worn till November 17,
1881, when helmets with bronze ornaments took their
place. The 9th Corps (Luss) was in 1864 clothed in
green doublets and Colquhoun tartan kilts, and continued to wear this uniform till its disbandment in
1882.

On April 28, 1880, the battalion was consolidated
under the title of 1st Dumbartonshire R.V.C., the
headquarters being removed to Helensburgh, with twelve
companies, lettered as follows : A, Helensburgh (late

1st Corps); B, Cardross (late 7th); C, Dumbarton
(late 6th); D, Bonhill (late 3rd); E, ·Jamestown
(late 4th); F, Alexandria (late 5th); G, Clydebank (late
14th); H, Maryhill (late 2nd); I, Milngavie (late
13th); K, Kirkintilloch (late 10th); L, Cumbernauld
(late 11th); and M, Luss (late 9th).

In 1882 the Queen's Prize at Wimbledon was won
by Serjeant A. Lawrance of the battalion. In this
year also (on January 1, 1882) the "M" (Luss) Company was disbanded, and a new "M" Company was
raised on February 12, 1882, at Renton. In 1884
"L" Company at Cumbernauld became a detachment
of "K" Company, and a new "L" Company was raised
on April 1, 1884, at Yoker. In 1900 a company of
mounted infantry, lettered "O," with headquarters at
Maryhill, and a cyclist company, lettered "Q," with headquarters at Dumbarton, were added to the battalion.

On March 8, 1887, sanction was given for the
battalion to adopt the scarlet doublet with yellow
facings and the glengarry with red-and-white diced
border of the Argyll and Sutherland Highlanders, to
be worn with Sutherland trews. The belts were
changed to white. Officers and staff-serjeants wore
blackcocks' tails in the glengarries in review order, and
all ranks white spats in review and black leggings in
marching order. Sashes were not worn. On March 29,
1904, a drab service dress with red piping on the
trousers was authorised, and this was the sole uniform
of the mounted and cyclist companies, which wore
brown felt hats with it.

During the South African War the 1st Dumbarton
contributed 98 of its members to the various new
formations. Of these, Lieutenant R. L. Stevenson and
24 non-commissioned officers and men served in
the 1st, 24 men in the 2nd, and 19 men in

the 3rd Volunteer Service Company of the Argyll and Sutherland Highlanders. Of the 1st Company, Privates J. C. Morrison, W. R. Kelly, and D. W. Moore died of disease in South Africa, and Lance - Corporal W. L. L. Fitzwilliam and Private R. M. Duncan after being invalided home, and of the 2nd Company, Lance-Corporal T. Stevenson died of disease in South Africa. One man joined the Scottish Cyclist Company, and 29 men the Imperial Yeomanry, of whom Private Neilson died of disease. Captain R. L. Stevenson also served a second period with the Imperial Yeomanry. One hundred and seven men of the battalion, in addition, joined the regular army and militia during the war, and 28 non - commissioned officers and men (including Staff-Serjeant Cumming, who was mentioned in despatches) of the A. & S. H. Brigade Bearer Company, attached to the battalion, served with the R.A.M.C. in South Africa.

In 1906 the battalion was placed in the 31st Field Army Brigade, 16th Division, and attended camp for fifteen days.

The distribution of the battalion since 1900 was—

A Coy., Helensburgh.
B Coy., Cardross, with a detachment at Dalreoch.
C and Q Coys., Dumbarton.
D Coy., Bonhill.
E Coy., Jamestown.
F Coy., Alexandria.
G Coy., Clydebank.
H and O Coys., Maryhill.
I Coy., Milngavie.
K Coy., Kirkintilloch, with a detachment at Cumbernauld.
L Coy., Yoker.
M Coy., Renton.

The battalion had a central rifle-range at Auchincarroch, in the Vale of Leven, up to 900 yards, and A, I, and K Companies had also ranges near their headquarters, that of the latter being held in conjunction with E Company, 4th V.B. Argyll and Sutherland Highlanders.

The lieutenant-colonels commandant of the battalion have been—

J. M. Gartshore, May 7, 1860.

John Findlay of Boturich (commanded at the same time the Highland Borderers Militia), October 13, 1862.

Colin J. Campbell, late Lieutenant 2nd Dragoons, December 2, 1876.

H. Currie, late Captain 74th and 79th Foot, and former Adjutant of the battalion (hon. col.), September 13, 1879.

James R. Thomson (hon. col.), December 8, 1888.

John McA. Denny (hon. col.), March 20, 1895.

Henry Brock, V.D. (hon. col.), January 17, 1903.

7TH (CLACKMANNAN AND KINROSS) VOLUN-TEER BATTALION, PRINCESS LOUISE'S (ARGYLL AND SUTHERLAND HIGHLANDERS).

Regimental District, No. 91.

(PLATE XLV.)

"SOUTH AFRICA, 1901-02." | ORDER OF PRECEDENCE, 219.

*Honorary Colonel—*W. J. F. EARL OF MAR AND KELLIE, August 5, 1896.

*Headquarters—*ALLOA.

THE first meetings with a view to the formation of volunteer rifle corps in Clackmannanshire were held at Tillicoultry on the 4th, and at Alloa on the 5th November 1859, but it was not till March 10, 1860, that the services of the Tillicoultry Corps, of one company, and June 2 that those of the Alloa Corps, of two companies, were accepted, the delay being due to the absence of the Lord-Lieutenant. The Tillicoultry Corps was at first numbered " 1," but this was afterwards changed, the Alloa Corps becoming the 1st and the Tillicoultry Corps the 2nd, the officers of both being gazetted on June 29, 1860. Each member paid for his own uniform and equipment, which consisted of medium grey tunics and trousers, with black braid and lace on the breast of the tunics and green facings, a grey cap with green band, and brown belts. A band of Graham tartan was worn round the caps at the Royal Review of 1860 as a battalion badge (see 4th V.B.), and was retained by the Clackmannan Corps till 1863, when a grey, green, and white diced band was substituted for it.

In 1862 both corps were attached to the 1st Administrative Battalion, Stirlingshire Rifle Volunteers, and in 1865 it was decided to re-clothe the two corps in green doublets with black braid and red collars and cuffs, Graham tartan trews, round green caps without peak and with red, white, and green diced band, and brown belts.

On November 5, 1867, the 1st Corps was increased to four companies, the fourth (D) being at Dollar, and it and the 2nd Corps were taken away from the Stirlingshire Battalion and formed into the 1st Administrative Battalion, Clackmannanshire Rifle Volunteers, with headquarters at Alloa, to which the 14th Stirlingshire Corps at Alva (raised on October 17, 1868) was added in 1868, and the 1st Kinross Corps in 1873. The latter corps had been raised as a subdivision at Kinross on October 31, 1860, and increased to a company on May 1, 1861, and had hitherto been attached to the 1st Administrative Battalion Fifeshire R.V. (see 6th V.B. Black Watch), whose changes of uniform it had followed. On the battalion being formed, it was determined not to proceed with the change of uniform decided on in 1865, which had only partially been carried out, and instead a uniform of dark grey doublets with scarlet collars, cuffs, and piping, the cuffs being pointed and with black lace, Murray tartan trews (out of compliment to Lord Mansfield, the Lord-Lieutenant), dark grey forage caps without peaks and with red, white, and green diced band, and brown belts was adopted. The officers had black braid on the breast of the doublet and silver lace round the top of the cap. The 14th Stirlingshire were clothed in this uniform on their formation. In 1874 the doublets were changed to scarlet with blue facings, and plain glengarries (with blackcock's tail for officers) were substituted for the caps, the Murray tartan trews and brown belts being retained.

In February 1880 the battalion was consolidated as the 1st Clackmannan and Kinross Rifle Volunteers, with headquarters at Alloa, and seven companies, lettered as follows: A and C, Alloa; B, Sauchie; and D, Dollar (all late 1st Clackmannan); E, Tillicoultry (late 2nd Clackmannan); F, Alva (late 14th Stirling); and G, Kinross (late 1st Kinross). In 1882 a section was formed at Clackmannan, and in 1883 it was increased to a complete company and lettered "H." Since then, with the exception of the formation in 1900 of a section of "H" Company at Kincardine and of a cyclist section at Kelty, attached to the Kinross Company, in 1903, there were no changes in the organisation of the battalion.

In 1887, by General Order 181 of December 1, the battalion assumed the title of 7th (Clackmannan and Kinross) V.B. Argyll and Sutherland Highlanders, and on February 21, 1888, it was authorised to wear the uniform of the regular battalions, but with trews and glengarry bonnets with red-and-white diced borders, the brown belts being changed for white. Officers wore shoulder-plaids, claymore belts, claymores, and dirks.

During the South African War, 85 members of the battalion, including 3 officers, saw active service. Of these, 11 men joined the 1st Volunteer Company, Lieutenant C. W. L. Ross and 17 men the 2nd, and Lieutenant H. R. Rae and 24 men (of whom 5 had already served in the 1st) the 3rd Volunteer Company of the Argyll and Sutherland Highlanders, and 16 men joined the Scottish Volunteer Cyclist Company, Lieutenant A. M. Muir and the remaining men joining other corps.

As headquarters for the battalion, Alloa prison was purchased in 1882, and enlarged and completed with drill-hall, offices, armoury, &c. The battalion had its rifle-range up to 900 yards at Hillend, near Alloa, and G Company had a separate range up to 600 yards at Blairadam.

The lieutenant-colonels commanding have been—

Alexander Mitchell, Major, November 5, 1867; Lieut.-Colonel, February 10, 1871.

John B. Harvey (hon. col.), December 21, 1887.

James Porteous, V.D. (hon. col.), January 24, 1891.

Andrew T. Moyes, V.D. (hon. col.), March 3, 1897.

Robert Haig of Dollarfield, January 25, 1902.

James Craig, September 13, 1906.

7TH MIDDLESEX (LONDON SCOTTISH) VOLUNTEER RIFLE CORPS.

(*Rifle Depôt.*)

(PLATE XLVI.)

" SOUTH AFRICA, 1900-02." | ORDER OF PRECEDENCE, 11.

Honorary Colonel—J. D. S. DUKE OF ARGYLL, K.T., G.C.M.G., G.C.V.O., V.D., August 11, 1900.

Headquarters—59 BUCKINGHAM GATE, LONDON, S.W.

ON May 21, 1859, at a meeting of the Highland Society of London, it was announced that a movement was on foot to raise a corps of Scottish volunteers in London, and the outcome of this was a meeting at the Freemasons' Tavern on July 4, 1859, with Lord Elcho in the chair, at which it was resolved to form such a corps. On November 2, 1859, the services of the corps as the 15th Middlesex (London Scottish) Rifle Volunteer Corps, with an establishment of six companies, were accepted. The companies originally formed were distributed over London as follows, and their recruitment was confined to Scotsmen resident in the Metropolis :—

No. 1 (Highland) Company. Headquarters, 10 Pall Mall, East.

No. 2 (City) Company. Mainly recruited from employés of the Oriental Bank, with headquarters there.

No. 3 (Northern) Company. Headquarters, Rosemary Hall, Islington.

No. 4 (Central) Company. Headquarters, Scottish Corporation House, Crane Court.

No. 5 (Southern) Company. Headquarters, 68 Jermyn Street, S.W.

No. 6 (Western) Company. Headquarters, Chesterfield House, W.

The corps was largely aided at first by the subscriptions of Scotsmen in London, and had a large
number of honorary members. The entrance-fee was
fixed at £1 and the annual subscription at £1,
members providing their own uniform and equipment; but of the 600 men originally recruited, 340
were "artisans," who paid no entrance - fee and only
5s. a-year subscription, and of these only 50 provided
their own uniforms, the rest being equipped from
corps funds. The corps was thus thoroughly representative of all classes of Scots in London. Two of
the companies were mainly, but not entirely, composed
of such "artisans," the others were mixed. In 1862
the entrance - fee was abolished, and since then the
necessary qualifications for entrance have been only
the introduction of a member and Scottish nation-
ality.

The original uniform was, for the 1st Company,
Elcho grey tunics, short skirted and with the skirts
rounded in front, with blue collars and cuffs, white-
metal buttons, grey lace on the collar, and grey
Austrian knot, Elcho grey kilts, goatskin sporrans
with two black tails, grey hose, laced boots, blue
glengarries with thistle badge, and brown belts; for
the 2nd to 6th Companies similar tunics with long
skirts, grey trousers with blue piping, brown canvas
leggings, and grey caps with sloping peak, blue-and-
white diced band, and blackcock's tail on the left
side. In 1862 the glengarry bonnet with blackcock's
tail was adopted as head-dress for the whole battalion.

In November 1860 the establishment of the battalion was officially increased to ten companies; but
this increase appears never to have been carried out,
for in 1861 No. 2 Company became No. 7, a new
No. 2 was raised, and a new No. 8 was formed as

Y

a kilted company, thus only raising the actual strength to eight companies, the two flank companies being kilted, the others wearing tunics and trousers, and all the glengarry with blackcock's tail.

The first honorary colonel of the corps was Lieutenant-General Colin Campbell, Lord Clyde, appointed in 1861, and, after his death in 1863, another distinguished Scottish officer, Lieutenant-General Sir James Hope Grant, was appointed to the same honour, which he held till his death in 1875.

In 1865 No. 3 Company was absorbed into the others, and in 1866 a new kilted company was formed under the Marquis of Lorne and lettered "B," the former 1st (kilted) Company becoming "A," the 2nd and 6th being amalgamated as "E," and the 4th, 5th, 7th, and 8th Companies becoming "C," "D," "F," and "H" respectively, letter "G" being left vacant. "A," "B," and "H" were then the kilted companies. In 1870 "E," and in 1872 "C," "D," and "F" Companies were kilted, thus completing the corps as a kilted battalion. On November 1, 1881, a new "G" Company was formed, thus attaining to the establishment of eight companies, which had been laid down in 1865 though never reached. In 1884 authority was given to increase the establishment to ten companies, and on November 1 of that year "I" and "K" Companies were formed.

In 1880, in accordance with an announcement in the 'London Gazette' of September 3, the corps was re-numbered the 7th Middlesex (London Scottish) Rifle Volunteers. No further changes in the establishment of the battalion (except the increase in the number of privates in 1901) took place after 1884.

The original kilted dress underwent few changes. In 1868 all the companies (including those not kilted)

were permitted to wear grey belted plaids, and in 1872
bronze buttons were introduced in place of those of
white metal, but in 1880 the latter were reverted to.
In 1882 doublets with gauntlet cuff and blue piping
replaced the tunics hitherto in use, and grey linen
spats, worn with shoes, were taken into wear, the
grey spats being exchanged for white ten years later.
In 1890 the valise equipment was introduced, the
shoulder-belts and expanse pouches being done away
with. Till 1882 it had been the custom for each
company to wear a separate badge in the glengarry
on special occasions (thus, "A" Company, deer grass;
"B" Company, the Clan Campbell badge of myrtle,
&c.; the companies which had no special badge wearing holly), but in that year the holly badge was made
common to all companies, and was worn when specially
ordered.

In 1872 Colour-Serjeant Michie of the London
Scottish won the Queen's Prize at the National Rifle
Association meeting at Wimbledon.

During the South African War no fewer than 218
members of the corps saw active service in the field.
Lieutenant B. C. Green and 45 other ranks joined
the City of London Imperial Volunteers in December
1899, and of these Lieutenant Green, Serjeant-Major
T. Smith, Armourer-Serjeant E. A. H. Gordon, and
Serjeant J. T. Hutchison were mentioned in Lord
Roberts' despatch of September 4, 1901, and Serjeant-
Major Smith and Serjeant Hutchison received the
medal for distinguished conduct. Nine more men
followed as a draft for the City Imperial Volunteers
in June 1900.

To the 2nd Volunteer Service Company of the
Gordon Highlanders the London Scottish contributed
Captains A. W. Buckingham and 56 other ranks, the

remainder of the company being made up from the 5th and 6th Volunteer Battalions Gordon Highlanders. This company left Aberdeen on February 23, and joined the 2nd Battalion at Ladysmith on March 25. Captain A. E. Rogers of the London Scottish served with it as a volunteer, and commanded it after Captain Buckingham was invalided. At the action of Rooikopjes on July 24, Corporal E. B. M. Murray of the London Scottish was dangerously wounded, and afterwards died, and Captain Rogers was slightly wounded. On September 8, near Lydenburg, a shell burst immediately above the company, which lost 3 killed and 16 wounded, of whom Serjeant W. F. Budgett, killed, and 10 men wounded belonged to the London Scottish. During the campaign Lance-Serjeant W. H. Kidd, Private D. E. Thomson, and Private T. P. Menzies died of disease. The company returned to Aberdeen on May 3. Serjeant E. Gavin and Corporal F. C. Thorne were mentioned in Lord Roberts' despatch of September 4, 1901.

To the 3rd Volunteer Service Company of the Gordon Highlanders (see 1st Volunteer Battalion) the London Scottish sent Captain B. C. Green (who had already served with the City Imperial Volunteers), 2nd Lieutenant H. G. H. Newington, and 26 other ranks, of whom Serjeant W. Steven was mentioned for gallantry on August 10, when a derailed train was attacked near Pietersburg (Lord Kitchener's despatch of October 8, 1901), and Serjeant F. H. Harris died of disease. To the 4th Service Company the London Scottish contributed 4 men, and Captain Gun was transferred to the command of it from the 3rd. Lieutenants J. H. Torrance and C. J. Dyke, 2nd Lieutenant W. N. Clark, and 27 men joined the Imperial Yeomanry in 1900, and 29 men in 1901, and in the latter year 1 man also joined Lovat's Scouts. The remainder of the 218 served in various corps.

The headquarters of the corps were first established at 8 Aldephi Terrace, and in 1873 removed to 1A Adam Street, Adelphi, W.C. There they remained until 1886, when newly built headquarters, with drill-hall, armoury, &c., at 59 Buckingham Gate, S.W., were taken into use. The musketry of the corps was carried out on the Pirbright Ranges, near Aldershot.

The lieutenant-colonels commanding the corps have been—

F. Lord Elcho (afterwards Earl of Wemyss), Colonel, A.D.C., January 30, 1860.
Henry Lumsden, late Captain Royal Aberdeen Militia (hon. col.), December 7, 1878.
William E. Nicol, March 14, 1891.
Eustace J. A. Balfour, April 28, 1894.
W. E. Edmonstone Montgomerie, V.D. (hon. col.), December 3, 1902.
James W. Greig, V.D. (hon. col.), December 3, 1904.

ARMY SERVICE CORPS (VOLUNTEERS).

(PLATE XLVII.)

THE Army Service Corps companies date from 1902, and were allotted one to each Volunteer Infantry Brigade. They were attached to volunteer battalions for administration as follows:—

Argyll and Sutherland Brigade Coy. A.S.C.(V.)—1st Dumbarton V.R.C.

Black Watch Brigade Coy. A.S.C.(V.)—4th V.B. Royal High-
  landers.
Gordon Brigade Coy. A.S.C.(V.)—4th V.B. Gordon Highlanders.
Highland Light Infantry Brigade Coy. A.S.C.(V.) — 3rd V.B.
  Highland Light Infantry.
1st Lothian Brigade Coy. A.S.C.(V.)—Q.R.V.B. Royal Scots.
Scottish Border Brigade Coy. A.S.C.(V.)—2nd V.B. King's Own
  Scottish Borderers.
Seaforth and Cameron Brigade Coy. A.S.C.(V.)—1st V.B.
  Cameron Highlanders.

No companies had been formed for the Clyde,
Scottish Rifles, and 2nd Lothian Brigades.

Each company consisted of a headquarters and a
supply section. The headquarters consisted of 1
major or captain, 1 subaltern, 1 company serjeant-
major and quartermaster - serjeant, 2 serjeants, 2
corporals, 1 wheeler, 1 shoeing-smith, and 1 saddler;
and the supply section numbered 1 captain, 1 staff-
serjeant, 1 serjeant, 1 corporal and 2 privates as
clerks and issuers, 1 corporal and 2 privates as
butchers, 1 private as labourer, and 2 drivers for
each vehicle. The vehicles were one 2-horsed waggon
for each battalion of the brigade and one for company headquarters. This *personnel* belonged to and
was borne supernumerary to the establishment of one
or more battalions of the brigade.

The uniform was that of the Army Service Corps—
blue with white facings and helmets, but with white-
metal buttons and silver lace.

ROYAL ARMY MEDICAL CORPS (VOLUNTERS).

(PLATE XLVII.)

THE Royal Army Medical Corps (Volunteers) were first formed as the "Volunteer Medical Staff Corps," and received their later title under Army Order 27 of February 1902. The force in Scotland was divided into the Edinburgh Company, the Aberdeen Companies, the Glasgow Companies, and a number of Brigade Bearer Companies, the establishments of which are given in Appendix G. The uniform was the same as that of the Royal Army Medical Corps — blue with dull cherry facings and helmets, but with white-metal buttons and silver lace.

EDINBURGH COMPANY.

This company was raised in Edinburgh, mainly from medical students of the University, as the 2nd Division Volunteer Medical Staff Corps, on May 22, 1886.

Thirty-four of its members served in South Africa during the war, of whom Captain David Wallace was mentioned in despatches ('London Gazette,' April 16, 1901).

Its commanding officers have been—

Surgeon David Hepburn, M.D. (afterwards Major), May 22, 1886.
Lieutenant D. Waterston, M.D. (Captain, August 11, 1906), January 7, 1903.

ABERDEEN COMPANIES.

The formation of one company, as the 7th Division Volunteer Medical Staff Corps, at Aberdeen was authorised on May 13, 1888. It was composed entirely of medical students of the University of Aberdeen, and its officers were first commissioned on April 17, 1889. In 1905 a second company was added, and also transport sections for two field hospitals and the bearer company of the Gordon Volunteer Infantry Brigade. Headquarters were at the Albert Hall, 14 Union Wynd, Aberdeen.

Six members of the company served during the South African War, of whom one, Private Alexander Watt, was killed in action.

The commanding officers have been—

Surgeon Alexander MacGregor, M.D., April 17, 1889.

Captain (Major, 1902) James Mackenzie Booth, M.A., M.D., September 8, 1891.

Major John Scott Riddell, M.V.O., M.A., M.B., July 2, 1904.

GLASGOW COMPANIES.

Two companies were formed on July 11, 1894, and these were increased to five in 1901. To the companies were also attached transport sections for six field hospitals and two bearer companies. Headquarters were at Gilbert Street, Yorkhill, Glasgow.

Forty-nine members of the companies served in South Africa during the war.

The commanding officer was—

Lieut.-Colonel Sir George T. Beatson, K.C.B., V.D., M.D. (hon. col.), who was appointed Captain Commanding June 23, 1894, Major on July 25, 1900, and Lieutenant-Colonel May 8, 1901.

BEARER COMPANIES.

The following Brigade Bearer Companies were independent units :—

Argyll and Sutherland—21 Jardine Street, Glasgow.
Black Watch—107 Victoria Road, Dundee.
Highland Light Infantry—81 Greendyke Street, Glasgow.
1st Lothian—71 Gilmore Place, Edinburgh.
Seaforth and Cameron—10 Bank Street, Inverness.

The Bearer Company for the Gordon Brigade formed portion of the Aberdeen Companies R.A.M.C.(V.), and its strength was included in that unit. That for the Scottish Border Brigade was borne supernumerary to the establishment of the 3rd Volunteer Battalion, King's Own Scottish Borderers, and the other bearer companies had not, up to 1908, been formed, but would have been found by the Royal Army Medical Corps (Volunteers).

APPENDIX A.

LIST OF RIFLE CORPS FORMED IN THE COUNTY OF ABERDEEN.

No.	Headquarters.	Date of Officers' Commissions.	Remarks.	Included in Records of—
1	Tarves	Feb. 15, 1860	2 companies. Became 2nd, July 19, 1860, and increased to 3 companies	2nd V. Gordons
2	...	...	Apparently never existed. 1st (see above) became 2nd on July 19, 1860	,, ,,
3	Cluny	Apr. 16, 1860	Formed as "1st Subdivision." Increased to 1 company and became 3rd Corps, July 19, 1860	4th ,,
4	Alford	Mar. 12 ,,	Formed as "2nd Subdivision." Became 4th Corps, July 19, 1860. Raised to 1 company, October 2, 1860	,, ,,
5	...	...	Apparently never existed	...
6	Aberdeen	Nov. 19, 1859	Became 1st Corps on July 19, 1860, the 7th, 8th, 9th, 11th, 12th, and 13th Corps having been added to it on March 16, 1860, making 9 companies in all	1st V. Gordons
7	,,	,, 19 ,,	Added to 6th, March 16, 1860	,, ,,
8	,,	,, 26 ,,	Raised to 2 companies, December 30, 1859. Added to 6th, March 16, 1860	,, ,,
9	,,	Dec. 23 ,,	Added to 6th, March 16, 1860	,, ,,
10	...	...	Apparently never existed	...
11	Aberdeen	Jan. 13, 1860	Added to 6th, March 16, 1860	1st V. Gordons
12	,,	,, 27 ,,	Raised as 2 companies. Added to 6th, March 16, 1860	,, ,,
13	,,	,, 21 ,,	Added to 6th, March 16, 1860	,, ,,
14	...	...	} Apparently never existed	
15	...	...		...
16	...	...		
17	New Deer	Apr. 12, 1860	Formed as a subdivision. Became 5th Corps, July 19, 1860. Increased to 1 company, November 1861	3rd V. Gordons
18	Ellon	,, 18 ,,	Became 6th Corps, July 19, 1860	2nd ,,
19	Huntly	Mar. 6 ,,	Became 7th Corps, July 19, 1860	4th ,,
20	Echt	June 9 ,,	Raised as 2 companies. Became 8th Corps, July 19, 1860	5th ,,
21	Peterhead	Apr. 4 ,,	Raised as 2 companies. Became 9th Corps, July 19, 1860	3rd ,,
22	Inverurie	,, 20 ,,	Became 10th Corps, July 19, 1860	4th ,,
23	Kildrummy	June 20 ,,	Raised as 1 subdivision. Became 11th Corps, July 19, 1860	,, ,,
12	Old Aberdeen	July 21 ,,	Disbanded, 1863. Reformed at Udny, 1864	2nd ,,
13	Turriff	Aug. 8 ,,	...	,, ,,
14	Tarland	Oct. 29 ,,	Raised as 1 subdivision. Increased to a company, May 7, 1861	5th ,,
15	Fyvie	,, 1 ,,	...	2nd ,,
16	Meldrum	,, 2 ,,	...	,, ,,
17	Old Deer	,, 29 ,,	Raised as 2 companies	3rd ,,
18	Tarves	June 11, 1867	Formed from remains of 2nd Corps	2nd ,,

No.	Headquarters.	Date of Officers' Commissions.	Remarks.	Included in Records of—
19	New Deer	June 30, 1861	Raised as 1 company, but amalgamated with 5th Corps in November 1861. A new 19th was formed at Insch in 1867	3rd & 4th V. Gordons
20	Longside	July 30 ,,	...	3rd V. Gordons
21	Aboyne	Nov. 22 ,,	" Marquis of Huntly's Highland "	5th ,,
22	Auchmull	June 18, 1862	...	4th ,,
23	Lumphanan	Mar. 29 ,,	...	5th ,,
24	St Fergus	Dec. 23, 1867	Raised as 1 subdivision. Amalgamated with 9th Corps, 1875. A new 24th Corps was formed at Fraserburgh in 1875	3rd ,,
25	New Pitsligo	Apr. 14, 1868	...	,, ,,
26	Cruden	Sept. 25, 1872	...	,, ,,

Note.—A "6th Subdivision" was formed at Glenkindie in July 1860, but no officers were appointed to it, and it disappeared from the Army List in July 1861; its members probably joined the 11th (Kildrummy) Corps.

APPENDIX B.

LIST OF RIFLE CORPS FORMED IN THE COUNTY OF FORFAR.

No.	Headquarters.	Date of Officers' Commissions.	Remarks.	Included in Records of—
1	Dundee	Nov. 15, 1859	Raised as 5 companies	1st V. Black Watch
2	Forfar	,, 15 ,,	Raised as 1 company; a second added, January 10, 1861	2nd ,,
3	Arbroath	,, 15 ,,	Raised as 1 company; a second added, May 1860. Raised to 4 companies, 1864	,, ,,
4	...	...	This number was borne for a few weeks by the 2nd Company 3rd Corps	...
5	Montrose	Nov. 15, 1859	Raised as 1 company; a second added, April 10, 1860	2nd V. Black Watch
6	...	...	Apparently never existed	...
7	Brechin	Mar. 26, 1860	Raised as 1 company; a second added, April 18, 1865	2nd V. Black Watch
8	Newtyle	Apr. 4 ,,	Designated " The Wharncliffe "	,, ,,
9	Glamis	May 8 ,,	...	,, ,,
10	Dundee	Apr. 10 ,,	Raised as 1 company; a second added, June 29, 1867	3rd ,,
11	Tannadice	Oct. 8 ,,	Raised as 1 subdivision. Increased to 1 company, September 29, 1867. Disbanded 1869	2nd ,,
12	Kirriemuir	Sept. 17 ,,	...	,, ,,
13	Friockheim	June 4, 1861	...	,, ,,
14	Dundee	,, 14 ,,	Raised as 1 company; a second added on June 29, 1867	3rd ,,
15	Cortachy	Aug. 16, 1865	Disbanded 1872	2nd ,,

APPENDIX C.

LIST OF RIFLE CORPS FORMED IN THE COUNTY OF LANARK.

No.	Headquarters.	Date of Acceptance of Services.	Date of Officers' Commissions.	Remarks.	Included in Records of—
1	Glasgow	Sept. 24, 1859	Oct. 1, 1859	"1st Western"	1st Lanark
2	,,	,, 24 ,,	,, 3 ,,	"Glasgow University"	,, ,,
3	,,	,, 9 ,,	,, 4 ,,	"1st Southern"	3rd ,,
4	,,	Oct. 10 ,,	,, 15 ,,	"1st Northern"	4th V.B.S.R.
5	,,	Sept. 24 ,,	,, 17 ,,	"1st Eastern"	3rd V.B.H.L.I.
6	,,	Oct. 10 ,,	Nov. 4 ,,	...	4th V.B.S.R.
7	,,	,, 10 ,,	,, 4 ,,	...	,, ,,
8	,,	,, 10 ,,	,, 4 ,,	...	,, ,,
9	,,	,, 10 ,,	,, 4 ,,	"Bankers"	1st Lanark
10	,,	,, 19 ,,	,, 4 ,,	...	3rd ,,
11	,,	Nov. 4 ,,	Dec. 13 ,,	"2nd Western"	1st ,,
12	,,	Dec. 5 ,,	,, 20 ,,	...	4th V.B.S.R.
13	,,	,, 5 ,,	,, 20 ,,	...	,, ,,
14	,,	,, 5 ,,	Feb. 2, 1860	...	3rd Lanark
15	,,	,, 5 ,,	,, 20 ,,	"Procurators"	1st ,,
16	Hamilton	Feb. 24, 1860	,, 29 ,,	...	2nd V.B.S.R.
17	Glasgow	Dec. 5, 1859	Dec. 28, 1859	...	1st Lanark
18	,,	,, 5 ,,	,, 20 ,,	...	,, ,,
19	,,	,, 5 ,,	,, 30 ,,	...	1st V.B.H.L.I.
20	This corps was to have been	raised from the	Western shipbuilding yards, but never existed.		
21	Glasgow	Dec. 5, 1859	Dec. 20, 1859	...	3rd V.B.H.L.I.
22	,,	,, 5 ,,	,, 24 ,,	...	3rd Lanark
23	,,	,, 5 ,,	,, 20 ,,	...	1st V.B.H.L.I.
24	,,	,, 6 ,,	,, 26 ,,	...	,, ,,
25	,,	,, 14 ,,	,, 26 ,,	...	2nd ,,
26	,,	,, 14 ,,	,, 26 ,,	...	,, ,,
27	,,	,, 14 ,,	Feb. 28, 1860	...	,, ,,
28	,,	,, 22 ,,	Dec. 30, 1859	...	1st ,,
29	Coatbridge	Feb. 13, 1860	Feb. 22, 1860	...	5th V.B.S.R.
30	Glasgow	Dec. 28, 1859	Jan. 7 ,,	...	3rd V.B.H.L.I.
31	,,	,, 21 ,,	,, 7 ,,	...	,, ,,
32	Summerlee	Jan. 10, 1860	Feb. 11 ,,	...	5th V.B.S.R.
33	Glasgow	Dec. 22, 1859	,, 6 ,,	"Partick"	1st Lanark
34	,,	,, 27 ,,	Jan. 7 ,,	...	3rd V.B.H.L.I.
35	,,	,, 27 ,,	,, 7 ,,	...	,, ,,
36	,,	,, 28 ,,	,, 7 ,,	...	1st ,,
37	Lesmahagow	Feb. 3, 1860	Feb. 11 ,,	...	9th Lanark
38	Glasgow	Dec. 29, 1859	Mar. 1 ,,	...	3rd V.B.H.L.I.
39	,,	,, 29 ,,	Feb. 6 ,,	...	1st Lanark
40	,,	,, 29 ,,	Jan. 7 ,,	...	2nd V.B.H.L.I.
41	,,	,, 31 ,,	,, 7 ,,	...	1st ,,
42	Uddingstone	Jan. 31, 1860	Feb. 17 ,,	...	2nd V.B.S.R.
43	Gartsherrie	,, 10 ,,	Jan. 31 ,,	...	5th ,,
44	Blantyre	Feb. 6 ,,	Feb. 17 ,,	...	2nd ,,
45	Glasgow	Jan. 10 ,,	,, 15 ,,	...	3rd V.B.H.L.I.
46	,,	,, 10 ,,	,, 17 ,,	...	,, ,,
47	,,	,, 10 ,,	,, 17 ,,	...	...
48	Airdrie	Feb. 11 ,,	,, 29 ,,	2nd company added Nov. 28, 1863	5th V.B.S.R.
49	Lambhill	May 3 ,,	May 16 ,,	1 subdivision only. Disbanded 1862	...
50	Glasgow	Jan. 10 ,,	Feb. 20 ,,	...	1st Lanark
51	,,	,, 11 ,,	,, 28 ,,	...	1st V.B.H.L.I.
52	Hamilton	Feb. 24 ,,	,, 29 ,,	...	2nd V.B.S.R.
53	Glasgow	Jan. 30 ,,	,, 17 ,,	...	1st Lanark
54	,,	,, 30 ,,	,, 22 ,,	...	3rd ,,
55	Lanark	Feb. 23 ,,	,, 29 ,,	...	9th ,,

No.	Headquarters.	Date of Acceptance of Services.	Date of Officers' Commissions.	Remarks.	Included in Records of—
56	Bothwell	Feb. 23, 1860	Feb. 29, 1860	...	2nd V.B.S.R.
57	Wishaw	Mar. 7 ,,	Mar. 14 ,,	...	,, ,,
58	Glasgow	Feb. 10 ,,	Feb. 22 ,,	...	3rd V.B.H.L.I.
59	,,	,, 21 ,,	,, 25 ,,	...	,, ,,
60	,,	,, 18 ,,	Mar. 1 ,,	"1st Highland"	4th V.B.S.R.
61	,,	,, 18 ,,	,, 1 ,,	"2nd Highland"	,, ,,
62	Biggar	,, 22 ,,	,, 6 ,,	Disbanded Sept. 1860. Re-formed Mar. 17, 1863	9th Lanark
63	Glasgow	,, 15 ,,	Feb. 24 ,,	...	1st ,,
64	,,	,, 18 ,,	Mar. 6 ,,	"1st Rutherglen"	3rd V.B.H.L.I.
65	,,	,, 18 ,,	,, 6 ,,	"2nd Rutherglen"	,, ,,
66	,,	,, 17 ,,	Feb. 29 ,,	...	,, ,,
67	,,	,, 17 ,,	,, 29 ,,	...	1st ,,
68	,,	,, 17 ,,	Mar. 1 ,,	...	2nd ,,
69	,,	,, 17 ,,	,, 1 ,,	...	,, ,,
70	,,	,, 17 ,,	,, 1 ,,	...	,, ,,
71	,,	,, 17 ,,	,, 1 ,,	...	1st Lanark
72	,,	,, 23 ,,	,, 5 ,,	...	9th ,,
73	Carluke	Mar. 12 ,,	,, 4 ,,	...	1st V.B.H.L.I.
74	Glasgow	Feb. 29 ,,	,, 5 ,,	...	3rd ,,
75	,,	,, 29 ,,	,, 7 ,,	...	1st Lanark
76	,,	Mar. 26 ,,	,, 14 ,,	...	,, ,,
77	,,	,, 8 ,,	April 2 ,,	...	3rd ,,
78	,,	,, 29 ,,	May 28 ,,	"Old Guard of Glasgow"	1st ,,
79	,,	,, 29 ,,	April 26 ,,	...	1st V.B.H.L.I.
80	,,	,, 29 ,,	,, 6 ,,	...	,, ,,
81	,,	April 2 ,,	,, 12 ,,	...	3rd Lanark
82	,,	,, 11 ,,	May 11 ,,	...	1st V.B.H.L.I.
83	,,	,, 24 ,,	,, 2 ,,	...	3rd ,,
84	,,	,, 24 ,,	June 12 ,,	...	1st ,,
85	,,	May 7 ,,	May 15 ,,	...	3rd ,,
86	,,	,, 7 ,,	,, 16 ,,	...	3rd Lanark
87	Busby	,, 18 ,,	,, 28 ,,	...	3rd V.B.H.L.I.
88	Glasgow	,, 9 ,,	,, 18 ,,	Disbanded 1864	1st ,,
89	,,	,, 9 ,,	,, 29 ,,	...	3rd ,,
90	,,	,, 24 ,,	June 5 ,,	...	1st ,,
91	Whitevale	,, 24 ,,	,, 5 ,,	...	,, ,,
92	Uddingstone	Offer of services not accepted.		...	
93	Glasgow	Aug. 8, 1860	Aug. 31, 1860	"3rd Highland"	4th V.B.S.R.
94	Douglas	Sept. 21 ,,	Oct. 4 ,,	...	9th Lanark
95	Bailliestown	Oct. 16 ,,	Jan. 15, 1861	...	5th V.B.S.R.
96	Glasgow	Nov. 29 ,,	Dec. 12, 1860	2nd company added Jan. 3, 1861	3rd V.B.H.L.I.
97	,,	July 30, 1861	Sept. 3, 1861	"Glasgow Guards." 4 companies. Amalgamated with 1st Lanark E.V., 1863	1st Lanark E.V.
97	Woodhead	Jan. 11, 1865	May 27, 1865	...	5th V.B.S.R.
98	Gartness	May 12 ,,	June 14 ,,	...	,, ,,
99	Clarkston	July 27 ,,	Aug. 3 ,,	...	,, ,,
100	Calderbank	,, 8 ,,	,, 4 ,,	...	,, ,,
101	Newarthill	June 7, 1866	July 26, 1866	...	,, ,,
102	Motherwell	Feb. 14, 1867	Mar. 7, 1867	...	2nd ,,
103	East Kilbride	June 6 ,,	June 25 ,,	...	,, ,,
104	Holytown, Bellshill	April 18, 1868	May 5, 1868	...	5th ,,
105	Glasgow	July 21 ,,	Oct. 19 ,,	"Glasgow Highland," 12 companies (1 in Partick, 1 in Crosshill)	5th V.B.H.L.I.
106	Strathaven	Oct. 1873	Oct. 1873	...	2nd V.B.S.R.
107	Leadhills	May 1875	June 2, 1875	...	9th Lanark

APPENDIX D.

LIST OF RIFLE CORPS FORMED IN THE COUNTY OF RENFREW.

No.	Headquarters.	Date of Officers' Commissions.	Remarks.	Included in Records of—
1	Greenock	Sept. 10, 1859	2nd, 13th, and 18th Corps added, making 4 companies, in February 1860	1st V.B. A. & S. H.
2	,,	,, 10 ,,	Amalgamated with 1st Corps, February 1860	1st ,,
3	Paisley	,, 22 ,,	...	2nd ,,
4	Pollockshaws	,, 22 ,,	...	3rd ,,
5	Port Glasgow	Nov. 15 ,,	...	1st ,,
6	Paisley	,, 23 ,,	...	2nd ,,
7	Barrhead	Feb. 15, 1860	...	3rd ,,
8	Neilston	Mar. 6 ,,	...	3rd ,,
9	Johnstone	Feb. 6 ,,	...	2nd ,,
10	Greenock	,, 3 ,,	"Highlanders." 11th Corps added as 2nd company, 1863	1st ,,
11	,,	,, 3 ,,	"Highlanders." Added to 10th Corps, 1863	1st ,,
12	,,	,, 3 ,,	Disbanded 1860	...
13	,,	Jan. 24 ,,	Amalgamated with 1st Corps, February 1860	1st V.B. A. & S. H.
14	Paisley	Feb. 8 ,,	...	2nd ,,
15	Kilbarchan	Jan. 20 ,,	...	2nd ,,
16	Thornliebank	Feb. 15 ,,	...	3rd ,,
17	Lochwinnoch	Jan. 20 ,,	...	2nd ,,
18	Greenock	Feb. 6 ,,	Amalgamated with 1st Corps, February 1860	1st ,,
19	Hurlet	Mar. 6 ,,	...	3rd ,,
20	Renfrew	,, 1 ,,	...	2nd ,,
21	Barrhead	,, 12 ,,	...	3rd ,,
22	Gourock	Apr. 6 ,,	...	1st ,,
23	Cathcart	,, 6 ,,	...	3rd ,,
24	Paisley	,, 10 ,,	...	2nd ,,
25	Thornliebank	May 15, 1862	...	3rd ,,

APPENDIX E.

ENROLLED STRENGTH OF THE SCOTTISH VOLUNTEER FORCE ON THE 1ST OF APRIL 1862.—(*Extracted from a Return prepared by Colonel MacMurdo for the Royal Commission on the Condition of the Volunteer Force*, 1862.)

		No. of Companies, &c.	Enrolled Members.	Total of Arm in County.
	ARTILLERY.			
Aberdeen .	1st Adm. Brig. (1st, 3rd, 4th, 5th, 6th, 7th Corps)	6	404	404
Argyll . .	1st Adm. Brig. (1st, 3rd, 4th Corps) .	4	284	
	2nd Corps	1	65	
	5th Corps	½	32	
	6th Corps	1	60	
	7th Corps	1	78	
	8th Corps	1	63	
	9th Corps	1	51	633
Ayr . .	1st Adm. Brig. (1st, 2nd, 3rd, 4th, 5th Corps) .	5½	320	320
Banff . .	1st Adm. Brig. (1st, 2nd, 3rd, 4th Corps)	5	280	280
Berwick . .	1st Corps	1	51	
	2nd Corps	1	50	101
Caithness .	1st Corps	1	61	
	2nd Corps	1	41	
	3rd Corps	1	58	160
Cromarty .	1st Corps	1	36	36
Dumbarton .	1st Corps	1	56	
	2nd Corps	1	54	
	3rd Corps	1	53	163
Edinburgh City	1st Corps	9	564	564
Elgin . .	1st Corps	1	53	53
Fife. . .	1st Adm. Brig. (1st, 2nd, 3rd, 4th, 5th, 6th, 7th, 8th, 9th, 10th Corps) .	10½	630	630
Forfar . .	1st Adm. Brig. (1st, 2nd, 3rd, 4th Corps)	6	374	374
Haddington .	1st Corps	1	69	69
Inverness .	1st Corps	4	234	234
Kincardine .	1st Corps	2	123	
	2nd Corps	½	25	
	3rd Corps	½	35	
	4th Corps	½	28	211
Kirkcudbright	1st Corps	1	50	50
Lanark . .	1st Adm. Brig. (1st, 2nd, 3rd, 4th, 5th, 6th, 7th, 8th, 9th, 10th, 12th, 13th, 14th, 15th Corps) . . .	14	888	
	11th Corps	1	52	940
Mid-Lothian .	1st Corps	8	463	
	2nd Corps	2	138	601
Nairn . .	1st Corps	2	125	125
Orkney . .	1st Corps	1	72	72
Renfrew . .	1st Corps	1	78	
	2nd Corps	1	56	
	3rd Corps	1	52	186

		No. of Companies, &c.	Enrolled Members.	Total of Arm in County.
ARTILLERY—*continued.*				
Ross . .	1st Corps	1	72	72
Stirling . .	1st Corps	1	61	
	2nd Corps	1	70	131
Sutherland .	1st Corps	1	71	71
Wigtown .	1st Corps	1	55	
	2nd Corps	1	47	102
	Total Artillery . . .	107¾	6582	6582
ENGINEERS.				
Edinburgh .	1st Corps	1	64	64
Lanark . .	1st Corps	1	105	
	2nd Corps	1	66	171
	Total Engineers . . .	3	235	235
MOUNTED RIFLES.				
Fife .	1st Corps	4	160	160
RIFLES.				
Aberdeen .	1st Adm. Bn. (3rd, 4th, 7th, 8th, 10th, 11th, 14th, 21st Corps) . . .	9	504	
	2nd Adm. Bn. (2nd, 6th, 13th, 15th, 16th Corps)	6	398	
	3rd Adm. Bn. (5th, 9th, 17th, 20th Corps)	8	428	
	1st Corps	11	695	
	12th Corps	1	48	
	18th Corps	1	80	
	22nd Corps	1	40	
	23rd Corps	1	60	2253
Argyll * . .	1st Adm. Bn. (2nd, 3rd, 7th, 11th Corps)	5	301	
	6th Corps	2	53	
	8th Corps	2	61	
	10th Corps	1	111	
	12th Corps	1	71	597
Ayr . .	1st Adm. Bn. (1st, 2nd, 3rd, 4th, 5th, 6th, 7th, 8th, 9th, 10th, 11th, 12th, 13th Corps)	12½	971	971
Banff . .	1st Adm. Bn. (1st, 2nd, 3rd, 4th Corps) .	4	215	215
Berwick .	1st Corps	1	81	
	2nd Corps	1	70	
	3rd Corps	1	59	
	4th Corps	1	66	
	5th Corps	½	37	313
Caithness .	1st Corps	1	61	
	2nd Corps	1	86	
	3rd Corps	1	78	225
Clackmannan (see Stirling).				

* For 9th Corps, see Perth.

		No. of Companies, &c.	Enrolled Members.	Total of Arm in County.
	RIFLES—*continued.*			
Dumbarton .	1st Adm. Bn. (1st, 2nd, 3rd, 4th, 5th, 6th, 7th, 8th, 9th, 10th, 11th, 12th Corps)	10½	804	804
Dumfries .	1st Adm. Bn. (1st, 2nd, 3rd, 4th, 5th, 6th, 7th, 8th, 9th Corps) . .	8½	570	570
Edinburgh City	1st Corps . . .	21	1801	1801
Elgin . .	1st Adm. Bn. (1st, 2nd, 3rd, 4th, 5th, 6th Corps)	6	439	439
Fife . .	1st Adm. Bn. (1st, 2nd, 3rd, 4th, 5th, 6th, 7th, 8th, 9th Corps, and 1st Kinross Corps) . .	11	920	920
Forfar . .	1st Adm. Bn. (3rd, 5th, 7th, 13th Corps)	6	621	
	2nd Adm. Bn. (2nd, 8th, 9th, 11th, 12th Corps)	6	433	
	1st Corps . .	8	630	1684
Haddington .	1st Adm. Bn. (1st, 2nd, 3rd, 4th, 5th, 6th Corps) . . .	5½	509	509
Inverness .	1st Adm. Bn. (1st, 2nd, 3rd, 4th, 5th, 6th, 7th Corps) . .	7	501	501
Kincardine .	1st Adm. Bn. (1st, 2nd, 3rd, 4th, 5th, 6th, 7th Corps) . .	6½	495	495
Kinross (see Fife).				
Kirkcudbright & Wigtown .	1st Adm. Bn. (1st, 2nd, 3rd, 4th, 5th Kirkcudbright, and 1st, 2nd, 3rd, 4th Wigtown Corps) . .	7½	534	534
Lanark . .	1st Adm. Bn. (16th, 42nd, 44th, 52nd, 56th, 57th Corps) . .	6	496	
	2nd Adm. Bn. (30th, 31st, 38th, 45th, 46th, 47th, 75th, 84th, 86th, 88th, 96th Corps) . .	11	813	
	3rd Adm. Bn. (37th, 55th, 73rd, 94th, Corps) . . .	4	313	
	1st Corps	16	989	
	3rd Corps . . .	9	579	
	4th Corps . . .	9	616	
	5th Corps	12	783	
	19th Corps . . .	15	924	
	25th Corps . . .	8	531	
	29th Corps . . .	1	83	
	32nd Corps . . .	1	57	
	43rd Corps . . .	1	55	
	48th Corps . . .	1	71	
	49th Corps . . .	...	3	
	95th Corps . . .	1	63	
	97th Corps . . .	4	254	6630
Linlithgow .	1st Corps . . .	1	84	
	2nd Corps . . .	1	91	
	3rd Corps . . .	1	91	266
Mid-Lothian .	1st Adm. Bn. (2nd, 3rd, 5th Corps) .	5½	372	
	1st Corps	8	449	
	4th Corps . . .	1	60	881
Nairn . .	1st Corps . . .	½	18	18
Orkney . .	1st Corps . . .	½	57	57
Peebles . .	1st Corps . . .	1	63	
	2nd Corps . . .	1	76	
	3rd Corps . . .	1	45	
	4th Corps . . .	1	...	184

	No. of Companies, &c.	Enrolled Members.	Total of Arm in County.
RIFLES—*continued.*			
Perth . . 1st Adm. Bn. (1st, 5th, 6th, 7th, 8th, 9th, 11th, 13th, 14th, 15th, 16th Corps)	12½	957	
2nd Adm. Bn. (3rd and 10th Corps, and 9th Argyll) . . .	6	446	1403
Renfrew . . 1st Adm. Bn. (1st, 5th, 10th, 11th, 22nd Corps)	8	602	
2nd Adm. Bn. (3rd, 6th, 9th, 14th, 15th, 17th, 20th, 24th Corps) . .	8	651	
3rd Adm. Bn. (4th, 7th, 8th, 16th, 19th, 21st, 23rd, 25th Corps) . . .	8	581	1834
Ross . . 1st Adm. Bn. (1st, 2nd, 4th, 5th, 6th Corps)	4½	330	
3rd Corps	1	68	398
Roxburgh and 1st Adm. Bn. (1st, 2nd, 3rd, 4th, 5th Roxburgh, and 1st and 2nd Selkirk Corps)	7	636	636
Stirling . . 1st Adm. Bn. (1st, 2nd, 3rd, 4th, 5th, 6th, 7th, 8th, 9th, 11th, 12th Corps, and 1st and 2nd Clackmannan) .	13	996	
10th Corps	1	76	1072
Sutherland . 1st Corps	4	354	354
Wigtown (see Kirkcudbright).			
Total Rifles	372	27,263	27,263
Grand total, all Arms . .	486¾	34,240	34,240

The totals in England and Wales were—

Light Horse	. .	11½ troops	662	enrolled members
Artillery .	. .	278¼ batteries	17,781	,,
Engineers .	. .	42 companies	2,669	,,
Mounted Rifles	. .	9 ,,	496	,,
Rifles *	. .	1430 ,,	106,833	,,
Total	. .		128,441	,,
Add for Scotland	. .		34,240	,,
Grand total, United Kingdom	.		162,681	,,

* Of these, 10 companies with 673 enrolled members formed the 15th Middlesex (London Scottish) R.V.

APPENDIX F.

RETURN OF THE SCOTTISH VOLUNTEER CORPS for the Year 1881.

(Extracted from the Official Return of January 1882.)

CORPS.	Author-ised es-tablish-ment.	Authorised num-ber of super-numeraries.	Effici-ents.	Non-effici-ents.	Total enrolled.	Proficients who have earned special grant of 50s.		Present at In-spection.
						Offrs.	Serjts.	
LIGHT HORSE.								
1st Fifeshire . . .	243	...	123	46	169	10	9	123
1st Forfarshire . .	61	36	48	3	51	1	7	34
Total Light Horse .	304	36	171	49	220	11	16	157
ARTILLERY.								
1st Aberdeenshire (Aber-deen and Banff) .	1130	...	1072	16	1088	28	59	890
1st Argyll and Bute .	1021	...	688	77	765	26	49	589
1st Ayrshire and Gallo-way . . .	890	...	757	59	816	24	48	674
1st Berwickshire . .	81	...	64	2	66	2	1	59
2nd ,, . .	81	...	58	3	61	2	...	43
1st Caithness (Caithness and Sutherland) .	647	...	561	8	569	15	35	385
1st Edinburgh City . .	724	...	604	41	645	23	34	562
1st Fifeshire (Fife and Stirling) . .	1054	...	918	24	942	27	55	837
1st Forfarshire (Forfar and Kincardine) .	1288	...	1202	67	1269	34	67	1103
1st Haddington . .	81	...	66	...	66	2	...	60
1st Inverness (Inverness, Cromarty, Nairn, Ross, Elgin) . .	1049	...	897	25	922	27	53	789
1st Lanarkshire . .	1366	...	1331	1	1332	42	69	1083
1st Mid-Lothian . .	644	...	467	45	512	23	34	452
1st Orkney . . .	730	...	536	43	579	21	40	464
1st Renfrew and Dumbar-ton	565	...	543	9	552	16	28	469
Total Artillery .	11,351	...	9764	420	10,184	312	576	8459
ENGINEERS.								
1st Aberdeenshire . .	201	...	197	3	200	6	10	163
1st Lanarkshire . .	603	...	586	17	603	13	34	506
Total Engineers .	804	...	783	20	803	19	44	669

Corps.	Authorised establishment.	Authorised number of supernumeraries.	Efficients.	Non-efficients.	Total enrolled.	Proficients who have earned special grant of 50s.		Present at Inspection.
						Offrs.	Serjts.	
MOUNTED RIFLES.								
1st Roxburgh . . .	61	25	50	3	53	3	4	50
RIFLES.								
1st Aberdeenshire . .	1104	...	842	2	844	31	47	731
2nd ,, . .	708	...	519	2	521	25	33	428
3rd ,, . .	910	...	608	62	670	26	41	577
4th ,, . .	767	...	552	22	574	22	33	450
1st Argyllshire . .	807	...	656	36	692	21	36	550
1st Ayrshire . . .	809	...	733	12	745	24	45	581
2nd ,, . .	707	...	653	8	661	20	39	571
1st Banffshire . . .	666	...	618	3	621	21	29	513
1st Berwickshire . .	708	...	532	27	559	13	34	503
1st Clackmannan and Kinross . .	706	...	655	23	678	26	33	602
1st Dumbartonshire .	1213	...	1200	13	1213	34	64	901
1st Dumfriesshire . .	1010	...	664	43	707	25	48	620
1st Edinburgh City .	2509	...	2002	27	2029	74	117	1755
2nd ,, ,, .	602	60	646	16	662	17	33	585
1st Elginshire . .	1069	...	1069	...	1069	25	51	1066
1st Fifeshire . . .	1211	...	976	41	1017	30	55	756
1st Forfarshire . .	804	...	660	22	682	18	37	603
2nd ,, . .	1410	...	1027	28	1055	32	60	927
3rd ,, . .	603	...	469	16	485	14	31	365
Galloway . . .	808	...	706	19	725	19	38	611
1st Haddington . .	607	...	384	22	406	13	21	359
1st Inverness . . .	1010	...	989	4	993	31	53	912
1st Kincardine and Aberdeen . . .	1011	...	684	36	720	22	39	526
1st Lanarkshire . .	1606	...	1534	18	1552	48	78	1207
2nd ,, . .	1010	...	967	19	986	26	51	746
3rd ,, . .	1205	...	1046	15	1061	39	63	901
4th ,, . .	904	...	754	6	760	31	48	622
5th ,, . .	1205	...	782	79	861	19	58	476
6th ,, . .	805	...	805	1	806	20	44	686
7th ,, . .	808	...	805	3	808	18	43	733
8th ,, . .	1205	...	1203	1	1204	27	64	946
9th ,, . .	607	...	544	9	553	15	34	507
10th ,, . .	1205	...	1025	9	1034	29	64	708
1st Linlithgowshire .	707	...	689	9	698	18	41	612
1st Mid-Lothian . .	1105	...	828	32	860	24	53	734
2nd Mid-Lothian and Peebles . .	1108	...	919	55	974	26	57	782
1st Perthshire . . .	706	...	535	16	551	16	36	496
2nd ,, . . .	809	...	693	18	711	20	35	624
1st Renfrewshire . .	907	...	882	5	887	26	42	768
2nd ,, . .	807	...	718	50	768	22	41	583
3rd ,, . .	807	...	772	18	790	20	40	645
1st Ross-shire . . .	910	...	896	8	904	26	50	712
1st Roxburgh and Selkirk	907	...	784	14	798	26	49	728
1st Stirlingshire . .	1008	...	758	17	775	27	48	674
1st Sutherland . .	1070	...	989	18	1007	25	50	802
Total Rifles .	43,170	60	36,772	904	37,676	1131	2106	31,184

CORPS.	Authorised establishment.	Authorised number of supernumeraries.	Efficients.	Non-efficients.	Total enrolled.	Proficients who have earned special grant of 50s.		Present at Inspection.
						Offrs.	Serjts.	
Grand total, all Arms .	55,690	121	47,540	1396	48,936	1476	2746	40,519
The totals in England and Wales were—								
Light Horse . .	306	9	48	209	257	1	4	44
Artillery . . .	32,551	50	26,755	1329	28,084	756	1684	23,636
Engineers . . .	9,114	90	8,057	304	8,361	163	458	7,129
Mounted Rifles . .	...	...	...	...	...	...	...	...
Rifles * . . .	147,768	340	117,762	4908	122,670	3208	6983	104,323
Total . .	189,739	489	152,622	6750	159,372	4128	9129	135,132
Add for Scotland . .	55,690	121	47,540	1396	48,936	1476	2746	40,519
Grand total, United Kingdom . . .	245,429	610	200,162	8146	208,308	5604	11,875	175,651
* Of these— 7th Middlesex (London Scottish) . . .	804	...	596	60	656	20	34	540

APPENDIX G.

ESTABLISHMENTS OF THE UNITS OF THE VOLUNTEER FORCE IN SCOTLAND FOR 1907-1908.

INCLUDING THOSE OF THE 8TH V.B. THE KING'S (LIVERPOOL REGIMENT) AND 7TH MIDDLESEX V.R.C.

(Issued with Army Orders dated 1st June 1907.)

ROYAL GARRISON ARTILLERY (VOLUNTEERS).

Corps.	Lieutenant-Colonels.	Majors.	Captains.	Lieutenants and 2nd Lieutenants.(a)	Quartermasters.	Medical Officers.(b)	Veterinary Officers.	Acting Chaplains.(b)	Total Officers.	Permanent Staff: Adjutants.	Active Sergeant-Majors.	Other Sergeant-Instructors.	Quartermaster-Serjeants.	Sergeant-Trumpeters.	Battery or Company Sergeant-Majors.	Battery Quartermaster-Serjeants.	Sergeant-Farrier.	Acting Armourer Staff-Serjeants.	Orderly-room Serjeants.	Serjeants.	Total Serjeants.	Corporals.	Bombardiers.	Trumpeters.	Gunners.	Drivers.	Shoeing-smiths.	Saddlers.	Wheelers.	Total, exclusive of permanent staff.	Total all ranks, inclusive of permanent staff.(c)
(P 2) 1st Aberdeenshire	2	2	13	20	1	4	1	1	44	1	1	6	1	1	11	2	2	1	1	39	58	52	26	22	768	60	4	4	2	1,040	1,048
1st Argyll & Bute	2	2	12	20	1	4	...	1	42	1	1	9	1	1	12	...	...	1	1	38	54	51	25	25	812	...	...	...	...	1,009	1,020
(P 3) 1st Ayr & Galloway	2	2	13	20	1	4	1	1	44	1	1	9	1	1	10	3	3	1	1	39	59	52	26	20	734	90	6	6	3	1,040	1,051
1st Banff	1	1	7	11	1	3	...	1	25	1	1	6	1	1	7	...	...	1	1	21	32	28	14	14	447	...	...	...	...	560	568
1st Berwickshire	...	...	1	2	1	1	...	1	5	1	1	1	1	1	1	...	...	1	1	3	5	4	2	2	62	...	...	...	...	80	81
1st Caithness	...	...	7	14	...	3	...	1	25	1	1	5	1	1	7	...	...	1	1	21	32	28	14	14	447	...	...	...	...	560	567
(P 2) 1st Edinburgh (City)	1	1	9	14	1	3	1	1	32	1	1	3	1	1	7	2	2	1	1	27	42	60	18	14	508	60	4	4	2	720	725
(P 1) 1st Fifeshire	1	2	15	28	1	4	1	1	50	1	1	9	1	1	14	1	1	1	1	45	65	56	30	28	982	30	2	2	1	1,200	1,211
(P 1) 1st Forfarshire	2	3	12	21	1	4	1	1	46	1	1	6	1	1	13	1	1	1	1	42	61	56	28	26	868	30	2	2	1	1,120	1,128
(P 1) The Highland	2	2	12	20	1	4	1	1	43	1	1	6	1	1	11	1	1	1	1	38	55	80	24	24	759	30	2	2	1	989	998
(P 3) 1st Lanarkshire	2	4	20	30	2	6	2	1	67	1	2	7	2	2	10	10	10	2	2	60	98	80	40	20	945	300	20	20	10	1,600	1,612
(P 3) 1st Mid-Lothian	2	2	8	12	1	3	1	1	29	1	1	8	1	1	5	3	3	1	1	24	39	32	16	12	407	90	6	6	3	640	646
1st Orkney	1	2	9	14	1	3	...	1	31	1	1	4	1	1	9	...	...	1	1	27	40	36	18	18	577	...	...	...	...	720	729
(P 1) 1st Renfrew & Dumbarton	1	2	7	11	1	3	...	1	26	1	1	3	1	1	6	1	1	1	1	21	33	28	14	12	412	30	2	2	1	560	565
Total	20	26	147	229	14	49	10	14	509	14	14	83	15	14	123	24	24	14	14	445	673	593	295	250	8678	720	48	48	24	11,838	11,949

(P a) Heavy artillery. (P 1, P 2, P 3) The corps includes 1, 2, or 3 heavy batteries. (a) The establishment of lieutenants is one per company, or two for a heavy battery. In addition to the establishment of subalterns, supernumerary 2nd lieutenants to complete the number of subalterns to two for each company (or four for each heavy battery) are allowed. (b) Additional surgeon-lieutenants and acting chaplains may be appointed, according to the requirements of the service, under paras. 56 and 66 Volunteer Regulations. (c) Including additional medical officers, additional acting chaplains, and all boys enrolled as trumpeters or bandsmen.

ROYAL ENGINEERS (VOLUNTEERS).

Corps.	Lieutenant-Colonels.	Majors.	Captains.	Lieutenants and 2nd Lieutenants (a)	Quartermasters.	Medical Officers (a)	Acting Chaplains (a)	Total Officers.	Permanent Staff — Adjutants.	Acting Serjeant-Majors.	Other Serjeant-Instructors.	Quartermaster-Serjeants.	Serjeant-Buglers.	Company Serjeant-Majors.	Acting Armourer Staff-Serjeants.	Orderly-room Serjeants.	Serjeants.	Total Serjeants.	Corporals.	Second Corporals.	Buglers.	Sappers.	Total, exclusive of permanent staff.	Total all ranks, inclusive of permanent staff (a).
1st Aberdeenshire	1	1	6	9	1	3	1	22	1	1	2	1	1	6	1	1	24	34	30	30	12	472	600	604
1st Lanarkshire	2	2	12	18	1	4	1	40	1	1	5	1	1	12	1	1	48	64	60	60	24	952	1200	1207
2nd Lanarkshire	1	2	9	14	1	3	1	31	1	1	4	1	1	9	1	1	36	49	45	45	18	712	900	906
Electrical Engineers—																								
Clyde Division (1 Coy.)	...	...	1	3	...	...	...	4	...	...	...	...	...	1	...	...	3	4	5	5	2	54	74	74
Forth Division (1 Coy.)	...	...	1	3	...	...	...	4	...	...	...	...	...	1	...	...	3	4	5	5	2	54	74	74
Total	4	5	29	47	3	10	3	101	3	3	11	3	3	29	3	3	114	155	145	145	58	2244	2848	2865

(a). See notes (a), (b), and (c) to R.G.A.(V.)

ESTABLISHMENT OF A COMPANY OF VOLUNTEER INFANTRY.

	Ordinary Company.	Cyclist Company.	Mounted Company (4 sections).	Mounted Section.	Two Mounted Sections.	Three Mounted Sections.
Captain	1	1	1	...	...	1
Lieutenants and 2nd Lieutenants }	1 or 2 (a)	4	4	1	2	2
Colour-Serjeant	1	1	1	...	...	...
Farrier-Serjeant	...	...	1	...	...	...
Serjeants	4	4	4	1	2	3
Corporals	5	6	7	3	4	6
Buglers	2	2	2	...	1	1
Privates	100 (b)	102	121	30	60	91
Total	114 or 115 (b)	120	141	35	69	104

(a) Namely, 3 for every two companies. See note (a) to Volunteer Infantry.

(b) The establishment of a company is nominally 116 of all ranks, but this number provides for a proportion of the battalion staff, leaving the company establishment proper at 1 or 2 below 116. For the same reason the number of privates varies from 99 to 101 per company.

VOLUNTEER INFANTRY.

No. of Regimental District	Corps	Lieutenant-Colonels	Majors	Captains	Lieutenants and 2nd Lieutenants (a)	Quartermasters	Medical Officers (b)	Acting Chaplains (b)	Total Officers	Adjutants	Acting Serjeant-Majors	Other Serjeant-Instructors	Quartermaster-Serjeants	Serjeant-Buglers	Colour-Serjeants	Acting Armourer Staff-Serjeants	Orderly-room Serjeants	Serjeants	Total Serjeants	Corporals	Buglers	Privates	Total, exclusive of permanent staff	Total, all ranks, inclusive of permanent staff (c)
1	Queen's Vol. Rifle Brig, Royal Scots (Lothian Regt.)	3	6	27	46	3	9	3	97	3	3	5	3	3	27	3	3	111	150	142	55	2795	3239	(d)3250
1	4th V.B. Royal Scots	1	2	8	12	1	3	1	28	1	1	2	1	1	8	1	1	32	44	40	16	800	928	982
1	5th " "	1	2	10	18	1	3	1	36	1	1	2	1	1	10	1	1	40	54	51	20	1003	1164	(e)1168
1	6th " "	1	2	11	17	1	3	1	36	1	1	6	1	1	11	1	1	44	59	55	22	1104	1276	1284
1	7th " "	1	1	6	9	1	3	1	22	1	1	5	1	1	6	1	1	24	34	30	12	598	696	708
1	8th " "	1	2	8	12	1	3	1	28	1	1	6	1	1	8	1	1	32	44	40	16	800	928	936
1	9th " "	1	2	8	12	1	3	1	28	1	1	6	1	1	8	1	1	32	44	40	16	800	928	932
8	8th V.B. " Liverpool Regt.	1	2	8	12	1	3	1	28	1	1	2	1	1	8	1	1	32	44	40	16	800	928	932
21	1st V.B. Royal Scots Fusiliers	1	2	10	18	1	3	1	36	1	1	7	1	1	10	1	1	40	54	51	20	1003	1164	(e)1173
25	2nd "	1	2	9	16	1	3	1	33	1	1	6	1	1	9	1	1	36	49	46	18	902	1048	(e)1056
25	1st Roxburgh and Selkirk	1	2	11	19	1	3	1	38	1	1	6	1	1	11	1	1	44	59	56	22	1105	1280	(e)1288
25	2nd V.B. K.O. Scottish Borderers	1	2	8	18	1	3	1	33	1	1	7	1	1	8	1	1	32	44	40	16	800	928	{f}937
25	3rd " "	2	2	10	18	1	3	1	36	1	1	8	1	1	10	1	1	40	54	51	20	1003	1164	1174
25	Galloway " "	1	4	8	12	1	3	1	28	1	1	6	1	1	8	1	1	32	44	40	16	800	923	936
26	1st Lanarkshire ;	2	2	16	24	1	4	1	52	1	1	4	1	1	16	1	1	64	84	80	32	1608	1856	1862
26	2nd V.B. Scottish Rifles	1	2	11	19	1	3	1	38	1	1	7	1	1	11	1	1	44	59	56	22	1105	1280	(e)1289
26	3rd Lanarkshire	1	2	13	22	1	4	1	45	1	1	3	1	1	13	1	1	52	69	66	26	1306	1512	(e)1517
26	4th V.B. Scottish Rifles	2	2	9	16	1	3	1	33	1	1	2	1	1	9	1	1	36	49	46	18	902	1048	(e)1052
42	1st V.B. Royal Highlanders	1	2	10	18	1	3	1	36	1	1	2	1	1	10	1	1	40	54	51	20	1003	1164	(e)1168
42	2nd " "	1	2	12	18	1	4	1	40	1	1	7	1	1	12	1	1	48	64	60	24	1204	1392	1401
42	3rd " "	1	2	8	12	1	3	1	28	1	1	2	1	1	8	1	1	32	44	40	16	800	928	932
42	4th " "	1	2	8	12	1	3	1	28	1	1	5	1	1	8	1	1	32	44	40	16	800	928	{f}935
42	5th " "	1	2	8	15	1	3	1	31	1	1	7	1	1	8	1	1	32	44	41	16	800	982	(e)941
42	6th " "	2	2	13	22	1	4	1	45	1	1	9	1	1	13	1	1	52	69	66	26	1306	1512	(e)1523

71	1st V.B. Highland Light Infantry	2	2	12	18	1	4	1	40	1	1	3	1	1	12	1	1	48	64	60	24	1204	1392	(f)1897
71	2nd ,, ,, ,,	1	1	10	18	1	3	1	36	1	1	3	1	1	10	1	1	40	54	50	20	1004	1164	(e)1169
71	3rd ,, ,, ,,	2	2	12	18	1	4	1	40	1	1	3	1	1	12	1	1	48	64	60	24	1204	1392	(f)1897
71	9th Lanarkshire	1	1	6	9	1	3	1	22	1	1	5	1	1	6	1	1	24	34	30	12	598	696	703
71	5th V.B. Highland Light Infantry	2	2	13	22	1	4	1	45	1	1	3	1	1	13	1	1	52	69	66	26	1306	1512	(e)1517
72	1st V.B. Seaforth Highlanders	1	1	9	14	1	3	1	31	1	1	8	1	1	9	1	1	36	49	45	18	901	1044	1054
72	1st Sutherland	2	2	12	18	1	4	1	40	1	1	10	1	1	12	1	1	48	64	60	24	1204	1392	1404
72	3rd V.B. Seaforth Highlanders	1	1	11	17	1	3	1	36	1	1	8	1	1	11	1	1	44	59	55	22	1104	1276	1286
75	1st V.B. Gordon Highlanders	1	1	9	14	1	3	1	31	1	1	2	1	1	9	1	1	36	49	45	18	901	1044	1048
75	2nd ,, ,,	1	1	7	11	1	3	1	25	1	1	6	1	1	7	1	1	28	39	35	14	699	812	(f)820
75	3rd ,, ,,	1	1	8	12	1	3	1	28	1	1	5	1	1	8	1	1	32	44	40	16	800	928	935
75	4th ,, ,,	1	1	10	15	1	3	1	33	1	1	7	1	1	10	1	1	40	54	50	20	1003	1160	(f)1169
75	5th ,, ,,	1	1	9	14	1	3	1	31	1	1	8	1	1	9	1	1	36	49	45	18	901	1044	1054
75	6th ,, ,,	1	1	7	13	1	3	1	27	1	1	6	1	1	7	1	1	31	42	38	15	748	870	878
75	7th ,, ,,	1	1	3	5	1	1	1	12	:	:	2	1	1	3	:	:	12	16	15	6	299	348	350
79	1st V.B. Cameron Highlanders	1	1	10	15	1	3	1	33	1	1	7	1	1	10	1	1	40	54	50	20	1003	1160	1169
91	1st V.B. Argyll and Sutherland High.	1	1	9	16	1	3	1	33	1	1	4	1	1	9	1	1	36	49	46	18	902	1048	(e)1064
91	2nd ,, ,,	1	1	10	18	1	3	1	36	1	1	4	1	1	10	1	1	51	54	51	20	1003	1164	(e)1170
91	3rd ,, ,,	1	1	9	16	1	3	1	33	1	1	5	1	1	9	1	1	36	49	46	18	902	1048	(e)1055
91	4th ,, ,,	1	1	10	15	1	3	1	33	1	1	6	1	1	10	1	1	40	54	50	20	1003	1160	1168
91	5th ,, ,,	2	2	10	18	1	4	1	36	1	1	7	1	1	10	1	1	(g)57	54	51	20	1003	1164	(e)1173
91	1st Dumbartonshire	1	1	14	26	1	3	1	50	1	1	13	1	1	14	1	1	32	75	73	28	1427	1653	(h)1668
91	7th V.B. Argyll and Sutherland High.	1	1	8	12	1		1	28	1	1	4	1	1	8	1	1	32	44	40	16	800	928	934
R.B.	7th Middlesex	2	1	8	12	1	3	1	28	1	1	2	1	1	8	1	1	32	44	40	16	800	928	932
	Total	58	97	476	777	50	157	50	1665	49	49	249	50	49	476	49	49	1911	2584	2409	954	47,866	55,478	55,825

(a) The establishment of lieutenants is one per company. In addition to the establishment of subalterns, supernumerary 2nd lieutenants to complete the number of subalterns to two for each company will be allowed.

(b) Additional surgeon-lieutenants and acting chaplains may be appointed, according to the requirements of the service, under paragraphs 56 and 66 respectively of the Volunteer Regulations.

(c) Inclusive of additional medical officers, additional acting chaplains, and all boys enrolled as buglers or bandsmen.

(d) Twenty-six ordinary companies, 1 cyclist company, and 3 mounted infantry sections.

(e) Includes 1 cyclist company.

(f) Includes a cyclist section.

(g) Includes 1 farrier-sergeant.

(h) Includes 1 mounted and 1 cyclist company.

ROYAL ARMY MEDICAL CORPS (VOLUNTEERS) AND VOLUNTEER BRIGADE BEARER COMPANIES.

Corps.	Lieutenant-Colonel.	Major.	Company Officers.	Quartermasters.	Acting Chaplain.	Total Officers.	Permanent Staff. Adjutant.	Serjeant-Instructor, A.S.C.	Serjeant-Instructor, R.A.M.C.	Quartermaster-Serjeants.	Staff-Serjeants.	Serjeant-Bugler.	Serjeants.	Total Serjeants.	Corporals.	Buglers.	Privates.	Total, exclusive of permanent staff.	Total, all ranks, inclusive of permanent staff.
Edinburgh Company	...	.	3	1	1	5	...	...	1	1	2	...	4	7	8	2	78	100	101
2 Aberdeen Companies	...	1	11	2	1	15	...	...	1	2	4	...	8	14	16	4	151	200	} 279
Transport sections for 2 field hospitals	...	...	...	...	...	...	...	...	...	2	...	...	2	4	4	...	34	42	
Transport section for 1 bearer company	...	...	...	...	...	...	...	...	...	1	...	...	1	2	2	...	32	36	
5 Glasgow Companies	1	1	32 (a)	5	1	40	1	...	3	5	10	1	21	37	43	10	370	500	} 708
Transport sections for 6 field hospitals	...	...	...	...	...	...	...	} 1	...	6	...	...	6	12	12	...	102	126	
Transport sections for 2 bearer companies	...	...	...	...	...	...	...		...	2	...	...	2	4	4	...	64	72	
5 Volunteer Brigade Bearer Companies	.	...	15	...	...	15	...	...	...	5	...	...	25	35	30	5	235	320	325
Total	1	2	61	8	3	75	1	1	10	24	21	1	69	115	119	21	1066	1396	1408

(a) Includes two transport officers,

SUMMARY.

ARMS.	Volunteer Officers.	Adjutants.	Serjeant-Instructors.	Volunteer Serjeants.	Total, exclusive of permanent staff.	Total all ranks, inclusive of permanent staff.
Royal Garrison Artillery (V.) . . .	509	14	97	673	11,838	11,949
Royal Engineers (V.)	101	3	14	155	2,848	2,865
Volunteer Infantry	1665	49	298	2584	55,478	55,825
Royal Army Medical Corps and Bearer Companies	75	1	11	115	1,396	1,408
Grand total . .	2350	67	420	3527	71,560	72,047

APPENDIX H.

RETURN OF THE SCOTTISH VOLUNTEER CORPS FOR THE YEAR 1907.

(*Extracted from the Official Return of* 1st *November* 1907.)

CORPS.	Estab-lish-ment.*	Efficients.†		Non-efficients.†		Total† all ranks.	Present at Inspec-tion, all ranks.	Cyclists included in fore-going.
		Officers.	N.C.O. and Men.	Officers.	N.C.O. and Men.			
Royal Garrison Artillery (Volunteers).								
1st Aberdeenshire . . .	1040	34	701	...	8	743	458	...
1st Argyll and Bute . .	1009	40	869	...	42	951	385	...
1st Ayr and Galloway .	1040	34	870	1	4	909	531	...
1st Banff	560	31	430	...	3	464	152	...
1st Berwickshire . . .	80	3	44	...	6	53	21	...
1st Caithness . . .	560	20	360	...	61	441	163	...
1st Edinburgh (City) .	720	28	602	2	33	665	378	...
1st Fifeshire	1200	39	946	3	45	1033	464	...
1st Forfarshire . . .	1120	36	885	1	21	943	632	...
The Highland . . .	989	41	743	...	16	800	277	...
1st Lanarkshire . . .	1600	37	1107	2	11	1157	604	...
1st Midlothian . . .	640	22	406	1	34	463	247	...
1st Orkney	720	30	521	1	3	555	266	...
1st Renfrew and Dumbarton .	560	20	504	...	6	530	279	...
Total R.G.A.(V.) .	11,838	427	9069	11	294	9801	4857	...
Royal Engineers (Volunteers).								
1st Aberdeenshire . . .	600	22	447	1	31	501	350	...
1st Lanarkshire . . .	1200	28	796	1	41	866	743	...
2nd Lanarkshire . . .	900	36	777	5	61	879	533	...
Electrical Engineers—								
Clyde Division . . .	74	7	64	1	4	76	70	...
Forth Division . . .	74	9	65	...	4	78	71	...
Total R.E.(V.) .	2848	105	2163	8	141	2417	1767	...
Volunteer Infantry.								
Q.R.V.B. Royal Scots . .	3239	106	2260	3	48	2417	2014	117(a)
4th V.B. do. . .	928	31	893	1	2	927	755	30
5th V.B. do. . .	1164	26	968	...	...	994	810	50
6th V.B. do. . .	1276	29	654	3	44	730	294	18
7th V.B. do. . .	696	17	454	1	5	477	224	...
8th V.B. do. . .	928	24	708	1	7	740	411	...
9th V.B. do. . .	928	24	661	3	46	734	551	...

* Excluding permanent staff.
† These figures for the *corps* refer only to volunteers, but the totals for each *arm* include the permanent staffs, which it is not necessary to show separately for each corps.
(*a*) And 75 mounted infantry.

CORPS.	Estab-lish-ment.	Efficients.		Non-efficients.		Total all ranks.	Present at Inspection, all ranks.	Cyclists included in foregoing.
		Officers.	N.C.O. and Men.	Officers.	N.C.O. and Men.			
*Volunteer Infantry—*contd.								
1st V.B. Royal Scots Fusiliers	1164	24	669	1	10	704	396	33
2nd V.B. do. do.	1048	22	730	1	29	782	337	57
1st Roxburgh and Selkirk .	1280	37	817	4	5	863	428	61
2nd V.B. K.O.S. Borderers .	928	33	483	1	19	536	300	29
3rd V.B. do. .	1164	28	569	1	8	606	340	41
Scottish Border Bearer Coy. .	...	1	41	1	1	44	26	...
Galloway V.R.C. . .	928	27	741	...	...	768	418	22
1st Lanarkshire V.R.C. .	1856	54	1194	...	18	1266	467	...
2nd V.B. Scottish Rifles .	1280	35	963	1	13	1012	620	99
3rd Lanarkshire V.R.C. .	1512	42	931	...	29	1002	614	65
4th V.B. Scottish Rifles .	1048	28	817	2	24	871	517	80
1st V.B. Royal Highlanders .	1164	29	844	...	9	882	698	60
2nd V.B. do. .	1392	26	606	1	16	649	369	13
3rd V.B. do. .	928	19	522	3	20	564	432	40
4th V.B. do. .	928	27	567	3	6	603	254	35
5th V.B. do. .	932	23	624	4	14	665	350	22
6th V.B. do. .	1512	49	1077	2	36	1164	700	50
1st V.B. Highland L.I. .	1392	25	761	3	55	844	327	33
2nd V.B. do. .	1164	27	951	1	18	997	544	59
3rd V.B. do. .	1392	37	987	...	18	1042	631	29
9th Lanarkshire V.R.C. .	696	23	540	...	3	566	397	12
5th V.B. Highland L.I. .	1512	35	1130	1	23	1189	628	65
1st V.B. Seaforth Highlanders	1044	33	789	1	12	835	421	...
1st Sutherland V.R.C. . .	1392	34	835	1	37	907	442	34
3rd V.B. Seaforth Highlanders	1276	28	695	1	9	733	359	15
1st V.B. Gordon Highlanders	1044	29	554	...	5	588	337	...
2nd V.B. do.	812	27	357	...	...	384	240	...
3rd V.B. do.	928	33	494	2	14	543	155	...
4th V.B. do.	1160	47	631	2	20	700	291	35
5th V.B. do.	1044	28	519	...	...	547	338	...
6th V.B. do.	870	30	517	...	6	553	307	...
7th V.B. do.	348	10	191	1	23	225	182	...
1st V.B. Cameron Highlanders	1160	25	866	1	10	902	435	29
1st V.B. Argyll and Sutherland Highlanders . .	1048	37	678	...	32	747	438	97
2nd V.B. do. do.	1164	29	862	2	30	923	653	36
3rd V.B. do. do.	1048	32	778	...	16	826	347	70
4th V.B. do. do.	1160	31	738	...	4	773	691	...
5th V.B. do. do.	1164	23	849	...	1	873	267	48
1st Dumbartonshire V.R.C. .	1653	56	1407	1	20	1484	1214	79 (b)
7th V.B. Argyll and Sutherland Highlanders . .	928	26	655	1	10	692	356	30
Total Infantry	53,622	1510	35,863	55	776	38,204	22,325	1593 (c)
R.A. Medical Corps (V.)								
Edinburgh Company . .	100	5	84	...	4	93	60	...
Aberdeen Companies .	278	14	263	1	...	278	219	...
Gordon V.I.B. Bearer Coy. .	...	2	59	1	3	65	45	...
Glasgow Companies . .	698	25	527	...	1	553	511	...
Total R.A.M.C.(V.) .	1076	47	940	2	8	997	835	...

(b) And 128 mounted infantry.   (c) And 203 mounted infantry.

CORPS.	Estab-lish-ment.	Efficients.		Non-efficients.		Total all ranks.	Present at Inspec-tion, all ranks.	Cyclists included in fore-going.
		Officers.	N.C.O. and Men.	Officers.	N.C.O. and Men.			
V.I.B. Bearer Companies.								
Argyll and Sutherland . .	64	2	59	...	1	62	55	...
Black Watch . . .	64	1	61	...	3	65	46	...
Highland Light Infantry .	64	3	58	...	5	66	65	...
1st Lothian	64	2	61	1	...	64	51	...
Seaforth and Cameron . .	64	2	46	...	...	48	34	...
Total Bearer Companies	320	10	290	1	9	310	237	...
Grand total, all Arms .	69,704	2099	48,325	77	1228	51,729	30,021	1593
The totals in England and Wales were—								
Royal Garrison Artillery (V.)	37,840	1108	27,566	56	1796	30,526	21,862	...
Royal Engineers (V.) . .	16,466	522	13,164	43	682	14,411	10,996	...
Volunteer Infantry * .	204,357	4459	141,060	227	4360	150,106	111,040	8776
Royal Army Medical Corps(V.)	2,838	79	2,336	5	52	2,472	1,603	...
Brigade Bearer Companies .	2,624	51	1,446	2	43	1,542	1,289	...
Total . . .	264,125	6219	185,572	333	6933	199,057	146,790	8,776
Add for Scotland .	69,704	2099	48,325	77	1228	51,729	30,021	1,593
Grand total, United Kingdom .	333,829	8318	233,897	410	8161	250,786	176,811	10,369
* Of these—								
8th (Scottish) V.B. Liverpool Regiment	928	23	623	2	49	697	340	...
7th Middlesex (London Scottish) V.R.C.	928	30	712	2	38	782	682	...

APPENDIX I.

ESTABLISHMENTS AND STRENGTH OF THE SCOTTISH VOL-
UNTEER FORCE, 1880 TO 1907.*—(*From the Official Annual Returns
of the 1st November of each year. No Annual Returns were published
prior to 1875, and those from 1875 to 1879 are not tabulated by
nationalities.*)

Year.	Establishment, all ranks, including permanent staff.	Efficient.		Non-efficients, all ranks.	Total enrolled.	Present at Inspection.
		Officers.	Other ranks.			
1880	55,245		45,303	1967	47,270	39,534
1881	55,690		47,540	1396	48,936	40,519
1882	55,992		45,734	1817	47,551	39,758
1883	56,453		45,902	1350	47,252	40,155
1884	56,699		47,730	1111	48,841	41,852
1885	56,945		50,530	903	51,433	44,987
1886	57,179		50,585	913	51,498	44,505
1887	57,342	Included in total of " Other ranks."	50,276	996	51,272	44,491
1888	57,797		49,677	1026	50,703	43,825
1889	58,094		49,351	1111	50,462	43,463
1890	57,986		47,981	1459	49,440	42,598
1891	58,289		48,248	1183	49,431	42,369
1892	58,428		47,420	1580	49,000	41,935
1893	58,268		47,595	1709	49,304	42,455
1894	58,067	1896	46,190	1548	49,634	43,613
1895	57,822	1916	46,960	1407	50,283	43,761
1896	57,904	1973	47,724	1508	51,205	45,127
1897	57,221	1973	46,801	1344	50,118	43,431
1898	57,221	1994	46,421	1305	49,720	43,128
1899	57,351	1983	45,972	1367	49,322	42,517
1900	70,484	2135	54,077	1273	57,485	49,361
1901	70,374	2163	55,786	1510	59,459	52,384
1902	71,002	2181	51,432	2186	55,799	42,111
1903	71,861	2194	50,096	1921	54,211	37,969
1904	71,441	2145	49,891	1561	53,597	40,440
1905	71,205	2095	49,458	1657	53,210	34,248
1906	70,945	2110	50,092	1550	53,752	32,440
1907	70,445	2099	48,325	1305	51,729	30,021

* Exclusive of the 7th Middlesex (London Scottish) V.R.C. and 8th (Liverpool Scottish) V.B.
The King's.

In connection with the above and the figures given on p. 57, it is interesting to note the following figures showing the proportion of ènrolled volunteers to male population in the years 1881, 1891, and 1901 in Scotland and in England and Wales. They are—

Year.	SCOTLAND.			ENGLAND AND WALES.		
	Male population.	Enrolled Volunteers.	Proportion of Volunteers to male population.	Male population.	Enrolled Volunteers.	Proportion of Volunteers to male population.
1881	1,799,475	48,936	1 in 36	12,639,902	159,372	1 in 79
1891	1,942,717	49,431	1 in 39	14,052,901	172,615	1 in 81
1901	2,173,755	59,459	1 in 36	15,728,613	229,017	1 in 68

APPENDIX J.

TABLE SHOWING THE UNITS OF THE TERRITORIAL ARMY
INTO WHICH THOSE OF THE SCOTTISH VOLUNTEER FORCE WERE
CONVERTED ON OR AFTER 1ST APRIL 1908.

Unit of the Volunteer Force.	Unit of the Territorial Army.
ROYAL GARRISON ARTILLERY.	
1st Aberdeenshire . .	1st and 2nd City of Aberdeen Batteries R.F.A. 2nd Highland Ammunition Column R.F.A. North Scottish R.G.A. (2 cos.)
1st Argyll and Bute . .	Forth and Clyde R.G.A. (1 coy.) Argyllshire (Mountain) Battery R.G.A. Buteshire (Mountain) Battery R.G.A. 3rd Highland Ammunition Column R.G.A.
1st Ayrshire and Galloway	3rd Lowland Brigade R.F.A. (Ayrshire, Wigtownshire, and Kirkcudbrightshire Batteries). 3rd Lowland Ammunition Column R.F.A. Lowland Mounted Brigade Transport and Supply Column A.S.C.
1st Banff	Banffshire Battery R.F.A. Banffshire Small-arm Section, Ammunition Column R.F.A.
1st Berwickshire . . .	Disbanded.
1st Caithness	Disbanded.
1st City of Edinburgh (except left half 1st Heavy Battery)	Forth and Clyde R.G.A. (4 cos.) 1st City of Edinburgh Battery R.F.A. Lowland (City of Edinburgh) R.G.A. (1 heavy battery and ammunition column).
1st Fifeshire (except No. 7 Company) . . .	North Scottish R.G.A. (2 cos.) Fifeshire Battery R.F.A. Highland (Fifeshire) R.G.A. (1 heavy battery and ammunition column).
1st Forfarshire . . .	North Scottish R.G.A. (2 cos.) City of Dundee Battery R.F.A. Forfarshire Battery R.F.A. 1st Highland Ammunition Column R.F.A.

2 A

Unit of the Volunteer Force.	Unit of the Territorial Army.
The Highland . . .	North Scottish R.G.A. (1 coy. and 1 detachment in the Hebrides). Highland Mounted Brigade Transport and Supply Column A.S.C. Inverness-shire (Mountain) Battery R.G.A. 3rd Highland Ammunition Column R.G.A. 6th Battalion Seaforth Highlanders (1 company in Nairnshire).
1st Lanarkshire . .	1st Lowland Brigade R.F.A. (1st, 2nd, and 3rd City of Glasgow Batteries). 1st Lowland Ammunition Column R.F.A. 4th Lowland (Howitzer) Brigade R.F.A. (4th and 5th City of Glasgow Batteries). 4th Lowland Ammunition Column R.F.A.
1st Mid-Lothian . .	2nd City of Edinburgh Battery R.F.A. Mid-Lothian Battery R.F.A. 2nd Lowland Ammunition Column R.F.A.
1st Orkney	Orkney R.G.A. (7 cos.)
1st Renfrew and Dumbarton	Forth and Clyde R.G.A. (2 cos. in Dumbarton, 1 coy. in Renfrew). 4th Highland (Howitzer) Brigade R.F.A. (1st and 2nd Renfrewshire Batteries). 4th Highland Ammunition Column R.F.A.
ROYAL ENGINEERS.	
1st Aberdeenshire . .	City of Aberdeen (Fortress) R.E. (1 coy.) 1st Highland Field Company R.E. Highland Div. Telegraph Company R.E.
Clyde Div. Electrical Engineers	Renfrewshire (Fortress) R.E. (1 coy.)
Forth Div. Electrical Engineers	City of Edinburgh (Fortress) R.E. (1 coy.)
1st Lanarkshire . .	1st Lowland Field Company R.E. Scottish Wireless Telegraph Coy. R.E. Scottish Air Line Telegraph Coy. R.E. Scottish Cable Telegraph Company R.E.
2nd Lanarkshire . .	2nd Highland Field Company R.E. Lanarkshire (Fortress) R.E. (1 coy.) 2nd Lowland Field Company R.E. Lowland Div. Telegraph Company R.E.
INFANTRY.	
Queen's Rifle Volunteer Brigade, The Royal Scots (except No. 4 Company)	4th and 5th Bns. Royal Scots.
4th V.B. Royal Scots . .	6th Bn. Royal Scots.
5th „ „ .	7th „ „
6th „ „	Mid-Lothian, 2 cos. Peebles, 2 cos. } 8th Bn. Royal Scots. Haddington, 4 cos.
7th „ „	
8th „ „	10th Bn. Royal Scots (Cyclists).
9th „ „ (except " H " Company)	9th „ „

Unit of the Volunteer Force.	Unit of the Territorial Army.
8th (Scottish) V.B. Liverpool Regiment	10th Bn. Liverpool Regiment.
1st V.B. Royal Scots Fusiliers .	4th Bn. Royal Scots Fusiliers.
2nd „ „ „	5th „ „ „
1st Roxburgh and Selkirk V.R.C.	Roxburgh, 3 cos. } 4th Bn. K.O. Scottish Selkirk, 3 cos. } Borderers.
2nd V.B. K.O. Scot. Borderers	Berwick, 2 cos.
3rd „ „ „	Dumfries, 4 cos. } 5th Bn. K.O. Scot- Kirkcudbright, 3 cos. } tish Borderers.
Galloway V.R.C. . . {	Wigtown, 1 coy. }
1st Lanarkshire V.R.C. (except "K" Company)	5th Bn. Scottish Rifles.
2nd V.B. Scottish Rifles . .	6th „ „
3rd Lanarkshire V.R.C. . .	7th „ „
4th V.B. Scottish Rifles . .	8th „ „
1st V.B. Royal Highlanders .	4th Bn. Royal Highlanders.
2nd „ „	Forfarshire, 4 cos. } 5th Bn. Royal City of Dundee, 4 cos. } Highlanders.
3rd „ „	
4th „ „	6th Bn. Royal Highlanders.
5th „ „	4 cos. of 8th Bn. Royal Highlanders (Cyclists).
6th „ „	7th Bn. Royal Highlanders.
1st V.B. Highland L.I. . .	5th Bn. Highland L.I.
2nd „ „ „	6th „ „ „
3rd „ „ „	7th „ „ „
9th Lanarkshire V.R.C. . .	8th „ „ „
5th V.B. Highland L.I. . .	9th „ „ „
1st V.B. Seaforth Highlanders .	4th Bn. Seaforth Highlanders.
1st Sutherland V.R.C. . .	5th „ „
3rd V.B. Seaforth Highlanders {	Elginshire, 6 cos. } 6th Bn. Seaforth Inverness-shire, 1 coy. } Highlanders.
1st V.B. Gordon Highanders .	6 cos. 4th Bn. Gordon Highlanders.
2nd „ „ } 3rd „ „ }	5th Bn. „
4th „ „	4 cos. 6th Bn. „
5th „ „ {	Aberdeen, 4 cos. } 7th Bn. Gordon High- Kincardine, 4 cos. } landers.
6th „ „	4 cos. 6th Bn. Gordon Highlanders.
7th „ „	2 cos. 4th „ „
1st V.B. Cameron Highlanders .	4th Bn. Cameron Highlanders.
1st V.B. A. and S. Highlanders	5th Bn. A. and S. Highlanders.
2nd „ „ „	5 cos. } 6th Bn. „ „
3rd „ „ „	3 cos. }
4th „ „ „ {	4 cos. 7th „ „ „ 4 cos. 8th Bn. Royal Highlanders (Cyclists).
5th „ „ „	8th Bn. A. and S. Highlanders.
1st Dumbartonshire V.R.C. .	9th „ „ „
7th V.B. A. and S. Highlanders {	Clackmannan, 3 cos. } 7th Bn. A. and S. Kinross, 1 coy. } Highlanders.
7th Middlesex (London Scottish) V.R.C.	14th Bn. County of London Regiment.

Unit of the Volunteer Force.	Unit of the Territorial Army.
MEDICAL UNITS.	
Aberdeen Companies, R.A.M.C. (Vol.)	1st Highland Field Ambulance R.A.M.C.
Seaforth and Cameron Brigade Bearer Company	Highland Mounted Brigade Field Ambulance R.A.M.C.
Gordon Brigade Bearer Company	2nd Highland Field Ambulance R.A.M.C.
Black Watch Brigade Bearer Company	3rd " " " "
Glasgow Companies R.A.M.C. (Vol.)	Lowland Mounted Brigade Field Ambulance R.A.M.C.
Argyll and Sutherland Brigade Bearer Company	1st Lowland Field Ambulance R.A.M.C.
Highland Light Infantry Brigade Bearer Company	2nd " " " "
1st Lothian Brigade Bearer Company	3rd " " " "

The following units continued to serve as volunteer corps under the Act of 1863, until a decision as to their transformation into " Officers' Training Corps " had been arrived at :—

Left half, 1st Heavy Battery, 1st Edinburgh
   R.G.A.V.
No. 4 Company Queen's R.V. Brigade, The Royal
   Scots   } Edinburgh University.
" H " Company 9th V.B. The Royal Scots
Edinburgh Company R.A.M.C.V.
No. 7 Company 1st Fifeshire R.G.A.V.   .   . St Andrews University.
" K " Company 1st Lanark V.R.C.   .   . Glasgow University.

THE END.

PRINTED BY WILLIAM BLACKWOOD AND SONS.